Permanent Revolution

Permanent Revolution

THE REFORMATION
AND THE ILLIBERAL ROOTS
OF LIBERALISM

JAMES SIMPSON

The Belknap Press of Harvard University Press

Cambridge, Massachusetts, and London, England 2019

Library of Congress Cataloging-in-Publication Data

Names: Simpson, James, 1954– author.
Title: Permanent revolution : the Reformation and the illiberal roots of
Liberalism / James Simpson.
Description: Cambridge, Massachusetts : The Belknap Press of Harvard University Press, 2019. |
Includes bibliographical references and index.
Identifiers: LCCN 2018026019 | ISBN 9780674987135 (alk. paper)
Subjects: LCSH: Reformation—England. | Social change—England. | Social change—
Religious aspects—Protestant churches. | Literature and society—England—History—
16th century. | Literature and society—England—History—17th century. | Religion and
literature—England—History—16th century. | Religion and
literature—England—History—17th century.
Classification: LCC BR375 .S56 2018 | DDC 274.2/06—dc23
LC record available at https://lccn.loc.gov/2018026019

*Not before time, I dedicate this book with gratitude and love
to my sister Julie, and to my brothers Bruce and John*

Contents

Preface

EVERY BOOK derives from the always unfinished business of unwriting and rewriting the self as one engages with history. Sometimes, however, books in long unconscious gestation also show themselves suddenly, by the flash of a single illumination. The sudden illumination that revealed this book in compacted, ideational form occurred in a session of the North-Eastern Milton seminar a few years ago.

I, as a late medievalist, had been very kindly invited, and sat demurely on the side benches, determined not to speak. I successfully restrained myself from intervention, but one remark left me speechless in any case. The group had been discussing Adam's permission, against his better judgment, to allow Eve to work alone in the garden of Eden, since, as Adam says, "Thy stay, not free, absents thee more" (PL 9.372). Adam's permission is grounded on a scrupulous sensitivity to Eve's right to exercise her free will, but this wasn't enough for one of the participants. This member of the group indignantly erupted: "Well it's a strange kind of freedom that insists on a precondition!" Everyone in the room seemed, so far as I could make out, to view this exclamation as anodyne.

By the current libertarian understanding of freedom, the remark was entirely just; indeed, one might have expected the comment to be regarded as anodyne by the Milton group precisely because Milton himself is such a plausible champion of the libertarian understanding of freedom. So the remark's lightning effect on me did not derive from any sense of it being absurd. The flash of illumination derived rather from its presuppositions: that agency had to be wholly located in and derived from the agent; and that if the action were to be described as "free," then it had to be chosen without any external, preexisting condition whatsoever. I suddenly understood, in the context of a Milton seminar, that the comment was itself Miltonic; and that its understanding of agency, in that Miltonic context, could only be understood as effectively ecclesiological in origin—one chose one's Church, and one made oneself at each moment. Not to choose, in absolute freedom, is, as Milton says, itself a heresy.[1] That important strand of Miltonic thought has remained dominant in liberal reception of Milton, even if it stands in stark contradiction to a strand of Miltonic thought less amenable to contemporary liberals (i.e. Milton's practical, authoritarian politics).

As I say, the seminar participants expressed no surprise at the remark; it was, after all, a standard liberal position that underlies, whether consciously or implicitly, default liberal anti-institutionalism. It confirmed the general tenor of the discussion of Milton as champion of liberty, even if, everyone rightly agreed, he was sexist.

To my own, silent self, however, the remark quickly produced a flurry of further, tacit questions: how could this assertion of free will be made without recognition that it stood at the extreme opposite of the theological, Calvinist, predestinarian culture into which Milton had been born? And, within a slightly wider horizon, how could it be that scholars of early modern English literature could champion Milton as a wholly consistent, if occasionally flawed, liberal, when Milton's most vigorous expressions with regard to the will of the people and for constitutionalism are disdainful, and when Milton's poetry and prose were (or so I saw and see them) riven and driven by contradiction? How could reformist liberals so admire a revolutionary working for a military junta, with all the attendant revolutionary violence?

In a wider horizon still, how could what I knew of the early Reformation (e.g. theological absolutism, predestination, iconoclasm, violence-producing literalism, intolerance, disdainful exclusivism) have no place whatsoever in a generally admiring discussion of Milton as proto-liberal? How did we get from the illiberal start of the Reformation to its proto-liberal end? I was also, in the context of contemporary America, conscious of that fact that this unexceptionable liberal statement of the center left was absolutely square with the presuppositions of the libertarian right.

The seminar set me on a course of self-instruction, then, to work out for myself how Milton's indisputably proto-liberal positions were shaped out of the larger and radically illiberal history of Protestantism, going right back to 1517; and to work out how Milton's proto-liberalism was hammered out of, and bore powerful traces of, that illiberal Protestantism.

The answers to my urgent, tacit questions posed then, in that seminar, are voiced now, in this book. They are, in sum, as follows: that Protestantism is a powerfully and necessarily self-conflicted tradition, precisely because its anti-formalism repudiates tradition. In flight from nothing so energetically as from prior forms of itself, Protestantism is best described as an anti-tradition tradition of permanent revolution, forever targeting earlier and / or competing versions of itself (rather than Catholicism) precisely as the source of most lethal threat. Once one understands that kinesis within Protestantism, it becomes possible to explain how 1688 was so very different from 1517. To understand that kinesis, one has to enter the long narrative; the only intelligible stories of Protestantism—and of any revolutionary movement—are long ones.

One also understands, however, how repudiation is never escape. The book's secondary theme is that the proto-liberalism of 1688, like our own liberalism, is deeply marked by the evangelical furnace in which it was forged, and from which it emerged. Many features of contemporary liberalism are intelligible only as the result of conflicted, ultimately ecclesiological histories. Belonging as one of the elect to the True Church is tough and searing work; the disciplines it imposes do not simply vanish. Finally, therefore, one sees that the evangelical revolution is not over, for two reasons: on the one hand, liberalism is the younger sibling of evangelical religion; and on the other, illiberal, revolutionary evangelical religion becomes visible as the other grand claimant, along with its younger sibling liberalism, to Anglo-American modernity.

The scholar to whom the book owes most is unquestionably Barbara Lewalksi, whose Milton is precisely the one I attempt to redescribe here, in my larger redescription of what may be called Puritan revolutionary cultures. The dauntingly immense learning and formidable clarity of Barbara's consistent, liberal Milton offers itself as a mighty model from which to learn, and against which to push. Barbara explicated her Milton to me at my very first lunch at Harvard, when I arrived in 2003. At another lunch many years later, in addition to critiquing of my account of Milton as iconoclast, she generously made space for me: as *Areopagitica* enjoins, she herself cheerfully enjoined, let the books fight it out, and see how Truth emerges.

These pages were written long before the immortal Barbara died on March 2, 2018, an occasion of immense and widely shared sadness.

Acknowledgments

My acknowledgments are many, and they belong with the story above, since scholarship inevitably takes shape from within the ecosystem of one's own most immediate, daily influences. It's been my immense good fortune to be influenced and nourished by all my colleagues in the Department of English, Harvard University, since 2003. This book derives most immediately from the privilege of working beside Barbara Lewalski, Nicholas Watson, Stephen Greenblatt, and Gordon Teskey. Conversation with, and awareness of, the proximate presence (both tutelary and critical) of Helen Vendler, Peter Sacks, Homi Bhabha, Daniel Donoghue, Werner Sollors, Jim Engell, and Elaine Scarry have also deeply inflected my writing.

Ecosystems of intellectual and personal friendship among other colleagues and graduate students have also been decisive. My luminously brilliant undergraduate teacher at the University of Melbourne, and now friend, Penelope Buckley understood the project with especial inwardness and enriched it with her preternatural perception. The constant generosity of three Davids and one Brian (Aers, Benson, Hall, and Cummings) has been crucial. I thank the following for key conversations and suggestions: Amy Appleford, Sarah Beckwith, Jason Crawford, Milad Doueihi, Jeffrey Hamburger, Rebecca Kastleman, Andrew Johnston, Andrew Lynch, Derek Miller, John Parker, Joanna Picciotto, Misha Teramura, and Valerie Traub. I warmly recognize the *Journal of Medieval and Early Modern Studies* and its consummately gifted managing editor, Michael Cornett, for sustained confidence in and support for my work.

Two year-long periods of research leave at radiantly generous institutions with extraordinary library resources were decisive: the Huntington Library (2013–2014) and the Wissenschaftskolleg zu Berlin (2017–2018). I thank Steve Hindle and Luca Giuliani for their humane, intellectually committed leadership. Three month-long fellowships, at, respectively, The Centre for the History of the Emotions, University of Melbourne (June 2015), The Principles of Cultural Dynamics Group at the Free University Berlin (June 2016), and the University of Paris, Sorbonne (June 2017), were much appreciated; I thank Stephanie Trigg, Joachim Küpper, and Milad Doueihi for their invitations and hospitality.

Regnal Dates

Richard II	1377–1399
Henry IV	1399–1413
Henry V	1413–1422
Henry VI	1422–1461
Edward IV	1461–1470
Henry VI	1470–1471
Edward IV	1471–1483
Edward V	1483
Richard III	1483–1485
Henry VII	1485–1509
Henry VIII	1509–1547
Edward VI	1547–1553
Mary I	1553–1558
Elizabeth I	1558–1603
James I	1603–1625
Charles I	1625–1649
English Republic	1649–1653
Oliver Cromwell, Lord Protector	1653–1658
Richard Cromwell, Lord Protector	1658–1660
Charles II	1660–1685
James II	1685–1688
William III	1689–1702

Permanent Revolution

Introduction

IN ENGLISH cultural history, the liberal, Whig tradition held that the English Reformation was about the following: the growth of individuality and interiority, now that each Christian had unmediated access to a personal God; liberty of conscience; rationality; the right of every person to interpret Scripture for him or herself; equality through the democratic priesthood of all believers; toleration; constitutionalism; and national independence. The Reformation, in short, produced the interdependent trifecta of the critically independent self, division of governmental powers, and the nation. The master code of this immensely powerful cultural package was liberty: personal, political, and national. The Reformation was, it might be said, a very good thing indeed.[1]

Without much effort, however, and with total plausibility, that same Whig tradition could have produced an entirely contrastive account of the Reformation, as (for a Whig) a very bad thing indeed. That account would instead stress the following: the Reformation's absolutist, cruel, despair-producing, humanity-belittling, merit-rejecting, determinist account of salvation; its closely related account of an exclusivist, invisible, ahistorical Church of the pure; its stringent insistence on the inerrancy of Scripture; its destructive iconoclasm; its initial political quietism—even in the face of tyranny. With each of these key features, the English Reformation

1

presents an especially somber aspect. By this account, the Reformation wasn't, by liberal lights at any rate, such a very good thing at all.

Both these apparently contradictory sketches of the Reformation are in my view *correct*. The dark picture is true of the sixteenth-century start of the process; the brighter picture of the late seventeenth-century provisional end. If both pictures are true, then how did we get from the illiberal start of the process to its apparent opposite, at the provisional end of that process? How did political quietism end up as constitutional government? How did a denial of free will end up promoting agency? How did a merit-denying culture arrive at meritocracy? How did a work-denying culture arrive at the Protestant work ethic? How did an intolerance promoting culture arrive at the ideal of tolerance? How did biblical literalism arrive at interpretative freedom? How did iconoclasm arrive at the art museum?

Whig historiography, so dominant throughout the nineteenth century, was subject to powerful critique by Herbert Butterfield in his *Whig Interpretation of History* (1931). Butterfield made a persuasive case that Anglo-American historiography consistently coded the triumph of Protestantism as the triumph of Anglo-American values (especially Liberty). Such historiography, he argued, accordingly produced a relentlessly teleological narrative that forever pointed to the triumph of Liberty.[2] Dissatisfied by that triumphalist, unidirectional narrative, Butterfield proposed a more complex narrative model. So far from it being the case that Liberalism was a *direct* result of the Reformation, he argued, liberty of sorts was the Reformation's *accidental* result. Herewith his elegant and profound formulation: the Whig historian, Butterfield says, "likes to imagine religious liberty issuing beautifully out of Protestantism when in reality it emerges painfully and grudgingly out of something quite different, out of the tragedy of the post-Reformation world."[3]

In my view Anglo-American historiography has yet fully to take up the challenge of this provocative, paradoxical historical resolution. Only apparently chastened by Butterfield's skeptical critique, for the most part Anglo-American historians of the Reformation centuries only seemed to withdraw into the domain of the professional historian, dispassionately to consider history non-teleologically, "in its own terms," and "for its own sake."[4] In fact, however, Whig triumphalism only went not so successfully underground, recoding the religious triumph of English Protestantism as secular triumphs of different kinds: of, for example, constitutional government; of characteristically English moderation; of working-class values; of rationality.[5] Protestant triumphalism thus remained a secretly, or not so secretly, embedded code of many influential professional Anglo-American historians up to the early 1970s. It remained, indeed, the code of a secularized *Heilsgeschichte,* or salvation history.[6] And after a relatively short hiatus, explicitly Whiggish accounts of triumphantly Protestant traditions have started recently to resurface, both religious, as well as secularist and republican.[7]

Since the early 1990s, a vigorous Catholic riposte to Protestant triumphalism has, influentially, also emerged. This riposte fails, however, to move beyond the Butterfieldian problematic, since it replicates the Protestant triumphalist narrative as a Catholic triumphalist mirror image.[8] With some admirable recent exceptions, Anglo-American historiography of the Reformation remains locked into a five-hundred-year agon, fighting a Catholic / Protestant struggle on one side or the other.[9]

Anglo-American institutional and social historians have, then, negotiated Butterfield, even if they often end up reproducing the positions (or their mirror images) to which Butterfield objected. By contrast with those historians, early modernist *literary* historians have tended to ignore Butterfield altogether. They have instead remained blithely in Protestant triumphalist mode, largely fixed in a Catholic / Protestant polarity, where "Catholic" is code for all that is illiberal.[10]

The very practice of Anglo-American literary criticism and pedagogy depends on presenting literature as resistant, anti-hierarchical and anti-institutional. To abandon the narrative that pitches the Reformation as the triumph of Liberalism will always be especially difficult for literary historians, since such a move knocks away a key support of the discipline itself; to question the Reformation is to question more than the discipline can manage. As a result, the chasm between the Catholic Middle Ages and the Protestant Reformation remains the deepest cultural divide in English literary historiography.[11]

Many Anglo-American literary scholars, both medievalists and early modernists, remain for the most part, accordingly, caught on either side of the break of 1534 (i.e. the Act of Supremacy). Many of the medievalists are caught in the bind, not only because they do not traverse the boundary line, but also because their work on pre-Reformation culture is often devoted to spotting the premonitions of the liberal order in medieval textual culture.[12] The early modernists are caught because they continue, despite some admirable recent exceptions, to ignore the pre-Reformation period except to rehearse inaccurate caricatures about it.[13]

How is it that literary scholars of the Reformation centuries can in such large numbers ignore the darkness of early European modernity? Herewith my answer: they approach the Reformation through one main door (1688), and avoid the other (1517).

There are two grand scholarly entry points to the Reformation centuries. An Anglo-American scholar of literature enters those centuries either through the front door of 1688 (the Glorious Revolution), or through the back door of 1517 (the Lutheran Reformation). One's point of entry tends to determine one's view of evangelical Protestantism. With some remarkable exceptions, Anglo-American literary scholarship had tended, until very recently, to approach the Reformation from the present going backwards.[14] Early modernist literary scholars, that is, tended, and tend still, to enter Mansion Reformation from the present going backwards, through its magnificent front door, the one marked "Glorious Revolution (1688)." Late medievalists, by contrast, come to the Reformation from the past going forwards, and so enter by the back door, marked "Luther, 1517."

The House of Reformation looks very different indeed according to one's point of entry. If one enters Mansion Reformation by the standard itinerary of the early modernists, then the front door of 1688 looks decidedly like the liberal tradition in formation. This is the moment of the relatively bloodless Glorious Revolution of 1688, and of both the Bill of Rights and the Toleration Act of 1689—those great, if qualified, victories for religious toleration and constitutional government. As I have said, most liberal scholars approach Mansion Reformation through that deeply inspiring front door.

Having once entered the mansion of Reformation via the 1688 front door of Liberty, (relative) Freedom of Conscience and Constitutionalism, it's easy to look back from the 1688 front rooms to imagine the 1517 back rooms of House Reformation with nonnegotiable approval: if 1688 was the result, then 1517 must have been desirable. Even the violent wars of religion must have been necessary to break, once and for all, with "Catholic absolutism." So, with some dark passages along the way (including wars and schisms among Protestants), Whiggish literary historians imagined the passages back to the 1517 rooms as a continuous, if long, corridor of Reform, not to say Liberty, between the sixteenth-century Reformation and its durable 1688 settlement. After all, 1517 was, wasn't it (as we have seen), about liberty of conscience, equality through the democratic, meritocratic priesthood of all believers, the right of every person to interpret scripture for him or herself, rationality, toleration, and (above all) the growth of individuality and interiority (an especial favorite with literary historians), now that each Christian had unmediated access to a personal God?[15]

Among Anglo-American early modernist literary scholars, the assumption of continuous, direct access down corridor Liberty, from front to back of Reformation House, has very often remained, however, precisely that—an assumption. Different factors encouraged literary scholars to forego any visit to the somber rear rooms of 1517–1580. Herewith some of those factors: relentlessly synchronic, anti-grand narrative New Historicism has favored small-scale chronologies; Anglo-American literary historiography has tended to skip the sixteenth century before 1580; and, until recently, Anglo-American literary history has tended to skip all religious literary history *tout court*.[16]

Anglo-American literary early modernists tended instead, accordingly, to stay up front in Mansion Reformation, and to choose between two glorious chambers: either the austere but hugely impressive, well-lit front room, marked "Milton," or the spectacular middle rooms, their ceilings "fretted with golden fire," marked "Marlowe to Shakespeare." Both these rooms are intensively visited, but the passages from those great chambers back to the beginning of the reign of Henry VIII tend to be almost wholly ignored (a quick peer back to Wyatt and Surrey writing poignant lyrics in prison excepted). Institutional historians have started again to venture grander narratives, but many literary historians remain locked, for the most part, in the mini-chronologies and demarcated rooms of Foucauldian revolutionary historiography.[17]

Late medievalist visitors have recently, however, been seen entering the back rooms of the English Reformation. For almost a century after the establishment of professional historical research in universities from the

1870s, late medievalists stayed at home; they didn't venture next door, beyond 1500, and into the early modern period at all.[18] In the 1990s, however, they started venturing forward; naturally enough, they entered Mansion Reformation from the past moving forward. They entered, that is, through the Lutheran back door.[19]

A frankly shocking sight met them as they entered Mansion Reformation by that 1517 back door. All the features mentioned above strike and shock: the Reformation's absolutist, cruel, despair-producing, humanity-belittling, merit-denying, determinist account of salvation; its closely related account of an exclusivist, invisible, ahistorical Church; its stringent insistence on the inerrancy of Scripture; its destructive iconoclasm; its early political quietism—even in the face of tyranny: with each of these key features, the early English Reformation presents an especially somber aspect.

Mansion Reformation's back entrance had, however, even greater shocks in store for the medievalist visitor. Entering by the 1517 back door, late medievalists discovered that many cultural forms routinely characterized by liberal culture as specifically "medieval" (e.g. iconoclasm, slavery, persecution of "witches," judicial torture in England, Biblical fundamentalism, political absolutism[20]) were specifically early modern phenomena. And the late medieval visitors discovered that capital persecution of religious difference was very much more pronounced from the 1550s, in England at any rate. And they certainly discovered a massive upshot in religious violence after 1547, revealing that the key differential is not, in England, Catholic / Protestant, but late medieval / early modern.[21] Late medievalists suddenly understood, that is, that liberal modernity retrojected its abject onto premodernity (aka, here, pre-Reformation Catholic later Middle Ages). The vast and ongoing popular history of the "gothic" (running from Spenser in the late sixteenth century to *Castle of Otranto* (1764) and well beyond to *Buffy the Vampire Slayer*) encapsulates, indeed, that inexhaustible liberal retrojection of the abject onto the Catholic Middle Ages.

In sum, Mansion Reformation looked glorious to literary liberals when entered by the front door of 1688. Let the same liberal enter by the back door, and s / he will be shocked to find the wholly illiberal culture of early modernity busily throwing its embarrassing abject over the back fence into the property behind, the Catholic ancien régime.

Both points of entry to Mansion Reformation are in fact vulnerable to the same disabling weakness, as long as scholars refuse to traverse the entire length of the Reformation: both entrances—front door or back—reinforce the standard antinomies of Anglo-American historiography. The radically simplified Whig picture of Catholic:bad / Protestant:good (roughly the way it looks from the front door) is reversed, by some of the revisionists, to become Catholic:good / Protestant:bad (the back door view). That way, the five-hundred-year agon of Anglophone historiography remains intact in both camps, forever paralyzed within the logic of a Catholic / Protestant contest. We remain, in short, caught in the agon so ably delineated by Butterfield in 1931.

II

Entrance via the front, 1688 door of Mansion Reformation explains why Protestant triumphalism should remain so powerful, even despite Butterfield's intervention. It therefore also explains why medievalists, who enter by the dark back door, find English cultural history so urgently in need of revision. Above all, the strikingly contrastive experience of such different doors to the same house impels us to connect them.

The stakes of connecting those two doors are high, since we stand to reconceive the following: the history of Liberalism; the relation of Liberalism to evangelical religion; and, by no means least, the nature of our own modernity. The stakes of such understanding are especially high in our own moment. Liberalism is in global retreat before evangelical religion.[22] And Liberalism in the West is becoming increasingly fragile on account of the following, for example: its minimalist anthropology and the abstract univeralist legal principles that flow from that anthropology; its default positions of institutional distrust; its impoverished conception of freedom; and, more recently, in a distorted offshoot of Liberalism, its inability to formulate persuasive models durable, flourishing cultural cohabitation, subject as it is to its own identity-driven exclusivisms.

Where the contested cultural investments in a given historical transformation are so deep (i.e., in the case of the Reformation, selfhood, the liberal political order, and the nation), the chances of definitive resolution with regard to understanding the logic of the Reformation centuries will remain, I concede, zero. Major historical phenomena of this kind, which continue to define our subjectivity and predicaments, are not susceptible of definitive resolutions of understanding. Traditions that emerge from the Reformation predicament are, nonetheless, susceptible of development and renewal, of the kind I hope to offer here. Precisely because we are part of history's problem, we can be part of its solution.

But what kind of history do we need to traverse the entire house? In a phrase: grand narrative. Or, in a slightly less crisp phrase: at least grander narrative than the micro-narratives to which we have been devoted for the last thirty years.[23] The liberal tradition is in my view profoundly and damagingly mistaken about its own genealogy, precisely because it promotes truncated forms of historical understanding, especially with regard to religion. Either it thinks, as nineteenth-century Liberalism thought, that the liberal tradition is a direct descendent of the sixteenth-century Reformation.[24] Or, in its more recent, militantly secularist form, the liberal tradition locates its origin in the eighteenth-century Enlightenment (with, perhaps, a glance back to Renaissance humanism), without reference to prior model cultures, and certainly without reference to religious culture of any kind. Liberal individualism, by this account, is inconceivable without the secularization thesis, and begins with the strenuous repudiation of religious culture *tout court*.[25]

Against those traditions, I argue here that the historiography of Protestantism needs to be diachronic for the same reason that the historiography of all successful revolutionary moments needs to be diachronic and relatively grand in its narrative. Like other revolutionary moments (e.g. the French Revolution), Protestantism, that is, has produced revolutionary historiography that renders one born-again historical period unintelligible to its predecessors. As Alexis de Tocqueville so astutely observed, "When great revolutions are successful, their causes cease to exist . . . the very fact of their success has made them incomprehensible."[26]

Without grander narrative, history also becomes irrelevant, since we cannot understand the ongoing, long-term *effects* of great events unless we are also prepared to understand the long-term *conditions and causes* of those same, great events. I am an adherent of the Zhou Enlai school of historiography, which holds that revolutions take about 150 years to find stable form (1517 to 1688, say; or 1789 to 1958).[27] As such, I am committed to grander narratives than either more recent Whig historians or New Historicism have permitted. We might wish to abandon some key teleological and triumphalist aspects of Whig grand narrative; that does not in itself necessitate abandonment of grand narrative per se. Put positively, I aim, insofar as possible, to make history whole, and thereby bring religious history into the story of modernity.[28] This demands a historiography that does not succumb to the temptation of supercessionism, by which I mean the practice of dismissing a prior historical period as culturally exhausted and definitively irrelevant.[29]

The most forceful historiographical commitment of this book is, then, to a non-supercessionist, and therefore longue durée cultural history, to a cultural history forever open to the ways in which relatively deep pasts (in this case religious deep pasts) resurface, and transform in new circumstances. Mighty historical forces do not vanish; they resurface in different form. Repress them, and they migrate to different cultural sites, with usually unintended results. Cultural systems are hydraulic. In the short and medium term they displace cultural energies; only in the very long term do they expel them. The proto-Enlightenment is less a clean break with, than an unintended transformation of, older evangelical materials.

III

Permanent Revolution, then, addresses the competing claimants to Anglo-American (and global) modernity (i.e. evangelical religion and the Enlightenment), and poses the following questions with regard to the British Reformations: (i) how did we get from the first, illiberal Reformation to the Protestant proto-Enlightenment?; and (ii) why did we need to?

Three perceptions animate the argument: (i) that dissident, repressive, non-conservative sixteenth-century evangelical religious culture was revolutionary; (ii) that revolutionary evangelical culture was simultaneously a culture of *permanent* revolution, repeatedly and compulsively repudiating its own prior forms; and (iii) that permanent revolution was, as it always is, punishingly violent, fissiparous, and unsustainable, so much so that it needed to invent self-stabilizing mechanisms. In the seventeenth century, I argue, English Calvinist Protestantism necessarily produced its opposite cultural formation (what I call the proto-Enlightenment), against the punishing, crushing, violent, schismatic logic of the evangelical Reformation. The Protestant proto-Enlightenment made the permanent revolution of evangelical religion at least socially manageable and personally livable, even if the liberal order remained scarred by the effort.

By contrast with the explicit claims of most academic historians, *Permanent Revolution* rebuilds one platform of the Whig narrative. Against, that is, the supercessionism of Enlightenment secularists, who aggressively insist that we can happily forget about the centuries prior to the eighteenth-century Enlightenment, this book *adopts* the Whig conviction that Liberalism does indeed derive from Protestantism. It also argues that the nascent liberal tradition was, in the late seventeenth century, the only set of resources that could save warring English and Scottish evangelical religion from itself.

However much each of the bald statements of the following positions requires careful qualification, in England these positions derive from, and, *as a package,* could *only have* derived from, Protestantism: qualified free will; correlative praise of works; democratic constitutionalism; division of political and judicial powers; consent-driven elections; freedom of religious and political conscience; religious tolerance; non-fundamentalist, non-literalist, non-institutional scriptural reading; freedom to read and interpret non-scriptural texts; and artistic autonomy. It's true, as we shall see, that some, though by no means all, these features of proto-Liberalism are recoveries of a late medieval inheritance (e.g. constitutionalism, modified versions of free will, anti-literalism). But the pressure to present them as a package of sorts derives from moving through the logic of Protestantism.

Insofar as my (admittedly large) claim about the ecclesiological genealogy of English and then Scottish Liberalism is true, this book therefore attempts to reinstate at least one very familiar platform of the Whig tradition, *pace* Butterfield and his legion of ostensibly observant followers: Protestantism *did* produce the package of liberal positions articulated in the last paragraph. It did so as a vital matter of survival after 150 years of European religious warfare. So far from it being the case that the late seventeenth-century proto-Enlightenment breaks utterly free of religion, as many proponents of the secularization thesis would have us believe, and so far from it being the case that English republicanism was driven by almost wholly secular, humanist traditions, I argue, on the contrary, that the British Enlightenment is in almost every key respect (except, perhaps, the history of science) the reflex of religious culture. To understand Liberalism, we need to understand early modern Calvinism. The most profound convulsions of our history, and the most profound determinants of our identity, are, so I contend, ecclesiological.[30] This book is in part a story of secularization, but that story understands the logic of secularization through the narrative of ecclesiology. It does not see secularism as the definitive escape from religion, and certainly not as the single option of modernity.

Permanent Revolution, then, attempts to reinstate one platform of the Whig tradition: Protestantism did produce the proto-Enlightenment in England and Scotland. With that one Whig platform duly back in place, however, the present book actively demolishes another. Not *pace* Whigs, the central argument of *Permanent Revolution* is that the liberal tradition derives from Protestantism by repudiating it. Sixteenth- and seventeenth-century Protestant culture is, despite both popular and popular scholarly persuasion, diametrically *opposed* to each one of the cardinal positions of the liberal tradition listed above. Those central features of early modern evangelical culture might be quickly and crudely summarized thus: enslavement of the will, with total repudiation of works as currency in the economy of salvation, and the permanent shadow of despair; a sense of self subject to an impossibly high bar of authenticity, and forever vulnerable to the charge of hypocrisy; a fear of dramatic performativity, now described as seductive, irrational, and lethal magic; repudiation of visual images, both material and psychic, as the destructive allurements of idolatry; obsessive focus on the literalist written as the source of salvation; and non-toleration for freedom of religious conscience.

So far, that is, from simply developing and secularizing forms of evangelical religion, Protestantism reversed itself in a profoundly agonistic relation to its own prior forms, though always within the kinetic cultural logic of Protestantism itself. The theme of Protestant history, that is, is very much less one of consistent, unidirectional development than of profoundly paradoxical, internally conflicted paradox. That history is, by the same token, much more dynamically intra-Protestant than it is Protestant / Catholic. Protestant history moves, as Butterfield (with some eighteenth-century predecessors) so acutely saw, under the master trope of historical irony.[31]

Each sequence of chapters focuses on one of these key issues, which are simultaneously key issues for early European modernity. In each case I adumbrate the evangelical lineaments of that cultural issue; point to the ways in which the pressures it imposed were clearly unstoppable and unsustainable; and show how English literary and theological culture crept out from under that crushing, intolerable evangelical heel. Each of the issues discussed here has relatively low, if visible, profile in late medieval Britain; rockets in significance in our early modernity; packed a mighty punch; and continues to inform our own, contemporary culture.

In fact, truth be told, just as often my enquiry started with my experience of what might be called the conditions of contemporary modernity, where "conditions" also designates pathology. The present is, after all (let's be honest), the place where most historical enquiry most urgently and frequently starts. Many cultural historians would describe their work as an act of discovery. My project is rather one of recovery, an exercise in what I call "cultural etymology," where one starts from the present and recovers immanent histories by which the present is freshly understood.

The substantial evidence for each chapter is drawn from poetry, literary prose, and drama. One justification for this evidential emphasis would be to give voice to literary artefacts in a larger discursive arena. Because I am more of a cultural historian than a literary critic, I do indeed wish to do this. The justification for this emphasis on literary artefacts is, however, stronger: works of art register cultural pressure and / or signal cultural change with greater, more luminous clarity than works from any other discursive field, not least because they were existentially threatened in this period of convulsive cultural transformation.

Chapters are grouped in thematic parts. Parts are themed as follows: Part 1: Religion as Revolution (Chapters 1–2); Part 2: Working Modernity's Despair (Chapters 3–5); Part 3: Sincerity and Hypocrisy (Chapters 6–8); Part 4: Breaking Idols (Chapters 9–11); Part 5: Theater, Magic, Sacrament (Chapters 12–14); Part 6: Managing Scripture (Chapters 15–17); and Part 7: Liberty and Liberties (Chapter 18). For each of these sequences except the last, I tell a tripartite story, whose narrative order runs roughly thus (with plenty of variation): appropriation of powers and carnivalesque, revolutionary energy (c. 1520–1547); revolutionary grief (c. 1547–1625); escaping revolutionary disciplines? (c. 1603–1688). Readers who are short of time will find each sequence self-contained.

PART 1

Religion as Revolution

1

Revolutionary Religion

THE QUESTION, then, is how do we resolve the two plausible but contradictory versions of the Reformation—the illiberal and the proto-liberal versions—in Anglo-American cultural history? How did the English Reformation get from its illiberal beginning in 1517 to its provisional proto-liberal stabilization in 1688? And why did it need to?

We require two historical concepts to answer these questions: one capable of adequately characterizing the cultural package of the early Reformation; and one capable of accounting for the generative dynamism within that cultural package, so generative as to produce its opposite. For the first, I appeal to a concept immanent within the practice of Reformation players themselves: that of revolution. For the second, I appeal to a phenomenon inherent in all true revolutions: that of permanent revolution. In this chapter, I sketch how the concept of "revolution" turns out to be remarkably illuminating as applied to the early modernizing evangelical program. This is a more static description. In Chapter 2, we see revolution in motion, for understanding of which I appeal to the idea of permanent revolution.

I

I label the illiberal theological package of early modern Protestantism "revolutionary." I do so because all the cardinal positions of early modern evangelical religion, except non-toleration, mark a radical break with the pre-Reformation past.[1] The adjective "revolutionary" is also applicable to evangelical early modern religious culture because that culture provides, for the first time, the recognizable blueprint for future European, and then later revolutionary political movements based on Western models, especially in Asia. The present chapter gives substance to the claim that Reformation evangelical religion is properly described as revolutionary.

Evangelical culture claimed the future by being revolutionary. Protestantism exhibits many features of something very distinctive and very new in what might be called early modernizing Europe.[2] The essence of all these revolutionary features is not the backwardness of the state, and not class struggle, but centralization, which sweeps whole pasts away.

In agreement with Stephen Pincus, I take centralization to generate the fundamental narrative of modernity.[3] Standard popular and scholarly liberal accounts of modernity not unreasonably accentuate the institution of individual legal rights evenly across jurisdictions as the essential narrative of modernity.[4] That optimistic, progressive, and decentralizing story is, however, underwritten by a more powerful and sometimes less optimistic story of centralizations—what Weber calls rationalizations—which create the very possibility of consistent national jurisdictions.[5] Revolutions that present themselves as expressions of individual liberties are sometimes susceptible of being read as expressions of the need for centralization.[6]

Pincus posits the Glorious Revolution of 1688 as the first true revolution of modernity. That may be. The story of centralizing modernity, however, starts well before 1688 in England, with the top-down revolution of the 1530s, itself part of the growth of the nation-state in sixteenth-century Europe. Here the prime narrative has nothing to do with individual rights and everything to do with centralization of powers. Henrician England experienced many forms of centralization, which were to reach their culmination in the distinctively early modern, largely seventeenth-century phenomenon of the divine right of kings. I focus first on forms of early modern centralization in Henrician England, before turning to their revolutionary effect.

Some centralizing, "rationalizing" features of the 1530s were legislative: above all, the abolition of any division between Church and State (the Act of Supremacy of 1534[7]), and the correlative abolition of the highly segmented orders of the pre-Reformation English Church. In addition, England also experienced legislated rationalizations of liturgical practice, law, church property, library localization, and language use.[8] Further forms of centralization were sociological, involving a powerful concentration of power in the hands of the monarch at the expense of the nobility, both greater and lesser.[9] They also involved abolitions of late medieval urban associational groupings, such as urban fraternities (broadly religious self-help associations).[10] Still other forms of centralization were produced by technological innovation, notably printing, which had the effect of speeding up the formation of a common linguistic standard, not to speak of common cultural standards.[11] The linguistic diversity of post-Conquest England (not to speak of post-Conquest Britain)—a diversity both within English and between English, Latin, French, Scots, and Welsh—had undergone a long process leading to the rapidly increasing status of English by the mid-fourteenth century. From the introduction of print into England (1476), that process of linguistic hierarchization between languages and linguistic centralization within English, in favor of a London standard, was markedly accelerated, with the loss of a variety of literary forms of English. Printing also prompted other forms of centralized control: for all its evident power ultimately to decentralize culture with the formation of the "private reader," printing also permitted and produced a much tighter, centralized surveillance of written production.[12]

These legislative, liturgical, social, and cultural centralizations of early modernizing England are indeed momentous.[13] Measured by ambition, however, they are small beer compared to the dream of centralization in Protestant theology, which most purely articulates the centralizing tendencies of early modernizing Europe. A monotheistic God has, by definition, absolute powers, but that God did not always act as an absolutist. On the contrary, the late medieval European Christian God was a constitutionalist of sorts: despite the fact that he *could* do whatever he liked, he freely made reliable agreements with humans according to which they could negotiate their way out of sin. Most (not all) late medieval theologies had imagined God working out from various combinations of his agreed, reliable, *ordained* power (*potentia ordinata*) and his wholly unrestrained *absolute* power (*potentia absoluta*). Of course the late medieval God had absolute powers at his disposal, but he freely decided to hold by his ordained, which is to say his established and rationally perceptible, power.[14]

Sixteenth-century Protestant theology was starkly different. The Protestant God acted, not coincidentally, like sixteenth-century monarchs, insisting on his absolute prerogatives. He actively repudiated any reliable agreements that would abrogate his "independent and illimited Prerogative."[15] Sixteenth-century Protestant theologians of all stripes invested God with massively concentrated, and newly opaque, executive praxis (notably predestination), at the center of a purified, utterly homogeneous True Church of the elect. In the matter of salvation theory (i.e. soteriology), evangelical theology demolished the elegant late medieval dialectical structures of grace (or gift) and wage by instituting one order—that of grace—distributed wholly at the divine monarch's inscrutable will. That is, Protestant theology gave precedence at every point to God's *potentia absoluta*. Pre-modern salvation was a wage of sorts; it implied that God owed something to humans who do their best. By contrast, the Protestant, early modern God owed nothing, certainly not by law, nor by agreement. He made no agreements, and he neutralized human agency altogether.

Centralization is both the parent and the child of revolutions: the centralizing of early modern nation-states permits the revolution, but the revolution also provokes greater centralization in its turn, until, of course, the unsustainable violence of the revolution produces the great counter narrative of modernity (i.e. decentralizing division of powers). Protestant theology, then, was in theory extremely centralized and revolutionary. This is, after all, unsurprising, since if the most powerful currents of a society are undergoing a process, it is only natural that theology should follow (or lead). Theology turns out, indeed, to be an especially precious index of cultural formations, since, in the pre-institutional stages of large-scale cultural change, theology has the luxury of imagining change, and of giving voice to cultural pressures, in their purest, least constrained form.

The sixteenth- and seventeenth-century evangelical movement is properly described as both centralizing and revolutionary because it:

- posited unmediated power relations between highly centralized, single sources of power on the one hand, and now equalized, atomized, interiorized, and terrorized subjects on the other;[16]
- looked aggressively upon, and sought to abolish, horizontal, lateral associational forms;[17]
- produced a small cadre of internationally connected, highly literate elect who belonged to the True Church, and who felt obliged by revolutionary necessity both to target the intellectuals of the ancien régime, and to impose punishing disciplines on the laity, who were expected, in this case, to become a "priesthood of all believers";[18]
- generated revolutionary accounts of both ecclesiology and the individual life: both could achieve a rebirth, wholly inoculated from the virus of the past;[19]
- demanded total and sudden, not developmental, change via spiritual conversion;[20]
- targeted the hypocrisy of those who only pretended to buy into the new order;[21]
- abolished old and produced new calendars and martyrologies;[22]
- proclaimed the positivist literalism of a single authoritative text, to be universally and evenly applicable across a jurisdiction, if necessary with violence;[23]
- demanded and enacted cultural revolution, through iconoclasm of the repudiated past's accreted, erroneous, idolatrous visual culture and by closing down its theatrical culture;[24]
- distributed the charisma of special place across entire jurisdictions, thereby legitimating the destruction of sites considered in the old regime to have compacted charisma most intensely, or to provide sanctuary;[25]
- actively developed surveillance systems;[26]
- legitimated violent repudiation of the past on the authority of absolute knowledge derived from the end of time. The saints were in a position confidently to judge and reshape the saeculum, or the world of everyday experience, precisely because, as elect members of the eternal True Church, they were saints; they beheld the everyday world from

the determinist vantage point of the *eschaton*, or the end of time. They knew how to see historical error (it was in fact easy), and they knew the denouement of History's narrative;[27]
- promoted the idea of youth's superiority over age;[28]
- appropriated the private property of religious orders and centralized previously monastic libraries;[29]
- redefined and impersonalized the relation of the living and the dead, notably by the abolition of Purgatory and the prohibition on masses for the dead;[30] and, by no means least,
- legitimated revolutionary violence by positing a much more intimate connection between violence and virtue than the Maoist dictum "no omelet without breaking eggs" would imply. In this culture, persecution and violence were a sure sign that the Gospel was being preached, that Christ was indeed bringing not peace but the (necessary) sword. The absence of tumult was symptomatic of somnolent hypocrisy.[31] Violence was a necessary obligation within the logic of History.

These key features of evangelical modernity find rather exact parallels in more recent revolutionary cultures, for example in France, Russia, China, or Cambodia. The fact that this typology of separate features can often be found together, as a package, in widely different historical moments might, indeed, embolden us to formulate an idea of a comparative revolutionary historiography / sociology. If we were so emboldened (as I am) to join such a tradition of scholarship, I would hasten to underline that sixteenth-century evangelical religion provides a robust template for later instantiations of the package.[32]

II

Is there any authorization from within early modernity to use the word "revolution," in its modern sense of "overthrow," with regard to events in the period 1642–1649, let alone the entire culture of evangelical religion between 1517 and the 1680s? The answer is yes, even if the semantic work done by the word "revolution" is more often effected lexically by the word "reformation," with its usual early modern sense of total (*not* reformist) change. The word "reformation" occupies a much higher profile than the word "revolution" in early modern Britain, though the word "revolution" in its modern sense does begin to displace "reformation" by the middle of the seventeenth century.

As in other European languages, astronomy is the primary discourse in which the word "revolution" itself was used in English in the late medieval and early modern periods.[33] Its primary sense is "return to beginnings."[34] In this sense, the word "revolution" is semantically parallel to the late medieval word "reformation," which had designated a return to beginnings, *ad pristinum statum ire*.[35] Usage of the word "reformation," indeed, for the Protestant Reformation, is itself a Catholic borrowing, since *reformatio* was the standard term for ecclesiastical renewal from at least the twelfth century.[36]

In early modern English, a frequent synonym for both "reformation" and "revolution" in this sense (of a return to beginnings) is "reduction."[37] Thus, in arguing against the existence of bishops, Milton (while still in his Presbyterian phase) declares that the Church must "*reform* her self rightly by the Scriptures, must undress them all of their gilded vanities, and *reduce* them as they were at first, to the lowly and equal order of Presbyters" (my emphases).[38] Milton's terms of choice are "reduction" and "reformation" rather than "revolution," and both mean, in keeping with the primary sense of "revolution," a return to pristine beginnings.

The senses of "reformation" and "revolution" can, however, very easily tip into full-scale change of a kind that looks very much like totalizing repudiation of the past and totalizing renewal. The new concept of revolution as totalizing change is perceptible as used in a sermon of Thomas Case (bap. 1598–1682), delivered to Parliament in 1641:

> Reformation must be universal . . . Let yours be so, I beseech you. Reform all places, all persons and callings. Reform the Benches of Judgements, the inferior Magistrates . . . Reform the Church, go into the Temple . . . Reform the universities . . . Reform the Cities, reform the Countries, reform inferior schools of learning, reform the Sabbath, reform the Ordinances, the worship of God.[39]

Case characterizes all that needs "reformation" as "Popery," and popery needs to be utterly destroyed, without pity: no matter how beautiful the flower, Case urges his parliamentary listeners, reformation must be effected by pulling up "the very roots," if the plant was not "of God's planting" (image 21). Should the work remain in any way incomplete, it will need to be done again: "You will find all your labor and cost carried away, as it were with a spring tide of profaneness and superstition. You will be still to begin your work of reformation" (image 20).

"Reformation," then, shifts into the territory of totalizing (i.e. revolutionary) renewal in the mid-seventeenth century. The word "revolution" itself, however, starts to make the same move at the same time, away from "return to beginnings," and toward "unprecedented overthrow of the established order." Thus Marchamont Nedham, in his *The Case of the Commonwealth of England Stated* (1650), defends the overthrow of Charles I as a "revolution." His first usage is in the older astronomical sense of "the perpetuall rotation of all things in a circle."[40] Very soon, however, with clear reference to the execution of the king, the word shifts into its modern sense: "Many Royall Families and famous Governments," says Nedham, "have had their fatall periods in a very short revolution of time" (image 9). Once that move is made, the way is open for the new sense: the frequent instances of governments being overthrown are referred to as "these national revolutions of government" (image 12).[41]

Nedham was well placed to understand sudden overthrow, since he was practiced at overthrowing his own former positions. He had begun as a spokesman for the parliamentarian cause, before switching sides to become a royalist defender, before switching back, after the execution of the king, to defend both the Rump Parliament, and then, finally, defending the Rump Parliament's overthrow by Cromwell in the coup d'état of 1653.[42] In his *The Excellencie of a Free-State*, published in 1656, after the military putsch of 1653, Nedham takes the case for "revolution" in the modern sense much further: he argues that no government should be allowed to settle into faction, and so each government must be subject to frequent change by "due succession and revolution of Authority in the Hands of the People."[43]

I am not, of course, the first to trace the revolutionary theological genealogy of the "saints." Indeed, the very term "Puritan Revolution" was first introduced by the French liberal politician, historian, and translator of Shakespeare François Guizot in 1826, by way of comparing the English Revolution favorably with the French version.[44] The term "revolution" was willingly taken up in the locution "Puritan Revolution" by nineteenth-century Whigs, who understood Puritanism as a vehicle for constitutional aspiration.[45] That Whig tradition was enabled by two moves. Whigs effected a softening of the edge of the word "revolution" to mean liberal, or proto-liberal, reformation on the one hand. On the other, they effected a redescription of Puritan politics as anti-authoritarian, whereby Christian liberty fed seamlessly into political liberty.[46] Absorption of the locution "Puritan Revolution" was also enabled by focusing on the "political" implications of Puritanism, as distinct from its "religious" content. The following claim by Guizot fed directly into the Whig tradition:

> Taking everything together, the English revolution was essentially political; it was brought about in the midst of a religious people and in a religious age; religious thoughts and passions were its instruments; but its chief design and definite aim were political, were devoted to liberty, and the abolition of all absolute power.[47]

In this book's account of the evangelical religion as revolutionary, I look less to the political character of Calvinist polities than to the politics of the theology itself. That is, I understand the theology as fundamentally expressive of European revolutionary modernity. Because "religion" as a category is, in our own times, presumptively pre-modern, and because the modern is also presumptively "progressive," very few scholars tend to regard religion as a key form of modernity. A good deal of *maxisant* scholarship of the 1960s and 1970s saw *premonitions* of modernity in the sectaries of the seventeenth century (in particular, premonitions of working-class, revolutionary political formations).[48] But very few scholars have understood the theology of Calvinism and its offshoots as substantively expressive of one key form of modernity itself.

The scholar who most persuasively worked from that premise is Michael Walzer, in his brilliant book *The Revolution of the Saints: A Study in the Origins of Radical Politics* (1965). Walzer's essential argument is that Puritanism is the "earliest form of political radicalism."[49] Puritanism is part of the process of modernization insofar as it was enabled by, and itself promoted the atomization of social agents and the correlative rise of large-scale political units that overwhelm "family, corporation, town," and which demand corresponding disciplines. Party rigor, enforced by internationalist intellectuals wholly dedicated to a totalizing cause, mark out Puritanism as a proto-revolutionary movement.

I hope Walzer would agree with me in arguing that the revolutionary force of Calvinism is expressive of modernity, without in any way making it "progressive" or liberal. Modernity has a variety of faces, one of which is revolutionary, illiberal evangelical religion.

III

The word "revolutionary" tends to evoke marginal sects who come, or fail to come, to occupy central power. There were, as we shall see, plenty of such sects in England, in the seventeenth century in particular. But the revolutionary package I am describing, both exhilarating and crushing, was not by any means the preserve of marginal sects. In addition to being the key doctrine of many varieties of unofficial Calvinism, it was also, as compacted in the doctrine of predestination, the official doctrine of the Anglican Church as defined by the Thirty-Nine Articles of 1571 (Article 17).[50]

Of course there were ecclesiastical ups and downs for evangelicals in the period of this book (1517–1689), moments when the evangelical package was more or less politically dominant. And, of course, much political theory (notably that of common lawyers) and actual governmental practice on the ground can, if by no means consistently, be described as fundamentally reformist, proto-constitutionalist and anti-revolutionary across these centuries.[51] But politically sustained, institutionalized religion affects, or comes to affect, everyone. Institutionalized Protestantism was by no means the only show in Britain in the Reformation centuries, but it was by far the most forceful and best-populated show, across the entire social spectrum. Above all, across the years from 1558, when the Act of Uniformity (requiring all English persons to attend church weekly) was enacted,[52] to 1571 (when swearing conformity with the Calvinist Thirty-Nine Articles was required of ministers), to the Religion Act and Recusants Act of 1593 (which specified capital punishment as the ultimate penalty for those refusing to worship inside the Church of England), Protestant ecclesiology became a source of national historiography, national identity, subjective identity of the most intimate kind, and intense national and intra-national conflict. Certainly in terms of media consumption, religion far outstripped secular literature for book production and sales in the Reformation centuries. Everyone who wished to participate in the English body politic, or who wished to avoid retribution or persecution, was, one way or another, a "Protestant," even if not a "Puritan." It was, furthermore, the driving force in the religious experience of brilliant writers from a very wide social and chronological range, from, say, the Linconshire martyr and writer Anne Askew (1521–1546), to Chancellor of the Exchequer Fulke Greville (1554–1628), to the Bedfordshire tinker and preacher John Bunyan (1628–1688). Those who defined themselves against that state church did so in ecclesiological terms.

The extremity of Protestant positions characterized mainline "Anglican" polity in at least the reigns of Elizabeth I (1558–1603) and James I (1603–1625). As long as we use the word "Puritan" to denote the risible likes of Jonson's Zeal-of-the-Land Busy, we tend to shield ourselves from the truth that Anglican polity was centrally Calvinist and predestinarian.[53] As long as we maintain the idea of a "moderate Anglicanism" in Elizabethan and Jacobean England, wisely and pragmatically occupying a via media between the extremes of Catholicism on the one hand and puritan Calvinism on the other, we remain in the beautiful confines of Herbert's Church Porch, unwilling to enter the dark and torrid interior space of his Temple.[54]

Once we do enter that Temple, we find something not in the least moderate. For there we find Herbert punningly crying from the rack to his torturing creditor God: "Stretch or contract me thy poor debtor!," where the call to "contract" in the legal sense underlines the fact that this God has abjured contracts, and so contracts the sinner in the torture chamber.[55] Predestinarian theology was orthodox English theology from 1559 to at least 1626 (the date of the York House Conference, after which the newly crowned Charles I effectively prohibited the promotion of predestination).[56] If we fail to enter the torrid space of Herbert's Temple, we fail to appreciate the punishing pressures and disciplines, and the astonishing extremities, of early modernity and evangelical, revolutionary Protestantism. In short, John Morrill's striking and oft-cited claim that "the English Civil War was not the first European revolution, but the last of the wars of religion," works within a mistaken antinomy.[57] The English Civil War (and its long prelude) mark the moment when religion lays claim to revolution.

To understand the cultural dynamics of revolutionary Protestantism, we need, however, to enrich the concept of revolution. I do that in Chapter 2, as I explicate the concept of permanent revolution.

2

Permanently Revolutionary Religion

ONCE STARTED, revolutions are difficult to stop, precisely because the logic of the revolution, for both practical and ideological reasons, is to turn aggressively against its own achievements and its own forebears, if not its own fellows. The proponents of revolution classically and now predictably fall victim, sooner or later (usually sooner than later), to the very movement they initiate. Before revolutions consume their children, however, they consume their own parents. This was no less true of the sixteenth- and seventeenth-century ecclesiological revolutions in England, even if not as violently, as it was true of the French Revolution's Terror of 1793–1794 (whence our word "terrorism"), of Stalinist Russian purges in 1937–1938 especially, and of China's Cultural Revolution between 1966 and 1976.

The fissiparous, permanently revolutionary nature of Protestantism is paradoxically built deep into Protestant identity, and can be seen in many features of evangelical institutional and discursive practice. Protestantism most actively repudiates itself, since early modern Protestants were, to use Edmund Burke's formulation in a different revolutionary context (1790), "rebels from principle," or, in a different Burkean context still, in 1775, promoters of "the dissidence of dissent."[1] Theirs was a practice of what Samuel Butler in 1663 called "thorough reformation / Which always must be carried on / And still be doing, never done."[2]

Do Protestant repudiations of prior Protestant dispensations amount, however, to "permanent revolution," as the title of this book would have it? In this chapter I delineate the logic of the English Reformation's permanent revolution—what has been called "scope creep" with regard to contemporary Islamic iconoclasm[3]—before turning in subsequent chapters to evangelical self-consumption and its attempted therapies with regard to specific issues. Here I focus on three decisive yet different moments: the 1540s; 1558–1580; and the 1640s. Each expresses a distinctive stage in the logic of permanent revolution, being, respectively: simplistic triumphalism (1540s); splintering of the revolutionary movement (1558–1580); and near exhaustion as the promoters and provisional beneficiaries of permanent revolution urge further revolution, even as they know they are about to be overwhelmed (1640s).

I

Revolutions in the modern sense naturally prompt the question as to when they are over. Both Louis XVI and Napoleon confidently proclaimed, in 1791 and 1799 respectively, that the revolution was over.[4] Very soon after the French Revolution in particular, however, it became obvious that the Revolution was not a historical moment but a historical process, and its processual nature was theorized.[5] The phrase "permanent revolution" is most famously associated with Leon Trotsky (1879–1940) (himself a victim of permanent revolution), who, having first used the phrase in 1906, argued in his book *The Permanent Revolution* (1929) that, even if the bourgeoisie had not established the conditions for the proletarian revolution, proletarians should in any case promote permanent revolution internationally, by way of establishing a global communist order (the model adopted by Lenin in 1917) (5:765–66). The phrase, however, had already been used long before, in 1830 in France with regard to the July Revolution (5:762), and by Pierre-Joseph Proudhon (1809–1865) with regard to the failed 1848 revolutions: "La révolution est en permanence . . . il n'y a qu'une seule et même et perpetuelle révolution" (5:763).

The phrase was used most forcefully, however, by Karl Marx in 1850, in his *Speech to the Central Committee to the Communist League*. Marx was addressing the German proletariat. Determined not to accept the defeat of the revolutions of 1848, he wished to maintain the revolutionary energy and program until the process was complete:

> It is our interest and our task to make the revolution permanent until all the more or less propertied classes have been driven from power, until the proletariat has conquered state power.[6]

Marx, then, contemplated the permanent revolution of class struggle with evident relish. He closed his speech to the Central Committee with a clear affirmation that the revolution can never end: "Your battle cry must be: Permanent Revolution!"[7] Even if they had no concept of class struggle at all, evangelicals, as I argue below, championed an idea analogous to that of permanent revolution, what they termed "reforming the Reformation." As with later revolutionaries, they also tended to make the claim for the permanence of the Reformation in moments of apparent defeat.

Permanent revolutionaries should, however, be especially careful what they wish for, since most often they are the victims of successive revolutionary waves. Permanent revolution is hard, exhausting, and dangerous work, which will by its own logic often consume its promoters. Revolutions occur, that is, under the sign of Saturn, who eats his children. Historical revolutionary consumption takes various forms—sometimes blade and flame, but more often consumption of spirit—as we shall see across this book.

II

Near the beginning of the English Reformation, in the 1540s, the matter seemed altogether straightforward. As in the initial, pre-institutional stages of all revolutionary processes, the clarity of distinction between the corrupt old and the revolutionary new was blade sharp. The path of swift movement from the fallen, complex old to the glorious, singular new was also plain, as plain as the text of Scripture. It was in fact a textual highway to the Promised Land.

Evangelicals of the 1530s and 1540s generation had necessarily undergone a conversion experience, having themselves been born into the Roman Church. The zeal of the convert is incomparable: the experience of having been personally born again into a new Church and a new identity was astonishingly energizing, so energizing as to produce complete confidence in a much greater conversion—the national, ecclesiastical conversion from the Church of Rome to the institution of the True (read evangelical) Church. The national transition was to be as definitive as the personal conversion, and the work of that transition was to be straightforward, since the unreal old Church, the material Church of the Papal Antichrist, was so easy to spot. She was rotten to the core, and dressed to match. The True Church was, by maximal contrast, utterly pure, wholly invisible, and totally real. Of course there was, in the 1540s, much evangelical suffering yet to be endured, and much work of stripping the old Church yet to be done.[8] The overdressed and tyrannical Roman Church would not go quietly into the dark. But the task was utterly clear, and the transition was to be definitive and rapid.

Take, for example, the evangelical convert John Bale (1495–1563). After having been sent at the age of twelve to the Carmelite Friars in Norwich, Bale began his study at, most probably, Jesus College Cambridge in 1514. Having produced a history of Carmelite writers, Bale experienced a conversion sometime in the mid-1530s. He married, rejected the Church of his upbringing, and started writing and acting in evangelical agitprop plays, under the protection of Vice-Regent Thomas Cromwell, in the late 1530s.[9]

After Cromwell's fall and execution in 1540, Bale fled to Antwerp. There he wrote and published *The Image of Both Churches* (c. 1545). This text presents itself as a paraphrase of the Book of Revelations, a text always guaranteed to provide fertile matter for the febrile. Bale's *Image of Both Churches* is, in fact, an extended prophecy of the victory of the True Church in England over the Church of Antichrist. The old Church is characterized, among other things, by infinite institutional complexity. It contained the following orders, listed by Bale at such length as to defeat syntax and degenerate into absurd nonsense:

> Benedictines . . . Carmelitanes, Ambrosianes, Rhodianes, Gregorianes, Purgatoryanes, Guilhelmytes, Jesuites, Johannites, Hieronimites, Niniuits, Cellites, Thaborits, Templars, Hospitelers, Crucigers, Augustinianes, Dominicianes, Franciscanes, Brygydanes, Basilianes, of Josaphats valley, and of the dark alley, and such other, with innumerable swarms of them every where. Peter prophesied afore of this smoky multitude.[10]

Bale clearly experiences a kind of verbal joy as he piles up these orders of the Catholic Church (and there are many excised here), including his own former order, the Carmelites. He itemizes the "smoky multitudes" at such length as to descend bathetically from "Josaphats valley" to "the dark alley" of absurdity. With that bathetic plummet, the institutions crash, so making the sentence itself a kind of bulldozer, driving all this institutional rubble into an imaginary corner, preparatory to definitive, hygienic disposal.

Bale also imagines a total transformation through the promotion of simplicity over hypocrisy. The martyred saints have stripped the gaudy Whore of Babylon (read The Roman Church),

> leaving her neither Relics nor Robes, sects nor Shrines, Abbeys nor Priories. . . . These [the martyrs] shall make her so desolate that no man shall in process of time regard her. They shall leave her so naked, that all the world shall abhor her that shall look upon her. Yea, in the conclusion they shall eat her flesh. . . . All these once plucked away by the evident word of God, no longer shall this harlot appear.[11]

Bale here compacts a series of generative evangelical oppositions in his lurid account of stripping, eating (!) and burning the Roman Whore of Babylon: simplicity versus complexity; probity versus illicit pleasure; naked truth versus hypocritical covering; true worship versus idolatry; upright male versus lascivious female; and (the master opposition, that drives all the others) the written, evangelical Gospel versus deceptive Roman ceremonies and mere traditions. The cumulative effect of these stark oppositions is to promote a simplistic historical scheme in which a single, pure institution will wholly replace a multiform, corrupt institution. The process has started, but the real work of change is ahead. That change will hurt; its attendant persecution will be a sure sign that the gospel is being preached.[12] But it will happen, and when it happens, it will be complete: "No longer shall this harlot appear."

As we shall see, however, history turned out to be less simple: the Lutheran movement represented by Bale will be successively overtaken by more radical forms of reformed Protestant religion, at first Zwinglianism, then magisterial Calvinism, then non-magisterial Calvinism. Already in 1556, Bale was conscious of splits within the Protestant camp. He wrote from Basel that the "new Catharites" (i.e. Cathars) were establishing "their church of the purity."[13]

III

With the accession of the boy-king Edward VI (aged nine) in 1547, Bale must have thought that the harlot was indeed about to be vaporized. He certainly expressed his well-grounded confidence in Edward's accession as a moment of evangelical victory—he returned to England from his first exile to be appointed Bishop of Ossory in Ireland, after a personal meeting with the king.

With Edward's accession, the atmosphere among evangelicals was certainly celebratory and full of hope for definitive purgation of Roman practice. Thus Archbishop Thomas Cranmer set the tone of a radical reform in his coronation sermon of February 20, 1547 (the first such speech before a monarch who did not recognize the authority of Rome). He compared the young king to the iconoclast Josiah, who became king of Judah (640–609 BCE) at the age of eight. Josiah's reign provided a deliciously apt blueprint for definitively purifying violence to be visited upon Catholics and their institutions from 1547. Resurgent evangelicals exploited the comparison for all it was worth. Thus Archbishop Cranmer directs Edward that his duty is

> to see, with your predecessor Josiah, God truly worshipped, and idolatry destroyed, the tyranny of the bishops of Rome banished from your subjects, and images removed. These acts be signs of a second Josiah, who reformed the Church of God in his days.[14]

Edward VI's reign was in fact subject to violent and internal political factionalism, but it was consistently radical in its ecclesiology. Already in 1545 a late Henrician statute suppressing self-help institutions of "Chantries, Hospitals, Fraternities and Brotherhoods" had been passed (before further reaffirmation under Edward VI in 1547), since these lay institutions had come to represent "superstition and Errors."[15] An Edwardian statute of 1550 attempted to enforce the total destruction of every religious image in England.[16] In 1552, the 1549 *Book of Common Prayer* was revised so as to strip England's liturgy, and particularly the Mass, of Catholic traces. That *Prayer*

Book also signalled a shift from Lutheran to Zwinglian formulations with
regard to the crucial issue of the Eucharist.[17]

The definitive evangelical purification of the Edwardian Church registered a decisive shift from a Lutheran to a more radical Zwinglian dispensation. That decisive shift was, however, insufficiently decisive for a new
generation of evangelicals who came to power after the death Edward's
half-sister and successor, Queen Mary (1553–1558).[18] The accession of
Catholic Queen Mary had provoked large-scale exile of Edwardian and
Scottish clerics (e.g. Thomas Becon, John Bale, Miles Coverdale, John Foxe,
Edmund Grindal, and John Knox) to Protestant cities such as Emden, Antwerp, Frankfurt, Strasbourg, Zurich, Basel and Geneva. When the exiles
returned to England at the accession of Elizabeth in 1558, one might have
expected them to applaud the Elizabethan settlement of 1559 as the fulfilment of the program they had promoted with such vigor under the
previous three monarchs (Henry, Edward, and Mary). Some of them, including John Bale, did in fact welcome it: against many of his fellow English
exiles, Bale accepted the *Book of Common Prayer* while in exile in Frankfurt
in 1554–1555, and returned from his second exile to England, under royal
protection, to a canonry in St Paul's Cathedral.[19]

Bale's approval was not, however, a sign of the times. On the contrary,
he was now of the older generation, born in the late fifteenth century, whose
Lutheran struggle had been with, broadly put, Catholicism. That Wittenbergian Lutheranism had been overtaken by Zurich-derived, Zwinglian
doctrine with regard to both the Eucharist and iconoclasm, but both those
guiding forces were now subject to a more radical force derived from
Geneva. Lutheran and Zwinglian English Protestantism were now overtaken, that is, by a yet more radical Calvinist wing, driven by a generation
born in the first half of the sixteenth century, whose aggression was targeted at fellow English Protestants.

The extended period of Protestant versus Catholic in England (1517–1558)
now gave way, that is, to a differently configured, more complex constel-
lation of oppositions, in which the most vigorous and dynamic fault lines
were not only between Catholic and Protestant but also between English
Protestants, and even between English Calvinists. Before their Marian
exile, English Protestants had actively promoted the ideal of persecution
as the surest sign of the justice of their cause: "where most persecution is,

there doth God's word most of al flourish," as Cranmer's chaplain Thomas Becon (b. 1512/13) had said in his *David's Harp* (1542).[20] At that time, however, the persecutors were Henrician, broadly "Catholic" conservatives, fighting a rearguard action against Protestant influences. By the time younger evangelical exiles returned to Elizabeth's England in 1558, they were still imagining the exhilaration of persecution, but now the persecutors were other English Lutherans or Calvinists. Despite the fact that the Elizabethan Settlement of 1559 and the Thirty-Nine Articles of 1571 were Calvinist in many respects (e.g. soteriology, iconoclasm, Eucharistic doctrine), these Calvinist commitments were insufficiently radical for many of the returning exiles.[21]

During their Marian exile of 1553–1558, divisions among English Protestants had arisen in Frankfurt and Geneva, when some exiles (in fierce dispute with others) adopted the liturgy of Calvinist Geneva and acted as independent, bishop-free congregations. Once those exiles had returned to England at the accession of Elizabeth in 1558, the English Church enacted the Act of Uniformity of 1559. That act established a distinctively "magisterial" Calvinist state theology (including predestination) and Calvinist state disciplines; it also confirmed an episcopal Church. Not all the exiles who returned from Geneva, however, were prepared to accept the *Book of Common Prayer.* Neither were they prepared to accept bishops. They wished, instead, to enforce "that reformation of religion which is grounded upon God's book, and somewhat to have opened the deformities of our English reformation, which highly displeaseth our eternal God."[22]

From this moment we see a main fault line opening up within English Calvinism, between a magisterial form in which the magistrate and the monarch stand at the center of a state-controlled, episcopal evangelical Church, and a more radical, anti-episcopal, proto-Presbyterian Calvinism (i.e. "puritan" Calvinism). This fault line within English Protestantism would widen across the following century. The resulting crevasse, along with the further, smaller crevasses it produced, swallowed two monarchs and more than 162,000 other victims, by far the great majority of whom were Protestants.[23]

To be sure, Catholic/Protestant aggression in Elizabethan England by no means vanished. In fact that confrontation reached extraordinary heights in Elizabeth's reign after the papal excommunication of Queen Elizabeth as a heretic in 1570: by Diarmaid MacCulloch's account, "England judicially murdered more Roman Catholics [261] than any other country in Europe" between 1580 and 1600.[24] The figure for capital punishment on religious grounds in early modern England between 1553 and 1603 (i.e. 544) beggars, it should be mentioned, the equivalent figure in late medieval England for the 150 years before 1547 (about 40, by one authoritative estimate).[25] The period between 1580 and 1600 also witnessed the majority of the 80 cases of judicially sanctioned torture (mostly of Catholics) inflicted between 1540 and 1640.[26]

The spectacular Elizabethan violence unleashed upon Catholics, however arresting, should not distract us from intra-Protestant conflict opening up from the beginning of Elizabeth's reign. Already between 1563 and 1567 the Vestments Controversy—focusing on clerical dress—produced fierce dissention among English Protestants, a dissention that produced the term "puritan" itself.[27] In the 1570s the stakes of these internal conflicts became much higher, since they became structural and institutional. They pitched an anti-episcopal, Calvinist Presbyterianism against a Calvinist episcopalian Church. The chasm between these positions would continue to strain and tear the fabric of the English Church until the end of the Civil War and well beyond.

We can observe these strains internal to English Calvinism in 1572 in two published addresses to Parliament, *An Admonition to the Parliament*, written probably by John Field (b. 1544/45) and Thomas Wilcox (b. 1549), and *A Second Admonition to Parliament*, attributed to, but possibly not written by, the most high-profile voice of this newly visible formation, Thomas Cartwright (b. 1534/35).[28]

At first the authors of the two Admonitions object to the appellation "puritanism" and its association with the charge of Donatism (i.e. the late antique North African heresy that insisted that membership of the Church be restricted to the pure who had not succumbed to compromises with persecutors).[29] The *Admonition to the Parliament* thus complains that the cruel and "Pope-like" governors of the Church of England call the "poor men" (i.e. those seeking more radical reformation) "Puritans, worse than the Donatists" (p. 33). Very quickly, however, the slander was taken up as a badge of pride. Already by 1573, the most articulate spokesman of the radical formation, Thomas Cartwright, had championed the charge of purity in his debate with John Whitgift (1530/31–1604), master of Trinity College Cambridge and later Archbishop of Canterbury: "The pureness that we boast of," says Cartwright, "is the innocency of our savior Christ, who shall cover all our unpureness and not impute it unto us."[30]

The core of the puritan position is the supremacy of scripture against human traditions—the fact that the "Word is above the Church" (p. 92). As it is, the Word of God is hedged in and confined—it "doth but peep out from behind the screen" of statutes and injunctions" (p. 93). Without "a reformation of religion that is grounded upon God's book," according to the *Admonitions*, England will prolong the "deformities of our English Reformation, which highly displeaseth our eternal God"(p. 81). The author targets "popish abuses" in the Church, but it's no longer papists who promote these abuses, but rather "hypocritical English protestants"(p. 92).

We should not, in fact, be misled by the omnipresent use of the abusive term "Papist" in Protestant polemic, since, as Michael Braddick has reminded us, "Anti-Popery was not necessarily about Catholics—it was a language with which to denounce the danger of all threats to the Reformation."[31] Focus on the important distinction between Protestant and Catholic in this period tends to blur one thing and efface another. It blurs the fact that much anti-papist rhetoric was, precisely insofar as it was rhetoric, not in fact anti-Papist, but anti-insufficiently-radical-fellow Calvinist, just as the lethal appellation "bourgeois" worked in Stalinist Russia, or "capitalist" in Maoist China.[32] It thereby effaces the fact that the much more dynamic cleavages were within Calvinism, not between Calvinist and Catholic. In any case, without wishing to minimize the importance of anti-Catholic action and culture, I here focus on the generative antagonisms within English Calvinism and Calvinists.[33]

The principal objects of attack in the *Admonitions* are twofold: on the one hand the liturgy and rites specified in *The Book of Common Prayer,* and, on the other, Church government. So much sacramental practice, the tracts argued, is not specified by Scripture, and should therefore be excised. Preaching is to be placed above mere scriptural reading; rituals for the burial of the dead and rites associated with childbirth are to be stripped of superstitious accretion; Sunday games are to be abolished; "copes, caps, surplices, tippets and such like baggage, the preaching signs of popish priesthood" (p. 35) should be done away with. Many of these demands are familiar from the 1560s and earlier. Demands for the abolition of the entire structure of Church government, including bishops, were, however, without precedent: "the names of Archbishops, Archdeacons, Lord bishops, Chancellors &c. are drawn out of the Popes shop together with their officers. So the government which they use ... is Antichristian & devillish, and contrary to the scriptures" (p. 30). Thus begins Presbyterianism in England.

John Whitgift, Master of Cartwright's own Cambridge college, Trinity, engaged in extensive defense of the forms, both liturgical and institutional, attacked by Cartwright. Whitgift was taken aback by Cartwright's demands that backsliders be executed. Those who signally fail to match the standards of the new order must, by Cartwright's judgment, be put to death: such are "stubborn Idolater, blasphemer, murderer, incestuous person, and such like should be put to death."[34] Challenged if he really would put those who failed thus to death, Cartwright replied unequivocally: "If this be bloody, and extreme, I am content to be so counted with the holy ghost."[35]

I focus on this important textual environment of the early 1570s not only to underline the viciously intolerant, uncompromisingly savage clarity of the initial steps of the Presbyterian Puritan movement, but also to underline two classic aspects of revolutionary culture expressed by these initial statements. In the first place, the *Admonitions* are revolutionary in the modern sense, of wishing to overturn an entire order:

> God hath set these examples before your eyes to encourage you to
> go forward to a thorough & a speedy reformation. You may not do
> as heretofore you have done, patch and piece, nay rather go back-
> ward, and never labor or contend to perfection. But altogether re-
> move whole Antichrist, both head and tail, and perfectly plant that
> purity of the word.[36]

In the second place, and above all, this moment reveals the ways in which a settlement in a given revolutionary culture (and especially in the inherently, ideologically anti-tradition culture of Protestantism) almost immediately produces "scope creep," a further boundary that must be traversed in order that the purity of the movement be reaffirmed and guaranteed. In the English Reformation, this was also therefore the moment in which the standard revolutionary practice of turning against one's "own" occurs.

This chasm within English Calvinism continued to widen at official levels under the archbishopric of John Whitgift (Archbishop of Canterbury 1583–1604) well into the 1580s.[37] The same fault lines also opened between English Protestants in texts of the 1580s. The narrative structure and dynamism of these texts, which point ultimately to Bunyan's *Pilgrim's Progress* (first published 1678) a century later, is generated by evangelical repudiation of lookalikes, but here the lookalikes are other, fake Protestants. The evangelical zealot's repudiation of the unbeliever takes the form not of violent eschatological exposure, but rather of face-to-face rudeness to, and humiliation of, fellow religionists. That rudeness and humiliation generates the propulsive movement of such texts.[38]

Take, for example, the dialogue *Countrie Divinitie* (1582), by George Gifford (1547/8–1600), which pitches Zealot (good guy) against Atheist (bad). Bad guy Atheist, however, turns out not to be an atheist at all; on the contrary, he's a God-fearing, run-of-the-mill Protestant.

Gifford had been deprived of his living by the same Whitgift who had debated with Cartwright; as chaplain to English troops in the Low Countries, Gifford had attended the dying Sir Philip Sidney in 1586, before being restored to his living in 1589. Gifford was certainly a radical Protestant, but in fact he was vigorously and actively opposed to a splinter group (that of congregationalist separatists such as Henry Barrow [1550–1593]), further to the radical edge than Gifford's own puritan wing.[39] In *Countrie Divinity*, however, there are no signs of compromise and community building. The divisive strategy is instead to separate, to push "atheists" (i.e. lukewarm Protestants) out of the Church of the elect.

Atheist quickly spots Zealot as the radical Protestant, who is one of these "curious and precise fellows."[40] Initially, as the names suggest, the contrast is wide, between someone who drinks and plays cards (Atheist), and someone who takes religion seriously (Zealot); very quickly and surprisingly, however, the gap narrows. Atheist turns out to be a person with whom many readers in the 1580s will identify: he candidly declares, "I mean well. I hurt no man, nor I think no man any hurt: I love God above all: and put my whole trust in him: what would ye have more?" (image 12). Atheist is no atheist whatsoever (except, of course, by the judgment of Zealot and of the text itself)—on the contrary, he's a Protestant, doing what a good Protestant is supposed to do: believe what preachers tell him; never put any trust in images; always have God in mind, worshipping only him; and detest the Pope ("I would both he and his Dung, were buried in the Dung-hill," image 27). Above all, Atheist has a true intention, even if he does not always understand theological doctrine (image 74).

Zealot, however, dismisses all these signs of "true" religion as false: the preachers in whom Atheist trusts have "no true knowledge" (image 12). Humble, believing, run-of-the-mill late sixteenth-century English Calvinist "Atheist" is in fact, by Zealot's judgment, a rank unbeliever: "There are a number of ye," says Zealot, "which are in deed very Atheists." Worst of all, Atheist is "a free will man" (image 36).

It will be obvious that the names used in this dialogue are less descriptive than prejudicial: Atheist is clearly a practicing Protestant. He is an "atheist" only by the extreme judgment of his interlocutor. It is Zealot who redescribes his fellow religionist as a nonbeliever:

> But see the blindness of men now-a-days, when they hear vain and brutish men boast of their faith, ye do well say they, to have a good belief, when as in deed it is no more but a proud presump-tion, wherewith God is highly displeased, because by it they would make him [i.e. God] a Liar. (image 41)

The text's own logic produces, that is, the force of the appellation "atheist"—it's an abusive name used by Zealot. The question of name-calling in fact arises explicitly in the text: Zealot would have it that Atheist has created the term "Puritan." When they resist true preachers, Zealot says, the ungodly call them "Puritans, rascals, and many such like." Zealot is roughly correct, since "puritan" is, by the *OED*'s account, first attested only in 1565.

So "puritan" is born, fittingly, of intra-Protestant dispute, but so, too (in English), are "atheist" and "zealot." In 1582 "atheist" is, in English, a new Calvinist coinage, first used in a translation of Calvin by Arthur Golding dated 1571.[41] The *OED* erroneously gives 1638 as the first attestation of "zealot," but my main point is that these terms of abuse come into roughly simultaneous usage, each creating the other, and they come into simulta-neous usage out of intra-*Protestant* division. Atheist makes this very point, objecting to Zealot that Puritans have brought dissention, and have fallen to dissention among themselves, where before there was harmony:

If they be so good and goodly, how cometh it to pass then, that there is so much debate among them? For I know towns my self, which are even divided one part against another, since they had a preacher, which were not so before. This they gain, that whereas before they loved together, now there is dissention sown among them. (image 50)

Like his contemporary, the hugely popular evangelical author Arthur Dent (d. 1607), whose *Plaine mans Pathway to Heauen* (1607) had gone through twenty-five editions by 1640, Gifford does not attack the actual, though disguised Catholics, whom he calls "Church Papists" (Gifford is reputed to have coined the phrase), so much as insufficiently radical Protestants.[42] His Atheist is the forerunner of Bunyan's god-fearing, well-intentioned, damned Ignorance. Gifford and Dent carry the Reformation to the "people," who, by this account at any rate, remain stubbornly resistant to it. Whereas the first generation of English Protestants referred to "the English people" in laudatory and sympathetic terms, as innocent victims, Dent's evangelical activist dismisses the people as "carnal Protestants" thus:

This age indeed aboundeth with many hollow hearted hypocrites, dissemblers & timeservers; which howsoever they make a face, and bear a countenance as though they loved the Gospel, yet their heart is not with it. Their heart is with Atheism; their heart is with Popery.[43]

In the last decades of the sixteenth century, then, the unending task of converting a still-blind populace, Protestant in name only by the judgment of so-called "Puritans," was conducted with withering evangelical contempt for backsliders. Gifford himself was subject to the same withering contempt, by congregationalist separatists who wanted nothing to do with "parish assemblies" (by which they meant parish churches under a bishop), since they are "a company of profane and ignorant people; gathered by the sound of a bell in the name of antichrist; worshipping God after a false and idolatrous manner."[44]

The main fault line between the Calvinist state church and anti-episcopal, anti-*Book of Common Prayer* Presbyterians had, then, started to produce sub-fault lines, between those anti-episcopal Presbyterians and those who wished for an even more exclusivist, congregationalist Church.[45] It produced further sub-fault lines, between, for example, Henry Ainsworth (1571–1622) and his former separatist coreligionists. Ainsworth's separatist faction in Amsterdam "seceded from Francis Johnson's 'ancient' separatist Church in 1610," but not before Ainsworth had attacked another, more radical separatist, the proto-Baptist John Smyth, in 1609.[46] These schisms also produced spectacular and self-authenticating rudeness among Protestants.

IV

Between the 1540s generation of Bale and the 1570s generation of Cartwright, then, Protestantism in England had been mobile as it repudiated "itself." It had moved, and overlapped, from Lutheran to Zwinglian to Calvinist state forms; and within Calvinism it produced state episcopal, state nonepiscopal, and non-state, nonepiscopal forms.

All these Protestantisms since 1547 may have been united in promoting, for example, opposition to Roman Catholicism; totalizing reformation; complete iconoclasm of every religious image; a doctrine of anti-works, predestination of the saved, regardless of human effort; and non-tolerationist disciplines. These points of unity only masked, however, widening disunities. On the one hand, puritan and separatist formations broke with the state Church from the 1560s, as we have seen. On the other hand, "conservative" (but Calvinist) reaction to the extremities of puritan Calvinist practice was articulated by, for example, John Whitgift in the 1570s, arguing against the premise that every aspect of Church practice and structure had to be explicitly grounded in Scripture, and arguing for the concept of adiaphora, or "things indifferent."[47] The situation in England was, thus, very different from that in France up to the beginning of the Wars of Religion in 1562, which lasted off and on until at least 1629, with appalling casualty figures: in that country the principal battle lines were between Catholic and Protestant; in England the cleavages that would produce civil war were cleavages between opposed forms of Protestantism.[48]

In England, the most thoroughgoing and reasoned champion of a historically tolerant, reformist Church, was Anglican clergyman and scholar

Richard Hooker (1554–1600). Hooker, indeed, generates his massive and humane *Of the Laws of Ecclesiastical Polity* (Books 1–4 published 1593 and Book 5 1597), precisely in response to what his contemporary Fulke Greville saw as the logic of the "outward Church, whose nature is her founders to devour."[49] Hooker saw as the logic of ever-further "scope creep" that produces intra-Puritan schism. Describing the ecclesiology of splinter groups in his own times, he says,

> So it was, that every particular Church did that within itself, which some few of their own thought good, by whom the rest were all directed … But a greater inconvenience it [i.e. Calvinist separatism] bred, that every later endeavored to be certain degrees more removed from conformity with the Church of Rome, then the rest before had bene: whereupon grew marvelous great dissimilitudes, and by reason thereof, jealousies, heart burnings, jars and discords amongst them.[50]

Hooker, however, had not seen the major "jars and discords" for the English Calvinist Church. They were yet to come, and would occur in the 1640s. The reign of Charles I (1625–1649) witnessed the most powerful, sustained, and royally authorized resistance to revolutionary puritan theology, liturgical practice, and Church government, under Archbishop William Laud (archbishop 1633–1645). In aggressive response to that, a Puritan-dominated Parliament prepared for Puritan victory in the 1640s.

As they did so, we observe three things with regard to our theme of permanent revolution: first, Puritans recognized that Protestant confidence and enthusiasm of the kind expressed by Bale in the 1540s were entirely misplaced; there had been no direct highway to the True Church. On the contrary, the path had been exhausting and inexplicably labyrinthine. Second, despite the awareness of so much failure behind them, Puritans played the same hand, continuing to call for an ever more complete, non-tolerationist, and if necessary violent purge of the English Church. Third, Puritans registered a melancholy, not to say exhausted understanding that they were being taken over (as indeed they were) precisely by the logic of their own permanent revolution.

Let us observe that triple understanding in the lively words of the Presbyterian Edmund Calamy (1600–1666), in a hugely popular sermon before

Parliament preached on December 22, 1641. In this very high-profile address, of which there were no fewer than five editions in 1642, Calamy complains of the English Reformation's unaccountably slow progress, after more than a century of sustained effort. In response, he promotes active, decisive Reformation. But he and his contemporaries also know (even in 1641), one way or another, that the game is up, given the unstoppable logic of the permanent revolution that Calamy and his fellow Presbyterians had themselves activated. They knew that they were about to become history's victims.

Calamy, who had been born into a Protestant family, became curate at St Mary Aldermanbury, London, in 1639, from which appointment he rose to become a key Presbyterian leader in the violent and fractious period leading up to and during the Civil War (1642–1651).[51] He had resisted the so-called "Et Cetera" oath of May 1640, which had sought to hold and enforce the conservative Laudian line, and had required clergymen to swear, without "equivocation, or mental evasion, or secret reservation whatsoever," that they would never seek to "alter the government of this Church by archbishops, bishops, deans, and archdeacons, &c., as it stands now established."[52]

Vigorous Puritan resistance to the exactions of this required oath produced the anti-episcopal, so-called "Roots and Branches" Petition of December 1640, signed by more than a thousand petitioners, which Calamy helped present to the Commons in January 1641.[53] And on December 22, 1641, he preached a vigorous and remarkable sermon, published as *England's Looking Glass*, to the House of Commons, urging further reformation of the English Church.[54]

Calamy's remarkable and popular sermon tries to be resolutely prospective. Even as he looks forwards, however, Calamy is conscious that the huge effort now required has uncomfortable, failed precedents: the true Reformation still lies in the future, and that future might, in fact, be just as confusing as the century and more of failed effort already behind Calamy. Far from consuming the Roman Church, it threatens to consume its evangelical proponents.

The sermon begins with confident claims about God's power to sort things out once and for all, in single strikes: "God hath an absolute power over all Kingdoms and Nations, to pluck them up, pull them down, and destroy them as he pleaseth." God has this power because the God whom Calamy favors can, interestingly, act precisely like the absolutist earthly king whom Calamy resists—God "hath an independent and illimited Prerogative over all Kingdoms and Nations to build them, or destroy them as he pleaseth" (image 6). If that's so, then, Calamy not unreasonably asks, how comes it that the Reformation—now under way for more than a century, and so confidently prophesied by its early promoters back in the 1540s— has taken so long to turn things around?

To answer that question, Calamy's account of historical agency shifts, not so subtly, from God to historical actors. A revolutionary God might be able to act decisively, but Englishmen were, regrettably, rather more tardy and inefficient. For, by Calamy's account, Englishmen are themselves responsible for the appalling slowness of the Reformation, and God is showing his displeasure at the tardy conduct of the business in hand. It's a slow birth:

> God speaks unto us by the great demur and delay of the reformation of the Church. For the Childe of reformation is come to the birth; but there wants strength to bring it forth. This is a sign, that there are some great obstructions in the Kingdom, that hinder the birth of this much desired Childe. (image 14)

The child has been a century in labor, and in the meanwhile has gone backwards as much as forwards. The house of the English Church (Calamy now changes his metaphor from birthing to building) is in urgent need of repair:

> And sure it is, that the House of this Nation is much out of repair: the House of the Lord lieth waste, and there is much rubbish in it. Many pollutions have crept into our Doctrine, much defilement into our Worship, many illegal innovations have been obtruded upon us; the very posts and pillars of this House, many of them are rotten, the stones are loose and uncemented; the House exceedingly divided and distracted with diversity of opinions. (image 28)

How to explain this creeping mess, after more than a century of reconstructive effort? The first, sixteenth-century Reformation had emerged, Calamy argues, from a thoroughly retrograde position of stinking Papal imprisonment. Now, however, we need a further, mighty push from parliamentarians of the Long Parliament to give birth to the true, new Reformation:

> Now this is the great work that the Lord requireth at your hands, Oh ye Worthies of Israel! To stub up all these unprofitable Trees, and to repair the breaches of Gods House, to build it up in its beauty, according to the pattern in the Mount, and to bring us back not only to our first Reformation in King Edwards days, but to *reform the Reformation itself*. For we were then newly crept out of Popery, and (like unto men that come newly out of prison, where they have been long detained) it was impossible but our garments should smell a little of the Dungeon from whence we came. (image 29; my emphasis)

At first the Spenserian metaphor of the dungeon applies to the faltering Reformation of Edward VI of the 1540s (the one that now needs reforming), which occurred almost precisely a century before Calamy's 1640s sermon. Without warning, however, the metaphor of the dungeon suddenly applies to the *present*, designating the retrograde conditions of the Reformation that the "worthies of Israel" (i.e. parliamentarians) *still* need to reform:

> A man that hath been for many years in a dark Dungeon, will rejoice exceedingly for a little crevice of light, though never so little. We have been in the Dungeon of despair, and we blesse God for the little crevice of light let in by your means. (image 29)

Calamy's triumphalist narrative, then, starts to collapse in upon itself. However much he starts, much as Bale had started a century earlier, with total confidence in God's unlimited power to effect the inevitable Reformation, Calamy retreats to various metaphorical schemes to account for the fact that, somehow, it just hasn't happened: the birth is slow; the house we built was ill-built; it's started to collapse in upon itself; we were weak in the first Reformation because we'd been weakened by the stink of the dungeon; the dungeon is somehow the *present*, and we *are still in it*, since we can see a chink of light *now*. And so on. In sum, despite the rousing and congratulatory tone of the sermon to the Puritan parliament, the actual turn of history is extremely negative. After a century, we are still, that is, talking about awkward births, slow beginnings, collapsing houses, stinking

Spenserian dungeons, and sightings of small shafts of light through the prison door.

So, enjoins Calamy, "reform the Reformation!," and this time no half measures. This is, in fact, precisely what the Long Parliament did. In 1641, 1643, and 1644 it enacted ordinances for the destruction of all religious imagery, anywhere.[55] In the same year, it established the so-called Westminster Assembly of Divines, which between 1643 and 1649, despite being highly riven itself, formulated the blueprint for Church government, theology, liturgy, and instruction for a fully nonepiscopalian, Calvinist, Presbyterian Church.[56]

Calamy is by no means alone in wanting to do failed reformation work well, once and for all. Another of Calamy's Presbyterian allies who, subject as he is to the personal logic of permanent revolution, will turn Independent before long, is John Milton. In the very year of Calamy's sermon (1641), Milton published *Of Reformation*.[57] This, the first of Milton's five antiprelatical tracts of the 1640s, is an extraordinarily vigorous attack on prelacy, which starts with a history of why the Reformation has failed in England, before turning to arguments about the lack of scriptural and historical justification for bishops, and no less vigorous arguments that abolition of the episcopy will not diminish the dignity of monarchy.

Of Reformation is driven by revolutionary millenarianism, ending as it does with a call for England to be ready for the "shortly-expected King," who, having opened the "clouds to judge the several kingdoms of the world . . . shall put an end to all earthy tyrannies, proclaiming . . . universal and mild monarchy through heaven and earth." Bishops shall, "after a shameful end in this life (which God grant them) . . . be thrown down eternally into the darkest and deepest Gulf of HELL," there to be subject to maltreatment by all the other damned, who will "exercise a raving and bestial tyranny over them as their slaves and negroes" (1:616–17).

This startling imprecation, published anonymously, ends the text. Milton begins with an account of why reformation of the Church in England has not yet reached this happy readiness. He moves consistently through the Reformation monarchs, pointing to the failures not of Catholic Mary but rather of, successively, Henry VIII, Edward VI, and Elizabeth I. The most striking account of failed Reformation is of the militant Protestant Edward's reign. "Reformation is not perfited [perfected] at a push," Milton concedes, but this indulgence is countered by a ferocious attack on the Edwardian bishops Cranmer, Ridley, and Latimer for blocking reformation. That they were martyrs (under Mary) counts for nothing.[58] All Christians, Milton confidently avers, will be martyrs, but that is not to say that everyone who suffers for religion is a martyr (1:533): "More tolerable it were for the Church of God that these names were utterly abolished like the Brazen Serpent, than that men's fond opinion should thus idolize them" (1:535). Whereas John Foxe praised these Protestant bishops as heroic martyrs to Catholic oppression in his *Actes and Monuments* (first edition 1563), in 1641 Milton presents them as traitors to the Protestant cause, subject to idolatry by misguided Protestant admirers.[59] More urgently than Catholic oppression, what now needs to be attacked is detestable Protestant shortcoming.

In this text Milton's historiography, that is, is driven not primarily by a Catholic / Protestant opposition; his main enemies are, rather, failed Protestants. Taken in the longer pattern of Milton's own career, we can see in retrospect that this very tract (Presbyterian, promonarchical as it is) would itself shortly become obsolete for Milton. The kinetic logic of Milton's revolutionary habit of repudiating not only prior Protestant dispensations but also his own prior persuasions determined his temporary habitation in a given position, however much each temporary sojourn was defended with ferocious self-confidence. Milton's career was propelled, without him ever saying so, by rejecting former versions of himself.[60] The stages through which he passed replicated the passage of powerful currents in English ecclesiology from the Elizabethan Settlement of 1559 until Milton's own times: anti-Catholic throughout, he first rejected Elizabethan, episcopal Calvinism for anti-episcopal Presbyterianism; then parliamentary Presbyterianism for non-parliamentary, puritan, Independentism, backed by military rule (his most publicly active phase); then ended with a Miltonic dissention all his own, from which position we find "John Milton, Englishman" addressing a doctrinal tract "To all the churches of Christ."[61]

In *Of Reformation*, he is still on the side of both Presbyterians and monarchy. Thus one category of those who obstruct true Reformation in 1641, he says, are "libertines," who refuse the discipline of a national Church, and who argue against a Presbyterian Church, and who foresee that "for one

Bishop now in a Diocese, we should then have a pope in every parish."[62] Milton himself will adopt precisely this "libertine" independence from Presbyterian discipline very soon after attacking it. Within a few years of writing *Of Reformation*, that is, Milton turned against his Presbyterian allies of 1641, and in 1646 famously formulated the charge that "New *Presbyter* is but old *Priest* writ large."[63] Milton relies on anti-Catholic language, that is, but not to attack Catholics: the targets now are fellow Protestants and former allies.

My point here is not the relatively trivial one that Milton changed his mind, even if Milton's was a mind that changed with remarkable frequency and extraordinary force. Neither is my point the only slightly less trivial one that a given figure changed his mind, sometimes repeatedly, to adapt to new circumstances, even if many figures did precisely that in the revolutionary decades of the 1640s and 1650s.[64] I am arguing, rather, that the shape of Milton's career, and the very language he used to describe the changes within that career, express the revolutionary logic of Protestantism, forever in flight from itself, forever deploying language previously used against Catholics now against former versions of Protestantism. Far from it being the case that Milton was consistent (as contemporary criticism insistently and unpersuasively affirms), Milton's mind *had* to change.[65] In 1644, after a sequence of intellectual revolutions in his own career, not to speak of more than a century of Reformation upheaval, Milton clearly felt, in fact, that the Reformation has *yet to happen:* he imagines writers defending "beleaguered Truth," "musing, searching, revolving new notions and ideas wherewith to present, as with their homage and their fealty, the *approaching Reformation*."[66]

For all Milton's repudiation of earlier forms of Protestantism, his *pattern* of repudiation is very Protestant. The only really consistent theme of Milton's career is an equally Protestant emphasis on being alone, or at best among an elite few, betrayed by an ignorant populace (in whose name the Protestant hero fights).[67] For all his changes of position, Milton is consistently antidemocratic, and often anti-parliamentarian. Instead of a regularly elected parliament, Milton proposed a "rigid oligarchy," a "Grand Council" whose members would sit for life.[68] So far from being emollient in the desperate straits of 1559, Milton, commissar-like, instead reaffirms the revolutionary necessity of the enlightened few directing the mentally enslaved many. It is necessary that the

> less number [should] compel a greater to retain ... their liberty, than that a greater number, for the pleasure of their baseness, compel a less most injuriously to be their fellow slaves. They who seek nothing but their own just liberty have always right to win it and to keep it whenever they have power, be the voices never so numerous that oppose it.[69]

V

Calamy and Milton are, then, from their different perspectives, conscious of living through, and keen to promote, a period of rapid and decisive revolutionary change. There have been errors and backsliding in the past; there is a certain exhaustion now; but reforming the Reformation will finally happen now, if Parliament has the iron resolve to enforce the demolition and rebuilding.

Or it would happen, were it not for the fact that Presbyterians have so many competitors as claimants to the True Church, each of whom claim authority within precisely the same historical and eschatological logic claimed by Presbyterians.

Calamy thus complains "the House is exceedingly divided and distracted with diversity of opinions" (image 28). Even, that is, as Calamy exhorts a glorious final push to reform the Reformation, he is conscious of the competition. There is so much resistance, and so much evidence of backsliding, even from this tenuous rebooting of the Reformation process. Luckily, the backsliders are not to be found among the parliamentarians, who have done sterling work. Apart from the benighted "people," the slackers are instead, according to Calamy, all those pesky troublemakers who have split off from, or never accepted membership of, the Presbyterian fold.

For by 1641 the True Church turns out to have many claimants. We can observe the burgeoning number of those claimants in action in *Gangraena, or, A catalogue and discovery of many of the errors, heresies, blasphemies and pernicious practices of the sectaries of this time* (1646) by Thomas Edwards (1599–1648).[70] His *Third part of Gangraena. A new and higher discovery of the errors, heresies, blasphemies, and insolent proceedings of the sectaries of these times* fol-

lowed in the same year.[71] Independents, with their own intense activity to
"reform the Reformation," were multiplying, by Edwards's estimation,
with hydra-like profusion. With the multiple splits among the evangelical
camp, into Presbyterians and Independents, the way was open for Presbyterians to diagnose the theological disease (i.e. Protestant heresy from
Protestant "orthodoxy") and to insist on the cure (i.e. merciless intolerance by evangelicals for other evangelicals). Whether or not Edwards's descriptive account is at all accurate, the indisputable point is that his most
vigorous enemy is definitely not the Catholic Church, or even Calamy's list
of "Atheists . . . Socinians [and] Arminians."[72]

The Catholic Church is old news. She has been dealt with. The new enemies are, instead, within and now adjacent, who have split in so many
ways from the Presbyterian movement.[73] In 1588 anti-Puritan Calvinists
had complained about the labile, restless character of evangelicals as "always seeking and searching; . . . men . . . [who] can never find whereupon
to rest. Now they are carried hither, now thither."[74] By the time of Civil War,
the Puritans are themselves complaining of the same phenomenon as
having led to schisms against *puritan* positions. Thus Edwards urges Parliament to exercise *intolerance*, against the full list of "sectaries within these
four last years" (image 13), and against their itemized list of no fewer than
176 errors and heresies. As Calamy was preoccupied by the agonizingly
slow birth of the truly reformed Church in England, Edwards is, instead,
horrified by the ease and frequency of misshapen births—by the monstrous shapes of religion. These unwelcome spawn are both already born
and yet to be born, once toleration is admitted. His own book is more
than eight hundred pages, but

> a great volume would not contain the Errors, prodigious, Opin-
> ions, and strange practices of these times. There is no question but
> there are many monsters conceived by some in this inter-mystical
> season, which are not yet brought forth, and others that are brought
> forth, yet like to bastard or misshapen children, are concealed from
> the public view, made known only to a very few, being the hidden
> works of darkness, the time not being yet come to publish them
> openly: waiting only for the midwife and nursing mother of a Tol-
> eration. (image 13)

The very group that had pushed for Church and national reform, and which by the 1640s was in a position to effect that full Reformation, was now faced with an entirely new set of challenges, as the revolutionary logic of their own position started to sideline them.

By the middle of the seventeenth century, then, it's clear that Reformation isn't remotely easy work, as Bale had so blithely imagined. Across more than a century of effort, it had instead been arduous labor, and there was a good deal left to do. The main reason why the work had been so hard, though, is because reformers had been entirely mistaken about the nature of the work in hand: each stage of the Reformation had produced a new horizon of reforming work yet to be done, and the ever new work of repudiating the work done to date. In addition to being hard, therefore, the work was also exhausting: each stage of the Reformation had turned aggressively on its predecessor. Achieved results themselves had fallen victim to the logic of a movement determined to repudiate tradition of any kind, especially its own tradition. Simple work had become very complex and exhausting work.

Edwards's passionate anti-tolerationist Presbyterianism might sound hysterical and paranoid, but Edwards was essentially correct: already in 1641, just before the outbreak of war between Parliament and royalist forces in August 1642, the schism between Presbyterians and Congregationalists (already visible since the 1560s) was starting to widen. In 1640 the moderate conservative Joseph Hall (1574–1656), while still bishop of Exeter (before his imprisonment by Parliament in 1642), acutely analyzed the dynamic of permanent schism facing the anti-episcopal parties, including Presbyterians:

> Some there are . . . which can be content to admit of an orderly sub-
> ordination of several Parishes to Presbyteries, & those again to
> Synods [i.e. Presbyterians]; others are all for a Parochial absolute-
> ness, and independence [i.e. Congregationalists]; Yea, and of these,
> there will be a division, in *semper divisibilia;* till they come to very
> Atoms: for to which of those scores of separated Congregations,
> known to be within and about these walls, will they be joined? and
> how long without a further scissure?[75]

By January 1644 divisions between Presbyterians and independents of various stripes were unavoidably explicit within the newly established Westminster Assembly.[76] As Michael Braddick says, "The most vituperative exchanges about the church settlement were within the parliamentary coalition, not between royalists and parliamentarians."[77] And despite the provisional victory of the Presbyterian party in that Assembly, the document of that Assembly was wholly bypassed by events as a blueprint for the national Church, notably by the military coup d'état, with its purge of parliament, in December 1648; by the dominance of Independents in the victorious New Model Army; by military dictatorship between 1653 and 1658; and, finally, by the formal repudiation of the Assembly's documents in 1660. By December 1648, Presbyterians had themselves been definitively swept aside by new and distinctively revolutionary forces.

In sum, whereas Bale had in the 1540s predicted rapid transition from old to new, and from complex to simple, a century later Calamy and Milton found themselves lamenting that the transition had not been swift; that the house was a mess and getting messier; that there was so much disagreement; that the situation was anything but simple; that the people were to blame; and that the new world was, in Matthew Arnold's much later words, despite the death of the old, "powerless to be born." Faced with that messy paralysis, we need, says Calamy, to push hard again, to "to *reform the Reformation itself.*" Protestants had to deal with the violence and mess of churches subject to the logic of Protestantism, the logic of permanent revolution.

PART 2

Working Modernity's Despair

3

Modernizing Despair

THE MOST DYNAMIC and widely diffused forms of early northern European modernity began with despair. A sense of spiritual hopelessness—what English vernacular penitential writers called both "despair" and, more evocatively perhaps, "wanhope," was a marginal issue in late medieval penitential treatises. It was one of the many sub-vices of Sloth, or *acedia*.[1] Despair produced by fear of predestination certainly figures in both the late fourteenth-century *Piers Plowman* (c. 1367–1388), just as amatory despair prompts dark reflection on predestination in Chaucer's *Troilus and Criseyde* (c. 1386).[2] Despair in the face of predestination is, however, extremely unusual in late medieval literature. It is abnormal. By stark contrast, the issue of despair rockets in significance across the sixteenth- and seventeenth-century religious writing and experience, across wide swaths of population.[3] It is the new normal. Why?

To be sure, despair is not the whole story. Certain Neoplatonic forms of extremely elitist fifteenth-century Italian humanism had promoted what was in fact a Classical idea of human perfectibility ("in apprehension how like a god!"), through intellectual mastery of the sciences.[4] To be sure, that tradition spread northwards in the late fifteenth century to find no less elitist, Neoplatonic expressions of perfectibility in works such as Thomas More's *Utopia* (1516).[5] To be sure, some rare early sixteenth-century figures, who were both humanists and theologians—most famously and gloriously

Erasmus (1466–1536)—courageously brought a modified version of human rational potential into theological discourse.[6] These traditions have long claimed the attention of cultural historians wishing to affirm a progressivist narrative of "Renaissance," and, even, of "Renaissance and Reformation."[7] Technical application of the tools of philology by both humanists and evangelicals does indeed create an overlap between the cultures of "Renaissance" and "Reformation." That, however, is where any overlap must end, given the astonishingly optimistic anthropology of many humanists, and the radically pessimistic anthropology of all evangelicals. The contrastive anthropologies of humanism and evangelical theology produce correlative contrasts with regard to the potential of human reason and nature, and therefore, with regard to the use of Classical culture. Humanist traditions of human perfectibility were, in any case, very much a minority affair, written by and produced for the republic of (usually Latin) letters, a numerically small and international group constituted by extremely cultivated, usually male intellectuals.

The central emphasis of sixteenth-century Lutheran and Calvinist religion in Protestant Europe, in fierce and unabashed contrast to those humanist traditions, placed despair-producing inadequacy and depravity ("this quintessence of dust") front and brutally center of a theological program. In England that human inadequacy and depravity was placed front and center of a national spiritual program. The very culture, that is, that has been, and in more covert ways continues to be, hailed as the fountainhead of liberty, was centrally committed to utter human imprisonment. This is a culture, indeed, that can properly be described as "post human," since "human" is consistently a term of abuse (along with "tradition") in the Lutheran and Calvinist lexicon, placed as it is, in the conceptual structure of evangelical thought, against, and forever obstructing, the idea of the divine.

Utter human incapacity to fulfill the Law through works stands at the heart of all evangelical theologies, whether Lutheran, Calvinist, or of most of the evangelical sects that splinter from both Lutheranism and Calvinism.[8] The very idea of any human agency whatsoever is understood as a threat to God: "I threaten'd to observe the strict decree / Of my dear God with all my power and might," vows George Herbert in his poem "The Holdfast," before he undoes each source of human impulse and agency—

even the impulse to trust in God—in a poem that finally comes to rest in a kind in paradoxical alienation from all that's ours: "all things were more ours by being His."[9]

This official consensus across wide ranges of otherwise fractured Protestant orthodoxy holds until, as we shall see, a break of sorts occurs in the second quarter of the seventeenth century, prompted initially by the administration of Charles I.

In any given society the relation between merit and reward will be a crucial indicator. Meritocratic societies in which the relation is close will tend to be dynamic. By contrast, societies in which the relation between effort and reward is aleatory, and in which widely dispersed effort is rewarded (or not) by parsimonious distribution of merit, apportioned by impenetrable rules, to an elite few, will usually be characterized by high incidence of depression, in which the pale cast of thought will shadow any proposed action.

The societies of early European Protestant modernity offer a perfect test case for the claims just made, since those societies adopted, and then enforced, especially extreme examples of the depression-production model. The official, sometimes state-backed theology of these societies was, like all truly revolutionary dogmas, determinist and free-will denying: history had its logic, regardless of individual human effort. But that did not let humans off a very sharp hook: huge effort was required to join the elect vanguard of history, despite vigorous denial of any perceptible relation between merit and reward. The only demanding rule driving the huge effort was "Believe!"

Sixteenth- and seventeenth-century Protestant Europe did indeed produce very high levels of depression, not to say psychic torture. Early modern Protestant societies, however, buck the trend of any simplistic alignment of meritocratic failure and psychic resignation. These revolutionary societies are extremely, if neurotically, dynamic, for reasons the following three chapters will seek to understand.

In this chapter I sketch the theology of this human depravity; the peculiar psychic cruelty of its necessary consequence (i.e. the doctrine of predestination, whether double or not); and the energy that exclusivism produces. I pursue that theological story up to the end of the reign of Elizabeth (1603). In Chapter 4, I turn to literary expressions of near-total subjection to predestinarian punishments, between 1530 and 1620 or so, in the form of brilliant, claustrophobic lyric poetry and endlessly recursive romance narrative, both forever unable to move out of or beyond the Cave of Despair.

From 1625 or so, the promise of a recovered freedom of will and then Miltonic epic seem to produce an escape route from the punishing disciplines of predestination and its attendant despair. In Chapter 5 I therefore look to the ways in which that apparent escape route to the proto-liberal future does not, in fact, offer its promised, full escape from early modernity's despair. Rebellion against the early modern absolutist God and his revolutionary theology themselves took revolutionary form, and thereby remain profoundly scarred by the struggle.

I

The Prologue to William Tyndale's 1525 New Testament is the very first welcome to the printed vernacular scriptures in English. At this very wellspring of the English Reformation, Tyndale (c. 1494–1536), following Luther, trumpets abject incapacity. A short introductory section of the text is a translation of the Preface to Luther's 1522 New Testament, while the rest is, apparently, Tyndale's own work.[10] The short section drawn from Luther warmly welcomes prospective evangelicals. "Evangelion," we are told, is a Greek word meaning "good merry, glad and joyful tidings, that maketh a man's heart glad, and maketh him sing, dance, and leap for joy" (p. 9).

The glad tidings quickly start, however, to look less than wholly glad. In the section for which no Lutheran source has been located, Tyndale underlines Luther's valuation of human worth, and here the news is decidedly morose. By Adam's fall we are "children of wrath and heirs of the vengeance of God by birth." We have

> our fellowship with the damned devils . . . while we are yet in our
> mother's wombs; and though we show not forth the fruits of sin . . .
> yet are we full of the natural poison, whereof all sinful deeds spring,
> and cannot but sin outwards (be we never so young) if occasion be
> given. (p. 14)

Tyndale's "welcome" has just begun. He goes on to summarize and empha-size all that's been said: our will "is locked and knit faster unto the will of the devil, than could an hundred thousand chains bind a man unto a post" (p. 17).

However dark this early English Protestantism, one might object that it is, after all, only the standard Christian theology of original sin. True, but pre-Reformation theologies had, from the beginning of the fourteenth century, developed a subtle, flexible, and reformist theological response to the grim predicament of abject human incapacity inherited from Eden. God, fourteenth-century theologies had it (we might take the English theo-logian William of Ockham, c. 1287–1347, as exemplary), can do anything he likes; he cannot be held to agreements, since that would infringe on his absolute power. But precisely because he can act at will, God can also freely agree to a pact. If a given human does what is in her or him (*facere quod in se est*), God will freely take that well-intentioned effort into consideration. This system involves subtle checks and balances between God's absolute power (*potentia absoluta*) and, on the other hand, his so-called ordained, or established, rule-bound power (*potentia ordinata*). It also involves checks and balances between God's unconstrained offer of grace (or gift) and his due payment of wage.[11]

The late medieval God, that is, provisionally yet reliably set aside the unpredictability of his absolute power and his right to give gifts as he will. He did this in order to establish a regime of ordained, or settled and pre-dictable power, whereby he would pay a kind of wage for human works that are in some sense deserved. There are variations of this dialectic of gift and wage in the broad stream of theology in the two centuries prior to 1517, with some versions stressing God's grace more or less as the enabling condition of human virtue.[12] But in all mainline versions, God was committed to taking well-intentioned human effort seriously, and he was certainly open to works performed in the world as wage deserving. He was also generously open to saving virtuous pagans.[13] This commitment to the value of works and the openness to non-Christian virtue accounts for the unjustified Reformation insult of "Pelagianism," derived from Augustine's enemy the British monk Pelagius (d. 418), who argued that works, without the need for grace, sufficed to achieve salvation.

There are also, it should be said, minority traditions from the mid-fourteenth century, some orthodox, some heterodox, that, with reference back to the late, predestinarian writings of Augustine (d. 430), insist only on God's absolute power.[14] Luther was educated in the Okhamist tradition sketched in the previous paragraph. As we shall see, he rejected its doctrine of salvation by turning to and developing the minority late-medieval traditions hostile to the notion of free will.

The Ockhamist tradition differed in crucial respects from the earlier, thirteenth-century scholastic doctrine of salvation, most closely associated with the great Italian, Paris-based theologian Thomas Aquinas (1225–1274). We need not explicate the grounds of those differences here, but whether Aquinian or Ockhamist, all mainline pre-Reformation, late medieval theologies awarded some place to human free will, and allowed that human effort, aided by divine grace, could in some way pay God back, through works, for the debt of sin.[15]

That consensus had immense institutional, sacramental, psychological, cultural, and economic consequences. The entire structure of the sacrament of penance and its appurtenances (penitential treatises, performance of penitential works, much religious art and literature, pilgrimage, purgatory, and the system of prayers for those in purgatory) depended on it. Repayment for the debt of sin through penitential works had to be negotiated through the Church, but the message was, one way or another, "You (often 'you' plural) can do it."

Theologies embed a politics. Across the later Middle Ages, theologians who opted for the model of checks and balances between absolute and ordained powers tended to favor conciliarism, whereby centralized Papal governance was subject to a kind of ecclesiastical constitutionalism by councils of bishops.[16] Theologians who, by contrast, opted for the absolutist, grace alone model opted, not coincidentally, for Papal absolutism.

Theologies also entail what might be called a sociology of salvation: the society of the saved is either a society sharing in common effort, conducted on the basis of agreements open to all (the dialectical model), or else the society of the saved is a society of the elect, who find themselves in heaven as a result only of God's impenetrable decision, leaving others damned for reasons known only to God (the absolutist model). The first of these societies—the otherworldly society of common effort—is open to help from the society of the benevolent living, through prayers for those in Purgatory.[17] The heavenly society of the elect chosen by the absolutist God was, by contrast, clean cut off from the society of the living, also in part because Protestants had closed down Purgatory.[18]

Luther, interestingly—like his proto-Protestant, pre-Reformation heterodox forebears, and like some elitist orthodox pre-Reformation forebears—chose the much simpler, anti-checks and balances, absolutist model. Harking back to the other great revolutionary period in Christian history—the transition from poly- to monotheism in late Antiquity—and its great theologian (Augustine), Luther adopted a strikingly unusual theology that was fiercely jealous of God's absolute prerogative. He broke directly through the elaborate checks and balances of ordained and absolute powers, and explicitly dismissed that dialectic in favor of just one element of the late medieval system—God's absolute power.[19] Luther wished to reinstate the wholly unpredictable God of the Hebrew Scriptures, and expel the God of scholastic, Aristotelian theology, who had absorbed classical notions of justice.

Luther's entire moment of breakthrough, indeed, begins as he understands that God's justice is God's justice, not ours. Luther had agonized, so he tells us in the autobiography of his conversion experience, over this passage of Paul: "For by it the just righteousness of God (*iusticia dei*), is revealed, from faith to faith. As it is written, the just shall live by faith" (Romans 1:16–17). The agony-producing word was "righteousness," in the phrase "righteousness of God" (here translated as "just righteousness of God").

Genitive phrases are ambiguous: "the justice of God" can mean either "the [recognized, common standard of] justice that God practices" (what grammarians call the "objective genitive"), or it can mean "the justice that belongs wholly to God" (the so-called "subjective genitive"). This second kind of genitive suddenly evacuates a word (here "justice") of any of its familiar meanings. Luther's conversion occurred when he suddenly realized that he should interpret "the justice of God" as a subjective genitive—as designating God's justice, not ours. The word should, that is, be understood wholly outside its customary usage.

That evacuation of human standards is here the semantic evacuation of just one word ("justice").[20] It is, however, an especially important word, and from that single interpretative act flows a corrosive for all human standards and initiative. Evacuation of human standards in order to make way for the alien standard of the divine is, indeed, the essence of Lutheran and Calvinist "post-human" theology.[21] God, the transcendent *deus absconditus,* or hidden God, is reinvested with his full and wholly unintelligible, inscrutable divine prerogatives. The text holds out just one human conduit—that of faith—to access this newly estranged God: "But to him that worketh not, but believeth on him that justifieth the ungodly, his faith is counted for righteousness" (Romans 4:5).

If humans cannot be saved by works as a wage, then how are they saved? Answer: by the alternative economic category of grace (i.e. gift). How do they secure that gift? Not through their own merits or deserving (since that would damage the status of the gift, which must by definition be given wholly gratuitously, without being owed). The Christian is saved, rather: (i) through Christ's sacrifice, which satisfied God once and for all for every elect sinner; and (ii) through God's imputation of worth to individual Christians, made for his inscrutable reasons. Paul's letter to the Romans (c. 80 CE), written from within a slave society in which the relation of merit to reward was forever very uncertain, provides the second of these answers:

> Even as David also describeth the blessedness of the man, unto whom God imputeth righteousness without works, saying, Blessed are they whose iniquities are forgiven, and whose sins are covered. Blessed is the man to whom the Lord imputeth not sin. (Romans 4:6–8)

All the Christian can now do is to have faith that God's decision has gone his or her way.

To reinstate God with his full and gracious prerogative—the "absolute givenness" of his gift—was inevitably and immediately to promote the doctrine of predestination. If humans were unable to contribute to their salvation through works, then either they were all damned, or else God saved them by imputing righteousness to them.[22] If the decision to impute or not was wholly God's, then it was wholly God's, and was taken by God from the beginning of the world, regardless of the unfolding of history, and regardless of human effort.[23]

Scholarly history frequently and incorrectly denies that Luther adhered to the doctrine of predestination, even if there is no getting around Calvin's very explicit acceptance of the full logical consequence of the idea that God makes all the decisions: not only salvation of the elect, but damnation of the reprobate (so-called "double predestination").[24] In his *Institution of Christian Religion* (first published in Latin in 1536, with significant revisions up to 1559, and translated into English in 1561, with eleven editions between 1561 and 1634, and three abridged editions between 1585 and 1587[25]) Calvin is unequivocal:

> That therefore which the Scripture clearly sheweth, we say that God
> by eternal and unchangeable counsel hath once appointed whom
> in time to come he would take to salvation, and on the other side
> whom he would condemn to destruction. This counsel as touching
> the elect, we say to be grounded upon his free mercy without any
> respect of the worthiness of man.[26]

Protestant soteriology (i.e. theory of salvation) therefore does away with human initiative and human history. The key determinations for reward of an individual life have all been taken before that life begins. The evangelical God has repossessed all the initiative in the event of one individual's salvation. That same God has evacuated the fundamental springs of human agency, except in the matter of belief.

Protestant soteriology also, therefore, psychologizes spirituality: the key question for every revolutionized Christian is no longer, as it had been for the narrator of the late fourteenth-century poem *Piers Plowman*, "How may I save my soul?" (B.1.84) but, rather, as it was for Bunyan in his *Grace Abounding* (first published in 1666), "Whether I was elected."[27] For anyone who took this soteriology seriously, the changed question amounted to a revolution of subjectivity. "Has my soul been saved?" left nothing for the individual evangelical Christian to work towards, but a lot to guess at, a lot to look out for, and a lot to feel. Calvin has it that the signs of justification are manifest: "Now in the elect we set vocation, to be the testimony of Election: & then justification to be another sign of the manifest shewing of it, till they come to glory wherein is the fulfilling of it."[28] Between the word "manifest" and the word "sign" in that sentence, however, a psychological slough of despond will inevitably and quickly open, a slough, or ditch, beside whose edges every sensitive Protestant will uneasily walk, and into which many will fall.

By 1547 the doctrine of human abjection and the incapacity of works to repair that abjection was aimed directly at, and reached, every adult in England, since it was an essential part of mandated, state religion. It aimed to govern the emotional life of very much larger numbers than the minority, elitist, generally Latin tradition of early modern humanism could ever have targeted. If cultural historians should attend to scale, then early modern mass despair wins by a large margin over coterie optimism. As John Stachniewski says in his searing book *The Persecutory Imagination* (1991), "Calvin himself was England's most published author between 1548 and 1650."[29]

And if cultural historians should attend to state mechanisms, then once again despair wins by a very handy margin over humanist promotion of human perfectibility. The Elizabethan Church was, it is true, instantly conscious of the dangers of Calvinist despair. Already in 1558/59, the very year of the Elizabethan Settlement, a set of "Injunctions for Religion" optimistically insists that preachers soft-pedal the hopelessness:

> Also, that the vice of damnable despair may be clearly taken away, and that firm belief and steadfast hope may be surely conceived of all their parishioners being in danger, they shall learn and have always in areadiness such comfortable places and sentences of Scripture as do set forth the mercy, benefits and goodness of Almighty God towards all penitent and believing persons.[30]

If, however, the early Elizabethan Church wished to go easy on "the vice of damnable despair," it went about generating that more "comfortable" message in a less than consistent way.

For other, high-profile state productions of the early years of Elizabeth's reign insist instead on despair production. Thus, for example, Article 17 of Thirty-Nine Articles (the official doctrinal statement of the English Church, printed in the *Book of Common Prayer*), ratified in 1571, is headed, "Of Predestination and Election." The opening is a forthright statement of Calvinist double predestination, whereby God, before the foundations of the world were laid, He hath constantly decreed by His counsel secret to us, to deliver from curse and damnation those whom He hath chosen in Christ out of mankind, and to bring them by Christ to everlasting salvation as vessels made to honour.[31]

The body of the article proclaims what terrific news this is for those who are elect. Even this upbeat official text, however, cannot help spot despair out of the corner of its anxious eye:

for curious and carnal persons, lacking the Spirit of Christ, to have continually before their eyes the sentence of God's Predestination is a most dangerous downfall, whereby the devil doth thrust them either into desperation or into wretchlessness of most unclean living no less perilous than desperation.[32]

Subscription to this simple yet terrifyingly simplistic distinction between the merry elect and the "curious and carnal" was required by statute, along with subscription to all the Thirty Nine Articles, of every minister of the Church of England in 1571, for the "establishing of consent touching true religion."[33]

Not only, however, was profound uncertainty about agency dangerously cemented, through double-predestination, into the doctrinal foundation of the Elizabethan Church. Doubt about works was also to be broadcast from every pulpit. No sooner does *The Book of Homilies* promote good works, than it also casts a shadow over them. This compilation of set sermons, designed for unlicensed preachers throughout England, was first published in 1547 under Edward VI, and then republished and expanded in an Elizabethan edition in 1563. Ministers were required by Article 35 of the Thirty-Nine Articles to read these sermons "in Churches . . . diligently and distinctly."[34] This is perhaps as close as sixteenth-century English culture gets to mass media, and it's quite close, since church attendance is mandated from 1559; every parish pulpit will therefore broadcast one of these handy formulations of evangelical doctrine to every adult once per week.[35]

The *Homilies* dismiss "traditions" as the "stinking puddles of men's traditions, devised by man's imagination for our justification and salvation."[36]

One of the stinking tradition-puddles so dismissed is the idea that works in any way contribute to our credit with God. The relevant homily presents the Calvinist truth of the matter of salvation in crisply depressing terms. God encourages us to do good works (Ephesians 2:10), but

> his meaning is not by these words, to induce us to have any affiance [trust], or to put any confidence in our works, as by the merit and deserving of them, to purchase to ourselves and others, the remission of sin and so consequently everlasting life, for that were mere blasphemy against God's mercy and a great derogation to the blood shedding of our Savior Jesus Christ. For it is by the free grace and mercy of God . . . without merit serving on our part, that our sins are forgiven us. . . . Good works then bring not forth grace, but are brought forth by grace.[37]

The neutralization of agency in this short but absolutely mainline, official state text can only produce depression: one is to do the good works, but one is not doing them (divine grace is the agent). One is to do the good works, but one is not to have any confidence in them whatsoever. They won't produce a reward from God, since God has already taken the decision with regard to reward. The only thing left to the agency of the individual Christian is to ponder whether or not his or her works are signs of the decision having gone his or her way. Works are no longer currency to effect a future decision; they have become opaque signs that reflect a prior divine decision, in which one could not have had any part.

II

All that sounds challenging enough when put into daily exercise. To appreciate fully the vicious psychic torture of this peculiar promotion and neutralization of action, however, we need to turn to Calvinist pastoral theology. After the liturgical and institutional failures of the Puritan mobilizations from the 1560s to 1580s, Puritanism turned to pastoral instruction and "comfort."[38] Let us listen to that comfort as articulated by the Cambridge theologian William Perkins (1558–1602), the most forceful English proponent of pastoral Calvinism in the 1590s.

Perkins published his long (334 pages) and popular *Golden Chain* in 1591;
it went through 10 editions up to 1621. The issue of election and damnation
was clearly felt to deserve a separate book; Perkins published the reworked
sequence on salvation as a single, shorter text (a mere 286 pages), devoted
to the issue of distinguishing the truly elect from those who merely think
they elect but are in fact damned. *A treatise tending unto a declaration whether
a man be in the estate of damnation or in the estate of grace* was published in 1590;
it went through eight editions up to 1619.

Perkins begins with a jaunty assertion that clearly invests him as author with divine perception, and yet simultaneously sows existential
uncertainty among his readers: "Good Reader, it is a thing to be considered, that a man may seem both unto himself and to the Church of God
to be a true professor of the Gospel, and yet indeed be none."[39] Setting
aside the issue of how Perkins can know that a person may think him
or herself saved when in fact that person is damned, the problem he
goes on confidently to thrust at his readers is this: the experience of the
elect and the reprobate turns out to be nearly identical; how do we tell
them apart?

Perkins wants to set a very high bar for election; or, rather, he sets the
bar high precisely in order to be able to sow doubt among those attempting
to clear it. The reprobate are not necessarily conscious hypocrites—they
accept the Word joyfully, they attend church willingly: "though they are
not sound, yet they are void of hypocrisy" (image 5). There is, indeed, a
profound "similitude and affinity between the temporary professor of
the Gospel, and the true professor of the same" (image 6). A religious
movement that began by distinguishing the invisible True Church from
the visible look-alike false Church, has now, by the 1590s, moved well
beyond the Catholic / Protestant distinction. The dangerous issue now is
look-alikes within the invisible Protestant Church, membership of which
necessarily involves unassuageable psychic torture, *huis clos*, of one kind
or another.

The elect may seem easily distinguishable from the reprobate, since they
accept the law with a "willing & ready mind . . . joined with love and liking"
(image 9). But (and here the distinction between elect and damned becomes
uneasily blurred), the reprobate believes that he, too, is saved, and "may seem
for a time to be planted in the Church: for he doth believe the promises of

God made in Christ Jesus, yet so that he cannot apply them to himself." The reprobate is among us:

> He is taken for one of God's sheep: he is kept in the same pastures, and is folded in the same fold with them. He is counted a Christian of the children of God, & so he taketh himself to be; no doubt because through the dullness of his heart, he cannot try and examine himself, and therefore truly cannot discern of his estate. (image 17)

Even if, however, the to-be-damned person cannot "truly" discern his actual condition, he *seems* to discern that the news is good. Thus the reprobate has, says Perkins in the *Golden Chain*,

> a tasting of heavenly gifts: as of Justification, and of Sanctification, and of the virtues of the world to come. This tasting is verily a sense in the hearts of the reprobates, whereby they do perceive and feel the excellency of God's benefits, notwithstanding they do not enjoy the same.[40]

So the reprobate perceives and feels, but does not enjoy. To many this will sound like a distinction without a difference. But the elect, too, are faced with experiences apparently identical to that of the reprobate, and yet told to take those very experiences as firm proof of election. In the judgment of Perkins's *Treatise tending unto a declaration whether a man be in the estate of damnation or in the estate of grace*, the elect have assurance of their acceptance, as when they "are persuaded in their harts by the holy ghost, of the forgiveness of their own sins, and of God's infinite mercy towards them." This assurance, however, is bought at a high price, since it necessarily involves profound doubt. Whereas the reprobate should know his fate by virtue of his dullness of heart, the elect will be assured of their future salvation only by virtue of the fact that their hearts must be broken by glum self-doubt in the "feeling of this sorrow":

> For look as men use to break hard stones into many small pieces and into dust: so must this feeling of God's anger for sin bruise the heart of a poor sinner and bring it to nothing. And that this may so be, sorrow is not to be felt for a brunt, but very often before the end of a man's life. (image 27)

Perkins goes further, arguing that total despair is a necessary sign of elective assurance:

> The fourth thing in true humiliation is an holy desperation: which
> is when a man is wholly out of all hope ever to attain salvation by
> any strength or goodness of his own: speaking and thinking
> more vilely of himself then any other can do; and heartily ac-
> knowledging himself to have deserved not one only but even ten
> thousand damnations in hell fire with the devil and all his Angels.
> (image 29)

Kafka cannot be far away when the only certain sign for a reprobate is
feeling yet not enjoying God's favor, and when the only way the elect can
tell themselves apart from the dull-spirited reprobate is by a feeling of
total, dull-spirited hopelessness. Reprobate and elect will flicker between positions at the slightest psychological provocation. The only winner
from this monstrous determination to sow existential doubt is the massively popular psychic bully William Perkins, who exudes gloriously self-
possessed certainty about how to distinguish one kind of despair from
another. In the *Golden Chain* Perkins accuses the Church of Rome of
erecting "a gibbet, which is set up to torment and to rack the consciences
of men" (image 149), but Perkins himself can surely lay claim to especially
fine workmanship in the matter of constructing psychological racking
machines.

For the individual Christian is left, by this theology, not only wondering
about the past event of God's decision that totally dominates his or her
future, and over which he or she has no control whatsoever. The individual
Christian is left having the world of works transformed into opaque signs
(irresolvable sign reading is exhausting). Even worse, there is no institutional comfort to be found, since the reprobate looks exactly like the elect.
One needs constantly to be on guard against oneself as a look-alike elect,
and against one's fellow evangelicals as fake, look-alike members of the
True Church. Repudiating Catholics is the easy work; distinguishing the
evangelical elect from the evangelical reprobate is much tougher. Toughest
of all is deciding whether or not one is saved.

III

The especially bleak account I have given of mainline, state-sponsored Calvinist depression-production follows John Stachniewski's pathbreaking *The Persecutory Imagination*. It does not follow in the grand, Whig tradition of identifying the Puritan revolution with liberty, or of immediately identifying those who courageously stand up against powerful Catholic institutions as the avatars of liberty.

Why, though, describe that determinist theology as revolutionary? I briefly offer three reasons why the word "revolutionary" is exact. In the first place, this soteriology fundamentally aims to restructure subjectivity in relation vertically to God and horizontally between one's "even Christians." The Catholic subjectivity against which Protestantism pushed was established by the dispensation of the Catholic Church in 1215, at the Fourth Lateran Council, in which it was specified that every adult Christian must participate in the sacrament of penance by confessing at least once per year.[41] Few political or theological interventions are more far-reaching than fundamental changes to systems of concerted effort and life-changing reward, especially when the life in question is eternal. The 1215 Lateran Council established a system of obligatory mediation, whereby the adult individual Christian connected the inner life with the divine through the mediating ministration of the Church and its sacrament.

The 1536 Henrician *Ten Articles* did not abolish, but did eviscerate, the sacrament of Penance. Penance just survived in those Articles (along with Baptism and the Eucharist), from the seven pre-Reformation sacraments.[42] By the 1549 *Book of Common Prayer*, however, only two sacraments remained (Baptism and the Eucharist). Penance had gone, the only trace of which was a general commination against sinners, a general confession, and a wish that open penance for notorious sinners be restored.[43] This statuted restructuring of subjectivity also entailed and required dismantlement of the institutions of penance, including fraternities and pilgrimages, along with destruction of their material fabric, such as pilgrimage shrines, chantry chapels, and, by no means least, from 1538, all religious images subject to "idolatry."[44] The functions of the Church that mediate the individual and the divine are stripped out, leaving the individual facing the unmediated source of power directly, and redefining the meaning of the

Church. Revolutionary cultures characteristically operate by abolishing mediating institutions and by bringing forward the face of power, so as to clarify the relation of central power and individual. This bringing forward is as much theoretical as aesthetic. The positive name for this process of bringing power forward so as to clarify its direct power flow to individuals is equalization. In the sixteenth century the name for that process was the priesthood of all believers.

The theology of the new dispensation was revolutionary in a second sense: it does away with an accretive, reformist process of self-reform through actions in and with one's society. In place of that reformist process through time, the revolutionary theology institutes a born-again notion of selfhood in which the past can be wholly rejected and a new life, inoculated against the viruses of the pathological past, be started afresh. "Conversion" replaces process.

A third way in which the word "revolutionary" is accurate is as follows: the invisible evangelical Church is intensely centralized. God has abolished all mediating structures, both vertical and horizontal, between each Christian and him or herself. So far from it being the case that Protestantism is anti-institutional, it is instead *arch*-institutional, so much so that it either abolishes or etiolates every material institution that might obstruct the key power flow of the True, eternal, invisible Church of the elect. The Church no longer offers mechanisms of its own, whereby Christians can negotiate their way out of the debt of sin through works of penitence. The visible evangelical Church, that is, serves as a gathering place, a meetinghouse, not an office. Like all revolutionary cultures since the Protestant Reformation, evangelical religion centralizes power and therefore atomizes individuals, laying bare the one claim on the individual that counts, that of the source of power.

Early critics quickly spotted the atomization that would necessarily follow from evangelical soteriology. Thus Stephen Gardiner, Bishop of Winchester, despite his promotion of Henry VIII's break with Rome, could by 1546 recognize where Protestant soteriology would lead. By his rhetorically shaped estimation, every man would be his own church under the evangelical regime, and "each one man to . . . be alone, alone, alone, my own self al alone, and then to be devoured of the devil alone, without comfort in the wilderness alone."[45]

For contemporary liberals, perhaps the greatest gain of the Reformation is precisely the growth of individuality and interiority, seen as signs of authentic agency. The claim of increased interiority has enjoyed long and very vigorous, triumphalist history, with many secular restatements.[46] From the perspective of William Perkins's pastoral theology, one might readily agree that evangelical religion certainly will produce an instantly heightened, not to say all-consuming, and intense sense of interiority. One might also, however, redescribe that newly discovered interiority as a sense of exposed self-consciousness before the surveillance of a wholly unpredictable God, "each one man to . . . be alone, alone, alone." Interiority arises responsively; faced by an alien and severe judge, we tend to feel self-conscious. One might, further, redescribe individuality as solitude.

The culture that experienced so much despair was, despite appearances, dynamic and energetic. How? To experience this soteriology from the inside was, to be sure, to experience a thoroughly abject, belittled subjectivity. The psyche is, however, a recalcitrant creature, and will not accept its minimized abjection lightly. Instead, the psychic belittling, through its own logic, produces psychic magnification. The orthodox Calvinist response to abjection was glorious, grace-produced, magnified assurance of being forever within the innermost in-group, a few chosen from history's reprobate many, as one of the elect. The unorthodox, though nonetheless frequent, response was, instead, the obverse of that assurance: a hugely magnified, inward persuasion of one's fate as a damned reprobate, a persuasion that provoked one possibly to truculent, obscene blasphemy and suicidal despair. The standard autobiographical narrative produced by these orthodox and unorthodox responses was a flip-switch pattern of up, and then down: a manic-depressive, bipolar narrative of brief rushes of grace followed by, and productive of, much longer periods of chronic, paranoid distrust and debilitating despair, as in, for example, Bunyan's *Grace Abounding* (1666).[47] Evangelicals did not forget either state, or the exhilarating, big-dipper experience of their dynamic boom and debilitating bust logic.

Above all, the denial of works produced endless work. Calvinists needed to read their lives, looking for signs of whether or not they had been saved. Material works in the world were the fruit of one's salvation, not its cause; one therefore had to work hard to produce fruit by which one would be persuaded of one's salvation. Uncertainty as to whether or not the fruit was real only produced more labor. In sum, a culture that was fiercely hostile to works produced a work ethic.[48]

Once we reach this hardworking, psychically intense state, we need to turn to where the meanings are (i.e. the arts, and in this case literature) to understand what existential doubt with regard to agency felt like to souls less muscular, but more sensitive, than William Perkins. There we will also see how English Protestantism worked its way partially out from under the predestinarian heel.

4

Modernizing Despair: Narrative and Lyric Entrapment

IF LITERATURE, according to a standard and plausible view, is where we go to find out "how it felt like," then only literature, we might suppose, will be capable of expressing the sheer intensity and extremity of Calvinist subjectivity, and the heroism of the existential psychic battles it necessarily entailed. Literature is also where we habitually look to see the readiest *dissent* from tyrannical regimes. Does English writing under evangelical regimes express, and does it dissent from, the torturous intensity of the Calvinist psychic rack?

In non-polemical evangelical poetry 1530–1547, lyric poetry certainly expresses, with searing poignancy, the psychic pain of the Protestant predicament. The closed, intensely personal, potentially claustrophobic rooms of lyric poetry are the literary spaces best adapted to express experience of absolutism. I begin by looking to Henrician poets' non-comforting adaptation of the lyric traditions of the Hebrew Psalms. In the next section (devoted to the period 1580–1630) I turn to lyric poets who transfer the Petrarchan predicament of unremitting and hostile power, as expressed in love poetry, to religious poetry. In this period, things only become more painful for the evangelical poet whose agency is neutralized.

What, though, of the slightly larger imaginative space of closet drama (i.e. Greville's *Mustapha*)? And what of the much larger imaginative space of romance narrative poetry (e.g. Spenser's *Faerie Queene*)? Closet drama and romance tell the same story as religious lyric poetry: theological absolutism is extremely painful on the receiving end, and there is no way out.

What of resistance? Such resistance as exists in the period, until the reign of Charles I, is expressed implicitly: that much pain can only be the product of tremendous, apparently insuperable and detestable existential threat. Only, however, from the second quarter of the seventeenth century does literature start explicitly to resist the tyranny of the Calvinist God. So in Chapter 5 we move out from the intense, claustrophobic rooms of lyric poetry, from the claustrophobic conditions of closet drama, and from the no less repetitive, endless work of Spenserian romance. The sum perception of these paired chapters is as follows: the insistent, not to say relentless focus of the Anglo-American Whig tradition on agency is a traumatic reflex of predestination. That insistent claim of agency is born of the agonies of a revolutionary discipline that denies every spring of agency.

I

Initially, the tone of polemical evangelical literature is upbeat, if not carnivalesque. Irreverent mockery and destruction of a powerful system can be great fun, even if it is dangerous work. Within a few years of theologians such as Tyndale trashing the sacrament of penance theoretically in 1528; within a few years of polemicists such as Simon Fish energetically dismantling Purgatory and redirecting the economy of prayers for the dead (1529); and just before Henrician agents under Thomas Cromwell were despoiling the shrines of saints (1536–40)[1]: evangelical poets were mocking the entire Catholic apparatus, including the sacrament of penance, with ebullient, hip-hop rhythms and irrepressible irreverence. Thus the poem *The Image of Ipocrisy* (c. 1534) has it that priests are like Judas, who ask "after Judas way / What will ye give and pay / As the matter falles / For pardonnes and for palles, / And for confessionalles. / We may have absolucions / Without restytutyons / And at our own election / Passe without correction / Besydes Christes passion / To make satisfaction. / We fear for none offence / So [as long as] they have recompence."[2]

Joyfully irreverent, *engagé*, and destructive writing of this kind trashes free will. This ebullient polemical moment quickly and unsurprisingly gave way, however, to a very different, less carnivalesque mood. Mockery of free will gave way, that is, to a very much more somber, intense, private, and privately circulated literary expressions from within the Henrician Reformation.[3] Even as the destructive work of dismantling the huge penance industry was actually being undertaken, cultivated Tudor courtier poets were wrestling with Lutheran psychic imprisonment from their actual imprisonment. Thus both Thomas Wyatt (1503–1542) and Henry Howard, Earl of Surrey (1516/17–1547) wrote psalm adaptations from and / or about prison, imagining themselves as penitents both before God and before their own king, who in fact bore striking resemblances to the newly absolutist God.[4]

Thomas Wyatt suffered two Tower imprisonments. In 1536, as part of the purge and executions of courtly figures surrounding Anne Boleyn, Wyatt was arrested and imprisoned, when from his cell he seems certainly to have witnessed the execution of the queen.[5] In 1541, Wyatt was again imprisoned for treason after the fall of his patron Thomas Cromwell in 1540. Wyatt also seems certain to have witnessed the execution of Cromwell, whose last words on the scaffold are reported to be addressed to Wyatt himself, "Farewell Wyatt, and gentle Wyatt pray for me."[6] On this second occasion of imprisonment, Wyatt was pardoned and spared execution on condition that he confess to the charges.

Wyatt's *Paraphrase of the Penitential Psalms* (written between 1534 and 1542) follows Wyatt's Italian source in filling out a biographical context for King David's inspired composition of the seven so-called "Penitential Psalms" (Psalms 6, 31, 37, 50, 101, 129 and 142 in the Vulgate Bible). The psalms generally, and the penitential psalms in particular, had been part of liturgical, para-liturgical, and sacramental structures throughout pre-Reformation Christianity.[7] In a sixteenth-century English context, the voice of the psalmist is cut off from human, liturgical, and sacramental support systems, not least because the sacrament of penance had been fundamentally weakened already by 1536 (prior to its abolition in the English Church by 1549). Whereas the sacrament of penance involves a process of negotiation, the new soteriology had effectively done away with negotiation, since all initiative was in God's hands.

The complainant of the penitential Psalms is imagined to be King David. David has as good as murdered the husband of Bathsheeba (2Samuel, 11–12), and so begs a silent God for forgiveness. His condition is one of terror, despair, and its corporal symptoms: I "Shake in despair unless thou me assure / My flessh is troubled, my heart doth fear the spear," he declares, in "horrible terror" (l. 195) before God.[8] We learn from the unspecified but authoritative narrator, who introduces David's voice, that none of David's good deeds, including, presumably, his singing of these psalms themselves, has any bearing whatsoever on God's decision to forgive David:

> But when he weigh'th the fault and recompense,
> He damn'th his deed and findeth plain
> Atween them two no whit equivalence.
>   (ll. 648–650)

There is no congruence between fault and reward; the gap between them is unbridgeable, and the standard terms of penitence therefore collapse. The psalmist inhabits a world in which spirit is almost entirely dislocated from formal practice. The narrator tells us that David "takes all outward deed in vain," except insofar as outward actions are "the sign or fruit alone" of God's already-given gift.[9] What is desperately needed in this predicament is a psychological persuasion that reward has been given as a gift (i.e. by grace) and that the works of penitence are the signs of that grace received. A crushed David feels a rush of gratitude toward his inscrutable God, who might have acted in his favor: "all the glory of his forgiven fault / To God alone he doth it whole convert" (658–659). All initiative belongs to God, even including the sinner's power and voice to declare his unworthiness in the first place: "Of thyself, O God, this operation / It must proceed by purging me from blood" (490–491). Wyatt imagines himself in a legal setting, but a legal setting determined by the logic of Luther's *deus absconditus*, and so evacuated of any recognizable relations of justice. David beseeches God to deal with him "after thy justice," which is precisely not "of law after the form and guise" whereby a lord judges his "thrall bondslave," since by that justice "no man his right shall save" (731–736).

For the Henrician courtier Wyatt, in both his razor-sharp, secular love lyrics and in his searing, finely-cut, word-by-careful-word religious poetry, resignation and sedition are poised (Wyatt's word) and balanced with extreme care: "In his heart he turneth and poiseth / Each word that erst his lips might forth afford. / He points, he pauseth, he wonders, he praiseth / The mercy that hides of justice the sword" (518–521). The very care taken by this poetry is of a piece with the charges under which Wyatt stood in 1541, when the capital charge of treason for which he stood trial turned on a syllable spoken or not.[10] The extreme care cannot help but expose the threat under which he stands: this level of care, that is, cannot help but implicitly protest at the (in)justice of the menacing sword (or, in Wyatt's case, the axe).

At the same time, despite this implicit protest at royal injustice, Wyatt has, in my view, quite clearly absorbed the devastating subjectivity required of the evangelical penitent. In fact, it is precisely his absorption of evangelical abjection that underlines and magnifies the threat under which his voice now stands. If the Lutheran God predestines souls without respect to works, for his own reasons, the same is true, mutatis mutandis, of the Tudor monarch. Both evangelical God and Tudor monarch dispense reward without respect to deserving: between deserving and reward there is, in Wyatt's words, "no whit equivalence." In his second, 1541 spell in the Tower, Wyatt was spared execution, as I mentioned earlier, on the understanding that he had confessed to the charges, "yielding himself only to His Majesty's mercy."[11]

In sum, within the period 1530–1547 the public, polemical repudiation of penance and of free will is wholly joyful. That repudiation entirely lacks any sense whatsoever that one should be careful for what one wishes, especially when one is wishing for the repudiation of any form of human agency. By contrast, the privately circulated poetry of one imprisoned Henrician courtier (I look to Surrey in Chapter 16) tells a very different, more complex story. Here the poet is paralyzed between two early modern absolutist rulers, one earthly and one divine. Neither ruler is prepared to act according to "law after the form and guise" of recognizable human justice. The terror of legal implosion impels the appeal to the divine judge, but that appeal merely replicates, as I say, the similarities of these two monarchs. The texts are nothing if not expressions of extreme fear; the intensity of that expression cannot help but expose the monstrosity of the threat, even if the theological response only finally redoubles that threat. Surrey, who was executed in January 1547 after having written Psalm paraphrase from the Tower awaiting execution, declares, "My eyes yield tears, my years consume between hope and despair" (Surrey, Ps 73, 45–50); if the quality of Surrey's astonishing psalm paraphrases are to be trusted, his life ended not in hope but despair.

II

Despair is, clinically, a chronic condition. So too was it an abiding, repetitive, even magnetic cultural condition in Elizabethan and Jacobean England, a consummation devoutly to be wished. That somber reflection comes ineluctably into view from the 1580s, when, to be sure, the Catholic threats, both external and internal, were being vigorously defined and addressed, both legally and militarily.[12] The testimony of English literature from this period underlines, however, a much more insistent, internal threat of despair to the revolutionary new order. Take, for example (if you have the time), the *Faerie Queene* (first published 1590, and then in longer form in 1596) of Edmund Spenser (1552–1599).

We meet the monster Error in Book 1, canto 1 of this very long text. Error is an obvious symbol for the Catholic Church: Redcross Knight (aka Saint George, aka Protestant England) encounters her first up; she is evidently a monster of the half-woman, half-animal kind, and she is simultaneously fertile and poisonous. Once attacked, she vomits both books and lumps of flesh; her spawn, "deformèd monsters," lap her blood so avidly that they swell and spontaneously burst (1.1.14–26). The initial fight requires courage, but the enemy is easily visible (she is seriously overweight, for a start), and must be confronted. Once decapitated, the hateful spawn have "slaine themselves, with whom he should contend" (1.1.26.9). The fight with the Catholic Church would seem to be over.

The *Faerie Queene* is itself seriously overweight; it sits heavy in our hand, weighing in at 984 pages of text in the Penguin edition.[13] Redcross's victory over Error takes place 8 pages into those 984. What will be the narrative of the remaining 976 pages? "God helpe the man so wrapt in Errours endlesse traine" (1.1.18.9), declares the poet in mid-fight with Error, but within short space that fight is in fact neatly over and the enemy survivors are conveniently self-exploding. There seems to be no endless train of error at all, except, of course, for those remaining 976 pages.

"Seems" is of course the operative word, for this first encounter turns out to be the easy one, for all its Gothic horror. Redcross Knight's real and much more demanding challenge begins immediately afterwards, when he meets the first incarnation of Archimago, the malevolent Catholic hypocrite who is capable of invading the psyche and of producing imaginative look-alikes.

Spenser's vast poem consists of many exhausting divagations and split narratives, in which heroes are beguiled by doubleness and lethally apparent likeness: their enemies are visually indistinguishable from friends, and their challenges much more psychic than physical. Error assumes many forms, and most of them are exceptionally difficult to decipher. Her circling, coiled "traine," or tail, is indeed endless, and the *Faerie Queene* is by no means over when she is dead; on the contrary, the narrative of the remaining five books is characterized by splitting, fragmentation, and unfinishable stories. Whereas medieval romance is characterized above all by closure, Spenser's Calvinist romance is forever open, driven as it is by dubiety and doubleness, and populated as it is by unkillable, zombie enemies (e.g. Archimago).[14] Heroes and villains are both "divided into double parts" (1.2.9.2), either literally or psychologically.

Above all, in Book One Redcross Knight must be tempted by unkillable suicidal despair, before being restored to psychic strength and rendered capable of another, victorious battle against another easy-to-spot monster (the Beast of the Apocalypse), as a prelude to his marriage with Una, the True Church, in Book 1, Canto 12. The nature and representation of Despair underlines the repetitive, irresolvable threat. Just as the poem is populated by Doppelgänger, despair itself is the inevitable, unkillable double of Calvinist certainty.

Redcross, like Marlowe's Faustus, witnesses the Seven Deadly Sins as a spectacle (Book 1.4.15–37) in Pride's palace.[15] Here the sins, and the penitential system they represent, have become an occasion for theatrically assured, mocking, complacent representation of old-order subjectivity. Despite its best intentions, however, new-order subjectivity is unable to remain complacent when faced with Despair. In Book 1.8.40–50 Una and Arthur accompany the exhausted, depleted knight Redcross out of the dungeon of Pride's palace, planning to take him to the House of Holiness to recuperate. The recurring experience of caves and dungeons is, however, by no means definitively contained. In the following canto (1.9), they come across a terrified young knight, Trevisan, in flight, who wears a halter around his neck, in readiness for suicide. Asked to recount the source of his ongoing terror, he tells the story of yet another knight, Terwin (Spenser strives to distance this narrative from Redcross). Trevisan tells how he and the loveless Terwin encounter "a man of hell, that cals himselfe *Despaire*" (1.9.28.5), who persuades Terwin to kill himself with a rusty knife.

The elect group returns to take revenge on the man from hell, Despair, who inhabits a cave in a visually arresting, infertile landscape of despair. Redcross's indignant rage against suicidal despair quickly ebbs as Despair advertises the attractions of suicide, quietly insinuating all the while that Redcross himself is susceptible to precisely the same self-cancelling desire: he, too, desires rest, "and further from it daily wanderest" (1.9.40.3). Despair's not unpersuasive theological arguments, delivered as blandishments to a profoundly self-doubting, wounded psyche, presage that other great early modern expression of desire for the consummation that suicide will bring, ending the "heart ache and the thousand natural shocks / That flesh is heir to." In the context of Spenser's poem, those arguments persuade another young man, Redcross, to choose the rusty knife in readiness for self-destruction. Only Una's unquenched indignation saves him from suicide. But Redcross's Despair cannot, like Redcross's unkillable enemy Archimago, be put from company so decisively. The elect group move on, but Despair is at it again, compulsively and repetitively rehearsing what William Perkins might have called reprobate "dullness of heart," or elect "holy desperation" (the sure sign of election).[16] As Una and Redcross leave, Despair returns to his endless work:

> He chose an halter from among the rest,
>> And with it hung himselfe, unbid unblest.
>> But death he could not worke himselfe thereby;
>> For thousand times he so himselfe had drest,
>> Yet nathelesse it could not doe him die.
> Till he should die his last, that is eternally.[17]

III

Spenserian romance cannot, then, escape the backward pull of despair. What of contemporary lyric poetry and closet drama of the 1580s until the 1620s? Fulke Greville, Lord Brooke (1554–1628)—passionate friend and biographer of Philip Sidney, and high-level civil servant to monarchs

Elizabeth, James, and Charles—was simultaneously an exceptionally acute critic of absolutist government, and a committed Calvinist.[18]

All Greville's work is characterized by compacted, penetrating analysis of tyranny through what may be called elitist pessimism. Amongst many other works, he wrote closet dramas (first composed 1594–1596); a biography of his friend Philip Sidney (which Greville left unfinished in 1611); and philosophical poems on various topics, including religion (1622–1628). His astonishing and largely unrecognized lyric sequence *Caelica* (written at various periods between 1577–1628) consists of 109 poems.[19] *Caelica* begins with love lyrics, but changes to religious lyrics at #84, vowing to Cupid, as Greville bids farewell to love lyrics, that he "bowed not to thy image for succession" (84.9). He promises now to turn to religion, to "thoughts that please me lesse, and lesse betray me" (84.14).

Both sets of poems in *Caelica*—the secular and the religious—are informed by an acute sense of the shapes and logic of tyranny. Together they constitute an astonishingly mordant, poetically dense, skeptical account of power and its corruptions, including the practice of both law and religion. Nothing escapes Greville's brilliantly caustic critique, or nothing except the actual experience of Calvinist despair. Before turning directly to *Caelica*, I begin with a brief account of the critique of absolute political power, and of the practice of state religion, as found in Greville's searingly intelligent closet drama and his discursive poetry.

None of Greville's writings was published during his lifetime, except *Mustapha* (published in a pirated edition 1609).[20] *Mustapha* was possibly written 1595–1600, but revised between 1603 and its pirated publication in 1609, and then again significantly revised before publication in 1633.[21] Greville sets his Senecan closet drama in the court of the Ottoman sultan Suleiman the Magnificent (r. 1520–1566). Suleiman is persuaded by his ambitious wife, Rossa, to murder his own virtuous son Mustapha, against whom Rossa has fabricated charges of sedition. Suleiman eventually agrees to the assassination, which is knowingly accepted by the virtuous and obedient son Mustapha. The popular rebellion at this act is stilled by play's end, with Suleiman still in power.

Mustapha's presentation of the Ottoman court is striking for the way in which its predicaments, political and religious, are used as a lens through which to understand the logic of absolutist English kingship, particularly under James I.[22] The play expresses foreboding about the permanent revolution set in train by the unholy alliance of absolutist state and cooperative, similarly structured religion. The chorus sees both past and future: the past of religion setting up a king, and the future of civil war between that same religion and that same king. It is the nature of the outward Church "her founders to devour" (p. 124, l. 18), and to blemish truth by helping kings. The logic of that process, however, produces a counter wave, whereby religion now seeks to destroy the king it established:

> Whence she that erst raised kings by pulling freedom down
> Now seeks to free inferior powers and only bind the crown.
>   (p. 124, ll. 23–24)

As a result, the chorus prophesies, in an extended passage, certain civil war between Church and State (pp. 123–125).[23]

So Greville understood the mechanisms of absolutism (he frequently uses the word "absolute") with unerring intelligence and searching acuity; understood the ways in which absolutism remakes the world in its own image (Greatness must "ever what it wills or fears make true") (p. 85, l. 5); and recognized, as he used the same language for, destructive secular absolutism as much as current theological absolutism ("grace alone") with particular resonance for an iconoclastic England: "though we make no idols, yet we fashion / God, as if from power's throne he took his being" (p. 98, ll. 97–98). He explicitly and accurately prophesies civil war between Church and State. In sum, Greville got it all right: he understood the logic of power, the mirroring interactions of state and religious absolutist power structures, and the inevitable civil war that issues from that unholy alliance.[24]

So after such a critique, what does the religion tightly embraced by Greville look like? The answer, in a word, is "absolutist." This most penetrating and prescient of analysts (and in the play Greville is, it must be said, more analyst than artist) apparently saw no alternative in his own religion to the very absolutism, though of an even more punishing kind, than the absolutism he critiques in the state. Greville perfectly understood the kinetic logic of revolutionary absolutism, but instead of rejecting that form in his own religion, he purifies it into its most sublime and despair-inducing shapes.

Greville's *Treatise on Religion* was probably written between his retirement in 1621 and his death in 1628. It consists of 114 stanzas, each a compressed, self-enclosed, discursive reflection on an aspect of Calvinist religion. It was published long after Greville's death, in 1670, having been excised from the planned publication in 1633.[25] Nothing is capable of lifting man up except grace, and grace is foreign to him, "in us but not of us" (stanza 3). Without that alien grace, man is a "slave of slaves", subject to "restless despayre, desire and desolation / The more secure, the more abhomination" (stanza 6). Science and nature help us not a whit to know God, and in using them we fashion only endless idols of error. As we look up from these idols, "justice there / Reflects self-horror backe upon the sinne" (stanza 22). Extrapolating this personal horror onto the public realm, when religion and politics merge into each other, then "this common traffique of abuse" leads inevitably to civil war (stanza 31). Only the onset of God's unmerited grace, producing the feeling of election, can provide any stable assurance. Until "you" (the reader) turn from "Atheisme to zeal," then "Thou feelst of thine Election no true seale" (stanza 44). God showers this glory on the best, while he appears in "clowdes of horror to the rest" (stanza 48). This resolution for the elect applies, however, only in death, since in life we remain subject to "temptation, error / So is our zeale warre, prayer, remorse and terror" (stanza 52). All mediums between God and the individual Christian are but sin's suggestion, and it is blasphemy to take the words and counsels of God as "a doctrine of despair." Though God's words "seeme severe, / Health of the chosen is the lost child's rod" (stanzas 101–02).

In sum, Greville embraces a religion that replicates, but in more purified, austere and sublime form, the absolutist political forms about which Greville the political observer is so trenchantly perceptive and so critically mordant. If Greville as learned courtier recognized that tyrannical politics neutralizes human learning, then Greville the Calvinist promoted a religion that dismisses human learning as utterly useless. If Greville as counselor searched most deeply for the sources of resistant agency, Greville the believer recognized no source of human agency whatsoever. If Greville the politician critiqued the subjective experience of political tyranny as self-destructively to serve power's "bent," Greville the believer embraced the experience of spiritual "zeale" as "warre, prayer, remorse and terror." If the problem with monarchical tyranny is the demolition of intervening mediums that ensure liberty, Greville promoted a religion that is relentlessly hostile to any medium whatsoever. As a politician, in short, Greville represented a tradition of the ancient constitution; as a believer, he is a modern.

If Greville's drama is the genre in which resistant political agency is explored most precisely, his discursive poetry offers, then, a declarative blueprint of a religious culture that seems to replicate, in heightened form, the structure of power Greville resists in his drama. What of Greville's lyric poetry? The question is especially interesting, since Greville innovates by carrying the crushing emotional disciplines of Petrarchan love poetry across to the territory religious lyric.[26] The 109 poems of *Caelica* were written across Greville's career, between 1577 and 1614. As stated above, Greville abandons love poetry at #84 and turns for the most part to religion. Shifts of this kind are usually critical: no more dallying with time-wasting amorous dalliance; now down to the serious business of religion. Does the shift in *Caelica* mark a salutary change, or more of the absolutist, despair producing same?

Petrarchan poetry, wholly derived from, though much darker than, Ovidian amatory poetry, is a study in tyranny.[27] The lover recuses himself from the world of public affairs, only to discover that private "affairs" are ruled by the same iron political law, since the boy-prince Cupid is a tyrant (child tyrants are possibly the worst sort). Greville wrote in this Petrarchan tradition, just as his dear friend Sidney did in *Astrophil and Stella*. Whereas Sidney's amatory poetry is delightfully insouciant, at its best Greville's is dark well beyond insouciance (darkness is Greville's specialty).

Take, for example, the last of the secular lyrics, "Who Grace, for Zenith had, from which no shadowes grow" (#83). This text begins by pointing to the happy lover, whose zenith position excludes the possibility of shadow. Should, however, that lover fall into despair—to "darke despaired warre of sprites" (83.6) then Greville will call on him as a fellow complainant, but only on condition that his fellow experiences "horror" for real. The truly despairing person knows that the despair is real precisely because (we are in Kafka territory) he cannot trust that despair ("Nor can I trust mine owne despaire, and nothing else receive./Thus be unhappy men, blest to be more accurst," 83.22–23). Greville as lover is as the living dead, whose despair is fed by desire; his heart is tortured as upon wheels, "With endlesse turning of themselves" (83.34). Nothing can satisfy the implacable judge Truth, "whom no desert can overcome, nor no distresse intreat" (83.46). The experience is self-divisive, humiliating and repetitive, productive only of the horror of despair:

> My Heart a wildernesse, my studies only feare,
> And as in shadowes of curst death, a prospect of despaire.
> My Exercise, must be my horrours to repeat,
> My Peace, Joy, End, and Sacrifice her dead Love to intreat.
>   (83.83–86)

Greville's subjectivity is so damaged as to corrode his very name; the only way of deciphering him is thematically: "For *Greiv-Ill*, paine, forlorne estate doe best decipher me" (83.98).

This, then, is the last poem in the secular sequence, a penetrating account of subjective self-destruction under the gaze of an unremittingly hostile, single power, in which the narrator is blessed only in the doubt-driven certainty that he's damned. Petrarchan lyric of this kind rocketed in prominence in France and Northern Europe, after a 150-year period between Petrarch's death in 1374 and the mid-sixteenth century.[28] Petrarch's sonnet form provided a small, though highly subdivided formal room for the exploration of highly subdivided, trapped subjective states, in which the experience of humiliation, self-division, and above all despair in the face of unrequiting and unrequitable power was expressed with brilliantly illuminating precision and beauty. The strange 150-year delay in the sudden, astonishingly powerful uptake of this set of poetic resources (surely unparalleled in European literary history) can be explained, in my view, by the fact of early modern absolutism. It is no accident that the first Petrarchan sonnets in English should be those of Thomas Wyatt and Henry Howard, Earl of Surrey, in the 1530s.[29]

Does, however, Calvinist religious lyric, working in the same forms (often the sonnet itself), provide any critical purchase of resistance to tyranny in this peculiarly enclosed space of emotional fragmentation, torture and despair?

Greville sets, as we have seen, Petrarchan love lyric and religious lyric into the same sequence. The religious poems also confront a power so transcendent that any imaginations of it become idolatrous obstacles and insults to that very power. Efforts to worship this inherently alien God are so inadequate as immediately to become themselves alien. When the charges of "superstition" and "atheism" are laid here, they refer to Greville's own, Calvinist Church, as in this text, "*Syon* lyes waste, and thy *Ierusalem,* / O Lord, is falne to utter desolation":

> Mans superstition hath thy truths entomb'd,
> His Atheisme againe her pomps defaceth,
> That sensuall unsatiable vaste wombe
> Of thy seene Church, thy unseene Church disgraceth;
> There lives no truth with them that seem thine own,
> Which makes thee living Lord, a God unknowne.

(109.13–18)

Efforts precisely to worship this God become acts of blasphemy, idolatry and iconoclasm by the visible Church, a Church inhabited by Greville himself. The voice of the poem accordingly beseeches the Calvinist *deus absconditus* to break from his transcendent cover, and make himself known: "Lord, thou no longer live a God unknowne" (99.24). If, however, human effort is precisely the cause of God's disgusted retreat, then the appeal for intimacy with that hidden, unknown God can only be made on the premise of alienation from fellow Christians in the same Church. To recognize God is to atomize oneself: "There lives no truth with them that seem thine own" (99.17).

Not only must the subject be wholly alienated either from his fellow Christians and from God, but that very position also guarantees that the subject's agency must be wholly denied in recognition of God's inviolate agential initiative. If, that is, human effort to represent God merely defaces God, then the speaker must both distinguish himself from the misguided human effort of his fellow Christians, and also somehow undo his own agency. To be an agent, that is, is to be an idolater.

This is clearly a position of extremity, even more extreme in its psychological challenge, perhaps, than Perkins's structure of subjection. (Greville makes no reference to good works being the fruit of grace.) It naturally produces desperation. In fact it produces a very peculiar mix of both desperation and gratitude, since the one form of agency this culture recognizes is divine; the desperation felt by the sinner turns to gratitude precisely as God appears. Only self-undoing at a profound level, however, can produce such gratitude: the Calvinist Christian needs to do much more than not attempt works; he or she must also undo the very impulse to work. The desperation thus produced also produces the assurance of election; conviction of one's worthlessness "beares the faithlesse downe to desperation; / Depriv'd of humane graces and divine," when "even there appeares this saving God of mine" (99.10–12, "Down in the depth of mine Iniquity").

The need to undo agency must also apply to the writing of poetry itself, taking it to the very edge of silence. And so, in another religious lyric, Greville's appeal to God shifts into subjunctive mood. Greville does not make the appeal, but only would if he could:

> *If* from this depth of sinne, this hellish grave,
> And fatall absence from my Saviours glory,
> I *could* implore his mercy, who can save,
> And for my sinnes, not paines of sinne, be sorry:
> Lord, from this horror of iniquity,
> And hellish grave, thou *wouldst* deliver me.
> (98.13–18, "Wrapt up o Lord, in man's degeneration,"
>   my emphases)

In sum, Greville's critique of political tyranny has no traction whatsoever in his religious writing. The lyrics of *Caelica* in particular expose a structure of subjective relations with God that are nothing if not extreme, perched as they are on the very edge of voice and agency. Greville's Calvinist God is himself an extremist, even within Calvinism. Not only is he an impenetrable and pan-initiative-possessing God. He also relieves the desperation his own hidden transcendence had in the first place provoked. In addition, any material form that aims to represent him, including the material form of lyric poetry, betrays him.

IV

Greville died in 1628. A younger generation of poets, most brilliantly the friends John Donne (1572–1631) and George Herbert (1593–1633), entered the same tightly confined lyric rooms inhabited by, for example, Wyatt, Surrey,

Anne Askew, the Countess of Pembroke, and Greville, there to produce astonishingly lucid poetry out of the predicament of "Despair behind and death before" casting "such terror" that the voice, no less than the flesh of the poet, struggles to find agency precisely as it struggles to abandon agency. Despite sometimes claiming that they pass beside the "gloomy cave of Desperation," the fragile fault lines of Calvinist spirituality recurrently threaten to open at the slightest provocation, thereby casting such poets into that gloomy Spenserian concavity.[30]

Judged by the terms of their institutional affiliations, Donne and Herbert were far from being what historians of religion call "the hotter sort of Protestant": Donne was a convert from Catholicism, who embraced Calvinist state religion from late in Elizabeth's reign (c. 1600), and, after his ordination as deacon and priest in 1615, flourished as a high-level clergyman under both James I (r. 1603–1625), and his religiously conservative son Charles I (r. 1625–1649), from 1625. Donne died in 1631, aged 59.[31] After a career as public orator of the University of Cambridge and MP, Herbert (b. 1593) was ordained as deacon by 1624, and as minister by 1630. His appointment to the parish of Bemberton, near Salisbury, in 1630, was, though by no means high profile, assisted by Charles I. (Charles also took comfort from reading Herbert's posthumously published *The Temple* (1633) in prison before his execution in January 1649.) Herbert died prematurely of ill-health in 1633.[32] Even, however, if Donne and Herbert were not the "hotter sort" of Protestant institutionally, their religious poetry is very hot indeed.[33] As religious poets, they work precisely up against the extremes of psychic challenge demanded by the likes of William Perkins.

The Calvinist psychic predicament is born of despair and necessarily produces despair. These poets struggle to build "broken Altars," with materials that they must themselves disown. Faced by the utter transcendence of this early modern God, language fragments.[34] Just as language had strained, cracked, and sometimes broken in some minority late medieval traditions of Platonizing, *via-negativa* Christianity, so too does it begin to break in the brilliantly iconoclastic lyric poetry of Donne and Herbert, so as to produce luminous, and sometimes lurid, effects of verbal and ethical paradox.[35]

Thus Donne's "Batter my Heart" (Holy Sonnet 14), first published in 1633, calls for God to treat him, Donne, as the revolutionary iconoclasts had treated religious images—to "break, blow, burn, and make me new": not mending but breaking, not polishing but burning, or, in the words of William Perkins, breaking "hard stones into many small pieces and into dust":

> Batter my heart, three-person'd God, for you
> As yet but knock, breathe, shine, and seek to mend;
> That I may rise and stand, o'erthrow me, and bend
> Your force to break, blow, burn, and make me new.[36]

Donne speaks (if unpublished while still alive) as a revolutionary, promoting renewal through breaking the idols of the old régime. God's iconoclasm of the self will, paradoxically, enable the self to "rise and stand." It will, in Donne's words, "make me new." In order that this act of self-breaking should happen, however, Donne engages in ethical paradox, breaking ethical norms in order to break, and break through, any doubt whatsoever about the extremity of his faith: he begs God to enslave and rape him in order that he, Donne, be free and chaste:

> Divorce me, untie or break that knot again,
> Take me to you, imprison me, for I,
> Except you enthrall me, never shall be free,
> Nor ever chaste, except you ravish me.
> (ll. 11–14)

This will to original novelty could just as easily be described as the subjectivity of sadomasochism, pleading with the implacable power to hurt by way of guaranteeing faith in one's utter subjection. Truculent obscenity is a frequent feature of Calvinist linguistic usage on the unstable edge of sanity, when the self is fragmenting.[37] It serves simultaneously as symptom of breakdown and token of the required self-hammering.[38]

Herbert, too, enters the torture chamber. He does so from outside the Church, where moderate folk living decently in society can counsel each other with the voice of moderation.[39] Once inside the church, however, almost all talk of society and moderation vanishes. To be sure, a poem like Love 3, coming at the very edge of *The Temple*, replays a courteous and generous welcome to the sinner by Love, to a comforting Eucharistic feast. In many of these poems within the temple, however, the wholly isolated poetic voice beseeches God to ease the pain, since "these cross-actions / Do wind a rope about, and cut my heart" ("The Cross," ll. 32–33). The torture may be painful, and the poet may beseech God to lessen the pain ("Oh rack me not to such a vast extent!," "The Temper (1)," l. 9). But calls to diminish the infliction of pain give way to readiness to accept a yet tighter turn of the wheel:

> Stretch or contract me thy poor debtor:
> This is but tuning of my breast,
> To make the music better.
>
> ("The Temper (1)," ll. 22–24)

As is frequently the case with both early modern Elizabethan and contemporary torture, paradox and euphemism are used to allude to, sharpen, and disguise the extremity of pain.[40] The "music" of the torture chamber equally underlines that there is and can be no legal "contract" between the irredeemable sinner and God. The new subjectivity of Calvinism has long ago rejected relations governed by contract, and has instead embraced only relations of absolute, unmediated power, where the source of power "contracts" and stretches bodies at will (where the word "contract" underlines the impossibility of any predetermined agreement between God and the sinner). Western literature has few analogues to subjectivity set on such an extreme and officially sanctioned knife-edge as early modern Calvinism, a subjectivity in which, as Herbert says, "My thoughts are all a case of knives" ("Affliction (4)," l. 7).

5

Modernizing Despair's Epic Non-Escape

LUTHERAN AND CALVINIST predestination certainly produced, as we have seen from the English examples, despair in early modern Europe, of the kind heralded by Dürer's *Melancholia* (1514). Carnivalesque verbal and physical trashing of pre-Reformation subjectivity in the early English Reformation, as presented in Chapter 4, quickly gave way to much less joyful conditions of stubborn, chronic, and intensely private despair. Religious poets expressing that condition, for almost a century from the 1530s, chose the confined space of lyric as the poetic space to do so. That private genre alone could express, and offer resistance of a kind to, despairing disintegration of self and voice. Desperation, it would seem, had nowhere to go, stuck as it was within the claustrophobic possibilities of sadomasochism. The endless wandering of Spenserian romance might have seemed like a deferral of sorts, but the religious books of the *Faerie Queene* are unable definitively to leave Despair's cave behind or alone.

The story of early modern English despair does not, however, end in the little rooms of lyric or the dark caves of Spenserian romance. Predestination also gave rise, paradoxically, to a great deal of inventive action. Total denial of the substantive value of works prompted, as we shall see, a great deal of epic work.

How so? Relatively recent, and certainly very influential, historians have mistaken Puritan devotion to work as Puritan devotion to work. Thus the hugely influential Marxist historian Christopher Hill, for example, writing in 1964, made comparisons between the pre-Reformation attitude to work and what Hill took to be contemporary African attitudes. Both the pre-Reformation and the contemporary African attitudes to work were, in Hill's eyes, degraded. Hill confidently set the medieval, in fact, a whisker ahead of the contemporary African: "Mediaeval society and religion had perhaps advanced too far to encourage the serf to think that his labor was degrading and evil [as per Hill's contemporary Africa, that is], but it was not honorable in itself."[1] Hill goes on jauntily and positively to align Puritanism and Communism: "In the U.S.S.R.," we can see the "education of the population in a new body of ideas which, like Puritanism, stresses the dignity and social value of labor."[2] Hill's multiply disgraceful cultural equivalences are straightforward: listless, work-hating Africa and pre-Reformation Europe on one side, with active Communism and Puritanism, both ennobling work, on the other. (Hill does not share his views on whether forced gulag labor—well known by 1964—was also ennobling.)

Objectionable and plain ignorant views such as those of Hill aside, early modern mainline Protestantism did have a justified reputation for working hard, as underlined so famously and analyzed so brilliantly by Max Weber in 1904.[3] Devotion to work among those who utterly repudiate works is certainly a paradox, but it's also a wholly intelligible paradox. Magisterial and Reformed Protestants worked hard precisely because they did *not* value works as currency that can satisfy God and change the future. The culture that produced the meritocracy did so, paradoxically, because it started out rejecting human merit through works altogether. Works, that is, did not produce meritoriously deserved election. Early modern Protestants worked hard, instead, because works were understood as the fruit of election; works, that is, were *signs* of the divine decision already taken. The Lutheran and Calvinist subject was therefore required to persuade him or herself, in good part through the signs of his or her labor, that the divine decision had in fact gone in his or her way.

To read one's own works as signs is unending and treacherous work. For one, the task can by definition never be complete; and second, total self-persuasion, or what Puritan divines called "assurance," about existential issues is for most souls (souls less muscular than those of John Calvin or William Perkins, at any rate) an arduous, slippery, and distressing business.

The only way to maintain high levels of faith in the worthlessness of works was, then, to work ceaselessly and to look for signs, knowing all the while that these works amount to nothing in themselves. The effort to persuade oneself that one was among the elect therefore produced extraordinary, if perhaps neurotic and self-deceptive dynamism. The uncertainty and necessity of the search produced the open-ended commitment to keep working until such a sign demonstrably appeared.[4] As long as the work continued to confirm the good signs, then, as per Mark Twain's comment about the music of Richard Wagner ("it's not as bad as it sounds"), it doesn't feel so bad.

The energetic, if neurotic works produced by predestination turn out, in fact, to be so energetic as to be world changing. The orthodox, persuaded of the savage purity of predestination, had a great deal at stake in energetically defending their orthodoxy. They needed, that is, to maintain their assurance that they were among the elect: the certainty and legitimacy of their entire revolutionary cause depended on it. So far from producing listlessness, the need to protect predestinarian certainty produced instead two classic and decisive orthodox responses. The orthodox either signalled readiness to command the state, if necessary by detonating a civil war in defense of what they took to be state religious orthodoxy (thus Calvinist parliamentarians from 1625); or, as super-orthodox, they rejected state orthodoxy altogether in the name of a further, higher boundary of orthodoxy (thus Puritan exiles, including exiles to America). The orthodox, that is, were determined either to remake the state in their own image, if necessary by civil war, or to abandon it altogether in search of a new state.

Another solution was theological and heterodox, from within Calvinism, but in opposition to Calvinism. That solution ("Arminianism") rescued a key element of pre-Reformation and pre-modern religious understanding (i.e. free will) from within the suffocating prison of early modern orthodox Calvinist predestination.[5] The prison house of predestination produced, as argued in Chapter 4, the tiny, lyric rooms of agonized lyric poetry and the recursive pathologies of unfinishable romance. In this chapter I look to the poetry of Arminianism—the poetry, that is, of a rescued free will. That poetry took the form of the apparently open vistas of Miltonic epic.

Even here, however, the epic landscape is scarred by the barely covered crevasses of early modern despair. Heterodox Calvinist escape from orthodox Calvinism turns out to produce the proto-liberal tradition, with the reclamation of free will. Here I will argue, however, that Miltonic epic never fully escapes the prison chamber. From the perspective of this and the previous chapter, we understand that contemporary liberal determination to apply the standard of agency as the key measure of approbation is but the historical reflex of Calvinist predestination. The relentless affirmation of agency seeks vainly, by its very determination, to hold predestination at bay.

I

For those who considered themselves the Calvinist orthodox after 1625, the kinetic logic of Puritan theology, which denied any value to human works, will produce both nation-changing revolutionary civil wars and what would become the world-changing colonization of America.

Already in 1609 Fulke Greville had accurately predicted the readiness of the orthodox to detonate civil war on religious grounds.[6] However accurate his prophecy, Greville was not preternaturally prescient, given that all he had to do was to look west and south from England to his contemporary European world: a sequence of eight especially vicious phases of religious civil wars (with between two and four *million* victims) had already ravaged France from 1562 and would last until 1629 (whence the word "massacre" arose for the first time in French and English, in response to the bloody events of St Bartholomew Day on August 18, 1572); and more complicated forms of civil war had also taken hold of the Low Countries from 1566.[7] Greville had seen the planned terrorism of the Gunpowder Plot of 1605 and the devastating Thirty Years War (1618–1648) was about to begin in the Empire, in which between 25 and 40 percent of the population of Central Europe was to die.[8] When religion and politics discover that their marriage will end in divorce, then, according to Greville, "massacres, conspiracie, treason, woe,/By sect and schisme prophanynge Deite" arise, and "teache confusion to rebell."[9]

Greville was also writing not long before the process in England that led to civil war started (i.e. the taxation crises between 1625 and 1629). It was not merely the case that Parliamentary readiness to trigger civil war was activated by those who happened also to believe in predestination. The case is much more interesting: even if we understand that "Arminianism" had a broader political meaning, it also designated an affirmation of free will, against orthodox Calvinist predestinarianism. Predestination, then, turned out to be one of the key sticking points between Parliament and the king, as we can see in the 1629 Parliament, which marked a key step in the collapse of parliamentary relations with the king.[10] The gap between Parliament and the king had been dramatically widened by Parliament's refusal to pass a taxation bill (tonnage and poundage); that issue, however, was secondary to another, ecclesiological one. Despite the Speaker's unwillingness to debate the motions put to him, the first of three motions (the other two devoted to taxation) put forward by Sir John Eliot read as follows:

> Whosoever shall bring in innovation of religion, or by favor or countenance seem to extend or introduce Popery or Arminianism, or other opinion disagreeing from the true and orthodox Church, shall be reputed a capital enemy to this Kingdom and Commonwealth.[11]

Although it did not formally pass this motion, Parliament vigorously acclaimed it while the Speaker was held in position against his will.[12] In response to this disorder and the refusal to grant the taxation, Charles I attempted to rule for the next eleven years without Parliament. The next time Parliament was recalled, in 1640, England was about to descend into the nightmare of civil war.

The other solution of the revolutionary, anti-free will, über-orthodox was, from 1620, to abandon the state altogether. Having first rejected England in dispute with fellow religionists for Amsterdam, and then having rejected Amsterdam in dispute with fellow religionists for Leiden, Puritans set off across the Atlantic to what became New England. It was precisely in 1629, the year of the Parliament that broke up amid dispute about predestination, that Charles I granted the Charter of Massachusetts Bay. Between 1630 and 1640, these self-imposed exiles would be followed by many thousand Puritan followers.[13] George Herbert recognized the world-changing, dynamic energy, or what I have called in this book the logic of permanent revolution, inherent in mainline Puritan culture. In his account of the Church Militant (published 1633), Herbert sees that new Churches will never satisfy. The new boundary reached will always a provoke a tension, through inferiority, with a superior antecedent:

> The latter Church is to the first a debtor.
> The Second Temple could not reach the first:
> And the late reformation never durst
> Compare with ancient times and purer years.[14]

The logic of this inherent tension will, according to Herbert, produce a new world, since "religion stands on tip-toe in our land, / Ready to pass to the American strand" (ll. 235–236).

These mighty revolutionary forces, then, which would reshape English constitutionalism and, no less, world history, were paradoxically driven by predestinarian Calvinists, who repudiated free will in the matter of achieving divine pardon.

There were also, however, consciously formulated heterodox *theological* alternatives within, driven by, and seeking to escape, the relentless logic of predestination. At least two emerged in England simultaneously. Thus Antinomians (i.e. those who reject law) not unreasonably believed (like many revolutionaries who claim to understand the logic of history) that they were freed from the moral law.[15] If God's irreversible decision had already been taken, then it made no sense to respect moral constraint. Only the extremity of predestination could have produced a no less extreme, if wholly logical, response.

Other heterodox Calvinists took a different, and much more impressive, theological route. They managed to recover some measure of free will from within the cramped logic of predestination. This Calvinist alternative, known as Arminianism, points most powerfully to the liberal future; it seems to escape from the predestinarian torture chambers of lyric, and takes us into the broad vistas of epic. Even there, however, as writers struggle to fight free of the predestinarian denial of free will and its attendant despair, we find more prisons of despair, even if relocated and newly refurbished. I now turn, then, to this theology's arrival in England and to the survival of despair in Miltonic epic.

By the time it arrived in England in the mid-1620s, Arminianism had already provoked major theological and political intra-Protestant fracture within the young Dutch Republic (declared 1581). Jacob Arminius (1560–1609) was educated in Leiden, Geneva, and Basel; he had been ordained as a pastor in Amsterdam in 1587. By 1603 he was appointed as a professor of theology in Leiden. From 1604 Arminius engaged in a widening dispute with orthodox Calvinists about predestination, despite the fact that Arminius himself held that his views were consistent with orthodox formulations of Calvinist faith. By the time of his death in 1609, a set of positions insisting on a modicum of free will was identified with his name.[16]

The essence of the Arminian claim for free will was that God's predestination was contingent upon an individual's decision freely to accept (or reject) grace sufficiently supplied.[17] The positions associated with Arminius were formulated and promoted in the *Five Articles of the Remonstrants* (1609). The differences between the heterodox Remonstrants (who also supported toleration) and orthodox Calvinists erupted in civil war in 1618; at the Synod of Dort (1618–1619), the orthodox Calvinist party duly proscribed the Arminian *Five Articles of the Remonstrants*. A court established by the States General of the Dutch Republic condemned the leader of the Remonstrants, Johan van Oldenbarnevelt, who had served the young Dutch Republic since 1586, to death. It also sentenced Hugo Grotius (another articulate supporter of the Remonstrants) to life imprisonment (from which he escaped). Oldenbarnevelt was beheaded in May 1619, at the age of seventy-two. Nearly two hundred Arminian ministers were deposed; eighty were banished.[18]

The divisions in the Dutch Republic were keenly observed in England, whence James I actively exercised his influence against the tolerationist, free-will promoting Remonstrants.[19] In the mid-1620s, however, Arminianism arrived in England, and duly replicated the civil divisions of the Dutch Republic by splitting the fragile coalition of forces that made up the English Calvinist Church (aka the Anglican Church). England's initial break with Rome in 1534 had been primarily jurisdictional. Potential schisms within English Calvinism of the 1560s and 1570s had been over liturgical and institutional issues. The division of the 1620s was, by contrast, provoked by theological difference with regard to the crucial matter of predestination. These theological differences within Calvinism concerning free will brought Puritanism (both Presbyterian and Congregationalist) into active and intransigent hostility, against the state Church. Those divisions would contribute to the outbreak of civil war in the early 1640s.[20]

With the publication of Richard Montagu's lively, irreverent, and extremely controversial *A Gagg for the New Gospell? No: a New Gagg for an Old
Goose* (1624), an Arminian defense of free will was suddenly available
in England.[21] Despite Montagu's denials of being either a Papist or an
Arminian, Parliament voted that Montagu's follow-up to *A Gagg* should be
burned and its author punished. By 1628, with royal protection and support, Montagu (bap. 1575–1641) was appointed to a bishopric, much to the
fury of Puritan opponents, who declared him fitter for "Fire and faggot than
further Preferment."[22] Already in 1626, the new king, Charles I (r. 1625–1649),
effectively broke the Calvinist consensus by proscribing any discussion of
predestination after the York Conference of 1626. By 1629, as we have seen,
the Commons in Parliament responded by announcing that "anyone promoting Arminianism or Popery . . . should be reputed a capital enemy to
this Kingdom and Commonwealth."[23]

Milton scholarship rightly agrees, for the most part, that Milton (1608–
1674) became an Arminian. Precisely when he did so is uncertain, since the
Church into which he was born officially repudiated free will, just as the
Presbyterian faction with which he briefly allied himself in the early 1640s
made that same repudiation, more vigorously.[24] By the time he started com-
posing *Paradise Lost*, however (c. 1658), his adoption of Arminianism seems
quite certain. In Book 5 the archangel Raphael explains to Adam that

> God made thee perfect, not immutable;
> And good he made thee, but to persevere
> He left it in thy power, ordained thy will
> By nature free, not overruled by Fate
> Inextricable, or strict necessity.
> Our voluntary service he requires,
> Not our necessitated; such with him
> Finds no acceptance, nor can find, for how
> Can hearts, not free, be tried whether they serve
> Willing or no, who will but what they must
> By destiny, and can no other choose?[25]

The main currents of Milton criticism have been driven by Whig conviction. For Whigs, speeches like this one by Raphael clearly signal the
proto-liberal Milton (seen either as a secularist interested only in political

liberty, or as a Christian humanist of a singular kind promoting freedom of choice).[26]

Before we readily accept that liberal understanding of Milton, we should apply at least two brakes. In the first place, we should note that Arminianism is a reflex of Calvinism. It shares with Calvinism beliefs in the total depravity of humans; in the absolute necessity of prevenient grace before humans are capable of exercising choice; that the choice so exercised is to believe or not believe; and in predestination. To be sure, Arminianism allowed some oxygen into the torture chamber, by opening a window onto the chamber: Christ's sacrifice was made for all (not only, as orthodox Calvinists had it, for the elect); and, above all, God's predestination was contingent on an individual's choice. We should not, however, forget that Arminianism tries to carve out a space within the logic of absolutism; it retains many cardinal features of the absolutist forms of early modern, revolutionary religion. Raphael's speech cited above is not inconsistent with these Arminian positions.

The second brake we should apply to the idea that Milton broke decisively free of Presbyterian, predestinarian Calvinism is the evidence of *Paradise Lost* itself. *Paradise Lost* is riven by paradoxes, the most glaring of which is that a poem written by a member of the inner core of a failed, anti-monarchical revolutionary junta should represent the inner core of a failed, anti-monarchical revolutionary junta as being led by Satan.

The Milton of paradox is perhaps the deepest theme in the history of Milton reception, brilliantly formulated by William Blake's comment (made 1790–1793) that Milton was of the Devil's party without knowing it.[27] In that single remark Blake points not only to the paradox of new Christian Milton being under the sway of old Satan but also to the possibility that the revolutionary inevitably, unwittingly, and paradoxically produces dark consequences by pursuing bright revolutionary programs, roads to hell being paved with good intentions. Liberal criticism of Milton, committed as it is to defense of the Revolution, tries to close these paradoxes down by making Milton consistent: God is a monarch, not a tyrant whose rules cannot be infringed. Rebellion against an earthly monarch is, say such critics, not at all inconsistent with knee-bending fealty to the divine monarch.[28]

In my view the effort to render Milton consistent robs his poetry of its roiling vitality, since it renders the poetry consistent with the polemical prose; in the context of this chapter, it also robs the poetry of any trace of Calvinist despair. Critics who defend Milton's consistency can, however, easily dismiss signs of Miltonic paradox by adducing the difference between theology and politics. Milton's God is an absolutist? Maybe, says the critic committed to Milton as a consistent, liberty-loving revolutionary, but that's God, and has nothing to do with Milton's politics. Milton's fallen angels look strikingly like Milton and his evidently failing fellows in 1658? Not a problem, says the consistentist: the devils rebelled against God, while Milton was rebelling against an earthly king.[29]

Rather, then, than directly prosecuting the case in which I believe (i.e. that Milton's representation of revolutionary devils is profoundly paradoxical and conflicted), let me instead pursue a different, almost purely descriptive case, which might be more difficult for the Miltonic consistentist to refute.

Does Milton the Arminian escape early modern, Calvinist despair? Or does he relocate it? I argue that Milton relocates despair to the predestinarian prison of Hell; he expresses it through the fallen angels. That descriptive case having been made, the argumentative case can follow: so far from banishing Calvinist despair, Milton augments it. In *Paradise Lost* despair becomes a potent, not to say cosmic, world-changing force, dwarfing the powers of those capable of profiting from the Arminian dispensation (i.e. humans). If we look to *Paradise Lost* for the formation of the democratic subject, we are shocked to find that the powers of that subject are miniscule in comparison with those of the fallen angels driven by despair. Humans are more a "pygmean race" set up against their implacably hostile enemies, the "thousand demi-gods," in their own vast and sublime "dimensions like themselves."

In the council session of Book 2, the fallen angels deliberate the best way to respond to defeat. The positions they articulate offer striking, point-by-point identity with the positions of seventeenth-century Calvinists, both orthodox and heterodox, as they confronted predestination. Milton cannot, so I argue, dissolve or escape despair. With his mighty poetic energy, he instead builds an adamantine, infernal prison for despair. By so doing, he shapes a distinctively new hero, "majestic though in ruin" (2.305), harrowed and hollowed out, but magnificent in his determination to build a mirror world within the concavity of despair. That hero is driven to run ahead of the knowledge of what he is fuelled by in the first place (i.e. despair). Satan thereby becomes a revolutionary rebel from principle. This dynamic produces astonishing scale and energy, but the energy is directed to the destruction of the power of choice in those who still possess it. Despite his effort to lock despair behind adamantine prison gates, in fact Milton starts from behind those gates, and quickly ends up opening the gates from within, thereby liberating and magnifying the world-changing power of early modern despair.

Paradise Lost begins in prison, "a dungeon horrible" flaming "as one great furnace" (1.61–62), the intensity of whose Statian gloom produces an effect of "torture without end," not least because the place is also hopeless: "Hope never comes / That comes to all" (1.66–67) says Milton in self-evident contradiction. Whether or not modern critics see Milton's God as a tyrant, the fallen angels readily ventilate precisely that persuasion: the initial dialogue between Satan and Beelzebub in Book One, and the positions articulated in Book Two's council session, are premised on the infinite, insuperable, and hateful power of the divine and absolutist monarch. The fallen angels attack God in precisely the terms that first Presbyterian Puritans and then Independents attacked Charles I, since God "sole reigning holds the tyranny of Heav'n" (1.124). "For what peace," Beelzebub asks, "will be giv'n / To us enslaved, but custody severe, / And stripes, and arbitrary punishment / Inflicted?" (2.332–335).

Faced with that apparently ineluctable, transcendent, and hostile power (all the more hostile for the modernist, monadic singularity with which anti-Trinitarian Milton invests his early modern heavenly monarch), what are the available escape positions? All are premised on despair, of course, and all are modelled on Satan's own rhetorical motive, as we witness him from the opening of the poem, "Vaunting aloud, but racked with deep despair" (1.126). The fallen angels pretend to seek what "reinforcement [they] may gain from hope" (1.190), when in fact, as they all know and frequently acknowledge, if hope fails, then they seek "what resolution [they may generate] from despair" (1.191, that last word appearing eight times in Books 1 and 2).

The first option for the fallen angels is the one chosen by Puritan Parliamentarians up to the point of their being marginalized and pushed aside by the Parliamentary purge by Independents in December 1648: outright civil war and rebellion against the king. Thus awesome Moloch proposes that the fallen angels "turn our tortures into horrid arms / Against the Torturer" (2.63–64), so that the monarch himself should experience his own "invented torments" (2.70).

Some orthodox Calvinists chose a different way of managing despair. They persuaded themselves, through subtle, if neurotic and ultimately exhausting, forms of self-persuasion that it wasn't so bad after all. To sleep, to dream, and even to forget the nightmare—that is the consummation devoutly wished by the devils who seek to drink from Lethe's stream of oblivion: they seek to drink from "the tempting stream, with one small drop to lose / In sweet forgetfulness all pain and woe" (2.607–608). The more sensitive even sit, not coincidentally like Milton's fellows in defeat, listening, ravished, to heroic poetry, sung "with notes angelical," of "their own heroic deeds," but only as long as they remain deluded by the idea that they acted in free will: they complain that "Fate / Free virtue should enthrall to Force or Chance" (2.550–551). Hell's aesthetic pleasure in the sublimity of heroic poetry is premised on, and sharpened by, despair (as is possibly the case with all aesthetic affirmation of sublimity).[30]

The desire for temporizing delusion and forgetfulness is most articulately voiced by Belial, who explores with acuity the shape of the prison from the inside. If, he argues, we attempt to confront God through open war, we'll fail. The result, or "final hope" of that approach would be "flat despair"; and who could bear that? Who, Belial lyrically argues, could bear to lose, "though full of pain, this intellectual being" (2.331)? So instead of "flat despair," Belial urges another kind of hopelessness. (Sufferers of absolutism become connoisseurs of the varieties of despair.) The more subtle form of despair he urges upon his fellows is to recognize that things could be even worse, and to wait, to self-habituate, to entertain delusive hope (ll. 2.119–225). Belial is the only angel who earns ever-active Milton's opprobrium, as offering counsels of "ignoble ease and peaceful sloth" (2.227).

If soft psychological delusion is no alternative to subjection, then imagining the exile of hell as "hard liberty" (the option in fact chosen and described thus by emigrés to America) is another possibility, as suggested by Mammon. The devils may in fact remain under subjection to God, but at least they will have the impression of noble independence, of seeking "our own good from ourselves, and from our own / Live to ourselves, though in this vast recess, / Free, and to none accountable, preferring / Hard liberty before the easy yoke / Of servile pomp" (2.253–257). Hell (unlike seventeenth-century America) was not inhabited before the exiled angels arrived.

With all these "choices" available, Satan and Beelzebub of course choose another course, that of invading already inhabited societies. Satan chooses lonely, New World discovery and ruination of the kind practiced by early modern Europeans from 1500. He takes off from the Mediterranean world, whose geography frames the opening of the poem, for the global age of discovery, flying alone,

> As when far off at sea a fleet descried
> Hangs in the clouds, by equinoctial winds
> Close sailing from Bengala, or the isles
> Of Ternate and Tidore, whence merchants bring
> Their spicy drugs: they on the trading flood
> Through the wide Ethiopian to the Cape
> Ply stemming nightly toward the pole. So seemed
> Far off the flying Fiend.
>
> (2.636–43)

All these escape routes are of course deceptive, despite plausibly promising to change the world. One might imagine outright war, spiritual independence, habituation, aesthetic pleasure in heroic poetry or the intellectual distraction of philosophy, or New World discovery and exploitation, but all these options "could charm / Pain for a while or anguish, and excite / Fallacious hope," before conscience strikes. Conscience, according to William Perkins, is like a "wild beast, which so long as he lies asleep seems very tame and gentle, and hurts no man: but when he is roused, he then awakes and flies in a mans face, and offers to pull out his throat."[31]

To score off the delusion of devils is easy and not uncommon critical work. Such work does render Milton's poetry consistent with his polemical prose and with his revolutionary action in history, but such dismissal underestimates the force of Books One and Two of *Paradise Lost*. To dismiss the despair of the devils as merely erroneous, and as merely deserved punishment for heretical rebellion, is to miss the fact that the shapes of their despair give a local habitation to the despair of orthodox Calvinists; it is also to miss the fact that Milton's Arminianism, for all its mighty struggle with hopelessness, does not have the resources to dissolve despair.[32] On the contrary, Milton's poem in these books reveals the inevitable despair of the revolutionary. Satan's subjectivity is such that his will to power must despairingly and heroically attempt to mimic and mirror the early modern absolutist God. The attempt is doomed to failure, since revolutionary Satan will remain forever unable to recover original, Edenic purity and bliss. The most powerful energies in this cosmos are liberated not by believers in modified free will but rather by the despairing. Despair turns out, paradoxically, to energize the world-changers, with their "unconquerable will": their ambitions and capacities are vast; and they vastly out-scale the domestic proportions of their victims. We can perceive their despair in every one of Milton's mighty, bondage-breaking sentences.

II

Milton's heroic reinvention of muscular epic, then, is in good part designed to repress despair. The very muscularity of the adamantine construction of *Paradise Lost* is a necessary response to the mighty force of despair. Milton's epic is, for many reasons, the last epic in English. Its determination to isolate and contain world-damaging, Satanic despair fails. By 1678, within fourteen years of the first publication of England's last epic (1664), despair is back, in another genre—prose fiction—that points forward to the novel. The progress of Bunyan's Christian in *The Pilgrim's Progress* (1678) has hardly begun before it is frustrated by the Slough of Despond into which Christian immediately falls.

After more than a century of chronic depression in the face of predestination, the prose-narrative of Calvinist Bunyan (bap. 1628–1688) knows more than the epic of Arminian Milton. For Bunyan does not try to repress despair about agency. Help, who pulls Christian out of the bog of Despond, explains that "this *miry slough,* is such a place as cannot be mended: it is the descent whither the scum and filth that attends conviction for sin doth continually run, and therefore it was called the *Slough* of *Despond.*"[33] Even the King (i.e. God) is incapable of fixing the ground: for more than 1,600 years, he has been sending his surveyors to shore up the spongy ground. Despite their pouring "at least twenty thousand cart-loads; yea millions of wholesome instructions" into the slough, and despite the fact that those instructions were "the best materials to make good ground of the place," nothing has changed. No one sees the solid steps of the Law that would lead across the bog, covered in mud as they are, and everyone falls in. There is no getting around chronic despair, for, despite the massive efforts to see "if so be it might have been mended ... it is the *slough of Despond still*; and so will be, when they have done what they can" (p. 21).

Bunyan is dead accurate about the inevitability of Calvinist despair, but he is wrong in his dating of the age of slough: not so much 1,600 years as 150, coincident with modernizing early modern Europe. He is, however, movingly frank and in my view correct about the inevitability of Calvinists and post-Calvinists falling into the slough; his movingly correct claim is, in fact, a literary critical reflection on his own project, since *The Pilgrim's Progress* is itself one of "the millions of wholesome instructions" unsuccessfully designed to solidify the ground. That despondency will remain spongy territory is implicit in the further narrative of Christian's travails, since he will soon meet the former "professor" in the "iron cage of Despair" in a room of Interpreter's house (p. 41); and he will be captured by the Giant Despair of Doubting Castle, who casts Christian and Hope into his stinking dungeon, there to be tempted by suicide, recalling, yet unable to escape the experience of, Spenser's Redcross (pp. 129–135).

However much *The Pilgrim's Progress* seeks to shore up the spongy passage of despair with one more set of solid instructions, that is, it cannot help being pulled down by the ever-recurring gravitational pull of evangelical despondency. *Paradise Lost* would also, by the argument of this chapter, count as an especially heroic example of those million unsuccessful early modern instructions against early modern despair, a poem forever despairing of the port, rowing against the current, despite the Herculean energy of its rower.

The history of evangelical agency denial narrated in these two chapters produces the relentless search for, and affirmation of, agency and its partner individuality, in contemporary liberal culture. In horrified recoil from divine election, we seek out our own unmediated elections in the most minute agential interstices of our experience. Without that pure agency, our thoughts become, to cite Herbert again, "all a case of knives."

PART 3

Sincerity and Hypocrisy

6

Pre-Modern and Henrician Hypocrisy

IN DECEMBER 1545, just over two years before his death, Henry VIII delivered a sermon of sorts to Parliament. The custom at this event was as follows: the Speaker would welcome the king, to which the Lord Chancellor would respond. On this occasion, however, the king himself chose to respond. His speech was recorded in person by Edward Hall, in his *The union of the two noble and illustre famelies* (1548). Hall places his record of the king's speech near the very end of his long narrative of late medieval dynastic civil war. Henry is reported to have chastised both temporal and spiritual lords, and all members of Parliament, for religious name-calling: "Discord and dissension beareth rule in every place." After citing St Paul's encouragement to Christian charity, Henry went on to note the lack of charity as of Christmas 1545:

> What love and Charitie is amongst you, when the one calleth the other, Heretic and Anabaptist, and he calleth him again Papist, Hypocrite, and Pharisee. Be these tokens of charity amongst you? Are these the signs of fraternal love between you?

The clergy were especially to blame, since, instead of preaching "truly and sincerely the word of God, according as they ought to do," the clergy "preach one against another."[1]

Without being able to know it, Hall was finishing his story of late medieval dynastic civil war (of "The Roses," 1455–1485) by pointing to the conditions that would ultimately produce England's next bout of civil war, the distinctively early modern religious conflict of the seventeenth century. That next war would be provoked in good part by religious identity rather than by dynastic competition. Among Henry's chosen terms, the gap between "sincerity" and "hypocrisy" will turn out to produce most violence; it will produce manifold cleavages not only between Catholic and Protestant, but also within Protestantism. Henry's perception that the clergy are especially given to sectarian name-calling is revealing, since, as we shall see, hypocrisy turns out to be a specifically ecclesiological charge, directed usually by and against clerics. Whenever it is laid, the charge of hypocrisy points to potential violence ahead.

Hypocrisy accusation and sincerity claims have a history within revolutionary moments, since the kinesis of revolution produces an intelligible sequence of phases, each of which seeks to exploit and/or to manage the impossible demands of revolutionary sincerity, and the impossible burden of avoiding hypocrisy. In this and the following two chapters, I aim to delineate the story of early modern English hypocrisy. As I do so, my essential argument is that sincerity and hypocrisy are of ecclesiological origin; that they are inevitable, unmanageable products of the centralizations and disciplines of revolutionary early modernity; and that the only way to deal effectively with the threat of hypocrisy (the Shakespearean solution) is to become a hypocrite.

In this chapter I tell the story from its late medieval sources up to and including the first, energetic outburst of Reformation hypocrisy accusation in the first half of the sixteenth century. In Chapter 7, I turn to the subsequent, more somber trajectory of hypocrisy accusation, as it rebounds back onto Elizabethan evangelicals. Chapter 8 looks to hypocrisy management (or lack thereof), from Shakespeare to Bunyan.

I

The words "sincere" and "sincerity" are attested in English only from the first third of the sixteenth century, when the tension between sincerity and hypocrisy suddenly and uncontrollably expanded.[2] Why should the charge of hypocrisy have arisen with such virulence in early modern England?

Two broad answers present themselves: the tactical and the conscience driven. The tactical reasons why the charge of hypocrisy flourishes in revolutionary contexts are easy to understand. Revolutionary cultures polarize: one is either for the revolution or against it. For the counter-revolutionary, it's often safer to pretend that one is for it, by active, chosen hypocrisy. The revolutionary, in turn, will almost certainly target counterrevolutionaries as masked hypocrites. The revolutionary might also often find it convenient tactically to extend the charge of hypocrisy: he will accuse *pro*-revolutionary competitors of hypocrisy, by way of accruing power within the power vacuum that revolutions always produce. Revolutionaries habitually target all their enemies as treacherous hypocrites. The charge is especially damaging since it implies that the enemy in fact recognizes the force of the true position (hypocrisy being, as is well known, the homage "vice" pays to "virtue"). The word "hypocrite" also implies that the enemy deserves only to be unmasked and then eradicated (hypocrites, as we shall see, are unreformable).[3] Then, in turn, the counterrevolutionaries also tend tactically to label the revolutionaries as hypocrites, since revolutionaries cannot ignore that charge, and it's likely to be plausible.

All these phenomena applied in the French Revolution (not to speak of Stalinist Russia), when, according to Hannah Arendt, "the war upon hypocrisy . . . transformed Robespierre's dictatorship into the Reign of Terror."[4] To understand the genealogy of this more recent revolutionary targeting of hypocrisy, however, we need to look especially to the Reformation centuries.

The tactical motives for adopting or exposing hypocrisy isolated in the previous paragraphs are, however, only the most obvious and predictable, and least interesting, sources of hypocrisy accusation in revolutionary moments. The more interesting sources of hypocrisy accusation are instead conscience driven. They arise from interior and self-reflexive sources.

Revolutionaries impose exactingly high levels of personal disciplines on their adherents. In particular, they demand completed, "sincere," singular subjectivities, from which any trace of sympathy for the past, and any trace of doubleness, has been expunged. The pre-modern world was characterized by divided jurisdictions, and so inevitably produced divided models of selfhood; the modernizing, revolutionary order will, by contrast, posit a single source of authority, and so demand rigorously singularized identity. Even God, by the judgment of Unitarians, must become just one person. The centered, revolutionary present is always simple and singular; so too revolutionary subjectivity will be radiant with what Donne calls "my mind's white truth."[5]

This is when the story of hypocrisy becomes really interesting. For maintaining fidelity to a Spenserian Una always turns out to be impossible. Revolutionaries therefore often fall victim to profound self-doubt and doubleness precisely because they set the bar for wholly consistent, unitary authenticity at so high a level. Hypocrisy accusation levelled at newly defined counterrevolutionaries is the prelude, that is, to the revolutionary's self-accusation, in all but ironclad Robespierres.

Given these many sources of hypocrisy accusation, the main narrative of such accusation will be one of widening fragmentation. One starts by accusing others, and yet others still, of hypocrisy, before falling victim to the second stage in the hypocrisy story, that of self-accusation, as the charge of hypocrisy inevitably produces a rebounding, echo charge. Once the chain reaction of fragmentations becomes unsustainable, counterrevolutionary, reformist cultures enter a third stage of the hypocrisy curve: they attempt to manage the distemper of ever-widening distrust and fragmentation by reintroducing positive models of personal doubleness and discreet concealment. They reintroduce, that is, what evangelicals would continue to call "hypocrisy," and what others might call social competence, decorum, irony, and playfulness.

The claimed virtue of "being authentic" will also, of course, continue to persuade evangelicals and their puritan descendants. That personal authenticity will continue to justify, and can only in fact be expressed by, outright, nonpolitically correct rudeness in once-Protestant cultures.

II

In Chapter 5, I spent very little time excavating late medieval religious despair, since the story was relatively easy to relate: there wasn't much.

Such is not the case with hypocrisy: here there is a late medieval story, but one that leads, as we shall see, directly into the much larger early modern narrative.

What status did hypocrisy have in late medieval culture? Hypocrisy is not one of the seven deadly sins. It does not figure significantly in late medieval penitential treatises. There are, for example, only two mentions of hypocrisy, and two of "hypocrite," in Chaucer's voluminous penitential analysis, *The Parson's Tale* (1390s). Hypocrisy is one of sixteen "twigs" on the branch of Pride; it is mentioned as a feature of false confession: "Hypocrite is he who hides showing himself such as he is and shows himself such as he is not."[6]

That situation might suggest that we need not pursue late medieval hypocrisy further, as we did not pursue late medieval despair. Perhaps hypocrisy, like despair, rocketed unexpectedly in significance in early modernity, as if out of nowhere. The profile of hypocrisy did indeed rise with disquieting rapidity and force in the sixteenth century, but we cannot leave the late medieval history there. For one vibrant, non-penitential late medieval tradition of hypocrisy allegation turns out to be the key to the later, Reformation story.

Penitential treatises directed toward the laity were, as I have said, largely uninterested in hypocrisy. The situation was dramatically different, however, in late medieval ecclesiological satire (satire, that is, not only of clerical failings, but satire that diagnosed existential dangers to the institution of the Church). In ecclesiological satire directed against clerics, written by other clerics, hypocrisy became the key charge, especially in polemic directed against the mendicant friars, from the middle of the thirteenth century.[7] The fountainhead of the vast late medieval river of anti-fraternal satire was William of St Amour's *De periculis novissimorum temporum* (*Concerning the Dangers of the Last Days*) (1256).[8] William presents the friars as fundamentally corrupt because fundamentally hypocritical, "pseudo" preachers. Basing his polemic on Paul's prophecies, in both letters to Timothy, that the last times will be heralded by the teaching of "hypocritical liars" (1Tim 4:2), William warns against preachers and prophets who may appear saintly but who (again following Paul) are "penetrators of homes and who are false."[9]

William of St Amour's principal charge against the friars—their hypocrisy—is underwritten by at least three further features of fraternal deception, each of which flowed directly into early modern polemic.

First, hypocrisy is not a sin like others, since it characterizes the irreducibly malicious. In fact hypocrisy is not essentially a sin at all, since it is not an individual failing so much as inherently a collective, institutional posture and practice. The true hypocrite's wickedness is not susceptible of penitential treatment, since he is properly a dead soul, at most a *personification* of disguised malicious intent, and therefore unable and uninterested in repentance. Hypocrisy does not elicit the response of pardon; on the contrary, there is no reforming a confirmed hypocrite, who is too far gone. Fighting hypocrisy is, therefore, a zero-sum institutional game; the hypocrite and his ecclesiastical order must be eradicated before he kills you and destroys the Church.

Second, if there can be no moral change in the hypocrite, then he becomes a fit sign of the end of days. Irreducibly malicious sinfulness is characteristic of Antichrist, and so portends the end of time and the destruction of the Church. The hypocritical friars are signs of the last times, forerunners of Antichrist, who "are false; it even appears that through such men the dangers of the last times will threaten or already are threatening the entire Church" (p. 59). Hypocrisy is an intra-ecclesiastical charge, with ecclesiological consequences for the imminent destruction of the Church.

Third, hypocrisy destroys communities. For hypocrisy is, by definition, hard to spot. Laying the charge of hypocrisy against another order of the Church might seem like an ideal way to galvanize one's own readership: everyone who is not in the ecclesiastical order of hypocrites becomes a textual community in the face of the hypocrite's threat. But the charge is dangerous, because there's no way of telling who is the hypocrite. William of St Amour attacks the friars as hypocrites but pauses to admonish caution among all, and therefore mutual distrust among all, his readers: "The ensuing dangers will be so great that the just and faithful will find no refuge among men, Jer.9: let each and every one guard against his neighbor, and have no faith in his brother" (p. 65).

From the thirteenth century we have, then, at least four mutually reinforcing charges against the friars: that they are hypocritical; that they deserve only eradication, not reformation; that they are signs of danger for the entire Church, portending its end; and that they provoke endemic distrust.

In her discussion of anti-fraternal satire in the great late fourteenth-century poem *Piers Plowman* (written in at least three versions, 1365–1380s), Wendy Scase elucidated a generative pattern of ecclesiastical satire whereby satirical topoi directed against one order of the Church were redeployed, in a widening application of satire, against another.[10] The charges of anti-ecclesiastical satire—in particular the charge of hypocrisy—are, that is, multiplicative: they start by targeting one order of the Church but are then taken up and deployed against other orders. As we shall soon see, the charge of hypocrisy inevitably extended to incorporate the very people who laid the charge of hypocrisy most vigorously against others in the first place. Lay the charge of hypocrisy against someone else, that is, and next thing you will find yourself being called a hypocrite, in a widening circle of accusation.

Most late medieval anti-fraternal satire blithely attacks friars without apparent awareness that the charge might rebound. In mid- to late fourteenth-century England, both pre-Lollard orthodox and heterodox Lollard texts attack friars especially as the source of ecclesiastical corruption.[11] In *Piers Plowman* (B Text, c. 1378), William Langland is, however, more self-reflexive: at poem's end, after rebuilding a thoroughly reformed Church, the psychological source of greatest spiritual perception, the figure of Conscience, effectively destroys the Church through the admission of hypocrisy. Conscience admits the hypocritical friar, Friar Flatterer, into the newly reformed Church. Suddenly the enemy of the new Church is *inside* the new Church, admitted by its strongest guardian (B Text, XX.305–373). Langland understands how dangerous it is to lay the charge of hypocrisy, since even Conscience can become confused, and effectively becomes a dangerous hypocrite himself.[12]

Just a decade or so later, in the 1390s, Chaucer was equally self-reflexive about the charge of hypocrisy. Extending the tradition of calling the friars hypocrites, Chaucer applies that tradition to a separate ecclesiastical officer—the Pardoner—in *The Canterbury Tales*. The Pardoner, a self-confessed hypocrite, and the Host's violent response to him threaten to undo the entire company of the Canterbury pilgrims, before the Knight steps in and works to reabsorb the Pardoner into the Canterbury company. To forgive and to accept a hypocrite, as in Jean de Meun's *Roman de la Rose,* and as in Langland's *Piers Plowman,* is, however, to step onto a very treacherous line.[13] The play of the tale-telling is reestablished, but only just, and with great risk. Chaucer's *Pardoner's Tale* became hot property in the sixteenth and seventeenth centuries, when it was repurposed to the new and non-fictional situation of the Reformation; it was also plausibly taken as evidence of Chaucer's proto-Protestantism.[14]

As for Langland, then, so too for Chaucer in the *Pardoner's Tale:* embracing the hypocrite, in apparent forgiveness, is potentially poisonous. In these literary artists, hypocrisy is not static; it refuses to stay out there, beyond the pale; instead it spreads, and insinuates its powerful way into those who attempt to manage it: thus Chaucer's Friar and Summoner both dangerously penetrate, or at least try to penetrate, the homes of the unlearned (cf. 2Tim 3:5). Chaucer models his Pardoner on Faux Semblant from Jean de Meun's *Roman de la Rose* (1260s), a text that Chaucer himself translated. Jean's Faux Semblant underlines just how dangerous he is: "several who never recognized my fraud have received their deaths through me, and many are receiving them and will receive them without ever recognizing it."[15] One can be unconscious of one's own murder even as it is being perpetrated by a hypocrite. Hypocrisy can take you by surprise, by suddenly coming inside.

III

As we turn to early modern hypocrisy, we begin with Thomas More, whose career traces the move from multiple social competence to early modernization's relentless sincerity. As Catholic More increasingly engaged with evangelicals, so too did he become early modern More of singular selfhood.

William Roper's biography of his father-in-law Thomas More (1478–1535) recounts how More would improvise in household plays.[16] When More served in the household of Cardinal Morton as a boy, he would, at the Christmas play, "suddenly sometimes step in among the players, and never studying for the matter, make a part of his own there presently among them, which made the lookers-on more sport than all the players beside."[17]

More's understanding of role-playing also had a central and profound role in his slightly later, playful, philosophical prose. Here he gives a powerful defense of play-acting in the matter of civic, deliberative persuasion. Thus in his *Utopia* (1516), the character Thomas More, who of course plays a part distinct from the historical Thomas More, forcefully opposes the pure philosopher Hythloday's refusal to play his part in counselling kings. Naked philosophy uncovered by a rhetorical mask, is, argues character More, both useless and absurd. Pure philosophy is almost by definition bad counsel, since it ignores what is perhaps the most fundamental rule of rhetoric, that of appropriateness, of adjusting one's mask to the scene at hand. A rhetorically inflected philosophy is a philosophy aware of place, time, and *scene*. Generic decorum, and especially the decorum appropriate to theatrical performance, will be its model. The More figure accordingly argues that there is "no place" ("non est locus") for the academic philosophy that thinks that everything is suitable to every place. There is, however, another, more civil philosophy ("alia philosophia civilior"), more practical for statesmen, which "knows its stage, adapts itself to the play in hand, and performs its role neatly and appropriately."[18]

The memory of More's admirable, impromptu conciliar shape-shifting was long-lasting. Delightful scenes of the kind Roper reports were recalled in very different cultural conditions in the Jacobean *Thomas More*. This play was written, censored, and revised by various hands, including that of Shakespeare, by 1605 (though never, apparently, performed), and represents More as a Londoner. At one point Lord Chancellor More and his wife entertain the Lord Mayor of London and his wife to dinner. Players offer a choice of interlude for entertainment, and More chooses one called *The Marriage of Wit and Wisdom*. A player, one Luggins, has, however, run off to get a beard for Wit, and is therefore missing when due to deliver his lines. More adroitly rescues the situation by stepping up among the players; the role he assumes is that of Good Counsel, warning Wit not to mistake Vanity for Wisdom:

Wit, judge not things by the outward show:
The eye oft mistakes, right well you do know.
Good Counsel assures thee upon his honesty
That this is not Wisdom, but lady Vanity.[19]

This little scene is nothing if not situated advice: the play is itself giving a contentious history lesson about the quality of More's counsel to a Jacobean audience, a century or so after the event in More's boyhood. The play embeds that advice in various layers of theatrical "situatedness," since it's a play within a play, full of apparently ludicrous or old-fashioned absurdities. The interlude is itself one such old-fashioned "absurdity." But just as that old, but not so old, mode is capable of bearing significant truths, so too does the play itself remind its audience of the contemporary significance of More's courageous and adroit counsel, theatrically delivered. Paradoxically and playfully, More assumes a mask not his own, as an actor, to warn his audience of the dangers of not penetrating masks.

By 1605 this rhetorical model had come under tremendous pressure from the evangelical demands of personal sincerity, which must be invulnerable to the charge of hypocrisy. Paradoxically, the historical More had himself actively participated in the formation of the new, early modern charge of hypocrisy. As much, that is, as More had been such a brilliant exponent of articulate, civilized, amusing, and effective insincerity in the first phase of his career, up to and including *Utopia,* his polemical, anti-Lutheran career (from 1520 or so) sees him participating in a tradition committed to stripping masks and denouncing hypocrites. The memory of More's earlier, brilliant improvisations was long-lasting, perhaps as a reminder of the liberties of pre-Reformation culture. The reminder also recalled all that had been lost in the later, religiously polemical phase of More's career.

I ended the last section by saying that Hypocrisy can take you by surprise, by suddenly coming inside. By 1534 in England, outside (i.e. Protestantism) had come inside, and inside (i.e. Catholicism) had been expelled outside. The language used in the long process of both expulsions—the language of hypocrisy—is, however, the same. In 1401, for example, the draconian statute *De Haeretico Comburendo* (the first instance of an English statute legislating burning as a punishment for heretics) targeted the proto-Protestant sect of Lollards as hypocrites, operating "under color of dissembled holiness."[20] That statute defending Catholic doctrine against hypocrisy finds its Calvinist echo 155 years later in the Elizabethan Settlement of 1559. The main aim of the relevant 1558/59 proclamation for that momentous Settlement is "to plant true religion to the extirpation of all hypocrisy, enormities and abuses." All "ecclesiastical persons" are to promote the Settlement "purely, sincerely, and without any colour or dissimulation."[21] To "the intent that all superstition and hypocrisy crept into divers men's hearts may vanish away," no relics or images are to be displayed or extolled.[22] Extirpation of hypocrisy was by 1559 a national, state project in a simplified state, without jurisdictional difference from Church.

From the beginnings of the English Reformation the language of hypocrisy was a key charge, to be deployed strategically. Both sides used such language, as by a mirror effect. By using it, both sides were effectively saying that the opposition really did in fact buy into the true position, but pretended not to, only out of self-interested malice. Thus the highest profile combatants in the 1520s and early 1530s, Thomas More and William Tyndale (1494–1536), each accused the other side of hypocrisy. In his *An exposycyon vpon the v.vi.vii. chapters of Mathewe* (1533), for example, Tyndale argued that More was in fact persuaded by evangelical theology, but acted hypocritically through covetousness.[23] Covetousness, says Tyndale, persuades many whom the truth at first pleases to persecute the truth. More, who by Tyndale's reckoning "knew the truth and then forsook it again," is a good example. At first More conspired with Wolsey to deceive the king, but

> when the light was sprung upon them, and had driven them clean
> out of the scripture, and had delivered it out of their tyranny, . . . and
> had wiped away the cobwebs which those poisoned spiders had
> spread upon the face of the clear text, so that the spirituality . . . were
> ashamed of their part . . . yet for all that, covetousness blinded the
> eyes of that glaring fox more and more and hardened his heart
> against the truth, with the confidence of his painted poetry . . .
> grounded in his unwritten verities, as true and as authentic as his
> story of Utopia. (image 95)

More mirrors Tyndale's strategy in the same year (1533), labelling Protestants as hypocrites who did not really believe false doctrine but who maliciously purvey it. In his massive *Confutation of Tyndale's Answer* (1532–1533), More accused his accusers of the identical charge:

> For when our savior said of hypocrite heretics "ye shall know them
> by their fruits," he meant that ye should perceive the same persons
> for heretics and hypocrites by the evil fruits of their false doctrine,

that under a cloak of virtuous living and cleanness they should secretly sow and set forth false heresies contrary to the known
doctrine.[24]

If Tyndale targeted More's use of artistic disguises in *Utopia*, More targeted
Lutheran evangelicals as actors, conscious as he is of the Greek meaning
of "hypocrite" (a stage actor).[25] More would seem to wish in 1533, when he
published the *Confutation of Tyndale's Answer*, that he was still Lord Chancellor in 1529, with the power to unmask those who were, in his view,
hypocrites: "If," he says, "men took heed & watched them [i.e. heretics]
well," and "cause them to be deprehended and taken," then "their masks"
would be "taken of and their hypocrisy . . . discovered."[26]

IV

In these ferocious encounters, the stakes were extremely high. There are
intense dangers for the individuals (both Tyndale and More will be executed
within three years of 1533). There are also cultural dangers for all artistic
practice (e.g. acting, assuming masks, writing fictional narrative), since
those who target hypocrisy will also always target and / or abandon art
making.[27]

More's attack on the hypocrisy of his enemies was borrowed from those
very enemies. By the late 1520s, the dangers of dramatic role-playing rose
dramatically, since the charge of hypocrisy had become revolutionary.
Whereas late medieval hypocrisy discourse had singled out one religious
order (especially friars, and the different orders of friars) as ecclesiastical
hypocrites, by the 1520s the charge was being applied globally to the entire Catholic Church. There was no safe place within that Church, since the
entire institution, from its Antichrist papal head down, was thought to be
committed to the destruction of Christian souls: ecclesiastics had provoked
a globalized catastrophe by destroying the entire Church. There could,
therefore, be no half measures in hypocrisy eradication: as with individual
hypocrites, so too with a hypocritical institution—there was no reforming
it; revolutionary eradication of the entire corrupt edifice (and not just one
corrupt order of the Church) was the only way forward. Reformist satire
ceded place to revolutionary ecclesiological critique.

The rhetorical temperature of hypocrisy attack therefore rose to red hot levels. And the Biblical models for that attack were drawn from specifically ecclesiological diatribes and narratives, when one lethal hypocritical Church encounters, and seeks to subvert, the True Church. These Biblical sources are driven by anger against priests: Christ's fierce attacks on the hypocritical "whited sepulchers" of the Scribes and Pharisees (e.g. Matt 23:27; 24:13); the prophecies of Paul's letters to Timothy about hypocritical preachers in the last times (1Tim 4:2, and 2Tim 3:5); and, above all, the febrile Book of Revelations, with its malicious and gaudy theater of the end of days.

Revolutionary, all-or-nothing anger at an entire institution's hypocrisy had characterized the vitriolic tone of Reformation polemic from its inception. Near the very beginning of his polemical career, in an open letter to Pope Leo X (1520), Luther defended his polemical aggression on the model of Christ's own example: "He Himself was keenly hostile to his opponents, and called them a brood of vipers, hypocrites, blind, children of the devil."[28] In his *Common places of scripture* (translated into English by Richard Taverner in 1538), the early Lutheran Erasmus Sarcerius (1501–1559) devoted a section to how members of the True Church should rebuke members of the Church of hypocrites. Answer: very rudely indeed, consequences be damned:

> So that the chief effect of this offending by Christ's words is that the
> hypocrites be confounded & destroyed, which by the just judgment
> of God ought to perish ... And albeit these effects be evil & horrible,
> yet the godly ought not to regard them. For it behoveth rather to
> obey god, than men: though the guts of the hypocrites should burst,
> & of the whole world.[29]

England's first Protestants also adopted the model of Christ's own candid authenticity to mount a total attack on the Catholic Church. Thus Tyndale appeals to the model of a wholly transparent selfhood deriving from Christ: "Nay," he says in 1528, "Christ is no hypocrite, or disguised, that playeth a part in play, and representeth a person, or state, which he is not."[30] As evangelicals modelled themselves on the undivided selfhood of Christ, they adopted a position outside time, in the *eschaton*, from the vantage point of the end of days, where all was certain. As they judged the hypocrite, evangelicals also therefore claimed themselves to be immune from any kind of hypocrisy, and claimed members' access to the immaterial, True Church.

Evangelicals, that is, not only considered Catholics to be profoundly mistaken about salvation. They also judged that Catholic opponents *knew* they were mistaken. Catholics were, that is, hypocrites, and had to be treated aggressively as such. Antichrist, in Tyndale's words again (from 1531), "disguised himself after the fashion of a true apostle and preached Christ wilily, bringing in now this tradition, now that."[31] The charge of hypocrisy is almost always directed at clerical figures. Thus language originally drawn from Christ's words about Jewish clerics (the Pharisees) (Matthew 23:14), and then deployed against Christian clerics (the friars) in the later Middle Ages, is now extended in application: the entire clergy of the Catholic Church are masked, "juggling," diabolic hypocrites maliciously betraying souls. Every cleric knowingly participates in this theater of damnation: each is a sign of the end of days, and so the subjectivity of each is entirely subsumed by their institutional, historical role as forerunners of Antichrist. The fit, though fallen, ethical state for the end of days is hypocrisy, as the dead end of personal change and development at the dead end of time. And so ecclesiastical satire is swallowed by ecclesiological critique; the time for debate, encouragement, and change was over. For, as Tyndale says in 1531,

> We understand . . . the pope, cardinals, legates, patriarchs, archbishops, bishops, abbots, priors, chancellors, archdeacons, commissaries, officials, priests, monks, friars, black, white, pied, grey, and so forth, by (I trow) a thousand names of blasphemy and of hypocrisies, and as many sundry fashions of disguisings.[32]

Tyndale's rhetoric is powerful, but not lurid. That rhetorical niche is most forcefully occupied in the early English Reformation by John Bale, who, in his *Image of both Churches* (first published 1545, with six editions up to 1570), for example, exhibits the standard, utterly polarized schema drawn from Revelations. Bale reads the apocalyptic Book of Revelations as a code for the events of recent English Church history. On the one hand, that Biblical book presents "the true christian church (which is the meek spouse of the Lamb without spot) in her right fashioned colors described" (aka evangelical

Lutherans).[33] On the other hand, St John (the putative author of the Book of Revelations) targets "the proud church of hypocrites [aka The Catholic Church], the rose colored whore, the paramour of Antichrist, and the sinful synagogue of Satan, in her just proportion depainted, to the merciful forewarning of the Lord's elects" (image 3). The "great Antichrist of Europa" is the "king of faces, the Prince of hypocrisy, the man of sin, the father of errors, and the master of lies, the Romish Pope" (image 86).

Bale wrote *The Image of both Churches* from his first exile, into which he took himself after the more conservative Henrician period initiated by the Six Articles of 1539 and by the execution of his patron Thomas Cromwell in 1540. *The Image of both Churches* is tremendously energizing, because it is also tremendously simple. Hypocrisy eradication is the essential activity of the evangelical; it's physically dangerous, but psychologically energizing. As Tyndale says in his *Exposycyon . . . of Mathewe* (1536), "He that is not ready to give his life for the maintenance of Christ's doctrine against hypocrites, with what so ever name or title they be disguised, the same is not worthy of Christ nor can be Christ's disciple."[34]

Just as sensitive literary artists discovered in the late fourteenth century, however, attacking hypocrisy is more dangerous work than one might at first think, since the charge can, without warning, rebound on its user. We will observe that disconcerting boomerang effect in action in Chapter 7, from the moment that the English Church becomes Calvinist.

7

The Revolutionary Hypocrite:
Elizabethan Hypocrisy

LAYING THE CHARGE of hypocrisy against the Catholic Church in the period 1517–1547 or so was tremendously energizing and rhetorically spectacular. The tremendous energy derives from the fact that revolutionary cultures characteristically aim to simplify not only states and institutions but also, necessarily, selves. The multiple jurisdictions of the self cede to the austere demands of centralized control, which are identifiable with the logic of History. Central control also demands that the centralized, simplified, unitary self be open for inspection. Until the inevitable backlash set in, this newly grounded, simplified, inspectable self produced extraordinary self-confidence and energy.

Laying the charge of hypocrisy against malicious representatives of the Church, and thereby against the Church itself, was rhetorically spectacular because the simplified, energized revolutionary self has rhetorical license for rudeness. The claim of totally self-assured, judgmental integrity, whole and transparent to itself, and utterly free of hypocrisy, inevitably produces rudeness: to be an authentic, sincere, visible self is to be an offensive self, wholly indifferent to decorum, hierarchy, and emotional sensitivity. One signals one's authenticity precisely by the level of one's bad manners (the ruder, the more authentic). The history of sincerity, or authenticity, is also in part the history of rudeness.[1]

Unabashed rudeness became a fixed feature of evangelical discourse from the sixteenth century; it has remained an essential weapon for those whom Burke was to call "rebels from principle."[2] In the later sixteenth century, however, the energized, simplified revolutionary self was struck by its own accusation of hypocrisy. This put a dampener both on the energized self and on the fun of polemical rudeness to hypocritical others. This is the moment, fifty or so years after the revolution had started, when the charge of hypocrisy boomeranged back onto and into the evangelical camp, splitting it from within.

The ideal of a wholly transparent selfhood was especially demanding and unstoppable; evangelicals assumed it to their cost. If hypocrisy had always been principally an ecclesiological charge, projected against priests, then evangelicals had a problem, since they were themselves priests, members of the "priesthood of all believers." They were all, to use a late medieval technical term reserved for especially robust, spiritually elite souls, *"perfecti."*[3] The heightened disciplines of revolutionary religion demanded, that is, that lay Christians assume much higher and more demanding institutional—not to say priestly—identification with the institution of the True Church. The polemical gain of unmasking the ecclesiological hypocrite therefore came with a very heavy price, since the claim of totally self-assured, priestly integrity also inevitably produced the answering charge of hypocrisy against oneself.

As we have seen, in pre-modern England the charge of hypocrisy migrated from one order of the Church to adjacent orders. By 1580, every Christian was, in evangelical theory, a priestly representative of the True Church in the Calvinist state, whose monarch is the Head of the state Church. The hypocrisy charge was therefore set to expand, as indeed it did, onto the priests of the new and True Church. The boomerang effect was partly a matter of being called a hypocrite by one's enemies, as Puritans famously were from the later sixteenth century. It is also, much more powerfully, a matter of charging oneself with hypocrisy. The totally confident elect assume an impossible burden, which makes them, frequently, totally unconfident, since they inevitably fall victim to believing that they are themselves the hypocrites.

From at least the 1580s, then, hypocrisy is no longer an external threat, practiced by wicked Catholic ecclesiastics out there. It becomes an internal threat, practiced by wicked Protestant ecclesiastics (in this case the elect priesthood of all believers) from within the deceptive recesses of the human soul. Hypocrisy is internalized; it is the permanent shadow that accompanies the evangelical's attempt to persuade him or herself of his or her own election. An evangelical's act as action is forever shadowed by its Doppelgänger, an act as theater, or hypocritical show, especially in a theological culture that distrusts all acts. Confronted directly with the absolutist God, the Calvinist subject feared, naturally enough, that he or she was faking it. The exercise of eschatological judgment that empowers hypocrisy detection equally, therefore, disempowers the psyche; it sends the wounded evangelical right back into history from the eschaton.

I

As we have seen, lurid description of the Roman Church as one giant and menacing hypocrite clearly energized early evangelicals in the first flush of the Reformation. Within, however, a few decades of Bale's lurid attacks on the Papal "king of faces, the Prince of hypocrisy," by the later sixteenth century, the charge of hypocrisy had begun to take queasy forms.[4] The charge now became more irksome and less manageable as it rebounded onto those who had projected it with such confidence.

Thus less "hot" English Protestants start calling Puritans "hypocrites."[5] This new turn is registered both by anti-Puritans and by Puritans. In the 1590s, the fiercely anti-Puritan Richard Bancroft (bap. 1544–1610, Archbishop of Canterbury 1604–1610) astutely analyzed the discursive tactics of Puritans, by arguing that they adopted arguments previously deployed against the Pope, but now against the monarch. Bancroft himself then plays the same polemical game. He calls Puritans hypocrites, since they deploy "forged lies, their poisoned tongues, and their hypocritical outcries," to provoke "a general mislike of her *Majesties* reformation."[6]

For their part, Puritans were themselves also conscious of the frequency and force of the charge that they were the hypocrites, that "they be but a company of hypocrites, and precise fooles," in the words of Arthur Dent's pro-Puritan, popular *Plain Man's Pathway* (1607), which raises the charge only to repudiate it.[7] Jonson's *Bartholomew Fair* (1614) exemplifies the kind of mockery Puritans faced, especially on the point of their hypocrisy. The risible Zeal-of-the-Land-Busy is early on set up as "a notable hypocritical vermin."[8] Like one of his companions, he is "a most elect hypocrite" (1.5.185). The tradition of labelling Puritans as, in the words of Andrew Marvell in 1655, the "race most hypocritically strict" is a very large and long one that extends well beyond the early modern period.[9]

Further, the nascent Puritan movement of the 1560s and 1570s began to lay the charge of hypocrisy, along with "Papist," against other English Protestants. Already in the fierce persecutions of Marian England (1553–1558), the issue of Nicodemism (i.e. hiding sympathies for a new religion, a term derived from the Pharisee Nicodemus who comes secretly to Christ by night [John 3:1]) was a key issue. Exiled Marian evangelicals lambasted their fellows who remained behind and disguised their evangelical sympathies.[10] So far, however, from being restricted to the period of Marian persecution, Elizabethan evangelicals, in ways characteristic of revolutionary movements, also pursued other Protestants with the charge of hypocritical Nicodemism, as well as applying the broader charge of hypocrisy to many fellow Protestants.[11] Queen Elizabeth may not, famously, have wished to "make windows of men's souls."[12] Elizabethan Puritans observed no such discretion, rudely pulling away the curtains of their fellow English Protestants' souls to expose and hunt out less than absolute commitment.[13]

Aspirant official Elizabethan policy was not itself, in fact, especially discreet about observing the curtains over souls. Thus in the third Elizabethan Parliament (1571), the playwright, parliamentarian, pamphleteer, and later torturer Thomas Norton proposed a bill demanding that, in addition to church attendance (already the law since 1552), obligatory participation in communion be enforced. Norton argued that "not only the external and outward show is to be sought, but the very secrets of the heart in God's cause . . . must come to a reckoning."[14] The views propounded by Edward Aglionby that "the conscience of man is internal, invisible, and not in the power of the greatest monarch on earth," prevailed with the Queen, in 1571, as they did again in 1576 and 1581.[15] That reluctance to make windows into men's souls may have activated the evangelical author of the *Second Admonition to Parliament* (1572), who marks out battle lines with new enemies (fellow Protestants) with old charges (hypocrisy). His enemy is less Nicodemite Catholics than insufficiently godly Protestants. He shamelessly adapts Christ's words to present need, arguing that "he that is not with me—take he the Jews' parte, the Turks, the Papists, or the hypocritical English Protestants' part—he is against me saith Christ."[16]

Most interestingly, Puritans fall victim to the self-destructive persuasion that they are themselves hypocrites. The most far-reaching pre-Reformation literary representations of clerical hypocrisy involve, as we have seen, a self-reflexive awareness that the charge will rebound, that it will come inside as a house breaker, a *penetrans domum*. The later sixteenth century also witnessed that same profoundly self-reflexive moment whereby Puritans register that they are indeed the worst hypocrites. This is the terrifying moment whereby Conscience, "when he is roused, he then awakes and flies in a man's face, and offers to pull out his throat."[17]

This more intimate and therefore more savage charge of self-hypocrisy derives directly from Calvin himself, in the very first chapters of his *Institutes*; it receives extensive airplay, as we shall see, from Calvin's English theological promoters (the 1559 edition of the *Institution of Christian Religion* was translated into English by Thomas Norton in 1561, with eleven editions up to 1634).[18] Norton, co-author of the first English Senecan tragedy *Gorboduc* (1561), was later in his career a keen hunter of hypocrisy, since he was named as a commissioner of torture in the case of Edmund Campion in 1581, and was one of those responsible for administering the torture. In addition to his being listed as torturer to Campion, Norton's name appears four further times on the inglorious torture warrants between 1574 and 1581.[19] He was probably the author of *A Declaration of the favourable dealing of her Maiesties Commissioners appointed for the Examination of certaine Traitours, and of tortures unjustly reported to be done upon them for matters of religion*, published in 1583 in the wake of Campion's torture between August and September 1581.[20] That text defends torture on a variety of grounds (e.g. only those who said they would not tell the truth were tortured). Nothing had been done to the tortured, affirms the *Declaration*, but what was "gentle and merciful."[21] A Catholic text published in 1582 was unpersuaded by talk of soft treatment. Confronted by the fact of having racked Campion and pulling his finger nails, those accused of torture are said to have made sport of it:

> Twit (said they) it was a merry pastime: he was cramped or pulled a little, not in earnest, but in jest. After the same manner they jested of others, which had been racked before. So great delight these

merry conceited fellows do take, in making scoffs and sports of the afflictions of sorry poor men.[22]

From his close reading and translation of Calvin's *Institutio christianae religionis*, Norton should have known that detecting hypocrisy is not in fact easy work for a Calvinist torturer, because the spiritual experience of the elect and the reprobate turns out to be unsettlingly similar. The only way to distinguish the two experiences is by capacity to detect psychic hypocrisy in oneself. For a Calvinist (for anyone, in fact), self-confirmation of pure authenticity is a tall order, since, as Calvin himself tells us, "the heart of man hath so many secrete corners of vanity, is full of so many hiding holes of lying, is covered with so guileful hypocrisy, that it oft deceiveth himself" (Book 3.2, image 192). The reprobate will believe the Word for a while, and (Norton's translation):

> we doubt not that such delighted with a certain taste of the word do greedily receive it, and begin to feel the divine force of it: so far that with deceitful counterfeiting of faith, they beguile not only other men's eyes, but also their own minds. For they persuade themselves, that that reverence which they show to the word of God, is most true godliness, because they think that there is no ungodliness but manifest and confessed reproach or contempt of his word. (Book 3.2, image 192)

Calvin's judgement on these self-deceived is harsh indeed: "But let them that glory in such shadows of faith understand, that therein they are no better than the Devil" (Book 3.2, image 192). Calvin's analysis of self-deception is brilliantly sensitive to the way in which people can fool themselves, but never once does he pause to reflect on how his account of self-deception might apply to every one of his readers, who are presumably trying to work out, from the 1,021 pages of the self-help book that Calvin has written on the subject, whether or not they have been chosen, whether or not they are fooling themselves.

Calvin himself insists that the elect can enjoy the assurance of their election only through severe doubt about that assurance.[23] He simultaneously distinguishes the hypocritical reprobates who think they are saved from the way in which they

receive the gift of reconciliation, although confusedly and not
plainly enough: not that they are partakers of the self same faith or
regeneration with the children of God, but because they *seem* to have
as well as they, the same beginning of faith, under a cloak of Hypocrisy. (Book 3.2, image 192, my emphasis)

All men are hypocrites, but one needs to be an expert in hypocrisy detection before one can be assured of one's own election, which assurance can
in any case only be grounded in profound self-doubt.

This same knife edge of assurance and despair, differentiated only by capacity to detect self-deception, is also articulated by the Cambridge theologian William Perkins (d. 1602), the most forceful English proponent of
pastoral Calvinism in the 1590s. I cite both from his massive and popular
Golden Chain (first published 1591) and from his even more massive *Exposition of the Symbole or Creed* (1595). For Perkins, as I argued in Chapter 3, the
faith of the reprobate and that of the elect look very similar; the signal difference is that *"the faith of Gods elect . . . also is called faith without hypocrisy."*[24]
By the faith of the elect, the Christian "may sever himself from all false
Christians, from Atheists, hypocrites, and all false seducers whatsoever"
(*Exposition of the Symbole*, image 15).

Reprobates are not, unfortunately, so easily distinguished from the
elect, since "in God's Church there be many hypocrites which receive
infinite benefits from God, by reason of his elect children with whom
they live" (*Exposition of the Symbole*, image 27). Perkins uses the received
language of hypocrisy about the reprobate experience, saying that they
manifest "outward holiness of life for a time, under which is compre-
hended the zeal in the profession of Religion, a reverence and fear
towards Gods ministers, and amendment of life in many things."[25] The
key word here is "outward," since the portmanteau concept for the reprobate is "hypocrisy, which giveth to God painted worship, that is, if
you regard outward behavior, great sincerity: if the inward and hearty
affections, none at all" (*Golden Chaine*, image 49). The only way of distinguishing is, as Perkins says in another text, *The Case of Conscience* (1592),
through inner persuasion:

We say, that the elect alone may be, and indeed are made sure of their
Election: that so we may exclude the reprobate hypocrites: for con-

sidering they are not elected, they can never be truly persuaded, that they are elected. I say truly: because it may come to pass, that many in their own thinking shall be predestinate: yet in truth they are not persuaded so: for they are deceived. . . . for their Faith is in hypocrisy.[26]

By the later sixteenth century, then, the charge of hypocrisy threatens to rebound on the priesthood of all believers, after they had themselves projected it on other priests with such force and assurance. The mobile charge of hypocrisy, which had moved from one ecclesiastical order to another across the late Middle Ages, now expands onto and into the priesthood of all believers, members of the True Church, each of whom must bear the psychic burden of the wholly transparent, non-hypocritical, elect and singularized selfhood of the saints.

II

In Calvinist England the burning psychological issue preoccupying evangelicals was, then, less the hypocrisy of the Catholic Church, and more the hypocrisy of evangelicals. It's true, as we have seen, that the Elizabethan Injunctions for Religion of 1559 declare that they aim to suppress "superstition through all her highness' realm and dominions, and to plant true religion to the extirpation of all hypocrisy, enormities and abuses."[27] For Calvinists, however, the ecclesiological battle line had been internalized. Attempted extirpation of hypocrisy had started to produce hypocrisy. The challenge now was to persuade oneself of one's election, and that effort required confident repudiation of all psychic hypocrisy, constant reaffirmation of what Donne called his "mind's white truth."[28] The only guarantor of election is the persuasion of election, which comes only through doubt of election. By believing in one's despair, one avoids the charge of hypocrisy.

Hypocrite hunters will always be hostile to art making, since art making involves the assumption of masks, personae, and voices. What Patrick Collinson calls English iconophobia in the 1580s is another symptom of this anti-hypocritical stripping, just as the hostility to theater is another.[29] William Prynne's *Histriomastix* (1633) attacks theater as hypocrisy. God "is truth itself, in whom there is no variableness, no shadow of change, no feigning, no hypocrisy." God has

> given a uniform, distinct and proper being to every creature, the
> bounds of which may not be exceeded: so he requires that the ac-
> tions of every creature should be honest and sincere, devoid of all
> hypocrisy, as all his actions, and their natures are. Hence he enjoys
> all men at all times, to be such in show, as they are in truth: to seem
> that outwardly which they are inwardly; to act themselves, not
> others.[30]

Elizabethan England, it is true, effectively demanded hypocrisy from Catholics and many puritans by legislating weekly outward religious observance from 1558.[31] But that legislative imposition of Nicodemite religion
might seem an easy yoke compared with the internal, psychological demands produced from within Calvinist theology itself. Unsurprisingly,
then, hypocrisy became a runaway charge from the 1580s, splintering
churches and individuals as they each attempted to confirm their authentic
membership of the True Church.

We can see just how internalized the charge of hypocrisy had become
throughout the central Reformation in the 1580s, by looking briefly to a
little-known play, the Norwich evangelical Nathaniel Woodes's *The Conflict of
Conscience* (1581), that may have influenced Marlowe's *Doctor Faustus* (?1592).[32]

Evangelical culture was not, as is frequently asserted, exactly hostile to
theater: for John Foxe, every evangelical martyrdom is a public, open-air
theater in which the sincere, iron-fast authenticity of the new religion is
made visible.[33] William Prynne (1600–1669), that great seventeenth-century
self-styled scourge of theater, makes this very point. Early Christian martyrs were, he says, on show, as in a theater. They were "drawn to the place
of execution called [*Theatrum*] a Theatre, where the innocent Martyrs for
the most part suffered in the view of all the people." So too, he recognizes,
"our Traytors [by which means evangelical martyrs] usually suffer on a
Stage or scaffold, erected for that purpose." The analogy in no way justifies
stage plays, however, for many reasons, including the following: martyrs
do not act voluntarily; they are "memorable public Spectacles of admiration"; and, not least, "they were real, not hypocritical, histrionical person-
ated Spectacles, consisting of representations only, as all Plays and Actors

are."[34] In the *Conflict of Conscience*, we will see how that orthodox theatrical visibility has its dark Doppelgänger of the punishing theater of the no less visible, divided, and inevitably hypocritical Puritan.

The Conflict of Conscience is a "Tudor Interlude," a technical term of literary history that disguises the fact that many "Tudor Interludes" share fundamentally the same structure, and were written for the same performance conditions, for a similarly sized troupe of professional actors, as the so-called late medieval "morality play," a late medieval theatre of instruction.[35] There are in fact many English evangelical interludes written between 1560 and 1585 or so.[36] Such plays are based on the structure of a medieval morality play (i.e. a tripartite comic structure of rise, fall, and recovery). The late medieval version of this instructive genre is fundamentally comic (i.e. ending happily), and the happy ending is premised on the reabsorption of the errant protagonist into the culture presented as official by the play. In the 1580s, however, that comic structure is fascinatingly inflected, if not destroyed, by Protestant theology, since, in the absurdist world of Calvinist theology, the ending can just as appropriately be tragic as comic.

The plot of *The Conflict of Conscience* is quickly told. In Act 1, Satan begins the action by declaring that he'll call on Avarice and Tyrannical Practice to help his "darling boy," the Pope. These two will, however, need Hypocrisy to win hearts to their self-interested domination. The scene then shifts to the private space of the evangelicals where Philologus is the authority figure who explains why persecution of the True Church is both necessary and salutary in the fight against "Romish Hypocrisie." Meanwhile Roman Hypocrisy, who prays that the Church may be replenished by the ability to distinguish truth from falsehood, out of "mere sincerite," announces his intention to go to England. Avarice and Tyranny impatiently await the arrival of Hypocrisy, who arrives pretending to speak like an evangelical, complaining that, "instead of the pure floud of thy Gospell," the Pope "Hath poysoned our soules with divelish Hypocrisie" (2.3). He then discloses his "true" nature to the obtuse Avarice and Tyranny, whom Hypocrisy renames Zeal and Careful Provision. In 3.1 Philologus reappears, complaining that evangelicals are now persecuted by Rome, which persecution we see planned by Hypocrisy and his fellows. Philologus is betrayed to the papal agents by an ignorant priest.

Act 4 is a scene of interrogation, in which the evangelical Philologus is brought before the Cardinal. Philologus is effectively persuaded to recant. His agony of conscience begins in Act 4.4, in which Spirit warns him against hypocrisy. Conscience and Suggestion verbally fight over the soul of Philologus, a debate lost by a despairing Conscience.

Act 5 opens with Hypocrisy announcing to the audience that they will now witness the spectacle of Philologus's despair. That collapse begins with the arrival of Horror, when the play suddenly bursts into life. Horror takes Philologus prisoner, announcing himself as "confusion and horror of the mynde" (5.4). He declares that he has been assigned by God, and that he brings "the Spirit of Sathan, blasphemy, confusion and cursing" (5.4). Horror will present a mirror to Philologus of "deadly desperation" (5.4). The evangelical hero Philologus falls to truculent and sacrilegious abuse of God, before falling victim to despair. He is incapable of trusting the promise of divine pardon promised by Theologus. In one ending, Philologus commits suicide by hanging himself. In another ending (this is absurdist theater, after all), he converts. The opposite endings are dependent on an identical plot.

On the face of it, the principal struggle in this play is, we might say, between Una and her look-alike Duessa, to use Spenser's almost contemporary cast of characters to designate Roman hypocrisy. Philologus represents the True Church in here, with Hypocrisy playing the part of the Roman Church out there, wholly dominated by diabolical and malicious intent. If we left our account of this play there, we'd have something similar to, say, John Bale's drama of the 1540s, in which figures like Dissimulacion or Pseudodoctrina wage unremitting attack on the True Church in England.[37] That placing, however, neglects the most intense drama of Act 5, which is *not* between Roman Hypocrisy and the true Church; it is, rather, a struggle of hypocrisy *within* the True Church, when the evangelical falls victim to "horror of the mynde," as Philologus is wholly unable to read the signs of his own state. In this play, fear of Catholicism cedes in horror, by a long margin, to the Calvinist's fear of his own punishing psyche.

A determined Theologus welcomes the signs of election. By his account, God will "pardon them that call to him unfainedly for grace," since "it is

God's propertye, to pardon sinners quight." So the bad news of psychic torture is good news:

> The Lord be praysed, who hath at length thy spirit mollified,
> These are not tokens unto us of your reprobation,
> You morne with teares, and sue for grace, wherfore be certified,
> That God in mercy giveth care, unto your supplication,
> Wherfore dispayre not thou at all of thy soules preservation,
> And say not with a desperat heart, that God against thee is,
> He will no doubt, these paynes once past, receive you into blisse. (5.2)

Philologus, however, falls victim to profound self-doubt. Horror-stricken, he considers himself "refused utterly, I quite from God am whorld [whirled]" (5.4). Any terror he experiences in the face of this rejection serves merely to confirm his hypocrisy. As a self-convinced hypocrite, distrusting himself, he also, therefore, distrusts everyone around him.

The dialogue of drama starts to wind down here, as Philologus dismisses the salutary effect of evangelical encouragement. Evangelicals had generated a tradition utterly hostile to hypocrisy in others. Here, however, we witness the inevitable result of that posture. For here we witness what happens to those who assume an utterly pure, end-of-time, authentic, fully visible selfhood, endowed by membership of the True Church. The inevitable product of that posture is to fall victim to hypocrisy, and to be propelled back, in the full visibility of public display, in horror to the saeculum from the unsustainable disciplines of being one of the elect. The long tradition of ecclesiological hypocrisy is now visited on its purveyors:

> No, no, my friends, you only heare and see the outward part,
> Which though you thinke they have don wel, it booteth not at all,
>   [helps]
> My lyppes have spoke the wordes in deede, but yet I feele my
>   heart,
> With cursing is replenished, ...
> I am secluded cleane from grace, my heart is hardened quight,
> Wherefore you do your labour loose, and spend your breth in
>   vayne. (5.2)

The fact that the two versions of the play conclude an identical plot with wholly opposite endings (suicide or conversion) points to the Kafkaesque, absurdist quality of this theological world, in which despair is simultaneously the surest sign both of election and of damnation. The events of this drama are wholly dependent on a divine action from outside; the psychic agonies of the protagonist are fundamentally disconnected from reward, and so the same action can produce totally opposed endings.

In sum, the history of hypocrisy from the late medieval period to early modern Calvinism is a history of dramatically rising profile and pressure. Whereas the charge of hypocrisy had been aimed at certain orders of the Church from the thirteenth century, its application widens dramatically once we have a priesthood of all believers in the sixteenth. Whereas evangelicals had aimed the projectile of hypocrisy at others, by the 1580s that weapon had boomeranged, and is now wounding horror-stricken evangelicals themselves. The disciplines of this modernity are unsustainable, and await attempted resolution from outside the Church, as from, for example, the false seeming friar / Duke of Shakespeare's *Measure for Measure;* or from mighty Milton; or from Bunyan; or, finally, from legislation in 1689. To these *essais* I now turn.

8

Managing Hypocrisy?: Shakespeare, Milton, Bunyan, 1689

THE CONFLICT OF CONSCIENCE of 1581 points to a new phase in the English Reformation. The key issue in this new phase is, despite the ferocity of anti-Catholic persecution from 1570 in England, less the Catholic Church as enemy, and more the intense and debilitating struggles within the evangelical tradition itself. The long tradition of ecclesiological hypocrisy is now visited on its purveyors.

How did English culture manage the contagion of hypocrisy? By the early seventeenth century, Shakespeare began to educate audiences out of the revolutionary discipline of sincerity, by inventing partial escape routes from the schismatic and intolerable logic of early modernizing authentic, singular selfhood. The provisional Shakespearean solution was, however, by no means the end of the story. Revolutionary Milton attempted an alternative solution in the mid-seventeenth century—that of reducing classical epic by outsourcing hypocrisy to only one, irreducibly malevolent and nonhuman, side in an epic contest. At the end of the seventeenth century, with *The Pilgrim's Progress*, the early modern ecclesiological couple hypocrisy and sincerity—not tamed at all by their early modern experience—stand ready to step into the narratives of the novel, whence they will continue walking into the nineteenth century and well beyond into liberal modernity (one might think of the novelistic evangelical hypocrites Square, Slope, Bulstrode, and, in North American literature, Hawthorne's Williams and Atwood's Commander, evangelicals all).[1] And after Bunyan, we will consider the key moment for hypocrisy release: the 1689 Toleration Act, which does its best to liberate English people from the singularity of modernizing subjectivity. In this chapter I look to all these different solutions or nonsolutions.

I

Puritans were themselves conscious of the frequency and force of the charge that they were the hypocrites, that "they be but a company of hypocrites, and precise fooles," as we saw in Chapter 7.[2] In Shakespeare's *Measure for Measure* (first performed 1604), however, the hypocritical puritan Angelo is anything but risible, especially in the context of the puritan Millenary Petition's struggle to gain the ear of the new king in 1603, at the Hampton Court Conference (January 1604). Instead, Angelo, and the play of which he is a part, expresses the wholly unfunny "form and pressure" of the early modern age.[3] Vienna may certainly be represented as a Catholic city (as indeed it was in the seventeenth century), with Catholic institutions and sacraments, notably confession (e.g. 2.3). Shakespeare takes care, however, to mix evidently Puritan features into this Catholic setting: Angelo's very name signals his claim to eschatological vision; the Duke describes him as "precise" (1.3.50) (an unmistakable buzzword for the puritan godly in early modern England);[4] and Angelo seeks to impose an actual puritan legislative proposal (the death sentence for adultery), which was in fact enacted in 1650.[5]

And, yet, there are no actual major religious figures in this play. This is not for a moment to say that the play has only secular interests, as a great deal of Shakespeare criticism would have had it until the last decade or so.[6] The setting of the play is, to be sure, secular, but only because religion has *more deeply penetrated* the secular realm in early modern Europe: this is the world of the priesthood of all believers, or at least of a few of them—those of spiritual athletes who are to be treated "in sincerity / As with a saint" (1.4.35–36). These figures are still in the putatively secular realm, whether the would-be nun Isabella or the precise magistrate Angelo, for whom hypocrisy remains an ecclesiological charge. This is also the distinctively early modern world as desired by Puritans, a world of non-priestly earthly magistrates who exercise power in ways exactly congruent with Puritan ministers.[7] It is also the world of the Tudor and Stuart Church post 1534, of princes who wield both secular and religious power.[8]

The Vienna of *Measure for Measure* is, in short, neither a Catholic Counter-Reformation nor a Protestant, Puritan city; it is, instead, expressive of the early modern world of revolutionary clarity and "terror," a word used more than once in the play, of secular power: the departing Duke says of Angelo that "we have lent him our terror" (1.1.19); Angelo himself insists that the law be preserved as a "terror" to birds of prey (2.1.4). This is a world in which secular power assumes spiritual prerogatives but (that word "terror" again) applies those spiritual prerogatives as from the perspective of the last judgment, empowered by eschatological vision. It is, in short, a world in which pardon has become irrelevant.[9] The secular power has taken upon itself the privileges of the predestining God, since Angelo proclaims that the law has become a prophet who foresees "future evils" and ends them before they live (2.2.95–99).

Shakespeare is not interested in the moment of the saint's transformation to hypocrite: the evangelical ideally has no interior life separate from the exterior, and so cannot claim the soliloquy. Angelo delivers three soliloquies: the first (2.2.164–189) occupies ninety or so seconds play time, and in this short span Angelo transforms from evangelical to its apparent opposite—the hypocrite. The two further soliloquies (2.4.1–17 and 4.4.17–32) merely confirm his settled disposition as hypocrite, or "false seeming." Angelo uses that phrase about himself (2.4.15), thereby evoking the longer history of hypocrisy from Jean de Meun's Faux Semblant, available to Shakespeare in Chaucer's translation of the *Romance of the Rose*.[10] Precisely because the saint has no interiority hidden from us, he cannot offer soliloquy as saint; his only privacy can be his status as hypocrite, but the change from saint to hypocrite must be without extended transformation, since it has to happen quickly, so deeply grounded is it in the structure of puritan sainthood. The puritan saint's subjectivity sits on the edge of time, straining for eternity, inevitably vulnerable to the trigger switch of hypocrisy. The moment of switch is precisely that: a moment without narrative.

Langland, Chaucer, and Nathaniel Woodes are, as we have seen, all self-reflexive about the way hypocrisy moves from the outside in. They offer, however, no account of how to *expel* the hypocrite; their texts therefore end in either crisis or extreme doubt. Shakespeare, too, represents the hypocrite come inside—Angelo is at the very heart of Vienna's system of law and punishment. But by contrast with earlier writers so far considered, Shakespeare does imagine how the hypocrite might be managed.

The only roughly viable solution at which he arrives, is, however, dark and slender: it involves a recognition that the ideal Calvinist relation between Church and magistracy will only work by being ignored through the lucky accident of a moderate, non-Calvinist magistrate; that politics must absolutely have priority over evangelical religion; and, most surprisingly, that *the only way to manage the hypocrite is to be a hypocrite,* or at least a player, adopting the "habit," and, for the Duke, learning how he may "formally in person bear / Like a true friar" (1.3.47–48).

The Duke, that is, wants to observe Angelo to see "what our seemers be" (1.3.54), but to do that he must himself become a seemer. He must pretend to act like Hypocrisie in the *Conflict of Conscience,* coming as a foreigner from Rome "in special business of his Holiness" (3.1.452). He must be the "old fantastical Duke of dark corners" (4.3.150), or, to use John Bale's formulation with regard to the Pope, the Duke must become the "king of faces, the Prince of hypocrisy."[11] He must, like Woodes's Hypocrisy, provoke his own startling "horror of mind."

The charge of hypocrisy began, as we have seen, as an ecclesiological charge against friars, and especially against friars who penetrate houses under cover of their ecclesiastical habit. Surprisingly, *Measure for Measure*'s Duke renders the priesthood of all believers just livable by himself becoming precisely that—a hypocrite friar, a *penetrans domum.* When we see *Measure for Measure* in its longer cultural history, that is, we can see that Shakespeare produces an astonishing if provisional solution to evangelical hypocrisy: instead of repudiating it head on, Shakespeare *embraces* hypocrisy, and he does so in its most celebrated historical form of the hypocritical friar. Isabella threatens to expose the hypocrite publicly, but in a Calvinist world of parallelism between magistracy and secular power, that avenue is blocked, since the tyrannical, hypocritical magistrate controls all discourse. The rescue by power in this world can only be made by absolute power; so the Duke must expel himself from the center of power and return in disguise as a friar, penetrating houses and offering fake absolutions.

The moment the Duke disguised as friar enters, he acts exactly like the friars of late medieval anti-fraternal polemic: he pretends "formally" to search Juliet's conscience to see if her penitence be "sound / Or hollowly put on" (2.3.22–23). In this short scene we witness the privacy of the confessional, and the movement through contrition and confession, all performed as if "formally" by a friar whose habit is itself "hollowly put on."[12] From this moment on, the Duke / friar must perform a series of further deceptions: he conceals himself from Isabella and Claudio in 3.1; he pretends to Claudio that he is Angelo's confessor in the same scene; he brutally pretends to Isabella, as she witnesses what she imagines is Claudio's head, that Claudio has been executed (4.3.108); in 5.1.386 the Duke continues to pretend that Claudio has been executed, well beyond the necessity of any plan to expose Angelo. What's more, in exactly the manner of hypocrisy's classic pattern, the Duke's feigning spreads to others: in 4.6 we see Isabella and Julia preparing to act roles not their own, to say their "part," in order to "veil full purpose" under the directions of the director Duke (4.6.1–4); in 5.1. Isabella "lies" to the assembled court about Angelo having slept with her, in response to which the Duke demands that she "confess the truth," and pretends to have her taken to prison.[13] The Duke orders that both the friar and Mariana be tortured so as to find out who is setting them on to slander Angelo—"there is another friar that set them on" (5.1.245). If this play is not interested in the moment of transformation from saint to hypocrite, it is fascinated by the repeated and sometimes excessive hypocrisies of the Duke.

In Act 5 Isabella charges Angelo in exactly the same terms as friars had been attacked in late medieval anti-fraternal satire: he is a "murderer . . . and adulterous thief, / An hypocrite" (5.1.43–45). That expresses everyone's disgusted view of the precise Angelo, but Shakespeare knows just how dangerous it is to attack hypocrisy. It's especially dangerous when the hypocrite embodies the power of state and church. The legal danger of attacking hypocrisy is, however, secondary to the psychological danger of the Calvinist magistrate becoming a hypocrite himself. There are no neat solutions to this exacting challenge in *Measure for Measure*: the danger of

Angelo's apparent absolutism can be checked only by the absolutism of the Duke; that absolutism effectively diminishes the socially restorative sacramental power of confession, since in this world legal and sacramental confession have become identical. ("Let my trial be mine own confession," says Angelo in 5.1.374.)[14] The strangeness of the larger situation is underlined by the oddity of a comedic ending being achieved by the imposition of law. (Shakespearean comedies and romances, in keeping with the vast genre of medieval romance behind them, are almost all happily resolved by the constructive logic of providential virtue, not by legal mechanisms.)[15]

However ethically diminished this early modern world, and however strange this ending, Shakespeare knows that part of the long process of managing hypocrisy among the priesthood of all believers will be the application of what looks like hypocrisy. Shakespeare, that is, doubles down on hypocrisy, by way of neutralizing the charge of hypocrisy. Across the play, but especially in the very long single scene that constitutes the entirety of Act 5, the Duke applies homeopathic medicine, or what Isabella calls "a physic / That's bitter to sweet end" (4.6.7–8). Angelo acts like a predestining God, while the Duke plays the part of the inscrutable *deus absconditus* of Protestant theology, playing by his own rules and eliciting our political faith alone.

For all the unresolved darkness of the play's solution to its even darker problem, Isabella voices the psychological light at the end of this particular tunnel, as she pleads for Angelo's pardon: "Thoughts," she declares, "are no subjects" (5.1.455). Shakespeare points to a way out of the appalling and vicious disciplines of the priesthood of all believers and of wholly sincere, unitary selfhood. We escape that Church by recognizing that wholly integral, united subjectivity of the Calvinist saint, with its "mind's white truth," is both dangerous and destructive for its promoters as much as for everyone else. To escape that Church, we need to recognize that thoughts have visors; we play roles; our sanity depends on our doubleness. To elude hypocrisy, we must first embrace the basic condition of the hypocrite. But, this play tells us in somber tones, we now need the state to be able to underwrite our multiple identity. In 1603, only the absolutist state, in which we must have faith alone, will be capable of managing the corrosive powers of revolutionary religion.[16]

II

Self-disgusted Calvinist consciousness of internal hypocrisy by no means disappeared after Shakespeare's *Measure for Measure*. Fulke Greville, ever the most sophisticated poetic analyst of the dark recesses of Calvinist spirituality, expresses the Calvinist experience of hypocrisy's inward aridity most uncomfortably. In his relentlessly pithy and intellectually pitiless *Treatise on Religion* (written probably 1622–1628), Greville effectively denies any alternative to "bottomless hypocrisie" in the translation of "true religion" into a given human, material form.[17] Neither, therefore, is there is any alternative to the inner experience of hypocrisy, or any turning away from the desolating aridity of that experience:

> For in this painted tomb, let man's own spirits
> Reallie judge what that estate can be,
> Which he begettinge in himselfe, inherits,
> Other than deserts of hypocrisie,
> Within the darkninge shadowes of his witte
> Hidinge his staines from all the world, but it.[18]

We see the same posture in another episcopalian Calvinist, Thomas Adams (1583–1652), whose 1613 Paul's Cross sermon *The white deuil, or The hypocrite vncased* (republished four more times up to 1621), describes with almost touching candor how it's impossible to escape hypocrisy.[19] "Who will totally cleare himselfe" of hypocrisy, Adams asks rhetorically. He answers: "Let me tell thee, if thou doest, thou art the worst hypocrite. . . . He that . . . sayes, he hath not sinned in hypocrisie, is the rankest hypocrite" (image 19). Eradication of one's own hypocrisy is quite impossible; anyone who thinks he can succeed is the greater hypocrite:

> Take heed: a Bible under your arms, will not excuse a false conscience in your bosoms: think not you fathom the substance, when you embrace the shadow: so the fox seeing sweet meats in the vial, licked the glass, and thought he had the thing. (image 21)

The sermon is moving because it undoes its own raison d'être: it simultaneously promises to expose hypocrisy and avers that the task is no more effective than the fox licking the glass containing the object of his hunger. Adams wishes he could not be talking about this self-defeating subject:

> I am haunted with this *white Devil, Hypocrisy*: I cannot sail two leagues, but I rush upon this rock; nay, it will encounter, encumber me quite through the voyage of this verse.... Shall I be rid of this Devill at once, and conjure him out of my speech? God give me assistance, and add you patience, and I will spend a little time, to uncase this white Devill, and strip him of all his borrowed colors. (image 17)

Despite these penetrating seventeenth-century accounts of the desolating experience of Calvinist hypocrisy, the charge of hypocrisy was about to take on its most lethal, and apparently unstoppable, force of fragmentation in the properly revolutionary period of the 1640s. This is a large topic, but one can take the rain check on the state of the traditions so far considered in this chapter in 1646, from Thomas Edwards's *Gangraena*. This text is a perfectly Presbyterian expression of accurately feeling as if one's revolutionary project is about to be overtaken by new, more revolutionary forces.

Edwards, as we saw in Chapter 2, describes and attacks new theological groupings as "heresies"; he enjoins absolute refusal of toleration for these new movements; and, in the context of this chapter, we can see him drawing on a tradition at least four hundred years old by describing these heretical clerical movements as hypocritical. He uses language that had been used against every heterodox ecclesiastical movement since the mid-thirteenth century. That language had been used, indeed, by Presbyterians against the Catholic Church; it was then used by episcopalian Anglicans against Presbyterians from the later sixteenth century. Faced with 176 heresies, Edwards now uses it as a Presbyterian against new, more revolutionary sects. He lambasts

> their damnable hypocrisy, and abominable dissimulation; and I am persuaded there never was a more hypocritical, false, dissembling, cunning generation in *England* then many of the Grandees of our Sectaries. Now their gross hypocrisy plainly manifests it self in these particulars, 1. they have covered all their practices and designs under the pretenses of godliness, honesty, saintship, purity of Ordinances,

tenderness of Conscience, a perfect thorough Reformation, new
glorious truths, giving to themselves and their party the name of
Saints, Saints, the godly party, tender Consciences, and under that
covert they destroy all godliness, good Conscience, truth.

Milton participated in the culture that produced Edwards. Revolutions
do not immediately provoke inward self-reflexivity; the desperate struggle
for power turns accusations outward. In the resurgence of revolutionary
aspiration that was the English Revolution, the charge of hypocrisy against
others, notably against prelates and the king, was used in very high-profile
circumstances. Milton is a good example of the wholly non-self-reflexive,
polemical usage, especially in his anti-prelatical works, but also against
Presbyterians, and finally against the king. In his anti-prelatical, Presbyterian tract *Of Reformation* (1641), Milton tarred bishops with the brush of end-
of-days clerical hypocrisy: "The sour leaven of human Traditions mixt in
one putrified Mass with the poisonous dregs of hypocrisy in the hearts of
Prelates . . . is the Serpent's Egg that will hatch an *Antichrist*."[20]

By 1648 Milton was charging his erstwhile allies, the Presbyterians, for
whom he had spoken in 1641, with hypocrisy, without any signal that he
had changed sides. Thus in the *Tenure of Kings and Magistrates* (1649), written
after the military coup of December 1648 and the execution of the king in
January 1649, Milton attacked the Presbyterians, who had now turned
against regicide, and identified them with the hypocritical prelates. Those
fainthearts support tyrants

> and fall notoriously into the same sins, whereof so lately and so loud
> they accused the Prelates; as God rooted out those immediately be-
> fore, so will he root out them their imitators: and to vindicate his
> own glory and Religion, will uncover their hypocrisy to the open
> world.[21]

In *Paradise Lost*, Milton simplifies the issue of hypocrisy. He projects the
act wholly onto Satan, the only hypocrite—but a perfect example of classically inveterate, irredeemable, ecclesiological, lethal hypocrisy—in the
poem. As hypocrite, Satan is especially dangerous, because hypocrisy is,
says Milton as narrator, "the only evil that walks / Invisible, except to God
alone, / By his permissive will, through Heav'n and Earth" (3.683–685). If a

polemicist ever believed that God alone is capable of detecting the hypocrite, that polemicist might, one would think, exercise especial care in
labelling others as hypocrites. Not so Milton in his pre-*Paradise Lost* career,
as he assumes, and then liberally exercises, the divine freedom of hypocrisy detection. Not only does he label the prelates and the Presbyterians as
hypocrites, but, in what can only be described as, perhaps, an especially
inconsistent (hypocritical?), and certainly pitiless way, he targets the executed king as a masked dissembler in the matter of literary plagiarism.

After the total defeat of royalist forces in August 1648, faced with the
question of what to do with the king, Oliver Cromwell affirmed that "thou
shalt not suffer a hypocrite to reign."[22] After the execution of the king in
January 1649, neither was Milton prepared to let the memory of what he
regarded as a royal hypocrite to reign. During Charles's imprisonment
awaiting execution, ghostwriters had produced a set of meditations and an
apologia, entitled *Eikon Basilike, the Image of the King*, as if in the king's own
voice from prison. The book was published in 1649, only days after the execution; it was a runaway success, with forty English-language editions
in 1649 alone.[23] Milton quickly and derisively rejoined, with *Eikonoklastes*
(1649), which aimed to neutralize the massive success of the king's book.
Milton's book went through three editions between 1649 and 1652, with one
more in 1690, published in Amsterdam.[24]

Eikonoklastes champions regicide as an act of iconoclasm but levels the
charge of hypocrisy as a powerful weapon in its polemical arsenal.[25] Milton
begins by ascribing the "low dejection and debasement of mind in the
people" (who are opposed to the regicide) to the "perpetual infusion of servility and wretchedness" inculcated by bishops, whose lives are "the type
of worldliness and hypocrisy" (p. 344). He next accuses the executed king
of hypocrisy in religion, given that he was influenced by his Catholic wife:
"But what is it that the blindness of hypocrisy dares not doe? It dares pray,
and thinks to hide that from the eyes of God, which it cannot hide from
the open view of man" (p. 422).

Dismissing Charles's private meditations in his *Eikon Basilike* as absurd,
as the "vows of hypocrites use to be," what incenses Milton especially is the
adoption of a prayer from Sidney's *Arcadia* as if it were delivered in the voice
of Charles: "A Prayer stolen word for word from the mouth a of Heathen
fiction praying to a heathen God; & that in no serious Book, but the vain

amatorious Poem of Sr *Philip Sidneys Arcadi*" (p. 362). Milton pretends to Pauline shock at the blasphemous offering to a pagan idol, but he focuses more on derision than on wounded religious sensibility. The borrowing reveals that Charles has left the stage of the world "ridiculously" (p. 364), offending the principle of Protestant authenticity, that one should only express one's own prayers; or that one should borrow prayers from fit places; and that one should not infringe copyright. How disgraceful that the "ignorant and wretched people" should have been fooled "by this deception, worse then all his former injuries, to go a whoring after him" (p. 367).

Hypocrisy remains signally and revealingly untamed in *Paradise Lost*. Milton reduces classical epic by reducing the confrontation to two ethically opposite combatants. Classical epic, whether Homeric or Virgilian, presents a conflict between ethically equal protagonists, who share the same culture and the same gods. Miltonic early modern epic, by contrast, suffers the discipline of early modernizing singular identity: there can only be one source of identity, to which all alternate centers must submit. Unlike Homer's or Virgil's, then, Milton's epic accordingly presents a wholly asymmetrical confrontation: the main protagonist of *Paradise Lost*, forever up against the very source of putative goodness (i.e. God), is ethically impoverished, is driven by despair, and projects only hypocrisy to his interlocutors. A confrontation thus structured permits Milton to outsource and concentrate all that he most fears in himself and his Calvinist culture to Satan. The domestic content and scale of action between Adam and Eve point to the future, but the epic content and scale of *Paradise Lost* are distinctively early modern for its absolutisms.

In sum, Milton's place in the hypocrisy tradition is that of the Protestant polemicist, who claims easily to penetrate the hypocrisy of others; who attacks divided subjectivity in others in the name of singular, personal authenticity; and whose claim to authenticity justifies pitiless rudeness. For Milton, hypocrisy is out there, among the enemies of the revolution. That self-righteous, proudly offensive tradition will of course have a long history ahead of it in the Protestant tradition, and in secular versions of that tradition, particularly in the United States. As we approach the end of our period, we can also, however, see the still vital, darker, alternative Protestant tradition of hypocrisy having come inside, or at least playing on the edges of the sensitive psyche. How to manage the contagion of hypocrisy remains a major cultural challenge up to and beyond *The Pilgrim's Progress*.

III

Bunyan's *The Pilgrim's Progress* was first published in 1678; it became an immediate best seller and one of the most influential books in English culture thereafter. On the face of it, *The Pilgrim's Progress* is a narrative driven by repudiation in the name of singular authenticity. Christian not only repudiates his former self and the Earthly City to generate his voyage in the first place, but also the following: Obstinate, Pliable, Worldly Wiseman, Civility, Beelzebub, Formalist, Hypocrisy, Timorous, Apollyon, Vanity Fair, Pope, Pagan, Wanton, Adam the First, Moses, Talkative, Lord Hate Good, Envy, Superstition, Pick-Thank, Mr By-Ends, Demas, Giant Despair, Ignorance, Flatterer, and Atheist. The narrative presents all these tempters and destroyers as external to Christian, whose salvation depends on his capacity to preserve his singular selfhood, produced in response to an absolutist God, against apparently insuperable odds. Faithfully to preserve that Calvinist stability of self, Christian exemplifies the punishing disciplines of evangelical early modernity in extreme form. Christian must, that is, reject earth and hell to achieve heaven. Whereas Milton's lost paradise is implicitly the paradise of the earthly republic sustaining Miltonic ecclesiology, Bunyan's narrative of paradise gained abandons earthly forms altogether. It sublimates the pain and humiliation of Christian's (and Bunyan's) earthly experience as progress in his route to heaven.

Bunyan's work of prose fiction was extraordinarily fertile for the novel in formation, while Milton's epic of military struggle between absolutist rulers could have no plausible epic followers in English verse after 1688. One reason for those very different Nachleben was the respective treatment of otherness in these works. Milton deals with doubleness by projecting it onto Satan alone: he outsources what had become internal Calvinist demons (e.g. despair, hypocrisy) onto the Satanic other. Any argument that *The Pilgrim's Progress* might also seem to externalize Calvinist demons must, however, take into account the genre of *The Pilgrim's Progress*. As psychological, personification allegory, Bunyan's "other" in *The Pilgrim's Progress* is Bunyan's "me."[26] That "me" turns out to include ... precisely the same list of tempters and opponents listed above, including Despair and Hypocrisy. Bunyan is dealing with internal challenges to Calvinist sincerity. Unlike the relentlessly self-confident Milton, Bunyan becomes, in his own moving words in *Grace Abounding* (1666) "a burden and terror to myself":[27]

> Thus, by the strange and unusual assaults of the tempter, was my soul like a broken vessel, driven, as with the winds, and tossed sometimes headlong into despair; ... I was but as those that jostle against the Rocks; more broken, scattered, and rent. O, the unthought of imaginations, frights, fears, and terrors that are affected by a thorough application of guilt, yielding to desperation! This is the man that hath his dwelling among the Tombs with the dead; that is always crying out, and cutting himself with stones. (Mark 5:2–5)[28]

Christian has many inner tempters, but the two most recurrent and tenacious are Despair and Hypocrisy, or, in other words, despair and hypocrisy. In the syntax of Calvinist emotional narrative, Hypocrisy follows Despair. Thus after escaping from the Slough of Despond, Christian's first encounter is with Mr Worldly Wise-Man, who points Christian to a much easier way, via the village of Morality where Legality, the father of Civility, lives. Christian is about to follow Worldly-Wise Man's directions, when Evangelist confronts him and explains that the way of civility, customary morality, and legality is, however tempting after the sheer terror of Despair, only a hypocritical façade: "Mr. *Worldly Wiseman* is an alien, and Mr. *Legality* is a cheat: and for his son *Civility*, notwithstanding his *simpering* looks, he is but an hypocrite, and can not help thee."[29]

The cruel pattern of escaping Despair only to meet Hypocrisy recurs: after witnessing the former "professor" (i.e. Christian evangelist) shut up in the cage of despair in a dark room in Interpreter's house, Christian almost immediately encounters Formalist and Hypocrisy, who come "tumbling over the gate" rather than enter the path by the narrow gate. Formalist and Hypocrisy answer in unison, thereby making an efficient point about the entire tradition of the Church (i.e. all form amounts to no more than hypocrisy) (p. 46). Later still, after escaping from the dungeon of the Giant

Despair (p. 135), Christian and Hopeful tearfully witness those blinded by despair stumbling around among tombs, before being shown a gate in "a door on the side of a hill" among the Delectable Mountains,

> and they opened the door, and bid them look in. They looked in therefore, and saw that within it was very dark and smoky; they also thought that they heard there a rumbling noise, as of fire, and a cry of some tormented, and that they smelt the scent of Brimstone. Then said *Christian, What means this?* The Shepherds told them, this is a by-way to Hell, a way that Hypocrites go in at. (p. 140)

Bunyan's world, not only in *The Pilgrim's Progress* but also in *Grace Abounding* and *A Relation of the Imprisonment of John Bunyan*, is the world of the priesthood of all believers. The Papacy is almost wholly irrelevant. As Christian survives the Valley of the Shadow of Death, for example, he comes across a cave "where two giants, *Pope* and *Pagan,* dwelt in old Time" (p. 79). The place is strewn, as one might expect in Bunyan's text (and as one would have with Spenser's), with the remains of Pope and Pagan's persecuted victims. Unlike the macabre passages of Catholic violence in Spenser's *Faerie Queene* (1590–1596), however, Christian moves on "without much danger, whereat I somewhat wondered."[30] The puzzle is solved by Christian's report of what he's since learned: that Pope is, "by reason of age, and also of the many shrewd brushes that he met with in his younger days, grown so crazy [broken] and stiff in his joints, that he can now do little more than sit in his Cave's mouth, grinning at Pilgrims as they go by, and biting his nails, because he cannot come at them" (p. 79). For Bunyan the Papacy is a figure of senile decrepitude, a source not of lethal threat, but of pathetic relief.

In this early modern world of massively raised ecclesiological standards for the laity, every single figure Christian encounters is a source of ecclesiological promise or threat. The ecclesiological status of individuals is so high, in fact, that any material notion of the Church itself dissolves in Bunyan's narrative, leaving individuals alone and agonized by their predicament, a terror to themselves. As individuals faced with such a menacing, singular demand on their authenticity, Bunyan's interlocutors therefore also necessarily manifest hypocrisy. Christian himself, indeed, acts like a cleric, becoming the (unsuccessful) catechizer of Ignorance and the successful detector of the hypocrite Talkative. Talkative, not the Pope or his followers, is the real and present danger, since Talkative talks the evangelical talk, sounding for the whole world like a professed Calvinist. Faithful is taken in, but quickly set straight by Christian in a snide conversation between Christian and Faithful, out of Talkative's earshot and behind his back. He is quickly and whisperingly exposed by Christian to Faithful as a "*Hypocrite or Talkative person*" (p. 97).[31]

Near the provisional end of the Reformation centuries, then, the four key features of hypocrisy charge from the thirteenth century are each fully functioning: representatives of the Church are hypocritical; they deserve only eradication, not reformation; they are signs of danger for the entire Church, portending its end; and they provoke endemic distrust. Bunyan's narrative is propelled forward by such atomization and distrust. The only big differences between the thirteenth- and the late seventeenth-century examples is that at the later moment the charge is diffused across all levels of society (all early moderns are clerical in this text), and the hypocritical enemy is one of one's own kind, and also, always implicitly, oneself. The principal enemies driving evangelical propulsion are now repudiated forms of hypocritical evangelical religion.

Across the period 1256–1678, the only thing that's changed with regard to the charge of hypocrisy is that it has spread, morphed, and penetrated an entire system, both its endo- and exo-structures, exhausting the energies of the system.

IV

And then (after a certain amount of further turbulence between 1660 and 1688!) something wonderful happened.[32] The first parliament of William and Mary, after the Glorious Revolution of 1688, passed "an Act for Exempting their Majesties' Protestant Subjects dissenting from the Church of England from the Penalties of certain Laws" (passed 1688, receiving royal assent 1689).[33] This act, normally known as the "Toleration Act," holds with the principle that the state must determine the ground rules of religious observance, but it significantly breaks from the principle that subjects must commit to ecclesiastical forms determined by the state (as expressed by the Ausburgian formula *cuius regio eius religio*).

Historians of toleration have dampened and corrected a long tradition of simplistic liberal triumphalism with regard to statutes of this kind, and what produced them. The word "toleration" should not, above all, be taken to mean "tolerance": in the early modern context, "forbearance" might be a better synonym, rather than *OED's* sense 3 for "tolerance": "freedom from bigotry or undue severity in judging the conduct of others." Neither is the story of toleration, as it was long understood to be, "the victory of the progressive thought of learned elites over a relentless and ingrained popular instinct to persecute."[34] From the evidence of this chapter, it is precisely the learned elites who generated the charge of hypocrisy, against other learned elites. And one should, furthermore, recognize the limits of the 1689 Act: all subjects were required to take the Oath of Supremacy, confirming the monarch as the head of the Church and State, renouncing fidelity to any foreign power; Catholics and anti-Trinitarians are excluded from its provisions; Dissenters remained unable to serve in public office.

All those qualifications duly recognized, from the *longue durée* history recounted in this chapter, the English liberal tradition surely can recognize this moment as foundational. It is certainly not the case that intellectual history alone drove this statute, as was often argued by the triumphalist narratives; on the contrary, it was the product of a very long and violent history on the ground.[35] But intellectual history certainly did contribute to its formulation: John Locke's Latin letter *De tolerantia* (1685–1686) was written from exile in the Netherlands (1683–1689), whither Locke had fled in the wake of the failed assassination attempt on Charles II in 1683, a plot in which associates of Locke had been implicated. The Latin letter was written in the wake of the revocation of the Edict of Nantes by Louis XIV in 1685, which had provoked the forced exile of about four hundred thousand Protestant Huguenots from France. *De tolerantia* was published anonymously in the Netherlands, in 1689. The Latin text develops the earlier vernacular *Letter Concerning Toleration* (1667), written from London, which was not published until 1876 but which seems to have circulated in manuscript.[36]

Locke would have had Parliament go much further than the Toleration Act. He astutely points out that religious groupings routinely appeal powerfully to toleration as long as they are weak, but, as soon as they gain power, revert to persecution.[37] We therefore need, Locke argues, a more coherent, grounded, sustained defense and practice of toleration. This Locke provides by arguing that no power external to a Church is capable of successfully determining orthodoxy for that Church. The magistrate is, therefore, wholly ill-equipped to attempt such an imposition of orthodoxy; only violence, which runs clean contrary to the Gospel, will result from the forced imposition. The example Locke gives, in a text almost wholly shorn of examples, is of "Arminians and Calvinists in Constantinople" (pp. 224–225), which example is clearly designed to point to the major players in England, with the exception that the setting is among the Ottomans.

Imposition from outside in this foreign setting is unthinkable, which clarifies the impossibility of effectively establishing orthodoxy in any other way, since "every Church is orthodox to itself" (p. 225). Only Churches are capable of establishing their own orthodoxy, in which case the magistracy and the Churches should be established as wholly distinct entities, with no overlapping jurisdiction, except that of the state determining that Churches are indeed separate jurisdictions and can act as they like as long as they do not infringe the laws of the land. The only groups and churches to be disallowed from this liberal dispensation are: atheists, because their word cannot be trusted (p. 246); such religions as claim to exercise dominion over the magistrate (implicitly targeting Puritans) (p. 245); and such religions as necessitate allegiance to a foreign power (thus Locke's implicit disallowance of Catholicism and explicit disallowance of Islam) (pp. 245–246). Near absolute jurisdictional separation was not the path chosen by the English Act of 1688–1689; in the Anglo-American legal tradition, that separation had to wait for the First Amendment to the Constitution of the United States, ratified in 1791.

The context and history of the Toleration Act is beyond the scope of this chapter. From the perspective of clerical hypocrisy, and the hypocrisy of the priesthood of all believers, however, we can say that Locke's solution offers the most persuasive management of the schismatic charge of hypocrisy, by establishing the potentially divided identity of individual subjects—divided between Church and State—as well as by establishing the grounds of acceptable difference between subjects, owing allegiance to different Churches. Locke does not, however, try to dissolve the issue of absolute fidelity. Part of the genius of his solution is that he grounds his defense of separately existing Churches precisely on the need to offer full and unforced commitment to one's Church: "All the life and power of true religion consists in the inward and full persuasion of the mind; and faith is not faith without believing" (p. 219). By forcing religious commitment of any kind upon subjects is "to add to the number of our other sins, those also of hypocrisy, and contempt of His Divine Majesty" (p. 219). Locke paradoxically promotes avoidance of hypocrisy in order to diminish the schismatic force of hypocrisy.

By lowering the temperature of the hypocrisy charge, Locke begins to open the way to a new culture, one in which divided sympathies and identities are permissible, and in which other words begin to replace, or at least give a much wider range of meaning to, the word "hypocritical"—words like "playful," "improvised," "decorous," "urbane," "artistic," "strategic," "amusing," "private," "discreet," "ironic."[38] Being one self (the modern, evangelical self) is really tough; it only exists in response to an absolutist God. Trying to be that self had produced massive social and internal fracture. And apart from the violence, being an evangelical self produces no delight in being in the world. 1689 sees the way back to playfully divided selves, in which thoughts are no subjects, in which multiform subjects play many parts, in which aspirational selves (what classical civilization called *daemons*) inhabit and encourage multiply layered selves, in which one can be honest without forever being the same unitary, sincere, and singular person.

PART 4

Breaking Idols

9

Liberating Iconoclasm

EVERY REVOLUTIONARY MOVEMENT practices iconoclasm: public destruction of the symbolic order of the ancien régime is the surest and readiest way of attacking the old order itself. The English Revolution, the French Revolution, the Russian Revolution, the Chinese Cultural Revolution (not to speak of many other revolutionary moments and places, including contemporary Mesopotamia) all encouraged, if not legislated, destruction of the visual culture of the dispossessed orders.[1] Image and statue destruction in ancient Israel, late Antiquity and eighth- and ninth-century Byzantium offered models for Protestant image de- struction; the archetype for later revolutionary image destruction in the West is, however, the early modern Protestant Reformation of the sixteenth and seventeenth centuries.[2]

That revolutionary moment serves as an especially powerful model because the motives for iconoclasm were so much deeper than in many later revolutions. The standard revolutionary reason for image destruction is symbolically to signal demolition of the old order itself. Protestantism's many reasons for image destruction were, however, even more deeply grounded, and were all powerfully categorical.

In the first place, the Decalogue forbade the making and worshipping of images and likenesses of what are "in heaven above, neither that are in the earth beneath, nor that are in the waters under the earth," promising

to visit the punishment of the sins of the fathers "upon the third generation and upon the fourth of them that hate me" (Exodus 20:4–5).

Second, Protestants saw themselves through the lens of ancient Israel,
both at the moment of invasion of the Land of Canaan under Moses and
Joshua, and then in the larger narratives of the Books of Kings. At the
moment of invasion (thirteenth-century BCE), God commanded total destruction of the idols of the various peoples inhabiting Canaan (e.g. Deuteronomy 12:2–3). The Books of Kings narrate the later history of the Kingdoms
of Israel leading up to the Destruction of the First Temple (586 BCE) as a repeated history of backsliding into idolatry, followed by dramatic, not to
say violent, iconoclastic purification.[3]

Third, Protestantism targets representation, in various senses. The early
modern centralized God wished to clear away all mediating layers between,
and all representation on behalf of, individuals and God. The most obvious
instances of penitential or votive mediation and representation were, precisely, representations of the saints and the Virgin Mary. For that reason
all visual representations of both saints and the Virgin (accounting for a
huge proportion of images) had to be destroyed.

Fourth, and above all, Protestantism was anti-formalist, and post-
human: its more revolutionary forms were obliged, that is, to demolish
anything that was not divinely mandated, and anything that was considered to be merely invented by human tradition.

This last, anti-formalist motive for iconoclasm will turn out, as we shall
see, to be the most insistent and the most difficult to manage. In fact that
fourth motive reveals that "iconoclasm" is too restricted a concept to designate the phenomenon of early modern image breaking. The images are
but one example of a much larger category—that of the idol. The idol is
that which is treated improperly as divine, with lethal results. The charge
of idolatry spread very quickly in early modern England from material images (merely the most obvious examples of "idols") to many other nonmaterial objects, which were also categorized as idolatrous. Fear of idolatry
and the destructive impulse toward idols moves in two self-generating
directions: it spreads outwardly, across the entire geography of the new
revolutionary jurisdiction, but it also spreads inwardly, into the psyche.
From things in the world, both material and nonmaterial (e.g. the Mass),
fear of idolatry migrated to the psychological realm of improper desire and

the cognitive realm of false doctrine. From that inward storehouse of idols, it also spread back outward, generating an ever more vigilant destructive impulse with regard to the material world, and to the very concept of special, charismatic place.[4]

England experienced more than a century of legislated iconoclasm of every religious image, from 1538 to 1644. This project of state-driven iconoclasm was longer and more systematically legislated than anywhere else in Reformation Europe. The legislated English iconoclasm beginning in 1538 produced what I have elsewhere called the "kinesis of iconoclasm," or, in other words, an intelligible historical pattern of iconoclastic practices, along with a set of attempts to manage the runaway action of attacking all forms of idolatry, both material and psychic.[5]

The kinesis of iconoclasm begins with energetic and irreverent evangelical destruction of physical religious images. That first phase of material destruction (c. 1538–1553) was, however, just the easy start, before a much more painful, unjoyful second sequence (c. 1558–1625) began. Iconoclastic hygiene around the absolutist, modernizing God targeted all forms of idolatry, not only visual images. It therefore worked its way into the liturgy, to be sure, but also into the most intimate recesses of the soul, breaking visual imaginations, and breaking the idols of false doctrine.

In that second phase, lovers of the image needed to invent ways of managing the punishing dynamism of iconoclasm. One key form of management was to stabilize and rename our love of, and need for, salvific representations of ourselves and others, otherwise known as images. Long before the drama of physical iconoclasm was over in England, we see how Shakespeare helped invent a new space for the restorative image, the space of Art. Shakespeare uses the potentially idolatrous reception of the marble statue of Hermione to undo idolatry. By welcoming Hermione back into the land of the living, Shakespeare also welcomes not only images, but salvific statuary, back into English culture.

A third phase (c. 1625–1670s) is mixed: on the one hand, the counterrevolutionary is determined to replace the images; on the other, the revolutionary is determined to return to iconoclastic business, precisely in response to counterrevolutionary attempts to reinstate images. Shakespeare's solution, then, comes well before the agony of idolatry destruction is exhausted in England. After counterrevolutionary efforts to reintroduce images, the need to purge the mind of potentially idolatrous forms grew stronger; so too did treatment of the external world become ever more severe, to the point of undoing the very concept of material place. Seventeenth-century Puritans theorized revolutionary space as what one recent historian aptly calls "a time and space of homogenous sanctity."[6] This theological attempt to theorize the even distribution of charisma across space has aesthetic implications, producing as it does what might be called abstract architecture and monuments—forms in space that attempt nonetheless to deny their spatiality; places that repudiate place.

An unrelenting program of iconoclasm must, however, inevitably almost fail, since the iconoclast's job is never finished. The most consistent psychological trait of the iconoclast is exhaustion. The "vast and intractable task" will remain undone, partly because the iconoclast must pursue the idol into the tricky recesses of the imagination itself; partly because the revolutionary order will never successfully repress images as special, representative places; and partly because the potential victims of idolatry fury always expand across the long revolutionary period.[7] These aspects of iconoclasm also have aesthetic implications: exhaustion and acute awareness of inevitable failure are built deep into artefacts that attempt to *further* the iconoclastic enterprise.

The English Revolution's most energetic artistic figure will produce, in exhaustion, a final push at the idolatrous edifice. In 1649 Milton laid the groundwork for the later revolutionary political practice of iconoclasm by explicitly extending religious image breaking to a political target. To the end, Milton sees himself as the iconoclast, not only the iconoclastic champion of regicide. In 1671, after the failure of the Revolution, he will also see himself as the blind Samson seeking to bring down the entire idolatrous edifice of deceptive religion, and purify sacred geography.

The agony will finally become roughly manageable not through legislation but rather through the Shakespearean solution—the invention of the category of Art. But the charge of idolatry will also survive, in evangelical religion, in revolutionary ideology critique, and, by no means least, one way or another, in the modern, liberal museum of art.[8]

In this chapter I delineate phase 1, the carnivalesque, fun phase of iconoclasm (1538–1553 or so), before turning in Chapter 10 to phases 2 and 3: the less amusing matter of breaking the psyche's images (c. 1558–1625); and the further, overlapping struggle between lovers and destroyers of the image in England (c. 1625–1670s).

I

Deuteronomy 12:3 makes the call to iconoclasm explicit (God is the speaker):

> ³ Also ye shall overthrow their altars, and break down their pillars, and burn their groves with fire: and ye shall hew down the graven images of their gods, and abolish their names out of that place.

Just as the ancient Israelites must demolish idols of competing Canaanite religions, so too were they prohibited from erecting any likenesses of their own. The drama of a written law as distinct from an image-based practice is violently played out as Moses descends from Mount Sinai with the tables of the law written by God (Exodus 32). The Decalogue, as recorded in Exodus 20:4–5 (and presented as a separate commandment by sixteenth-century evangelicals),⁹ forbade the making of images:

> ⁴ Thou shalt make thee no graven image, neither any similitude of things that are in heaven above, neither that are in the earth beneath, nor that are in the waters under the earth.

No sooner does modernist Moses bring this law to the Israelites than he finds them worshipping the Golden Calf. "Moses' wrath waxed hot" (Exodus 32:19); he smashes the Tables of the Law in anger; pulverizes the Golden Calf; has the Israelites drink the potion in which the gold powder is mixed; and orders the execution of three thousand men (Exodus 32:19–28). This extraordinary narrative is generated by a set of key oppositions: writing versus image; divine command versus human making; elite reader versus popular custom; new writing versus old idol. God confirms the justice of Moses's violence inflicted on the idolaters, and adds plagues for good measure (Exodus 32:35).

This exemplary narrative of monotheistic writing narrates the infliction of violence on polytheistic images as the prelude to possession of the Land of Canaan. Early modern evangelicals and their late fourteenth-century predecessors in England understood narratives of this kind to be the prelude to their own possession of a fully Reformed Church in the geographies of early modern Europe.

Even before official iconoclasm, however, the image had come under threat in pre-Reformation England. The image is never wholly secure in Western literate culture. Despite the decisive defenses of the image by Gregory the Great in 599 and 600, the Christian image was forever subject to attack from its powerful competitor, writing (a potential threat embedded, indeed, in Gregory's defense of images as "books for the unlettered").[10]

A vast tradition of orthodox late medieval spirituality, known as "devotional piety," had, however, from the thirteenth century, promoted imaginative, theatrical, *visual* engagement with the narrative of Christ's life.[11] The forms of this devotional culture are as follows: highly visual rendition of the life, and particularly the sufferings, of Christ; intense emotionality represented within, and provoked by, the text and / or image; and high theatricality, with time foreshortened by the dramatic presentation of Christ's sufferings. Devotional images were designed to instruct and to move, in both senses: the images were pre-cinematic, designed to produce the effect of movement, and they were designed to move the emotions of an illiterate or moderately literate laity.

Such treatment of images came under pressure in England from the late fourteenth-century proto-Protestant movement, known as Lollardy. Lollard hostility to the idolatry provoked by images had high profile in the heterodox attack on the orthodox Church.[12] The *Twelve Conclusions of the Lollards* (1395), for example, declares that the prayers made to "deaf images of tree and of stone, been near of kin to idolatry." The learned Lollard author acerbically evokes, in order to invert, St Gregory's famous late sixth-century dictum about images being books for the illiterate: deaf images of tree and stone are, he asserts, "forbidden imagery"—that is, they are "a book of error to the lewid [ignorant] people."[13]

Late medieval orthodox defenses of the image had a relatively low profile in the campaign *against* the Lollard "heresy."[14] To be sure, the draconian orthodox, anti-heresy *Constitutions* of Archbishop Arundel (1409) targeted, among other issues, dispute about orthodox use of images.[15] Thus Article 9 refers to images as part of a general interdiction on disputing "established articles of the Church": let no one teach contrary to the determination of the Church, "especially about the adoration of the glorious cross, of images, the veneration of saints, or pilgrimages to places, or their relics."[16] The *Constitutions* of 1409 gave much higher profile to the textual and Eucharistic issues raised by Lollardy, partly because isolating textual and sacramental issues (especially views on the Eucharist) provided surer ground for heresy convictions.

Early fifteenth-century orthodoxy had, however, another reason not to stress Lollard hostility to images: the orthodox were themselves muddled about just how much an image should move. In the late fourteenth and fifteenth centuries in England, that is, orthodox theologians could not help but be conscious of the danger of the image culture they themselves promoted.[17] The more candid of those orthodox theologians recognized the fact that orthodox promotion of moving images, precisely because they moved, and seemed alive, had very uncertain borders with the illicit and dangerous practice of idolatry. Orthodoxy suddenly realized, that is, that it *shared* with heterodoxy a distrust of illiterate reception of moving images.

Take, for example, Reginald Pecock's *Repressor of Overmuch Blaming of the Clergy* (c. 1455), the most extensive and systematic vernacular treatment of the image question in the period between Arundel's *Constitutions* (1409) and the first iconoclastic legislation of 1538.[18] Pecock (?1395–?1460) was bishop of Chichester when he wrote the *Repressor*, for which text he was convoked by the Council of the English Church on charges of heresy.[19] He recanted, resigned his bishopric, and was confined for the rest of his life, without access to writing materials.

Pecock recognized the centrality of the image issue, describing "the having and using of images" as the "first governance for which the lay people overmuch and untruly witen [blame] the clergy."[20] Pecock's fundamental position with regard to religious images is that of the learned orthodox. Images are, he asserts, in no way forbidden in Scripture or by any ground of the faith (2:2, p. 137), but they are in no way to be treated as alive. Solomon may have become an idolater, but these days no one could be so "fond, masid [confused], and doted [foolish]" that they would worship "idols as Gods" (2:2, p. 145). This is the core of Pecock's entire, extensive defense of image use: they're dead.

Once stated, Pecock qualifies the standard position in various ways. Very quickly, he goes on to concede that iconoclasm is justified in cases of idolatry. "Images," he says, "may leefully [legitimately] be broken, when they been used in idolatry irremediably" (2:2, p. 147). But on what grounds might that be the case? The lay party (i.e. Lollards) erroneously assert that the "people trowen [believe] . . . that some goodly virtue [power] is in those images, or that those images do miracles, or that they been quick [alive] and see, hear, or speak at some while, or that they sweat at some while" (2:3, p. 148). Now that the charge of vivacity is more explicit, Pecock more explicitly repudiates it: no adult in Christendom, or none who is not, at any rate, simple minded ("a natural fool"), believes such a thing.

After a long defense of images and their affective power, however, Pecock moves to the intimately related question of relics and pilgrimage. Here he suddenly reverses position entirely. His orthodox defense of pilgrimage sites depends precisely on what he described earlier as the risible fancy of the credulous, or even of the "natural fool." God chooses one image over another as the fit destination of a pilgrimage; therefore, Pecock declares in his own voice,

> it is not inconvenient [improper] that God make thilk [that] image of stone or of tree for to sweat and that the image be moved from one place unto an other place without man's bearing and . . . that the eyes of the image be turned hitherward and thitherward verily or seemingly, as though the image saw, and that the image . . . [should] speak. (2:8, p. 186)

In short, Pecock shifts ground a good deal in the *Repressor*. In one section, images are most certainly dead; it is inconceivable that even the most dull-witted contemporary should think otherwise. In a separate section, he actively promotes the idea that the images have shown signs of life, by sweating, eye movement, and apparent speech. Late medieval orthodoxy, particularly candid orthodoxy, was, in sum, confused about religious image use. Devotional piety prompted orthodoxy to go as close as it could to an affirmation of image vivacity; conflict with proto-Protestant opponents prompted the contrary affirmation: images were pure, dead matter, useful only rhetorically as nonmoving movers of emotion.

II

The issue of images, then, was certainly a cause of significant disruption in the late medieval, pre-Reformation English Church. On the one hand, the orthodox needed to defend the imaginative, salutary vivacity of images: every church was painted with such images; pilgrimage sites and the entire system of pilgrimage depended on the presence of relics and statues; and the widespread and growing use of private devotional images was grounded in orthodox conviction.[21] On the other hand, those same orthodox needed absolutely to deny that the images were in any way alive. To consider the images as dead or alive was a fine balance across a fine psychic boundary; it produced serious trouble, since to get the balance wrong was to incur the charge of heretical idolatry. From 1401, heresy had become a burning issue in England, and orthodoxy remained uncertain about image use.[22]

In the first sequence of the English Reformation (c. 1520–1558), and especially with the legislation of 1538, 1547, and 1550, the confusion was put to an end. The fault line that ran beneath all sacred images opened dramatically. Iconoclasm of all religious imagery was legislated, and the charge of idolatry extended rapidly from images to many other "merely human" inventions.

This first stage of the legislative story is quickly told.[23] In 1538 all visible cult of the saints before their images was forbidden. Archbishop Cranmer (Archbishop of Canterbury 1533–1555) instructed bishops that all images that are "abused with pilgrimages or offerings . . . ye shall, for avoiding that most detestable sin of idolatry, forthwith take down and delay [destroy]."[24] Deciding which image was subject to idolatry and which not was, however, obviously impossible. In 1547, therefore, Cranmer produced a further, more sweeping, and simpler solution: "All the images remaining in any church or chapel . . . [shall] be removed and taken away."[25] By 1550, under the boy king Edward VI, who was actively promoted as a new Josiah (the iconoclastic boy king of Judah, 2Kings 18–20 and 2Kings 21–3), a further act was passed, this time by statute, ordering the destruction of all images in church except those of noble families: parsons having "any images of stone timber alabaster or earth, graven carved or painted," shall "deface and destroy or cause to be defaced and destroyed the same images and every of them."[26]

These legislative acts took immediate effect and radically transformed not only the interior of Churches but also what one might call the cultural geography of England. The practice of pilgrimage was forbidden in 1538; shrines of saints were unceremoniously destroyed; and the images of saints destroyed.[27] The statues that were objects of veneration at pilgrimage destinations were regarded as part of a pagan geographical network. Veneration of such objects was described, that is, as a resurgence of pagan polytheism, of local deities to whom "we attribute the defense of certain countries, spoiling [depriving] God of his due honor"; they are nothing but "*dii tutelares* of the Gentiles idolaters, such as were Belus to the Babylonians and Assyrians," says the author of the official *Book of Homilies* (originally published in 1547, but republished in 1563 and enlarged with what became the longest sermon in the collection, "An Homily Against Peril of Idolatry").[28]

The evangelical campaign against the sacred image was, however, only part of a much larger, and expanding, campaign against idolatry. In the few years of Henry VIII's reign when evangelicals were actively directing policy (1536–1539), the iconoclasm campaign also took to the stage and massively extended the campaign from images to other forms of idolatry. Take, for example, the plays of John Bale, written and produced in the late 1530s, immediately after the first iconoclasm legislation. After his 1537 release from imprisonment, at the instance of Vice-Regent Thomas Cromwell, Bale worked as an agitprop playwright, director, and actor. Along with a number of other plays, he wrote and performed *God's Promises* between 1538 and 1540 (when he fled to Amsterdam after the fall and execution of his patron Cromwell). *God's Promises* presents a sequence of figures from the Hebrew Scriptures in dialogue with Pater Coelestis, who begins the play by promising to send "plagues of correction most grievous and sharp" (ll. 58–59) to correct the idolatry of his people.[29] Each dialogue rehearses a passage of Hebraic history that has infuriated God. The only drama as such consists in the attempt of a given patriarch to restrain the irrepressible and punishing fury of God toward his chosen people. The causes of the divine fury are easily translatable into code for the Catholic Church, notably idolatry.

In *God's Promises*, God at first restricts idolatry to image making in the age of Abraham (ll. 315–317), and to worship of the Golden Calf in his dialogue with Moses (ll. 495–496). God, however, makes it clear to Moses that no form of idolatry will be tolerated: "Never will I spare the cursed iniquity of idolatry for no cause" (ll. 507–508). The punishment will be spectacular—"all Israel shall it see" (l. 512). Idolatry remains, however, the irreducible sin of the ancient Israelites: in his dialogue with King David, God starts to despair at Israel's inveterate idolatrous tendency. She "will not leave her old idolatry," says an exasperated God,

> Nor knowe me for God. I abhor her misery.
> Vexed her I have with battailes and decayes,
> Still I must plague her; I see none other wayes. (ll. 560–562)

The relationship between God and his people is clearly pathological; neither partner sees any way out of the chronic habit of mutual abuse and violence. The dialogue with David in particular begins to sound like a therapy session for God. He confesses that "I cannot abide the vice of idolatry," even if, he says, he should permit all other forms of vice (ll. 584–585). In his dialogue with Isaiah, he works himself up into yet another targeted fury against the "tyrants of Sodoma." (Bale frequently associates idolatry and sodomy, a practice legislated against for the first time in 1534.)[30] At this point, however, Bale's early modern God extends the definition of idolatry to the entire penitential and liturgical practice of the Catholic Church: "I abhorre your fastes and your solemnity. / For your traditions my ways ye set apart. / Your works are in vain: I hate them from the heart" (ll. 693–695).

This God thunders, as a prelude to rehearsing the terrible, unremitting violence he has visited upon the Israelites, who are hooked on idolatry: "Always they apply [fall back] to idols worshipping / From the vile beggar to the anointed king" (ll. 714–715). In another play probably of the same year, *Three Laws*, the identification of idolatry and sacramental practice is more explicit: idolatry is to be "decked like an old witch," who declares that "this is my common cast, / To hear Masse first or last / And the holy Friday fast, / In good time mowt [might] I it say" (ll. 503–506).[31]

Bale's extension of idolatry from images to the Mass presents what high-profile evangelical theologians such as Thomas Becon (1512–1567, chaplain to Archbishop Thomas Cranmer from 1547), were arguing very soon after Bale's play, from their exile in the reign of Queen Mary (1553–1558): idolatry was not at all restricted to images, but extended to many other forms of illicit and lethal worship, notably "the sacrifice, which our Savior Christ offered on the altar of the Cross"; Catholics "make a show of it to the people, that they may fall down and worship it as a god, yea, God himself Creator and maker of all things." We should, Beacon declares, "give over" this "Idolatrous massing."[32]

The very form of *God's Promises* expresses the drama of writing versus image, since not only is its content consistently directed against image worship and other forms of idolatry, but its form is also wholly dominated and suffocated by Biblical text: "action" as such consists of rehearsal of textually grounded, Biblical narrative.

As represented by this play, destruction of idolatry is the immediate and unavoidable prelude to the conversion of England. It ends with a final summation by John the Baptist of the history of national weakness and invasion produced by idol worship. God the father promises "John" (the Baptist) that he will be his messenger, just before the appearance on stage of another "John" (Bale), who clearly sees himself as a John the Baptist championing the image destruction and anti-idolatry campaign in the newly Protestantized kingdom of Henry VIII.

Breaking of physical images, is, however, only the easy start of a program of thoroughgoing iconoclasm. The inner recess of asylum for the image, the psyche itself, had also to be visited by the revolutionary purist, metaphorical hammer in hand.

This second phase begins with the most extreme, radical, and revolutionary recommendation for idolaters of all stripes and all social classes, and for the responsibility of delivering that treatment, by John Knox (d. 1572). Writing from Marian exile in 1558, Knox declares, "I suppose it be evident, that the punishment of idolatry doth not pertain to kings only, but also to the whole people, yea, to every member of the same."[33] The punishment that each subject must deliver is death: "I say, it is lawful to punish the idolaters with death."[34] This second phase also produced the proposition that all churches themselves be destroyed. The separatist Henry Barrow, for example, in keeping with a powerful evangelical repudiation of special places, and a no less powerful evangelical hatred of places that have housed the idolatry, recommended in 1590 that evangelicals follow both the second commandment and the divine mandates as expressed in Deuteronomy 12:2–3: "Thou shalt utterly deface and destroy all

these synagogues and places where such idols have been set up and worshipped."[35] The logical application of these divine prohibitions and commands is to destroy the churches themselves:

> How then doe they still stand in their old idolatrous shapes, with
> their ancient appurtenances, with their courts, aisles, cells, chancel,
> bells, etc.? Can these remain, and all idolatrous shapes and relics be
> purged from them? Which are so inseparably inherent unto the
> whole building, as it can never be cleansed of this fretting leprosy,
> until it be desolate, laid on heaps, as their younger sisters, the abba-
> cies and monasteries are.[36]

This first sequence of iconoclasm in England was, then, the first sequence
of a broader campaign against idolatry in all its forms. Those forms were
most obviously liturgical (the Mass) and material (images of all forms). Images, however, are deeply embedded in the psyche, beyond the reach of
the hammer. Whereas the first phase of English iconoclasm was ebullient,
irreverent, pitiless, and physical, the second phase (1558–1625), to which I
turn first in Chapter 10, was somber, pitiless, and psychic.

10

Saving Images and the Calvinist Hammer

IN THE FIRST PHASE of the English Reformation, then, the charge of idolatry spread rapidly and unpredictably through the evangelical nervous system, to attach itself to every salvific form, both psychological and material, that was judged to be human-made, and without scriptural foundation. The obvious targets of the virus were material and liturgical, and the tone, as we saw in Chapter 9, was confident. The job was to be short, pitiless, and complete.

The next phase of the Reformation (1558–1625) was, however, rather less ebullient. The job seemed never to be done, and the images found refuge from the purifying revolutionary hammer in the most elusive of corporal territories—the psyche itself.

Because Reformation evangelicals were Biblical literalists, so the argument goes, they felt compelled to destroy images of the old, Catholic order, images that provoked idolatry. They did it because the Bible told them so. That standard explanation, that Biblical prohibition provoked a century of iconoclasm, is persuasive as far as it goes: citation of the commandment (Exodus 20:4) against graven images is ubiquitous in Reformation polemic against images. In my view, however, this explanation does not go nearly far enough to explain the ferocity and duration of English iconoclasm, since it suggests that iconoclasm is (i) only a matter of observing Scriptural injunction; and (ii) only a matter of the physical destruction of images.

Historians have admirably chronicled the vast physical phenomenon of image destruction. In this chapter I address the second phase of iconoclasm in the English Reformation, between 1558 and 1625 or so.[1] I follow and develop the work of cultural historians, especially that of Margaret Aston, in tracing the more subtle, perhaps more ferocious, and certainly more painful matter of psychic iconoclasm.[2] We need to look for evidence of image destruction within the psyche, as evangelicals pursue what Francis Bacon in 1620 famously called "idols of the tribe," the idols of every human mind, which by its very nature produces idols.[3] These idols of the tribe are not only powerful visual images but also the idols of false doctrine.

Idolatry, indeed, is not at all restricted to adoration of images, but also applicable to incorrect *doctrinal* thoughts, along with pretty well every fabrication of the imagination. Evangelicals accordingly repudiated the category of the imaginative, just as they repudiated the category of the "human," as fabricated, merely constructed, and not grounded in the scriptural and the written. So idolatry will now apply especially to psychic experience: the hammer-wielding iconoclast needs above all to move into, and through, the psyche itself, there to lay waste to the imagination.

Images are, however, too powerful and resourceful to stay in the psyche, and to suffer mental iconoclasm indefinitely. Images save us; we need them; they devise ways of stepping back out of the embattled psyche, and back into the physical world where we need them to be; in this chapter we will observe, as we turn to Shakespeare's *Winter's Tale,* that return of the saving image, stepping carefully out into a newly protective space, the space of Art.

The anti-idolatry war will not by any means cease there, however. In a further, third phase of the English Reformation (1625–1670s) revolutionary iconoclasts such as Milton will extend the idol destruction to the realm of the political (an extension with a long history ahead of it), and pursue the personal, pitiless campaign of idol destruction to the very last push of a revolutionary career. Evangelical pursuit of idols into the world of commodities and into the novel will also remain vigorous, with Bunyan's *The Pilgrim's Progress.* I turn to that third phase of English reformation iconoclasm in Chapter 11. Let us begin, however, with the flight of idols into the apparent asylum of the psyche, and revolutionary, Calvinist pursuit of those fugitives.

I

The issue of the idols of the mind arose with especial force in, as one might expect, the second phase of the Reformation in England. The reign of Catholic Queen Mary (1553–1558) witnessed the annulment of the iconoclastic legislation of 1538–1551, and the restoration of images in churches.[4] The Elizabethan articles and injunctions of 1559 turned directly and decisively to the restoration of the image-destruction campaign. These injunctions directed bishops to enquire of their parish clergy as to whether they had "removed, abolished and destroyed . . . all images, shrines . . . pictures, paintings, and all other monuments of feigned and false miracles, pilgrimages, idolatry, and superstition."[5]

A few years after the Elizabethan iconoclastic injunctions of 1559, those injunctions were defended and theorized in the very high profile and massively diffused *Book of Homilies*. The 1547 edition was reissued in 1563 with, as mentioned in the previous chapter, a vigorous new sermon added, "A Homily against the Peril of Idolatry," now by far the longest sermon in the compilation. The text's basic argument is that national strength is produced by iconoclasm, and vice versa. The sermon generates the argument primarily from negative examples. It effectively produces a history of religion so as to unlock the secret of national strength and weakness, by identifying enslavement and national weakness with idolatrous practice. Every national disaster is traceable to idolatry: all this "captivity and most miserable thralldom" we "owe to our mighty gods of gold and silver, stock and stone, in whose help and defense, where they can not help themselves, we have trusted so long."[6]

The very length of the homily's world history of ever-resurgent idolatry, points, however, to a new phenomenon in the English war against religious images. The longer the story of idolatry, the greater the danger of exhaustion; the more frequent the image resurgence, the greater the need for total iconoclasm, including iconoclasm of the mind. "Idolatry," the author declares in the third section, "standeth chiefly in the mind" (image 123). Not only is it primarily a psychological issue, but it's a problem for weaker, less educated minds: idols are "worshipped of the ignorant sort of men" (image 131). In competition with the false doctrine generated by the seductive image, preaching always loses. The situation appears hopeless:

And that evil Opinion [concerning the idol] which hath been long
rooted in men's hearts, cannot suddenly by one Sermon be rooted
out clean. And as few are inclined to credit sound Doctrine; as many,
and almost all, be prone to Superstition and Idolatry. So that herein
appeareth not only a difficulty, but also an impossibility of the
Remedy. (image 131)

Writing and preaching are feeble against the irresistible seductions of
the image (and the broader category of idolatrous doctrine), says this
sermon (confessing its own weakness against addictive, lethal, and massively popular misconception). There is nothing for it but unremitting
and psychological iconoclasm. The "stumbling-blocks and poisons of
men's Souls, by setting up of Images, will be many, yea, infinite if they be
suffered" (image 133).

In any religion in which God is utterly transcendent, counter-idolatry
police work will need to be especially vigilant and severe, since the problem
is by no means restricted to material images. Repression of idolatry, that
is, required internal, psychic regulation even more pressingly than external
iconoclasm. The problem is much wider and deeper than physical iconoclasm can address, since idolatry now encompasses all humanly constructed figments and imaginations, including *false doctrine*. Any humanly
constructed idea or doctrine must now also fall victim to the prohibition
on idolatry.

Take, for example, what Luther says in his Commentary to Romans, published in 1515, before the beginning of Luther's public career.[7] Romans 1:23
charges that sinners are at root idolaters. "For," says Luther citing Paul, "they
turned the glory of the incorruptible God to the similitude of the image of
a corruptible man, and of birds, and four footed beasts, and of creeping
things" (p. 42). Paul, writing in the first-century Mediterranean world,
clearly has pagan statuary of the classical gods in mind here. Luther,
however, comments on this passage by defining the turn from the incorruptible God to the belated and fallen state of idolatry as a *psychological*
phenomenon. He locates that turn in the deepest habits of the human
psyche: "The human mind," he says, "is so inclined by nature that as it
turns from [worship of the true God], it of necessity becomes addicted to
[the worship of false gods, or idolatry]" (pp. 44–45).

Idolatry for Luther is not at all restricted to worship of images. Rather, idolatry is the psychic habit whereby humans change God into a "figment of the mind, when men neglect what He demands, and honor Him by works which they have chosen for themselves" (p. 45). This spiritual idolatry "of a finer kind" derives from love of one's "good intention," whereby a human "imagines" s/he worships a "merciful God, whereas . . . [s]he worships his own figment of reason more devoutly than the living God." This produces "idolatry, and idolatry leads to a whole deluge of vices" (p. 46). So the more refined form of idolatry for Luther is the psychopathology of believing bad—that is imagined, or humanly invented—doctrine. Idolatry is, as a result, located in the deepest habits of the human psyche.

For Luther, the hypocrisy of false doctrine is a form of humanly ineradicable psychic idolatry. "God," he says in his 1522 Preface to Romans, judges us "according to what is at the bottom of the heart . . . he punishes works that are done otherwise than from the bottom of the heart as hypocrisy and lies."[8] Every man, however, hates the law at the bottom of his heart. Those mistaken Christians who actively promote the value of works in addition to faith, "make for themselves . . . an idea in their hearts." But this is "a human imagination and idea that never reaches the depths of the heart" (pp. xvi–xvii). To rely on human imaginations is to commit "idolatry," which leads "to the most shameful sins" (p. xix).

Calvin, who was much more actively iconoclastic than Luther, agrees. In his *Institutes,* first published in 1536, and first translated into English in 1561 (from Calvin's 1559 edition), Calvin declared that scarcely

> a single person has ever been found who did not fashion for himself an idol or specter in place of God. Surely, just as waters boil up from a vast, full spring, so too does an immense crowd of gods flow forth from the human mind.[9]

Calvin targets the imagination in particular as the dangerous source of idolatry; he describes the imagination as "a perpetual workshop [*fabricam*] of idols."[10] The very intensity with which Reformation evangelicals imagined a transcendent God paradoxically, though perhaps predictably, spawned hundreds of all too material gods and goods potentially subject to idolatry. It also spawned very many more deceptive thoughts—practically every thought, indeed—of what the truth of God might be.

Mental idolatry bites especially hard in historical contexts of actual image removal. As the images are removed from sites for which they were designed, where do they go? One place was into private spaces of private homes, from which place they must be harried out and defaced by inspection and surveillance.[11] The Elizabethan injunctions of 1559 direct bishops, for example,

> whether you know any that keep in their houses undefaced any images, tables, pictures, paintings, or other monuments of feigned and false miracles, pilgrimages, idolatry and superstition, and do adore them, and specially as have been set up in churches, chapels or oratories.[12]

Another space into which images will inevitably creep, having being chased from church to domestic oratory, and from there to material destruction, is into the immaterial space of minds. They will not, however, be safe from the hammer there. Calvin's successor Theodore Beza claimed to have been successful in purifying his own psyche: "I have driven the crucifix from my mind," he claimed.[13] Weaker brethren clearly required more strenuous direction. As Laurence Humphrey (d. 1589), friend of John Foxe and John Bale, wrote from his Marian exile Basel in 1559:

> If the idols are removed from the churches but steal into the mind and statues are erected in the heart, that is deformation not reformation; a change of place, not a driving away of the thing, and so much the more dangerous because it is interior and personal.[14]

Humphrey wrote in the period described by Patrick Collinson as not merely iconoclastic but "iconophobic," which he dates to 1580–1620 or so.[15] In Section II I look to what's going on in the psyches of two sensitive late Elizabethan writers, notably Fulke Greville and Edmund Spenser, in that period.

II

Fulke Greville (1554–1628) was, as we have seen in Chapter 4, simultaneously an exceptionally acute critic of absolutist government, and a committed Calvinist. His lyric sequence *Caelica* (written 1577–1628) begins with love lyrics, but changes to religious lyrics at #84.[16] Both sets of poems, the

secular and the religious (109 in all), are informed by an acute sensitivity
to the multiple forms of tyranny, including the tyranny of idolatry. Here
I focus on just a few of the religious lyrics that deal with mental idolatry.

Greville promotes internal iconoclasm more unsparingly than any Puritan. The terrible weakness of human will and reason present humans
with a "true mappe of [their] Mortality" by which "many Idols are at once
defaced, / And all hypocrisies of fraile humanity, / Either exiled, waved, or
disgraced" (96, ll. 34–37). For Greville this defacement of mental idols is,
however, no easy or peaceful matter. As for Donne, who demands that God
renovate him by the hard-handling meted to idols themselves—to "break,
blow, burn, and make me new," so too does Greville see internal iconoclasm
as a violent and terrifying process.

This is especially true for those sophisticated Christians who will not be
deceived by physical idols. Thus the Manicheans, says Greville in a *Caelica*
lyric, had no idols, nor did they worship "gods of Wood." That did not, however, save them from internal idolatry: "Yet," says Greville, "idols did in
their ideas take," until "clearer faith this idol took away" (89, l. 6). This example of the Manicheans is clearly intended by Greville as a benchmark
for sophisticated Elizabethan Calvinists, now freed from adoration to
physical images, yet still subject to idols "in their ideas." Those Christians
might, he says, think the work is pleasantly done once they remove the
physical images, but they would be utterly mistaken: the intensely un-
pleasant work of violent internal iconoclasm must be a matter of self-
martyrdom and burning through textual commitment, before one might
properly dare a visual contact with Christ: "The heart must first beare witness with the book, / The earth must burne, ere we for Christ can looke"
(89, ll. 17–18).

The most penetrating of these lyrics—#100 in the sequence—is a sonnet
that confronts the terrible challenge of mental iconoclasm by taking us
into the dark recesses of the imageless psyche:

> In night when colours all to black are cast,
> Distinction lost, or gone down with the light;
> The eye a watch to inward senses plac'd,
> Not seeing, yet still having power of sight,
> Gives vain alarums to the inward sense,

Where fear stirred up with witty tyranny
Confounds all powers, and thorough self-offence,
Doth forge and raise impossibility:
Such as in thicke depriving darknesses,
Proper reflections of the error be,
And images of self-confusednesses,
Which hurt imaginations only see;
 And from this nothing seene, tells news of devils,
 Which but expressions be of inward evils.[17]

This exceptionally dark sonnet enacts the ghastly psychopathology of a disabled imagination. The visual power that operates in darkness is the psychological faculty of the imagination—the soul's "imaginary sight"—which remains capable of producing mental images in darkness, of presenting, as Shakespeare says, a shadow to the "sightless view."[18] Because, however, the imagination is subject to the tyranny of reason ("witty tyranny"), its habitual work produces nothing but "vain alarums." Here the vanity, or emptiness, does not signal a purified imagination. On the contrary, the imagination is alarmed, and these alarms are all the more terrifying precisely because they are *forged* by a tyrannous reason.

The process is also all the more terrifying, though also all the more painful, as the poet diagnoses the psychopathology as he experiences it: this is the work of a "hurt imagination," an imagination being turned back on its own proper operation so as to produce only reflections of error, or "self-confusednesses." In fact those reflections are nothing else than images, from which there can be no escape for the wounded imagination. The final line paradoxically defines the *image* of "nothing seen" as the incurable disease of the pathological imagination.

Greville both experiences and diagnoses a debilitating psychopathology within English culture in the late sixteenth century. Before we turn to Shakespeare's therapy for that illness, we should briefly look to a more famous and spectacular representation of that same psychopathology, in the great poem of another courtier-bureaucrat in late Elizabethan England, Spenser's *Faerie Queene* (Books 1–3, 1590, and Books 4–6, 1596).

In Book 1 of that poem, it's clear that mental images are very much more treacherous and debilitating than external images. As we saw in Chapter 4, spotting and destroying the monster Error is relatively easy work; managing the phantoms produced by Archimago, much more difficult. Already in Book 1, Canto 1, immediately after Redcross Knight's victory over Error, Archimago conjures an exact look-alike of Una from hell, and, "with charmes and hidden artes," implants it in the psyche of Redcross Knight: "So lively, and so like in all mens sight, / That weaker sence it could haue ravisht quight."[19] This moment of psychic image confusion provokes the primal division of Redcross Knight (a synecdoche for England itself) and the True Church. Canto 2 gives poetic form to the theme of the official "Homily on the Peril of Idolatry" (i.e. that national weakness can be identified with submission to sensual addiction to the image), when Redcross Knight is unable to distinguish the false image of Una from the True Una, who herself falls victim to Archimago. Seeing Redcross and Una "divided into double parts," Archimago transforms himself into the shape of Redcross to deceive Una, while Redcross is deceived by the Una look-alike Fidessa, who is in fact the Whore of Babylon Duessa. With remarkable ease and speed, then, we end up in a narrative in which we have two Unas, and two Redcross Knights. In each case, one is a phantom, capable of entering the psyche with deadly accurate likeness and lethal intent.

Of course Redcross, despite falling exhausted victim to the wiles of his psychic enemies, is finally rescued and, with the graceful aid of Arthur, recovers. From a lowest, near-death point of enfeebled weakness, with all resources "cleane consum'd, and all his vitall powres / Decayd, and all his flesh shronk up like withered flowres," Redcross regains his strength to marry Una at the end of Book 1, in an allegory of England's manifest Protestant destiny.

England's vulnerability is not, however, over. *The Faerie Queene* is the original Gothic horror. Like all best originals, this one contains the seeds of all that will follow. One of those seeds is the zombie, the unkillable revenant whose horror is simply inexpungible. The revenant zombie in this narrative is, precisely, the psychological image producer, Archimago, whose name means simultaneously and appropriately the original magician / the original image. Images in this profoundly imagistic text are lethally dangerous, produced as they are by irredeemably malicious and unkillable figures. As long as Archimago is on the loose, the narrative climax of Book 1 —the marriage of England and the True Church—remains vulnerable.

National history becomes vulnerable, that is, to the native movements of the psyche, in particular the native movements of the imagination. At the end of Canto 12 of Book 1, Archimago is imprisoned in chains. And how does Book 2 begin? Archimago easily slips his bonds: "His artes he moves, and out of caytives hands / Himselfe he frees by secret meanes unseene." With "subtile engins" (imaginations), Archimago is pursuing Redcross again. Before that narrative of manifest destiny can be fully stabilized, then, the imagination needs to be reeducated.

So it is that in Book 2 of *The Faerie Queene* Spenser represents the training of the knight Guyon, who stands for Temperance. The key phase of Guyon's training is psychological, as he accompanies Arthur into the soul itself for a science-fiction journey through the three cells of the psyche in Aristotelian psychology (i.e. imagination, reason, and memory).[20] The psychological terminology of cells is rendered monastic, with each personified faculty inhabiting a separate *cella*. The sequence begins with the cell of Phantastes (the imagination), before passing through the cells of, respectively, Reason, and Anamnestes (or memory) (FQ 2.9.47–60).

Spenser's *Faerie Queene* is extraordinary precisely for its imaginative visual painting of moral states. All the more extraordinary is it, then, in a poem so utterly dependent on brilliant visualization of inner states, that the cell of Phantastes should be dismissed as a place of weird extremes or idle fantasy. The chamber is filled with buzzing flies, which provide an appropriate aural backdrop for the visual frescoes:

> All those were idle thoughts and fantasies,
> Devices, dreames, opinions unsound,
> Shewes, visions, sooth-sayes, and prophecies;
> And all that fained is, as leasings, tales and lies. [deceptions]
>   (FQ 2.9.51)

We might expect that the richest stock of psychic materials for a poet of Spenser's cast would be archived in the cell of Phantastes—after all, this very science-fiction scene of an intra-psychic journey would itself be impossible without drawing on the imagination, "on all that fained is." One of the features of Spenser's poem that makes its fantastic narrative profoundly serious is, however, precisely the way in which Spenser attempts to disown the resources of his own art: Spenser is a committed Calvinist who fears the unkillable image maker Archimago, and yet who depends at every turn on precisely Archimagic resources. Where do those deeply conflicted pressures lead?

They lead, predictably perhaps, to scenes of shocking psychological violence. I end this section with the knight Guyon's journey at the end of Book 2, a journey that takes him across the Idle Lake to the Bower of Bliss inhabited by Genius and sexual desire, Acrasia. Spenser pulls out all the stops to underline the sublime beauty of this place, beautified precisely by Genius, the *ingenium* or imagination, who "guileful semblants . . . makes us see" (*FQ* 2.12.48). The Calvinist Spenser must, however, break the generative spell that produces his own poetry. The following scene has often been understood as a representation either of fallen sexual desire or of iconoclasm.[21] I see it in a more radical and psychic light, as an astonishingly intemperate representation of Calvinist Temperance seeking to break the habitual, beautiful, and generative processes of the imagination itself:

> But all those pleasant Bowers, and Palace brave,
> Guyon broke down, with Rigour pitiless;
> Ne ought their goodly Workmanship might save
> Them from the Tempest of his Wrathfulness,
> But that their Bliss he turn'd to Balefulness:
> Their Groves he fell'd, their Gardens did deface,
> Their Arbors spoil'd, their Cabinets suppress,
> Their Banket-houses burn, their Buildings raze,
> And of the fairest late, now made the foulest place.
>   (*FQ* 2.12.83)

Calvin, as we have seen, regards the human psyche as a perpetual workshop, or *fabrica*, of idols. Spenser's hero enters the workshop and attempts to break the machines and their beautiful setting. Spenser takes care to distinguish the destruction of this site of *engin*, or Genius, from *his* Doppelgänger (every figure in this poem has one). There is another Genius, the noble one who accompanies us always as a kind of conscience, serving as a moral guide through production of salutary images: "And straunge phantomes doth let us oft forsee, / And oft of secret ill bids us beware" (*FQ* 2.12.47, ll. 6–7). Late medieval texts, such as Gower's *Confessio Amantis* (1390), allow that function of the *ingenium*, or imagination, to work in simultaneous action with the sensual, more "genial" operations of a single Genius figure, persuaded as they are that the sensual Genius is, however powerful and seductive, inseparable from the healthy working of the psyche.[22] Spenser's hero, by contrast, must engage in a desperate, intemperate, Herculean, and of course doomed effort to separate the two operations of the imagination. In this scene of shocking psychological self-damage, Guyon seeks to annihilate the native functioning of the imagination. The effort can only produce yet more "vain alarums."

III

Shakespeare died in 1616, almost precisely a hundred years after Luther had initiated the internal iconoclasm of an absolutist God. As Shakespeare entered the last phase of his career, in 1610 or so, the kinesis of iconoclasm had many phases yet to run. After the attempted beautification of holiness, including the restoration of images, in the Laudian Church (from 1633), the Revolution witnessed one last, yet extraordinarily aggressive, legislated push against images of all kinds between 1641 and 1644.[23] Shakespeare is, nonetheless, his prescient self in his final plays, which seek to look forward by turning back, to offer therapy for England's "hurt imagination" by plays of restorative power, in particular *Pericles* (published 1609) and *The Winter's Tale* (1610–1611). I devote this section to reflection on the final scene of *The Winter's Tale*.[24]

The Winter's Tale is not an explicitly religious play—it is, indeed, set strategically in a pagan universe, apparently uncomplicated by the agonies of early seventeenth-century Christian theology. What we might nonetheless call the "romance theology" of *The Winter's Tale* allows for the restorative recovery not only of Perdita—that which is lost is found—but also, through penitence, of recovery from the "witty tyranny" of paranoia.

Leontes, and everyone subject to him, is trapped in the tyrannous grip of a "hurt imagination," or what Paulina calls a "weak-hinged fancy": which "something savours of tyranny" (2.3.118–119). Leontes inverts everything he sees with a fluid yet unhinged rationality, confirming itself at every turn, such that, in his own accurate but ignored self-diagnosis—"All's true that is mistrusted" (2.1.49)—the "center is not big enough to bear / A schoolboy's top" (2.1.103–104). This is a vertiginous world from which there seems no

escape, so tyrannously does Leontes's imagination leap to damaging sur-
mise. As Paulina fearlessly tells him when he threatens to have her burned,
"It is an heretic that makes the fire" (2.3.114): Leontes is the source of the
pathology, just as scholarship on iconoclasm frequently makes the point
that the true idolaters were the iconoclasts, so in thrall were they to images that they needed to obliterate them. The liveliness of the image is also
activated by the iconoclast's imagination, standing "in the level of" the iconoclast's "dreams" (cf. 3.2.78).[25]

The precise language of tyranny (language that would be used of Charles
I before long) is used by Leontes: "Our prerogative calls not your counsels"
(2.1.164–165), just as Leontes's passion is explicitly called "tyrannous" (2.3.27).
Like evangelical iconoclasts, Leontes is exhausted by his overwrought
imagination—"Nor night nor day, no rest!" (2.3.1)—and, also like evangelicals, once Hermione is announced dead and he comes to his senses, all
that remains for Leontes is the constant companion of the evangelical
mind-set, despair: "Therefore," says Paulina to the chastened king, "betake
thee / To nothing but despair" (3.2.206–207).

The unjustly accused Hermione avers that only a miracle—"powers
divine" would be capable of breaking into Leontes's closed and claustrophobic world so as to make "tyranny tremble at patience" (3.2.29–30).
When, however, that power divine does arrive in the form of the Delphic
oracle, Leontes immediately dismisses it as "mere falsehood" (3.2.139). But
if divine power cannot cure the wounds inflicted by Leontes's "hurt imagination," Shakespeare does not give up on the possibility of practicing an
alternative cure. In this play he looks not to religion but to the miracle of
performative art to effect the needed therapy.

In the play's last scene, Paulina takes the newly reunited father and
daughter, along with Florizel and Polyxenes, into her "gallery." By the time
this scene was performed for the first time, Elizabethan England had
experienced a fierce program of iconoclasm produced by what Patrick
Collinson, as we have seen, has called an "iconophobic" culture.[26] One inevitable product of that removal of images from churches was a correlative
development of a culture of "art" collecting, and the cultivation of private
collections in domestic spaces.[27] That physical transfer of objects from
Church to private home also necessarily involved a transfer of meaning:
the function of objects changed from cultic to aesthetic.[28] This transfer is

part of a much larger post-Reformation process whereby a new category, Art, must be invented in order to stabilize the destruction of beautiful arte-facts. There is nothing inherently secular about this desire, but the process does express a profound need for a category outside religion to answer to our need for, and love of, artefacts.

This process of moving from what Hans Belting calls the image to the work of Art, from cultic object to aesthetic artefact, is not complete until Kant's *Critique of Judgment* in 1790, even if it is not of course by any means complete then.[29] But Paulina's gallery makes a decisive move within these categories toward the work of art, even if in her case the resonance with the religious image is so much more powerful. Paulina—a kind of stage and gallery director in this multimedia performance—takes care to neutralize fears about unnatural magic of the kind Spenser feared in art making: as Hermione starts to move, Paulina says that "her actions shall be as holy as / You hear my spell is lawful" (5.3.104–105).

Leontes describes the event, as it is happening, in terms of performative magic: "O royal piece," he exclaims, "there's magic in thy majesty, which has / My evils conjured to remembrance" (5.3.38–40).[30] So too do many aspects of Paulina's gallery, and the showing within it, evoke religious forms, now described as magic in evangelical polemic: like Christ before the litur-gical resurrection of Easter Day, the "statue" of Hermione is hidden behind a curtain before her own resurrection; Hermione is, for the audience on and off stage, resurrected; the gallery in which Hermione is displayed is suddenly called a "chapel" (5.3.86); and just before Paulina commands Hermione to descend, she calls for the precondition of faith from her audience: "It is required / You do awake your faith" (5.3.94–95).[31] Above all, Perdita approaches the statue as a living embodiment of her mother in such a way as almost to produce the performative effects of bringing the statue to life:

> And give me leave,
> And do not say 'tis superstition, that
> I kneel and then implore her blessing. Lady,
> Dear Queen, that ended when I but began,
> Give me that hand of yours to kiss.
> (5.3.42–46)

Shakespeare does not explicitly label this as religious theater, partly because religious theater was officially prohibited in Elizabethan and Jacobean England.[32] Much more interestingly, Shakespeare stays just on the secular side of specifically nonreligious theater, even as he draws on the profound formal, restorative, and affective resonances of religious theater. All the framing details of the gallery visit are underlined, just as the revivifying effects of specifically aesthetic appreciation of great art are presented onstage in English theater for the first time. We are told the name of the sculptor (i.e. Giulio Romano) (5.2.90)—the only such instance of a named artist in Shakespeare's oeuvre; the statue is referred to as a work of art—as a "statue," a "piece," a "work" (5.2.88–91); we are told where the artefact is in the gallery (i.e. behind the curtain in pride of place, 5.3.10); and we are told who owns the "poor image" (i.e. Paulina), "for the stone is mine" (5.3.57–58). And we are also given access to the penetrating, almost idolatrous aesthetic effects of this wondrous art before we know it's not art at all. Leontes is spellbound by the marble, just as Pygmaleon was. Despite the pain of this showing, Leontes begs for more of art's painful homeopathic therapy:

> For this affliction has a taste as sweet
> As any cordial comfort. Still methinks
> There is an air comes from her. What fine chisel
> Could ever yet cut breath? Let no man mock me,
> For I will kiss her.
>   (5.3.76–79)

In sum, Shakespeare is deliberately *not* trying to reintroduce the religious by the back door, as it were, even if he most definitely is drawing on the resurrective resonances of late medieval religious liturgy, theater, and art.[33] Shakespeare knows, well before the convulsions of absolutist evangelical iconoclasm had run their revolutionary course—even, indeed, while they were running that destructive course—that resurrection needs something from outside the closed regime of evangelical religion: therapeutic resurrection needs the new experience of animating likeness we now call Art. The romance had seemed over before the statue, said to be "newly performed," or finished, is displayed. But only the work of art, through its ongoing performance, can bring the play to its own, revivifying end. That which had been lost—the work of art—is found again.

11

One Last Iconoclastic Push?

TRANSFORMATIVE REVOLUTIONS take a long time to settle down into manageable form. (My rule of thumb is 150 years.) The demanding and usually destructive cultural practices they unleash take a long time to achieve sustainable form. In the case of iconoclasm, one can isolate a classic sequence of phases in what might be called the kinesis of iconoclasm: material iconoclasm; mental iconoclasm; resurgence of prohibited images; further, more violent iconoclasm; and, finally, the gallery, the art market, and the art museum. The process by no means ends in the art museum, since it is only provisionally stabilized there. Shakespeare certainly points to the proto-liberal point of stabilization as Hermione steps out in 1610 from the gallery into our lives. But the process of stabilization in England needed at least one further bout of violent iconoclasm before that solution could gain traction.

In this chapter I look to two last iconoclastic pushes, produced by two great writers. Mighty Milton's last act is a hard push against the world's idolatry, both religious and political, seeking once again to transform that inveterate world. Tortured Bunyan, by contrast, pushes mightily against himself, as he seeks to abandon the idolatrous world of Vanity Fair altogether.

I

The need for more psychic and material purging was felt from the beginning of the revolutionary decade. Thus an anonymous text published in 1642, *The Crosses case in Cheapside,* justified the illegal defacement of the cross in Cheapside with a trial of sorts, in which the cross speaks in its own defense. The case for the prosecution insists that the real work of idolatry destruction is psychological; that work can only be effected by destruction of the material cross. The iconoclasts mistakenly think that "the main and chief work" is complete with material destruction. Not so, alas: "the hardest part of the work is" ahead: "all the defiling hitherto is done by the hand; now the *heart* must bee employed too, and then the work will be done indeed."[1] The work is not easy, since the heart will not yield its imaginations without a desperate fight; it will defend, it says,

> my strong holds there (the house of my Images, and guardians
> thereof) with my *Imaginations* and every thing that exalteth itself.
> The heart will stick here, nay it will die here before it will yield . . .
> up its Idol. (image 41)

In Book 5 of the *Faerie Queene*, Spenser had prophesied this further, more violent purifying stage of the process with his figure of Talus, the servant of Artegall, who represents Justice. In Book 2 of the *Faerie Queene*, Guyon and Redcross had attempted to manage Archimago by hard psychological handling. Those attempts had failed, since by Book 5 the struggle against ever resurgent idolatry remains unfinished; it is just as urgent as it had been in Books 1 and 2. Now, however, the struggle is external, and the weapons promise a clean sweep. Talus, who is made of iron, is armed with an iron flail; he is "Immoueable, resistlesse, without end." So there in Book 5, Canto 9, the hero Artegall and his cyborg Talus seek to destroy the protean Malengin (bad imagination), even as the imagination transforms into various creatures and natural forms before being trapped as a snake, and crushed by the unstoppable Talus, "that all his bones, as small as sandy grayle / He broke, and did his bowels disentrayle."[2]

In 1649 Milton was minded of Talus, and sought to fulfill Spenser's dream of the definitive solution for idolatry. His problem was more difficult, since he needed to grapple not only with religious idolatry but also, within the logic of permanent revolution's scope creep, with largely new forms of imagined idolatry. Milton sees monarchy itself as a form of political idolatry, and his *Eikonoklastes* (1649) champions regicide as an act of iconoclasm. Milton's title answers to that of the massively successful book published under Charles I's name earlier in the same year, *Eikon Basilike,* the *Image of the King.* Milton thinks the title of King Charles's book is perfect, since "by the shrine he dresses out for him, certainly would have the people come and worship him."[3] Milton's own book is, accordingly, entitled *Eikonoklastes,* the "famous surname of many Greek Emperors, who in their zeal to the command of God, after long tradition of Idolatry in the Church, took courage, and broke all the superstitious Images to peeces" (p. 343).

With just over a century of failed iconoclasm behind him, and with the targets of idolatry attack ever expanding, Milton accordingly longs for Talus *redivivus,* for one last, definitive push, and one very significant extension of the definition of idolatry, into the political, so paving the way for what to us are more recognizable forms of revolutionary iconoclasm, as in the French Revolution, for example. Milton wishes into being a "man of Iron, such as Talus, by our poet Spencer," who was "feigned to be the page of Justice, who with his flail could do all this, and expeditiously, without all those deceitful forms and circumstances of Law, worse than ceremonies in Religion." If he could wish such a pitiless iconoclastic creature of emergency into existence, then, says Milton, "I say send it down, whether by one Talus, or by a thousand" (p. 390).[4]

Another figure who, like Milton, was in late 1648 dismissive of "those decietful forms and circumstances of Law," or, rather, zealous in prosecution of Old Testament law, was one Henry Ireton. In early 1649 Ireton would sit on the committee that sentenced Charles I to death. In December 1648 he is recorded as judging that those guilty of idolatry in 1648 were no less worthy of the death sentence than idolaters in ancient Israel. "What," he asks, "should exempt the magistrate under the Gospel from punishing idolaters, what . . . should deter him from punishing them with death or other punishment?"[5] This is severe, to be sure, especially so when one remembers that idolatry is, as Voltaire pointed out, a charge only ever laid against another, never claimed by a practitioner.[6] Ireton defends the severity by appeal to its punishment as defined by the Old Law: "We shall desire no more than this ground of it [idolatry] made it sin, and the ground of the punishment, do remain the same now, then the sin is to be restrained as it was then, and that which was sin then, is sin now."[7]

Talus figures were indeed unleashed by the Civil War Parliament. In 1641, 1643, and 1644 Parliament produced legislation designed to repeat and extend all previous iconoclastic legislation since 1538. The 1641 "Order for the Suppression of Innovations" targeted crucifixes and "scandalous pictures of any one or more persons of the Trinity, and all images of the Virgin Mary";[8] 1643 ordered removal and / or destruction of all fixed altars, altar rails, chancel steps, and of "all crucifixes, crosses, and all images and pictures [including images in glass] of any one or more persons of the Trinity, or of the Virgin Mary and all other pictures of saints or superstitious inscriptions in or upon all and every church";[9] and in 1644 the scope creep moved to include pictures and representations of "any angel or saint," all church organs and organ cases, and all religious images in open space. The organs "shall be taken away, and utterly defaced, and none other hereafter set up in their places."[10] The attack on organs is striking enough, but the principal novelty here is the massive locational extension of the idolatrous image: no longer restricted to churches, the legislation applied to "any open space within this kingdom."[11] From 1643 some of this work was enacted by the Committee for the Demolition of Monuments of Superstition and Idolatry in Westminster and London, under the chairmanship of Sir Robert Harley.

The Earl of Manchester issued a warrant to one William Dowsing, of uncertain authorization, on 19 December 1643, to set this ordinance into action.[12] Dowsing's response was rapid and vigorous. He set to work on the chapels of various Cambridge colleges, but he assiduously also covered much of East Anglia. Of the 245 parish churches Dowsing visited, he destroyed more than 90 percent of the images. Dowsing's energetic application, minutely recorded by him, was but one example of a much larger campaign. Every parliamentary soldier had been both justified and primed to take the iconoclastic law into his own hand. Thus *The Souldiers Catechism* (1644) imagines the iconoclastic soldier faced by a question about the legality of independent image breaking: "Is it well done of some of your Soldiers (which seem to be religious) to break down Crosses and Images where they meet with any?" The prepackaged answer is that, while nothing should be "done in a tumultuous manner," the military is indeed justified in dismissing Milton's "deceitful forms and circumstances of Law," since they see themselves doing God's work that had been neglected by the magistrates:

> But seeing God hath put the Sword of Reformation into the Soldiers' hand, I think it is not amiss that they should cancel and demolish those Monuments of Superstition and Idolatry, especially seeing the Magistrate and the Minister that should have done it formerly, neglected it.[13]

Of course the matter was in fact often handled in a "tumultuous manner." Iconoclasts in both Norwich and Canterbury Cathedrals, for example, targeted both Laudian innovations along with the Edwardian service books, not to speak of the cathedrals themselves (the seat of the hated bishops, who would be abolished in 1646). Thus in September 1642 at Canterbury Cathedral, a letter by the sub-dean of Canterbury Cathedral, Thomas Paske, gave an eyewitness account of the targeted attack on the sacral fabric of the cathedral on August 26, 1642. The revolutionary soldiers "defaced the goodly screen ... violated the monuments of the dead, spoiled the organs ... and ... mangled all our service books, and books of Common Prayer."[14] The bishop of Norwich, Joseph Hall (d. 1656), already a victim of Milton's fury in 1641 and 1642, and a victim of the Act for the Sequestration of the Property of Malignants (April 1643), recounts a further, carnivalesque and parodic assault on Norwich Cathedral in 1643:

> Lord, what a work was here, what clattering of Glasses, what beating down of Walls, what tearing up of manuscripts, what pulling down of seats, what resting out of irons and Brass from the Windows and Graves, what defacing of Arms, what demolishing of curious Stonework ... what Tooting and Piping upon the destroyed Organ Pipes, and what hideous Triumph on the Market-day before all the Country, when in a kind of Sacrilegious and profane procession, all the Organ Pipes, Vestments ... together with the Leaden Cross ... were carried to the Fire in the public Market-Place.[15]

Faced with resurgent and the widening scope of iconoclasm in the English Revolution proper, those of evangelical temper were faced by two possibilities: either a mighty, final clean sweep of the empire of material imagistic signs, by way of transforming the idolatrous world on the one hand, or total abandonment of that idolatrous world on the other. These choices became especially acute after the final failure of the Revolution in 1660. In Milton and Bunyan, we see figures who chose one or other of these possibilities. Milton chose to imagine more outer iconoclasm, while Bunyan struggles in agony to abandon the idolatrous world altogether. I take these exemplary figures in turn.

II

In *Paradise Lost* the battle for jurisdictions is on again, though this time in the knowledge that the battle will be lost. The poet predicts in Book 1 how the fallen angels will repopulate the geography of the Land of Canaan with local idols. The poem starts with a characteristic revolutionary aspiration, that the wicked of the past be "blotted out and razed" (1.362); no sooner, however, is the aspiration for that *damnatio memoriae* expressed than we learn that these angels will soon be repopulating Canaan (1.375–527), as animated idols.[16] Milton thus recognizes that the long history of idolatrous backsliding recounted in the Book of Kings is uncontainable: it started in earliest Hell, and, implicitly, continues in postrevolutionary England.

   After the loss of Paradise and the failure of the Revolution in 1660, revolutionaries and evangelicals of all stripes reverted to postures of recusancy and / or lonely imagination. In John Milton's brilliant poetic drama *Samson Agonistes* (published in 1671), and in my view quite certainly Milton's farewell to the world, Milton chose to imagine himself in heroic, lonely, destructive material action against the idolaters. In his prologue he cites Aristotle's transactional account of the effect of tragedy on an audience: he rehearses the standard position cogently: by "raising pity and fear, or terror," tragedy purges "the mind of those and such-like passions, that is to temper and reduce them to just measure with a kind of delight."[17] By this criterion, however, it seems to me that *Samson Agonistes* fails entirely, partly because the poem is not transactional or even persuasive in ambition at all, but rather an apologia located wholly in aged, blind, heroic Milton's refusal to submit to failure.

   There is, however, a further reason why *Samson Agonistes* will not effect any catharsis in its audience: whereas the poem presents the Philistines as both Samson's enemies and enemies of Israel, the poem effectively addresses many of its own readers as enemies, who have submitted to the return of the king. The poem, that is, is delivered not into a situation of national war, but rather to a divided, post–civil war readership. It expresses a profound desire to destroy its own idolatrous readership, those who have bowed before the restored monarchy. Milton himself, as Samson, remains wholly untouched by fears of inner, psychic idolatry; he therefore directs his tremendous animus against idolatry in all its forms outwardly, in one last imagined, longed for, and completely destructive push against the columns of both state and state religion.[18]

Samson's position fairly brims with intense and painful echoes of Milton's own biography. Like Milton at one point or another in his life, Samson is blind, at least once unhappily married, and defeated. The Chorus comment magnificently on the Philistine giant warrior Harapha, "his giantship . . . somewhat crestfall'n" (l. 1244). This line could easily apply both to Samson, and also to Milton in the 1660s, subject to the humiliations inflicted by noble idolaters, as they celebrate their victory. At poem's start Samson sits where Milton had found himself sitting at many points in his career—dismissing the "people" as addicted to idolatrous slavery of sorts: "This day a solemn Feast the people hold / To *Dagon* thir Sea-Idol, and forbid / Laborious works, unwillingly this rest / Thir Superstition yields me" (*SA* 12–15). Across his career, Milton had frequently described himself as Samson describes himself—alone, in prison of sorts (here a real prison), among slaves, and conscious of the apparent failure of his destiny to liberate those very people whom he dismisses with such confident repudiation: "Promise was that I / Should *Israel* from *Philistian* yoke deliver; / Ask for this great Deliverer now, and find him / Eyeless in *Gaza* at the Mill with slaves, / Himself in bonds under *Philistian* yoke" (*SA* 38–42).

Samson blames himself for the fact that the Philistines are so flagrantly worshipping the idol Dagon on account of their victory over himself (*SA* 435–448). Like Milton, however, Samson emphatically does not question himself, remaining wholly confident in the probity of his rejection of idolatry and its attendant slavery; he resists appeals to accommodate the idolaters, to prostitute "holy things to idols" (*SA* 1358). Those at fault are his two wives, especially Dalila; Israel itself for not having taken advantage of his, Samson's, strength (*SA* 242–249); and, by no means least, the superstitious people.

In Milton's context of 1671, those superstitious people are not foreigners, but rather fellow English readers. If we are permitted to hear Milton's grieved and rancorous voice through Samson's, then we hear Milton blaming his readership, castigating his own people for loving "bondage more than liberty,/Bondage with ease than strenuous liberty" (SA 270–271). Not only that; much more than that: we hear how Samson brings iconoclastic destruction down upon the idolaters, and we witness the imagination of Milton destroying not, as I say, foreign enemies as Samson does, but his own countrymen through an act of anti-idolatry terrorism:[19]

> As with the force of winds and waters pent,
> When Mountains tremble, those two massie Pillars
> With horrible convulsion to and fro,
> He tugg'd, he shook, till down they came and drew
> The whole roof after them, with burst of thunder
> Upon the heads of all who sate beneath,
> Lords, Ladies, Captains, Councellors, or Priests,
> Thir choice nobility and flower, not only
> Of this but each *Philistian* City round.
>   (SA 648–656)

Revolutionary Milton, then, remains unwaveringly true to the revolutionary impulse violently to purge the material realm of all idolatrous forms, with accompanying violence against people if necessary. As we move toward the end of our Reformation centuries, we end with Bunyan, who provides a very different, more inwardly tortured instance—the inability to purge the psyche of all idolatrous forms.

III

Bunyan's Christian and Faithful in *The Pilgrim's Progress* (first published 1678) must, near the end of Christian's journey, pass through Vanity Fair on their way to the Celestial City. Everything is on sale at the fair, including all sorts of *Vanity*, and it lasts all year long:

> Therefore at this Fair are all such Merchandise sold, as Houses,
> Lands, Trades, Places, Honours, Preferments, Titles, Countries, King-

doms, Lusts, Pleasures, and Delights of all sorts, as Whores, Bawds,
Wives, Husbands, Children, Masters, Servants, Lives, Blood, Bodies,
Souls, Silver, Gold, Pearls, precious Stones, and what not.[20]

This is an arrestingly broad category of earthly engagements. Not only
must Christian avoid the obvious snares of "Whores, Bawds"—snares of
the kind one might expect in allegorical, spiritual narratives of worldly
danger. Without syntactic pause, however, as part of the very same list of
snares, Christian must also avoid "Wives, Husbands, Children, Masters,
Servants, Lives, Blood, Bodies, Souls . . . and what not." On the face of it,
this list is shocking, since families are categorized in exactly the same class
as family destroyers. Christian must repudiate them all.

The context gives the reader a momentary respite of sorts from this
shock: items in this list are only to be rejected as long as they are on sale
in Vanity Fair. Only as long, we are permitted momentarily to think, as
"Wives, Husbands, Children," for example, are treated as commodities, are
they to be rejected. That momentary respite (of sorts—are we really expected to reject our families?) does not, however, last long: the list effectively includes the absolutely necessary worldly entanglements with which
almost all social creatures will need to contend one way or another—
"Houses, Lands, Trades, Places," not to speak of the latter, more fundamental categories "Lives, Blood, Bodies, Souls." These last are shockingly
classed along with obviously dangerous enticements "Silver, Gold, Pearls,
precious Stones," before the entire list, the sum of earthly engagements
without which no social creature will be able to survive, is all tossed aside
with the dismissive and most terrible dismissal of all: "and what not." This
ruthless list offers nowhere and no way to cultivate earthly existence of any
kind.

As unwilling consumers at Vanity Fair, Christian and Faithful face the
apparent and relatively minor charge of disturbing the peace (a misde-
meanor) in the court of Lord Hate-Good. The spiritual tenor of the allegorical vehicle takes over, however, and produces a charge of heresy as
treason (a capital offense), for which Faithful is tortured and then burned
at the stake. In the religious allegory, the real charge is not disturbing the
peace, but the capital crime of resisting the law of Vanity Fair, and thereby
not committing the required idolatry. When Lord Hate-Good instructs the

jury, he reminds them of the law requiring idolatrous worship, a law with especial poignancy for Bunyan, who had chosen prison (a twelve-year confinement) in 1661, even before the Act of Uniformity of 1662, in part out of his refusal to accept the *Book of Common Prayer* ("a mere human invention and institution").[21] Lord Hate-Good recalls what for Bunyan would have been the Biblical types of English laws concerning observance of state church worship, most recently (by the publication of *The Pilgrim's Progress*) in the 1662 Act of Uniformity:

> There was also an Act made in the days of *Nebuchadnezzar* the Great, another of his Servants, that whoever would not fall down and worship his Golden Image, should be thrown into a Fiery Furnace. There was also an Act made in the days of *Darius,* that whoso for some time called upon any God but him should be cast into the Lions' Den. (p. 112)

Bunyan's Vanity Fair list, then, is a summary—startling in its limitless extension—of the sources of idolatry. In the context of Vanity Fair, the list certainly points to critique of consumerism as idolatrous—worshipping goods as gods—that will have a long future before it.[22] The tradition behind this list is, however and obviously, the broader Biblical prohibition against worshipping false gods. The remarkable and disquieting feature of Bunyan's list is, as I say, that it effectively tars all earthly practice with the brush of idolatry.

From the beginnings of European monasticism in the sixth century, monks sought to flee entirely the world and its entanglements. That demanding tradition was designed for spiritual athletes, who were capable of sustaining the extreme pressures of life in the heavenly Jerusalem of the monastery. With Bunyan, more than a millennium later, we can see a much broader tendency at work in the passage from the later Middle Ages to the early modern period: the extreme, world-renouncing disciplines of the monastery and the contemplative life, to be practiced by regular clergy, are now adopted by the laity in the active life.[23] Christian's narrative begins, indeed, in flight from family and the entire City of Destruction. Everyone who belonged to the early modern priesthood of all believers was monasticized, not so much a secular priest but a secularized monk.

In this and the previous two chapters we have seen how English evangelical culture could have arrived at such an extreme account of what was idolatrous. With Shakespeare we have seen how English culture could survive that monastic regime applied to the life of the laity, now known as the priesthood of all believers. In the eighteenth century especially, English culture, along with other northern European Protestant cultures, invented the category of Art, subtended by the discourse of the aesthetic, and the institution of the art gallery, to save itself from the destructive internal logic of labelling all earthly existence as idolatrous.[24] On the way to that provisional solution, however, we have seen that the destructive revolutionary energies of iconoclasm and idolatry pursuit are ever-ready to spring into action, with ever wider targets, both external and internal, both material and immaterial.

To describe the way those energies have inflected history following the Protestant Reformation turns out to be a vast subject. The kinesis of revolutionary iconoclasm never settles into manageable form. It turns out to shape national cultural histories born of revolutionary epochs (e.g. France, China); colonial history (e.g. South America); the history of contemporary warfare (e.g. ISIS); and histories of the subject, which must always centrally involve the image. Even if we look no further than the cultural history of Anglo-American cultures since the sixteenth century, the histories of the following cannot be told without reference to the early modern war against idolatry that erupted in the sixteenth-century: the history of the struggle between word and image after the indisputable Reformation victory of the Word; the history of the art gallery, which has simultaneously become a place of asylum for the image, but also the space in which the ripple effect of unending iconoclasm is played out in manageable ways; the histories of space and place, in which places of special charisma are destroyed in favor of a homogeneous concept of space, in which charisma is spread evenly across a rationalized jurisdiction, relevant also to the history of abstraction; the history of colonial iconoclasm; and the history of ideology critique, the practice of the intellectual elite designed to target the idols of the credulous tribe. Contemporary evangelical, no less than forms of liberal culture, remain unendingly enthralled to the enormous sways of iconoclasm's kinesis. The art gallery is but one area of relative and highly managed calm.

PART 5

Theater, Magic, Sacrament

12

Religion, Dramicide, and the Rise of Magic

WE ALL KNOW that magic was a key feature of medieval culture. We learned as much from our primary school lessons about the ducking stool as a test for witches in the benighted Middle Ages (if she's not a witch, she sinks; if she is, she floats: lose/lose for the woman in question, and a big loss for the legitimacy of late medieval religion).[1] If we were raised as Protestants, we also learned, or rather imbibed, that Protestantism was more "rational" than a superstitious Catholicism, an idea whose vibrancy extends from the sixteenth century well into our own time.[2]

When we put away childish things, we learned the same lesson as adult scholars. We learned it first from Weber's secularization thesis. Weber certainly did argue for a disenchantment of the world with Protestantism, even if his "rationalization" thesis was frequently misunderstood to be primarily about rationality rather than about bureaucratic "rationalization."[3] In Anglo-American scholarship, we relearned the lesson about the Middle Ages and magic from the main, most influential authority on the subject, Keith Thomas. Thomas's *Religion and the Decline of Magic* (1971) offered an extended reformulation of a very old position (i.e. that Protestantism is a "rational" and progressive repudiation of a pre-Reformation mix of magic and religion).

Thomas expresses due scholarly caution about describing the medieval Church as a repository of magical practice: "It would, of course," he says, "be a gross travesty to suggest that the medieval Church deliberately held out to the laity an organized system of magic" (46). Having cautioned against the gross travesty, however, Thomas goes on to recommit it. The following citations are all taken from within a narrow set of page extents: "the medieval Church did a great deal to weaken the fundamental distinction between a prayer and a charm" (42–44); "The medieval Church thus appeared as a vast reservoir of magical power . . ." (45); "Nonetheless, there were several circumstances which helped to consolidate the notion that the Church was a magical agency . . ." (47); "The Church's magical claims were also reinforced by its own propaganda . . ." (48).

By the time we reach the last of these claims, the word "deliberately" in the first has been disabled: if, that is, the Church did practice magic, but not "deliberately," what force can the word "propaganda" in the final citation have? Propaganda is nothing if not deliberate. Almost all Thomas's evidence about medieval black magic is taken uncritically from proto-Protestant or Protestant sources, just as his understanding of magic is grounded in a Protestant understanding of the performative as magical (thus allowing him to describe therapeutic and sacramental practice as "magical"). His recognition that early modern Protestants were themselves superstitious is accounted for as a hangover of medieval obscurantism. If Protestants were superstitious, then that was a medieval inheritance.

In short, the medieval and irrational magic fit hand in glove, or did so until recently, when the glove started to come off. In the last two decades, scholars have taken issue with Thomas's thesis. Alexandra Walsham's extraordinarily generous bibliographical essay, "The Reformation and the Disenchantment of the World," reviews the entire range of ways in which the Thomas position has been nuanced if not outright questioned, including the idea that Protestantism was any more "rational" than late medieval Catholicism. (There is nothing especially "rational" about predestination, even if it is a perfect example of perfect rationalization in the Weberian sense.)[4] Euan Cameron's recent *Enchanted Europe* (2010) also offers a much more nuanced account of the history of superstition.[5]

Neither of these scholars has, however, gone as far as I'd like to go in this chapter: so far from replacing pre-Reformation spirituality with a more "rational" religion, it is more nearly the case—or so I contend here—that the Reformation *reinvented* black magic. Reformation evangelicals reinvented black magic from a late Antique and early Christian cultural model, which described the practices of pagan religion as obscurantist magic.[6] Gothic horror is not, that is, gothic at all; it is instead early modern horror. Calvinist evangelicals in England targeted black magic not long, indeed, before the phrase "black magic" is first recorded by the *OED*, in Spenser's *Faerie Queene*, in 1590: "By strong enchauntments and blacke Magicke leare [lore]."[7]

Why should evangelical religion have revived the charge of black magic with such intensity? These chapters argue that evangelicals invented black magic primarily because they needed to attack Catholic sacramental practice, in which performative language (e.g. *"Hoc est enim corpus meum"*) makes something happen between earth and heaven. The Catholic Mass in particular needed to be described as juggling magic or as "hocus pocus" (plausibly a deliberate, mocking corruption of *"hoc est corpus meum,"* first attested earlier than the *OED*'s record of 1624).[8] This attack also applied to other sacraments, and from there extended to denigrate the entire Catholic Church, as William Perkins put it in his *Golden Chaine* (first published 1591): "And surely, if a man will but take a view of all poperie, he shall easily see, that the most part is meere Magique."[9]

Cultural history has rightly stressed that one of the key linguistic differences between pre- and post-Reformation cultures is that between allegory and literalism.[10] That is indeed a powerful and telling distinction, to which we will turn in Chapter 15. Single-minded focus on that important linguistic distinction should not, however, distract us from another linguistic distinction dividing pre- and post-Reformation cultures, that between performative and denotative language.

Performative liturgical and sacramental language is transactional: it presents itself as an action that might make something new happen between heaven and earth, in the here and now of its performance. If performative words are transactional acts, they thereby run directly counter to the linguistic predicament of Calvinism. With regard to God at least, the premise of transactional language is always already broken for the Calvinist, since there can be no transactions with the Calvinist *deus absconditus.* That God has already made all the irrevocable decisions in the very first place, before the creation of the world. Sacraments can change nothing. Evangelical religion drastically demotes performative language, then, in favor of denotative language. Performative language ends up, in fact, either in hell or "the Middle Ages," as black magic. One impulse of this and the following two chapters is, then, to reverse Thomas's title: not *Religion the Decline of Magic*, but a chapter whose theme is (evangelical) religion and the rise of (black) magic.

Fear of linguistic performativity in all its forms produces, in part, those putative specialists at performative language, "witches"; persecution of those new made witches is, accordingly, another specifically early modern phenomenon. Revolutionary orders habitually project their own embarrassing abject back onto the benighted, repudiated order. Once the new order has conjured its enemy, it must promptly retroject that abject back onto the previous, repudiated dispensation. Early modern black magic and witches are not, in short, medieval hangovers; they are, instead, much more authentic creations and retrojections of early modernity itself. Early modern religion needed to invent black magic as a parody of the Eucharist. It also needed, simultaneously, to disown that invention, by claiming that black magic and witches came from somewhere else (i.e. the late medieval Church).

This is obviously a huge topic. To look no further than the historical focus on the persecution of witches, it's also a site of intense if inconclusive historical labor.[11] In this chapter I narrow the subject by focusing on the effect of magic's rise, in early modernity, on theater. The theatrical space is delimited, to be sure, but also especially telling, since drama, perhaps even more than lyric, is the performative genre par excellence: drama depends on performative language (language making things happen in and on the world of the stage), and therefore has intimate connections with liturgy and sacramentality. The very etymology of "liturgy" ("public work") points both to its inherently public status and to its work in the world.[12]

My fundamental argument is that, as early modern fears of sacramental and black magic rose, so too did drama fall, or at least shrank its own magic circle. The immediate victim of evangelical horror at performative sacramentality in Protestant Europe was, of course, the Catholic Eucharist, with its real presence; the next victims were many old women, persecuted as witches. That same horror of performativity had, however, a further collateral cultural victim, which was theater.

The English stage took many centuries to recover from the banishment of the Biblical, and of religion generally, from the stage (legislation prohibiting Biblical matter on the English stage, first enacted in 1559, was not fully repealed until 1968).[13] In this chapter, I take the story up to the beginning of the reign of Elizabeth (1558). Chapter 13 narrates the evangelical persecution of witches and the correlative evangelical prosecution of theater in early modern England. Chapter 14 turns to the production and shrinkage of drama itself, from Marlowe and Shakespeare to Milton.

I

Evangelical religion was inherently hostile to drama for many reasons. These objections were most obviously moral (the theater promoted gender-bending, hypocrisy and licentiousness), but evangelical hostility, not to say horror at theater ran deeper than moral objection. Drama is most deeply committed to action, works, acts; evangelical religion denies human agency, and altogether dismisses acting (in both senses) as a way of accruing merit. Further, evangelical insistence on the absolute primacy of the pre-scripted Word above merely human invention sets Calvinism on a collision course with the improvised effects of theater. Yet further still, religious theater offends the Calvinist understanding of idolatry. Late medieval street theater could represent God (father and son), as often, for the son, as twenty-five times in a single day, played by different local artisans / actors.[14] This set pre-modern theater on a collision course with Calvinism's hostility to idolatry, or the merely human and imagined material forms that promised access to the transcendent.[15]

Perhaps, however, the deepest motive for evangelical hostility to theater is ontological: theater, like the Mass, stages the performative—words making something happen in the world. Theater works as a look-alike to the Mass (or vice versa), using words, staging, movement, and costume to underwrite and guarantee the performative happening.[16] Theater presents itself as "play," while never abandoning the claim that, by taking a holiday from work, in play, we might make something serious, even sacral, happen.

Theater, then, plays with and around the liturgical and sacramental. The Mass and the theater were also two of the highest profile, indisputably mass media performance events of early modern Europe (royal entries being another example). In Reformation Europe, indeed, the conditions of theater sometimes looked like liturgy precisely because the costumes had been repurposed from one (liturgy) to the other (theater).[17]

The set of evangelical threats to theater articulated in the last few paragraphs inhabits the theater itself in various ways, but the ontological objection that theater is a kind of lethal magic, just like the Mass, is the deepest and most generative challenge and/or opportunity for playwrights. In response to it, theater produced some extraordinary, brilliant dramatic responses, each of which presents as a kind of last call for theater, before evangelicals finally succeeded in closing theaters in 1642. The fall of drama from the 1570s was by no means unbroken, punctuated as it was by exceptionally brilliant last calls. Elizabethan theater was, however, part of a larger cultural trajectory, the overall effect of which would diminish and contain theater's power.

There has been some extraordinary work on magic and sacramentality in early modern drama, notably by Stephen Greenblatt.[18] Because, however, literary history tends to work within tightly periodic schemata (late medieval *or* early modern), there has been relatively little cross-periodic work on the genesis of magic in Anglo-American theatrical culture. This is a lost opportunity, for two reasons: on the one hand drama, above all, depends on performative language (language making things happen on the world of the stage), and, on the other, because the cross-periodic purview brings some striking features freshly into view.

In this chapter, therefore, I'll look to English dramatic history *across* the fifteenth and into the sixteenth centuries, a move that is especially appropriate since fifteenth-century drama continued to be performed throughout the sixteenth century, in one of the longest running shows in English theatrical history (each year, for approximately two hundred years, from at least the late fourteenth to the late sixteenth century, when the mystery plays were closed down). In powerful ways, late medieval is early modern theater.[19] When we set these finally simultaneous performances (mystery plays and sixteenth-century evangelical theater) in tandem, we are struck by something hidden in plain sight. Despite our deep-set persuasions about the identity of magic and the medieval, we understand that medieval drama manages performative magic with confident and sometimes comic ease, whereas early modern, Protestant drama is frequently tortured by it.

II

The intimate connection between sacramentality and theater was the premise of the vast, most ambitious and enduring theatrical phenomenon of the later Middle Ages, the Corpus Christi cycle drama that stood immediately behind Elizabethan theater. That cycle drama seems certainly to have emerged from liturgical drama—the *Quem Quaeritis?* (Whom do you seek?) of the Easter service, in which Mary Magdalen seeks the now risen body of Christ.[20] The cycle drama as it evolved was played annually; it was staged and played by amateurs (including women actors); it lasted for at least two hundred years in a number of northern cities; it took over the streets of entire cities as the theatrical space; it was free; it performed the entirety of salvation history in one or a few liturgically significant mid-summer days (Corpus Christi Day, or Whitsunday); and it was performed by the set of manufacturing and trade organizations—the crafts, or mysteries, or guilds—who could lay plausible claim to representing a very significant proportion of the working men of a given city.[21]

Like almost all other surviving medieval drama, the cycle plays stood in synergetic, though not at all wholly overlapping, relation with formally ecclesiastical, sacramental practice.[22] The body of Christ, the treatment of the body of Christ, and the brutal or merciful social works provoked by that multiply re-presented body are, in a variety of ways, the consistent focus of this astonishing workers' street theater of salvation history. Like almost all surviving medieval theater, cycle drama understood human identity as, broadly, ecclesiological: these plays direct self-understanding toward communal participation, through the sacraments of penance and the Eucharist especially, in the working body of the Church, very broadly understood. Without being sacraments themselves, they "perform" the origin of two sacraments (Baptism and the Eucharist), and they offer a massive penumbra—as long as a day, as long as world history—for collective participation in sacramentality of sorts. Like the sacraments, they perform representations in both the artistic and ontological senses.

Zwinglian and Calvinist understanding of the sacraments prohibit the very premises of the cycle drama. Apart from substance of the doctrinal splits within Protestantism with regard to the Eucharist, which appeared within the first decades of the Reformation, the very fact of such splits was no basis for communal drama. As Lee Palmer Wandel says, by the time Calvin wrote about the topic (1536), the Eucharist "was increasingly not a moment of unity, not a celebration of the living body of the faithful, but a vortex of dissent" (between Catholicism and Protestantism, and within Protestantism).[23] Only two sacraments (Baptism and the Eucharist) survive the Reformation, and the Eucharist is no longer a way of rechanneling the past into the present through sacramental performance; it is instead, by the Zwinglian account, a purely memorial event, remembering something that happened once, a long time ago, and, by the Calvinist account, an "effectual sign" of grace.[24]

By definitively breaking the nexus of words, performance, history, and presentation, Protestants rendered the specifically theatrical resources and events of cycle drama vulnerable to attack of the kind made by William Prynne in 1633. In his vast anti-theatrical text *Histriomastix*, Prynne argues that "Popish Priests and Jesuits in foreign parts . . . have turned the Sacrament of Christs body and blood into a Mass-play; so they have likewise transformed their Mass itself, together with the whole story of Christs birth, his life, his Passion, and all other parts of their Ecclesiastical service into Stage-plays."[25]

Performativity—words that make things happen in the world—are, then, presented either as divine in late medieval theater, or as diabolical magic in early modern theater. We can turn to exemplary texts to see this in action.

The York Cycle's Creation of Adam and Eve (written probably before 1415) has God conjure the first humans into being by voice alone. Just as he has brought the universe into being through the power of words (Play 2), so too does he conjure humanity forth performatively:

> For this reson and skyll alane [justification][alone]
> I sall make man lyke unto me. [shall]
> Rise up, thou erthe, in blode and bane, [bone]
> In shape of man, I commande the.[26]

Having produced the (presumably) inert forms of both Adam and Eve, God animates them on stage: "Takys now here the gast [spirit] of lyffe / And ressayve [receive] both youre saules of me"(3.41–42).

This is, of course, a biblical and theological moment, expressive of the exclusively creative power of the divine Word. The moment is also, however, a profoundly dramatic one, occurring nearly at the start of an entire day's theater on Corpus Christi Day (which fell between 23 May and 24 June), representing all of salvation history, from the beginning to the end of time. This moment occurs very soon after God has called light into being for the first time, presumably timed to coincide with a May sunrise in York (Play 1.147), and then, in Play 2, after God has called the cosmos into being, "Noght by my strenkyth [strength] but by my stevyn [voice] / A firmament I byd apere" (2.32–33). In this culture, all cosmic and human history, that is, begins with the dramatic act par excellence—the animation of natural forms and then of the first humans by the power of words. God offers the ur-example of the dramaturge's craft, bringing worlds and creatures to life before us, no less than he animates the world of the theater itself, in drama's preferred temporal zone of the present. Drama becomes most fully itself when actors create the illusion that they are not merely repeating lines written offstage, but when, instead, words or actions make other words or actions happen in the here and now—the re-presentation—of the performance. Performance, that is, is most fully itself when it is performative, miraculously taking place on stage as a unique event, *hic et nunc,* whether as the first sunrise or the creation of human beings.

Contrast that fifteenth-century instance of performativity and performance with a mid-sixteenth-century instance, in a play by John Bale, the *Three Laws* (c. 1538). Bale had been commissioned by Vice-Regent Thomas Cromwell to write and stage evangelical plays; *Three Laws* is one of a number of plays (*King John, John Baptist's Preaching, The Temptation of Christ,* and *God's Promises*) Bale wrote, staged, and performed in.[27] As in the York "Creation" play, God the Father starts *Three Laws* too, and his speech is likewise performative. But the performative word is an order: God orders the three laws (of Nature, Moses, and Christ) to step forth, and so they do:

> Steppe fourth ye thre lawes for gydaunce of Mankynde
> Whom most inteyrly in hart we love and faver, [entirely][favor]
> And teach hym to walke accordynge to our mynde.[28]

God calls forth personifications of law; laws are precisely that which pre-exist drama, since they are literally prescriptive and pre-scripted, written

before, and not voiced now. Their appearance on stage as characters announces that the ideal form of this play will be prescriptive declaration,
rather than performative performance. This is a play that, from its opening
at any rate, really should not be a play at all.

It is therefore no accident that the great hero of the play turns out to
be not Christ but Evangelium—a personification of the animated, action-
producing written Word. In this early drama of evangelical modernity,
script preexists and is designed wholly to subsume action. These plays
are so dominated by the authority of Scripture, indeed, that fidelity to
that pre-dramatic text effectively preempts the "unwritten verities" of
the dramatic itself.[29] "Drama" becomes the occasion for Scriptural summary. Deus Pater thus invests Evangelium with its legibility and inde-
structibility at play's end: "Thu [you], lawe of Gospell, though thu [you]
be last of all / In operacyon yet thu art the princypall"(ll. 1896–1897).This
drama produced printed play texts, which is in part simply a matter of
a technological possibility now available, but also totally in keeping
with the specifically, primarily written form that preexists and determines the live performance. Bale as playwright appears in the printed
edition (1548) as an evangelical divine, appropriately carrying a small
bible in hand.[30]

Bale's *Three Laws* does, however, offer a much more profoundly performative moment, when the vice figure Infidelity calls sub-vices Sodomy and
Idolatry into being, in order to attack Natural Law:

> Where are these vyllen knaves, [villanous]
> The devyls owne kychyn slaves,
>> That them I can not se?
>> I conjure yow both here,
> And charge ye to apere,
>> Lyke two knaves as ye be!
>
> *Sodomismus [offstage.]*
> *Ambo* is a name full cleane. [Both]
>> [*as*] *Monachus*
> Knowe ye not what I meane,
>> And are so good a clarke?

Infidelitas
By Tetragrammaton,
I charge ye, apere anon
    And come out of the darke.
    (ll. 222–230)

This is obviously much more seriously performative than God ordering the three laws to appear: Infidelity *conjures* figures, through a spell, to come out of the dark: the words do not merely make something happen in the world, but they bring that something into being, out of the darkness. The spell that works blasphemously deploys the four-letter Hebrew word for God (the Tetragrammaton) as a magic-performing character, simultaneously thereby acknowledging and hollowing out the power of the divine Word. The effect of this conjuration is also performative and bodily: Sodomy and Idolatry produce an infection, and leave Lex Naturae covered in lethal sores.

Why should the fifteenth-century play represent *God* as engaged in performative theater, while the sixteenth-century play reserves performative action for the *vice* figure?

We can broach the question by looking to the well-populated discursive field of sixteenth-century anti-theatricalism. There we observe a sixteenth-century hostility, not to say neurotic fear, of the performative. Bale's identification of the performative, and indeed the theatrical, with the maliciously, magically diabolical finds many echoes in evangelical discourse about the dangers of theater and the Catholic Mass.

As is well-known, despite being often strangely underplayed by scholarship, evangelical hostility to drama is profound and largely consistent across at least three centuries (and possibly beyond) in English culture.[31] From the late fourteenth-century proto-Protestant *Treatise on Miracles Playing,* to the polemics against theater that forced the closure of the mystery cycles in the 1560s and 1570s, to the virulent polemical attacks on urban theater and theatricality in the 1580s, to the vast *Histriomastix* of William Prynne of 1633, which precedes the banning of plays in the London theaters by parliamentary, Presbyterian fiat in 1642, a ban that lasted effectively until 1660:[32] across this long chronology, the set of anti-theatrical evangelical charges is remarkably consistent. Above all, plays are exemplary of hypocrisy (playing someone one is not), and they are idolatrous, treating dead matter as animate.[33] Behind these two mighty attacks—of hypocrisy and idolatry—lie many other explicitly made charges of what I call evangelical dramicide: plays provoke idleness; they involve cross-dressing and gender bending; and they encourage lust.[34]

The figures animated by the conjuration of Bale's Infidelity, along with Infidelity himself, confirm, and conform to, evangelical attacks on drama in just about every way: these vice figures are all hypocrites, maliciously pretending to be ecclesiastics, and dressed, as for example Sodomy is, in the habit of a monk (in precisely the years that monasteries were being destroyed). Their spectacular costumes as actors underline the fact that both the actors *and* the figures they represent are hypocritically dressed to kill. These vice figures are also all idolaters: Infidelity promises to promote idolatry just before he brings Idolatry into a life of maliciously deploying the sacred for financial gain. The figures are also presented as sexually suspect: Infidelity not only promises to promote sodomy (Bale is the first English dramatist to represent Sodomy on stage to my knowledge, soon after the first 1533–1534 statute against "buggery");[35] and Idolatry, once a "he" (and no doubt in reality a "he" as an actor) is now a "she," confirming evangelical fears of actors as gender bending hermaphrodites.

We have, then, something very interesting going on here: the conjuration of Bale's Infidelity introduces the truly dramatic, performative action of the play; but Bale is using drama to *attack* drama, since the vice figures are the most playful, overdressed, morally transgressive—in short, the most theatrical—figures in the play. Their characters evoke intense audience animus, but that very animus can only be turned against their status as actors, and therefore against the very form in which they participate as professional actors.

That vice figures are also the most theatrical figures is also true of fifteenth-century morality plays such as, for example, the lively morality play *Mankind* (between 1464–1479). Not only, however, does Bale build anti-theatricality powerfully into his theater, but he also makes a series of further identifications with the theatrical in ways uncharacteristic of fifteenth-century morality plays. In this play malicious theatricality is further identified with the following cluster of cultural practices: sacramentality; popular therapeutic superstition; and, above all, diabolical magic designed to blind and kill its believers.

Bale's Infidelity is, by definition, unnatural (he sets out to infect the law of Nature).[36] In fact Bale capitalizes on Infidelity's unnatural status to enlarge the very definition of the unnatural and popular medicine. Popular therapeutic practice of the countryside becomes, by definition, unnatural. Infidelity calls upon his helpers, who together constitute a new discursive category of the unnatural. The hermaphroditic figure of Idolatry thus unnaturally couples sacramental practice and rural superstition. She acts in very much the same range of operation as Robin Goodfellow, or Puck:

> With holye oyle and watter,
> I can so cloyne and clatter, [deceive]
> That I can at the latter,
>> Manye suttyltees contrive. [tricks]
> I can worke wyles in battle, [subterfuges]
> If I do ones but spattle [spit]
> I can make corne and cattle,
>> That they shall never thryve.
> Whan ale is in the fatt,
> If the bruar please me natt, [brewer]
> The cast shall fall down flat,
>> And never have any strength.
> No man shall tonne or bake, [make ale]
> Nor meate in season make,
>> But lose hys labour at length.
>
> (ll. 442–457)

Idolatry is to be "decked like an old witch."[37] So far as I know, this is the first appearance of a witch on the English stage, just four years before the first statute against, and specifying capital punishment for, witchcraft, in 1542.[38] Idolatry as witch relies on Catholic sacramental support: "And thys is my commen cast, / To heare Masses first or last, / And the holy frydaye fast" (ll. 503–505). Popular, rural therapeutic practice is being corralled in this play into a new discursive category—that of black magic—along with Catholic sacramentalism.

Idolatry takes us close to ecclesiastical practice; Sodomy, by small contrast, is wholly within the Church. He is costumed "like a monk of all sects,"[39] and takes orders of this kind from Idolatry: "Set thu fourth sacramentals,/Saye dirge, and synge for trentals,/Stodye the Popes decretals,/And mix them with buggerage" (ll. 671–674).

In short, the play redraws the boundaries of the "popular": it places witchcraft and sodomy in the dramatic space reserved by the morality play for immorality, and it contains both idolatry and sodomy under the category of the apparently "popular" figure of Infidelity. Above all, the dramatic and the sacramental are identified with popular superstition and magic.

These identifications are not by any means of course restricted to Bale, though Bale is an especially interesting figure, since, in addition to being an agitprop dramaturge and dramatist, he was also a theological polemicist. In 1552 Bale describes a priest with whom he had a dispute precisely about *Three Laws*. Bale mocks the priest as sacramental player:

> More apish toys & gaudish feats, could never a dysard [jester, player] in England have played (I think) than that apish priest shewed there at the communion. He turned and tossed, lurked and louted, snored and smirted [smirked], gaped and gasped, kneeled and knocked, looked and licked, with both his thumbs at his ears & other tricks more.[40]

In other texts, Bale goes very much further, to describe the Mass not only as theatrical but also as black magic. In *The First Examination of Anne Askew* published in 1547, for example, Bale lets rip with an account of sacramental, Eucharistic witchcraft. Having described the Mass as an "execrable idol," he goes on thus:

> Of popes hath it received disguisings, instruments, blessings, turnings and legerdemayns, with many strange observations borrowed of the Jews and pagans' old sacrifices . . . It hath obtained also to be a remedy for all diseases both in man and beast, with innumerable superstitions else . . . It serveth all witches in their witchery, all sorcerers, charmers, enchanters, dreamers, soothsayers, necromancers, conjurers, cross-diggers, devil raisers, miracle doers, dog-leches, and bawds. For without a Mass, they can not well work their feats.[41] (image 105)

Bale not only describes the Mass as theater and magic. Never one for half measures, Bale goes yet further to posit that the Catholic sacrament is the very condition of all black magical practice.

At this point, we can leave an early modern tradition with a long and especially violent, vicious future ahead of it, in both Europe and New England. As William Perkins was so confidently to argue in his *Golden Chaine* (first published 1591), witches certainly exist, who, by

> Enchantment, or charming, is that, whereby beasts, but especially young children, & men of riper years, are by Gods permission in-fected, poisoned, hurt, bounden, killed, and otherwise molested; or contrarily, sometimes cured of Satan, by mumbling up some few words, making certain characters & figures, framing circles, hanging amulets about the neck, or other parts, by herbs, medicines, and such like trumpery.[42]

III

The contrastive picture I have painted so far is a surprising but simple one: if we restrict ourselves to literate culture, and to the representation of magic on stage (and in literature) up to the end of the reign of Queen Mary (1558), say, then the first phase of Reformation English theater would seem to iden-tify black magic with the following: idolatry; the Catholic Mass; popular superstition regarding herbal remedies; and, finally, theater itself. What connects all these targets is performativity: each regards words as events that change the world.

Are there any fifteenth-century counterexamples (i.e. examples of per-formative magic being targeted on stage)? Fifteenth-century theater was being performed on Corpus Christi Day right up until the late 1560s, when it was banned both by official fiat and local evangelical pressure, in the very years that the London theaters were opening.[43] When, from consideration of Bale's theater, we look back and across to the urban, artisanal cycle plays in order to look out for an intimate connection between performativity and witchcraft, we do indeed see it. In these pre-Reformation plays, however, it's the *vice* figures who attempt to identify the sacramental and the mag-ical. These plays point prophetically, that is, to the way in which the charges of witchcraft and magic are laid against Christ, and against drama itself. And as they point to the potential death of drama, so too do they defend performative drama, in the same way that they defend Christ.

Like the image in religious contexts, drama is always dangerous; all forms of religious drama will, one way or another, register and address the dangers of dramatic re-presentation of the sacred. This is certainly true of the unabashedly drama-hostile theater of evangelicals, but it turns out to be no less true of fifteenth-century cycle drama. The fifteenth-century cycle plays preserve a remarkable, illuminating, unscripted sense of performativity; they preserve the experience of an unscripted, improvised happening on stage, but they do so precisely by repudiating any connection with witchcraft. In these plays the Pharisees accuse Christ of being a witch. Let me turn primarily to the York cycle, and especially to the brilliant York interrogation play, *Christ before Herod,* to substantiate this argument.

In both the York Cycle and the compilation of plays preserved in the Towneley manuscript, the authorities, and especially the Pharisees Caiaphas and Annas (habitually called "bishops"), have a PR problem.[44] Christ is demonstrably a miracle worker. He does so performatively, through the power of words that are themselves events, making things happen in the world. In the York Cycle, Christ raises Lazarus from the dead, for example, through verbal power:

> *Christ: Lazar, veni foras,*
> Come fro thy monument.
>
> *Lazarus:* A, pereles prince, full of pitee,
> Worshipped be thou in worlde alway
> That thus hast schewed thi myght in me.
>   (24.184–188)

The simplest way for the pharisaical-episcopal authorities to deal with these extremely disruptive, very public, and therefore highly embarrassing physical phenomena is to redescribe them: these are no miracles, but charms.

In Christ's trial before Caiaphas and Annas (Play 29), for example, the Pharisees label Christ as a witch: "With wicchecrafte he fares withall," Caiaphas avers with regard to Christ's miracles (29.57). In Play 30, the first of the two "Christ before Pilate" plays, Caiaphas tries to persuade Pilate that Pilate's wife's dream about Christ was sent by a dream-medium, in the manner of Spenser's Archimago, through sorcery: "He with wicche-crafte / this wile has he wrought" (30.294–295). And in *Christ Before Pilate* (2), the so-called York Realist takes up a scene from the apocryphal *Gospel of Nicodemus* in which first the standard soldiers and then the local heavy-weights are all unable to keep their banners standing upright in Christ's presence. As the banners turn, first the soldiers blame the bizarre phenom-enon on magic: "For all our force, in faith, did they fold, / As [if] this war-lock [wizard] worship they would" (33.189–190).[45] At first the Pharisees Caiaphas and Annas try to blame the soldiers, but soon they, too, resort to the charge of magic against Christ: "He enchanted and charmed our knights," says Annas, to be capped by Caiaphas: "By his sorcery, sir— yourself the sooth saw— / He charmed our chevaliers and with mischief enchanted" (33.287–289).

In these plays, then, the charge of witchcraft is certainly in the air, but it's laid by corrupt episcopal figures against *Christ*. The story does not end there, however. When we look to York's *Christ before Herod,* one of the most brilliant plays of all the cycles, we behold a luminous exploitation of *anti-theatricality*, used to finally theatrical effect. In this play the playwright himself paradoxically capitalizes on dramicidal practice to create extraor-dinarily powerful drama.

The play begins with Herod the bully's call for silence—he's off to bed and threatens to execute anyone who disturbs him. At this point he is dis-turbed by the entry of Christ, sent by Pilate for judgment by Herod. With Christ, Herod gets silence indeed, but silence of a kind that disturbs, not to say overturns, power structures. Once flattered by Pilate's emissary, Herod acccepts Christ into his chamber, on the premise that Christ will provide the kind of entertainment that bullies derive from terror. "These games were gradely [well] begun" (31.119), Herod declares once Christ is intro-duced. Even after Christ is strikingly unmoved, and therefore unenter-taining, Herod insists that he'll teach him to provide entertainment: "We shall have good game with this boy" (31.161). Still, the fun just can't get started with such a poor actor: Christ "deafens us with din" (31.189) (the din of total silence, that is). Herod and his henchmen conclude that Christ is overawed by the splendid (theatrical) courtly garments (31.281–283)—their "gay gear," and so decide to dress *him* theatrically. Building on the gospel reference (Luke 23:11), the playwright heightens the theatrical reference by aligning the white robe with that of performing fools. Still, however, the fun just won't start: "We get not a word" (31.362).

Christ is so recalcitrantly untheatrical in this play that one could be forgiven for thinking that the fifteenth-century playwright had imbibed an evangelical *distrust* of drama. For here Christ refuses play. The fulcrum of the play shifts from presenting Christ as expected actor, to Herod as actor. And acting turns out to be the negative of this play: Christ refuses to play, or to act at all. In fact he says nothing throughout the entire performance. Through Herod, the playwright promises a play within a play, with Christ providing the entertainment. Herod gives him a script, but Christ, as wholly recalcitrant nonactor, resolutely refuses to follow it.

If, however, Christ refuses to provide entertainment, he does provide extraordinarily powerful theater, though through the inversion and apparent repudiation of standard theatrical practice. For across the play it's the spectator Herod who becomes the foolish player. And it's Christ who creates the sense of an improvised, performative, sacred event, happening dramatically and unscripted in the here and now of the play itself.

By refusing to play, Christ redraws the jurisdictional boundaries of theatricality itself. For in the face of Christ's deafening silence, and refusal to play the part assigned by his new costume, it is Herod and his henchmen who are themselves finally reduced to the level of the court's unwitting fools, already theatrically dressed as they are. Precisely by attempting to make a spectacle of Christ by having him don a fool's robe, they become the spectacle themselves. There *is* a play within this play, but Christ is its director, and it's a stripped, minimalist theater that rejects the native resources of theater (i.e. dialogue, costume, entertaining action). By realigning the force lines of Herod's theater of trial and torture, Christ realigns the force lines of secular society. Herod's opening boasts of absolute power are dwarfed by the very thing that that pretended power began by demanding: silence.[46]

This is, then, a play of exceptionally powerful theater, but a theater whose power derives from a refusal of the standard terms of theater. Christ seems to act like an evangelical, apparently uninterested in acting, being only himself, unprompted by costume. He also refuses any verbal performativity.

There is nothing remotely magical about his performance. His ostensibly improvised action, however, is powerfully theatrical and performative, in triggering a dynamic that wholly restructures the power relations with which the play begins. That evangelicals might likely have modelled their own accounts of interrogations on plays of this kind seems likely and entirely fit.[47] Christ produces great theater by refusing the bad entertainment of watching someone being bullied. In the larger cultural movement of which this play is a part, Christ saves the magic of pure theater by anticipating, and paradoxically forestalling, attacks on theater. He also, not at all least, illuminates the sacramental sense of the entire cycle, here by having his exposed body totally transform the world around it.

An apparently anti-theatrical Christ, then, produces powerful theater. This fifteenth-century example prophetically underlines the ways in which theater will need to adapt to attacks on magical performativity in Calvinist England, a subject to which we turn in Chapters 13 and 14.

13

Enemies of the Revolution: Magic and Theater

THE FIRST PHASES of the Reformation in England up to the beginning of the reign of Elizabeth in 1558 produced, then, a drama that was hostile to drama. Evangelical anti-theatrical theater has Scriptural text trump theatrical moment, as it invents and then chases performative language of all kinds, both sacramental and magical, from the stage. The denotative Scriptural text aggressively targets and persecutes performative language. Bale takes up drama in order to kill it stone dead.

In Bale's plays Scriptural text prescribes action, wanting nothing more than to close down the improvised, sacral sense of an event taking place in the here and now of the theater. So intense is the anti-theatrical impulse in these scripts that it bundles all the most obviously theatrical resources (i.e. costume, performance, acting, works, and above all performativity) with the sacramental. It then makes the bundle bigger, by wrapping theatricality and sacramentalism up with popular, rural, therapeutic practice. The whole bundle is then labelled "unnatural witchcraft," and ready for disposal. The bundling is itself all very theatrical. The resultant theater is spectacular, lively, and irreverent, targeting as it does no less than the entire Catholic Church, and specifically the performativity of its sacramental system. Theater becomes a brightly painted garbage truck in action, where the garbage is what was, until yesterday, considered sacred.[1] Lively effrontery points, however, to a short life ahead, the half-life remaining to what's left of evangelical theater after this agitprop dump drop.

Early evangelical revolutionary modernity, by this reckoning, was hostile to theater, even when it deployed theater. Bale creates irreverent theater by consuming theatrical resources. The difference with pre-Reformation theater is not, however, absolute: the York *Christ before Herod* can see the writing on the wall; it sees ahead of time that theater has dangerous connections to magic, and so creates powerful theater by apparently abjuring theatrical resources. Either way, theater remains threatened: both sides— pro- and anti-theater—know that theater is dangerous, and both sides generate theatrical effect by undoing theatrical effect. Both sides know that performativity is adjacent to magic, and therefore certainly radioactive; both sides know that performativity is dangerous theatrical stuff if not handled with care.

If evangelical theater had a short life ahead of it, early modern, evangelical pursuit of witchcraft had, by complementary contrast, a long and vibrant life waiting to spring into action. With the reinvention of black magic and the persecution of old women as "witches," along with the persecution of Catholics, early modern England, and then early modern Britain, witnessed the rebirth of what one medieval historian, with reference to the later Middle Ages, has called the "formation of a persecuting society": 191 Catholics were judicially murdered in Elizabethan England—more than any other country in Europe for those decades—while upwards of 500 women were executed for witchcraft in England between 1566 and 1645 (the estimated figure for Scotland is 1,500).[2]

The resurgence and exponential extension of witchcraft persecution in early modern England is far too large a topic for this chapter and the next. We can, however, witness the correlative rise of magic and the attack on performative sacramentality in early modernizing England through the restricted lens of theater. Evangelicals themselves had largely abandoned theater by the end of the sixteenth century, but the vibrant Elizabethan and Jacobean professional theater of London was in no way indifferent to, or untouched by, the rise of magic and the attack on performative sacramentality. Theater could in no way ignore those cultural pressures, not least because theater is, as we have seen in Chapter 12, a para-sacramental space and practice; issues of conjuring life into the collective present of the here and now are existential issues both for Catholic sacramental practice and for theater.

In this and the following chapter, then, I look primarily to the distinctively early modern nexus of the following phenomena across the phases of the English Reformation from 1558 until, and just beyond, the English Revolution of 1649: black magic witchcraft; fear of the sacramental; and theatrical performativity. In this chapter I look to the cultural forces conditioning theater; in Chapter 14, to theater's own response.

I

England's first professional theatre opened, in Whitechapel, in 1567.[3] The staggeringly popular and brilliant theater of Elizabethan London—the theater of Marlowe, Shakespeare, and Jonson, to go no further—is rightly defined as a daring, exhilarating mass cultural phenomenon, whose time had definitely come: in one of Europe's largest cities (population c. two hundred thousand in 1600), on the assumption of full houses, many thousand people per week attended plays, from nearly the entire range of social classes.[4]

The amphitheater playhouses were initially situated near the borders, but outside the jurisdiction of, the City of London, either in Whitechapel (1567) or Shoreditch (1576, 1577) to the east, or across the river in Southwark (1587, 1595, 1599).[5] The hall playhouses, such as Blackfriars to the southwest (1596), were within the city walls, but Blackfriars enjoyed jurisdictional liberty, given its previous function as a friary.[6]

The geographical location of these theaters in the liberties of the city, for the most part just outside the jurisdiction of the City proper, has led some scholars of Elizabethan theater to exaggerate the "liberty" of Elizabethan theater. Stephen Mullaney, for example, declares that "of all the arts, drama is the most social, indeed the most metropolitan."[7] Metropolitan, but, in Mullaney's account, daringly adjacent to the center of power: "popular drama in England emerged as a cultural institution only by . . . dislocating itself from the strict confines of the social order and taking up a place on the margins of society, in the Liberties located outside the city walls."[8]

Mullaney's claims about Elizabethan London theater are vulnerable on at least two counts. First, the claim that theater is "the most metropolitan" of the arts is the mistaken product of a severely foreshortened history of theater in England, which by 1600 was a powerful and various art form of long standing that was increasingly brought into the metropolitan environment only in the 1560s. The opening of the metropolitan London theaters coincides almost exactly with the end of the nonmetropolitan cycles in York (1569), Wakefield (1576), and Chester (1575), which had been in operation for two centuries before the London theaters opened.[9]

Mullaney is also vulnerable on a second count. He is correct to point to the importance of the location of the theaters in the liberties of the city, but the need to carve out artistic "liberty" is itself the product of increasingly invasive government surveillance of theater across the sixteenth century. The London theater was indeed daring, but it was much more closely regulated, and much more closely within sight of royal and civic surveillance, than was the cycle drama of late medieval England. From the beginning of the Reformation in England, royal authority was attentive to what was happening on stage, and in particular with regard to religion. A 1542 statute for the "Advancement of True Religion" prohibited, for example, the printing or playing of any "printed books printed ballads plays rhymes songs and other fantasies" that ran counter to (more conservative) policy introduced since 1539.[10] In 1544 a proclamation expressed concern that "manifold and sundry interludes" were being played "in suspicious, dark, and inconvenient" places in London. All plays were accordingly banned in London, except those performed in the houses of noblemen, the lord mayor, sheriffs, aldermen, and gentlemen, or in the halls of "companies, fellowships or brotherhoods." The only outdoor theater permitted was that sanctioned by historical usage.[11]

This tightening of theatrical regulation continued in the reigns of Edward, Mary, and Elizabeth: an Edwardian proclamation of 1551 declared that all play scripts had now to be approved by the Privy Council; a Marian proclamation of 1553 prohibited the printing and playing of any "interlude" "concerning doctrine in matters now in question and controversy touching the high points and mysteries of Christian religion" without royal license.[12] From an entirely opposed ecclesiological ground, an Elizabethan proclamation of 1559 rehearsed almost exactly the same prohibition of interludes concerning religion: the queen's officers will prohibit interludes "to be played wherein either matters of religion or the governance of the estate of the commonwealth shall be handled."[13] Elizabethan legislation culminated in the extension of the office of Master of the Revels to include licensing of plays in 1581.[14]

The newly centralized metropolitan location of theater in the 1560s and 1570s was clearly the result of many factors—political, economic, social, and religious—but it was also clearly the result of a kind of compromise being worked out. The essence of the compromise, whether or not anyone could have articulated it quite like this at the time, went as follows: bring theater within the orbit of royal protection (even if the City of London does not like it!), cut the religion, and we'll allow it, with due government surveillance. But Elizabethan theater was nonetheless subject to "gradual tightening of government control over all theatrical activity."[15] The no less daring nonmetropolitan cycle plays of pre-Reformation England, which were amateur, nonpaying, and acted in the streets, were based in cities far from central governance. The fact that they survived for forty or so years after the Act of Supremacy itself implies how durably resistant they were to central government control.

None of the legislation from the middle of the sixteenth century designed to govern theater seems to have been aimed at Corpus Christi plays; it had in its sights, rather, the highly polemicized, small-troupe, nonmetropolitan drama of religious policy, of the kind represented by John Bale's drama, which also had the printing press at its disposal. All that changed, however, in the 1560s and 1570s, when the cycle plays were indeed specifically targeted by official central policy.

Despite the fact that scholarship has been strangely reticent to recognize centralized effort to close down the cycle drama, there is no doubt that, even if economic factors may have played a part, central Calvinist ecclesiastical authority (and therefore state authority) certainly aimed to close the cycle drama down in the 1560s and 1570s.[16] Even if, as we have seen, sixteenth-century legislation against religious plays may not have been targeting cycle drama, those plays started to feel evangelical pressure from the middle of the sixteenth century. Already in 1548 certain cycle plays (i.e. the Death, Assumption, and Coronation of the Virgin) deemed to be especially offensive to the theological line of the Edwardian regime were suppressed in York. They were definitively suppressed in 1561 after having been reinstated under Queen Mary.[17]

Theatrical treatment of the sacraments was in particular a key factor in provoking the ire of central authority. In 1548, early in the reign of Edward VI, the city of Hereford voted to cease performance of "diverse pageants of ancient histories in the procession in the said city upon the Day and Feast of Corpus Christi."[18] A document of 1576, from the Diocesan Court of High Commission, points to problems with the representation of the sacraments in the so-called Towneley cycle: "There are many things used" in those plays that "tend to the derogation of the Majestie and glorie of God, the pro-phanation of the sacramentes, and the mayteynaunce of superstition and idolatrie." The Commissioners therefore direct the citizens of Wakefield that

> no pageant be used or set forth wherein the Majesty of God the Father, God the Son, or God the Holy Ghost, or the administration of either the sacraments of baptism or of the Lord's Supper be coun-terfeited or presented, or anything played which tend to the main-tenance of superstition and idolatry or which be contrary to the laws of God . . . or of the realm.[19]

Prohibition of the representation of the two surviving sacraments (Baptism and Eucharist) is especially revealing. Anxiety about representation of the Eucharist almost certainly accounts for the loss of a folio in the manuscript of the York plays.[20] Sometime between 1462 and 1552 the Last Supper play in the Chester cycle was no longer performed.[21]

Moves of this kind are plausibly driven by metropolitan centers of power, and were clearly framed so as to close the plays down altogether. The 1576 document directed against Wakefield might pretend to be selective in its prohibitions, but it ends up leaving no room for any of the plays, since most represent a person of the Trinity one way or another (upwards of eleven local men would, for example, have played the adult Christ in separate plays, out of thirty-two plays). Even if plays did not concern a person of the Trinity, the clauses "contrarie to the lawes . . . of God," not to speak of "the realme," leave wide and untrammelled space for legal attack.

The same concerted, centralized forces are visible in the direction to close the York Cycle in 1568. The Town Corporation of York decided that it would substitute the so-called Creed Play for the cycle plays in that year, but only after having consulted Dean Hutton, appointed to Her Majesty's

Commission for Ecclesiastical Causes in the North. Dean Hutton judged the text of the Creed Play thus in 1568:

> I see many things that I cannot allow because they be disagreeing from the sincerity of the gospel, the which things, if they should either be altogether cancelled or altered into other matters, the whole drift of the play should be altered ... [so] surely mine advise should be that it should not be played, for though it was plausible years ago, and would also now of the ignorant sort be well liked, yet now in the happy time of the gospel, I know the learned will mislike it, and how the state will bear it, I know not.[22]

How the state bore the insistence of the Chester Whitsun plays to perform in 1575, against the express prohibition of Edmund Grindal, Archbishop of York, was clear: the Privy Council summoned the mayor, John Savage, to London to account for this civic disobedience.[23] In York, the entire cycle was not performed in 1568, and only once again, for the last time, in 1569. Only in 1930 were cycle plays grudgingly given performance license for the first time in England since the 1570s, and only in 1968 was all censorship of British theater removed.[24]

II

The cycle plays, then—the theater of the "rude mechanicals"—were closed, in good part by central authority, in exact synchrony with the opening of the professional London theaters, in the late 1560s and 1570s. In almost the same years as the first London theater opening in 1567, and the first cycle play closing in 1569, England also witnessed the first persecution of "witches" that involved *maleficium* with the aid of "familiars" (i.e. malevolent spirits in the service of the Devil, who took the form of household animals).[25]

Thus on July 26, 1566, in Chelmsford, Essex, one Elizabeth Francis is said, under interrogation by the Queen's attorney, to have confessed to learning witchcraft from her mother Eve from age twelve; of having given blood to "Satan," a talking spotted cat (who talked "in a strange hollow voice"); and of having provoked various deaths with Satan the cat's help before she gave the cat, after sixteen or so years, to Agnes Waterhouse, who was sixty-four years old at the time of the trial. Agnes Waterhouse also confessed to various standard rural mischiefs such as provoking the failure of brewing and the curdling of butter, in addition to various more than merely mischievous murders. Joan Waterhouse, daughter to Agnes, also confessed to using Satan the cat on her own initiative, despite not having been taught the art. Satan, now in the form of a fearsome dog, of which the trial pamphlet gives us two identical and disconcerting cartoon pictures, had agreed, we are told, to serve Joan.[26] He did so only on condition that Joan give him her body and soul. The document records that Agnes Waterhouse was executed on July 29, 1566; the entire trial, conviction, and execution had taken three days.

The 1566 trial and execution in Chelmsford precede many more executions.[27] The reign of Charles I, up until 1642, saw a fall in trials, before the period of the Civil War, which saw the largest instance of judicial persecution for witchcraft, in southeastern England. That concerted attack was driven by the self-styled "Witch Finder" Matthew Hopkins and his "zealous Puritan" assistant John Stearne between 1645 and 1647, when at least 250 people, mostly but not exclusively women, were tried, of whom at least 100 were executed.[28]

These persecutions were backed up by statute. The 1566 Chelmsford execution follows, not coincidentally, the Witchcraft Act of 1563, which confidently affirms that since the repeal of an earlier statute in the first year of the reign of Edward VI, many "fantastical and devilish persons have devised and practised invocations and conjurations of evil and wicked spirits, and have used and practiced witchcrafts, enchantments, charms, and sorceries."[29] First offenders will be put in the pillory; second offenders will suffer execution as a felon (i.e. hanging).

Anglo-Saxons also certainly practiced therapeutic magic in the crucial matter of crop fertility.[30] Evidence for the practice of lethal, black magic in the later English Middle Ages is, by contrast, extremely thin. Just two high-profile legal cases exist, of royal women (Joan of Navarre in 1419 and Eleanor Cobham in 1441) charged with and convicted of witchcraft.[31] The record of intellectual, learned discussion, equally thin as it is, expresses skepticism more than conviction about the existence and practices of witches. Skepticism, indeed, characterizes the main medieval legal text concerning witchcraft, the so-called *Canon Episcopi* (9c), whose influence derived from its inclusion in Gratian's *Decretum* (c. 1150).[32]

This situation changes dramatically in every way as Europe, both Catholic and Protestant, approaches the end of the fifteenth century.[33] The most famous texts promoting belief in witches, such as Heinrich Kramer and Jacob Sprenger's *Malleus Maleficarum* (published in Speyer, 1486–1487) are very late medieval. In England the history of statute against and capital punishment for witchcraft is all post Reformation, beginning with a Henrician statute of 1542, and following in a sequence 1563 and 1604.[34]

Evangelical fear of witches, no less than performative sacramentality, has, to be sure, its late medieval, proto-Protestant premonitions.[35] These quasi-Lollard texts are, however, but premonitions. In England by far the most vigorous set of treatises promoting the existence of witches and the need to execute them appears between 1580 and 1620 or so. The rarity of scattered pre-Reformation, proto-evangelical tracts contrasts dramatically with the high density of Elizabethan and Jacobean anti-witchcraft tracts from 1580. These were all written by Calvinists (even if from a wide spectrum within Calvinism), and all affirm the existence of witches and the need to execute them. The following, for example, authored such texts: Phillip Stubbes (1583), Henry Holland (1590), George Gifford (1587, 1593), James VI of Scotland (1593), William Perkins (1610), and Alexander Roberts (1616).[36] The list contains some very high-profile names: not only William Perkins, the principal Elizabethan purveyor of "pastoral" Calvinism, but also James VI of Scotland (later, of course, James I of England, when his *Daemonology* was republished).[37]

The crucial fact in any argument concerning the early modern genealogy of witch persecution is the chronology of the actual persecutions themselves. About this there is no doubt: "Most historians of English witchcraft, however, are generally agreed that an initial surge in prosecutions in the period from about 1580 to 1620 was followed by a lull in the 1630s, a further spike in the years of civil war, followed by a rapidly accelerating decline after 1660."[38] Persecution of witches was, if by no means an exclusively Protestant matter, certainly a phenomenon of European early modernity. From the beginning of the sixteenth century the frightening hobgoblins that had been firmly affixed as gargoyles to the outer faces of medieval churches started to move; they jumped off the churches and ran not only around and into the paintings of Hieronymus Bosch at the beginning of the period, but also, in the minds of many responsible for the execution of justice, into the cottages of old women.

Is the almost exact temporal coincidence of cycle closings and the persecution of witches a mere coincidence? At the least, we can say that there exists a large cultural overlap between those responsible for closing the plays and for initiating the persecution of old women for witchcraft. The most explicit element in common, aside from broad Calvinist commitment, is horror at performativity (i.e. the animation of words making things happen in the world).[39]

To see that horror of, and fascination with, performativity in the vicious persecution of old women, let us return to the trial record of the conviction of Agnes Waterhouse in Chelmsford in 1566. This is not an official document. It is instead an evangelical pamphlet, replete with bad poetry using the evangelical buzzwords ("Did Christ in vaine prepare the heavens, / for his elect to dwell?"), and lurid cartoons of the satanic pets (pussy, lizard / toad, Rottweiler devil dog).[40] The text provides a good sample of the topoi of witch trials (especially blood sucking), but it also focuses on the key issue of linguistic performativity. The last words we hear from Agnes concern her use of Latin. Does she go to church and participate in the "common prayer," asks her interrogator. Yes—the Lord's Prayer, the Ave and the Creed. In what language? "Latin." Why Latin, which is against the law?: "And she said that Satan would at no time suffer her to say it in English," before which Agnes gives herself over to "Christ her savior, which dearly had bought her with his most precious blood."[41] Agnes Waterhouse was hanged on July 29, 1566, three days after the start of her trial.

The same distinctively evangelical emphasis on issues of linguistic performativity, at the climax of a trial, is found in other trial accounts. Thus on April 14, 1621, Elizabeth Sawyer was tried for and convicted of witchcraft in Edmonton, just to the north of London.[42] Sawyer relates that the Devil insisted that she pray no more to Christ, but say only this (incorrect) Latin to him: "*Santibicetur nomen tuum.*" Sawyer confirms that she does not know or understand Latin, and that she learned this clause from the Devil alone. Once she makes this linguistic point, she declares herself "more quiet and the better prepared and willing thereby to suffer death, although I must confess, that I would live longer if I might."[43] Elizabeth Sawyer was hanged at Tyburn on April 19, 1621, three days after the start of her trial.

The linguistic charges in these trials are especially cruel since they are charges whereby the learned apply double jeopardy against the illiterate: not only are the old women culpable for using Latin, but they are also ignorant in not being able to understand it. The attack is not only cruel, but it is also revealing of the fact that Latin, the language of the Catholic Mass, is now invested with malicious, animate power to change things in the world. Whereas orthodox Catholic doctrine had it that words pronounced in that language could call forth the presence of Christ, they now call forth Satan, in what is clearly a distorted mirror image of performative sacramental practice, no less than Satan's sucking of the witches blood from a hidden but unnatural teat—the common denominator of all these trials— is also resonant with its sacramental original.

Within their larger diatribe against the spreading curse of witchcraft, many of the "learned" anti-witchcraft texts also demonize linguistic performativity, as derived from Catholic sacramentality. Thus in a text published in 1608, William Perkins follows earlier sixteenth-century Protestants by framing his attack on witchcraft with an attack on the Catholic sacraments, focusing on the spuriousness of any efficacy contained in ritual words and actions. Those who expect such words and actions to produce effects in the world replicate nothing better than the

> devil's sacraments and watchwords, to cause him to do some strange work. For the enchanter hath relation in his mind to the devil, whose help he hath at hand by covenant either open or secret; or at least some superstitious opinion of the force of the words, which is a preparation to a covenant . . . For there are and have been some learned men, in all ages, who maintained . . . that there is great virtue & power in words pronounced in time and place, to effect strange things.[44]

Belief in such practice derives directly from the sacramental practice of the Catholic Church, where, for example, by crossing of the body, we are

> blessed from the devil. A thing usual even of latter times, specially in Popery; wherein the cross carieth the very nature of a Charm, and the use of it in this manner, a practice of enchantment. For God hath given no such virtue to a cross, either by creation, or special privilege and appointment.

Just as J. L. Austin rightly determined that performatives need to have "felicitous" conditions, so too did early modern Calvinists focus on the fact that performative words and actions only work if produced in the appropriate circumstances.[45] Thus James VI underlines the fact that the conjured spirit will not appear until the performative conditions have been fulfilled—until, that is, "after many circumstances, long prayers, and much muttering and murmuring of the conjurers; like a *Papist* priest, dispatching a hunting *Mass.*"[46]

So the pursuit of witchcraft was, in England and Scotland, driven in part by evangelical sacramental persuasion: Calvinist denial of performativity of any kind in any of the sacraments produced a much larger attack on performativity. The need to deny liturgical performativity was so intense as to produce the correlative need to conjure magical performativity out of nonexistent shadows in order to persecute it. The "magic" of the Mass produced a toxic cultural formation with upwards of two thousand victims in England and Scotland.

There are few heroes in this lamentable story. One of them is the water engineer Reginald Scott (d. 1599), whose learned, forensic, and passionate *The Discovery of Witchcraft* (1584) denies of the whole vicious farrago of nonsense concerning witchcraft. Even Scott, however, begins his treatise by describing Catholic sacramentalism as conjuring magic. Addressing the witch persecutors, he makes the connection of witchcraft and sacramental practice thus:

> If I should go to a Papist, and say, I pray you believe my writings, wherein I will prove all Popish Charms, Conjurations, Exorcisms, Benedictions and Curses, not only to be ridiculous, and of none effect, but also to be impious and contrary to God's Word: I should as hardly therein win favor at their hands, as herein obtain credit at yours. Nevertheless, I doubt not, but to use the matter so, that as well the *Massemonger* for his part, as the *Witchmonger* for his, shall both be ashamed of their Professions.[47]

III

Evangelical attack on sacramental performativity and magic had consequences for theater. In Chapter 12 we observed the profound connection of "playing" and sacramentalism in the largest, longest theatrical phenomenon of English history, the cycle plays. We also observed evangelicals (e.g. John Bale), in the first phase of the English Reformation, making explicit and hostile connection between the Catholic Mass and theater. John Jewel (1522–1571), Elizabethan Bishop of Salisbury, makes the same connection in his influential *Apology in Defense of the Church of England* (first published in Latin in 1562, and translated twice by 1564), by mocking the fact that, according to Catholic practice, "the sacramental bread" is to "to be worshipped as God"; Catholics

> have brought the sacraments of Christ to be used now as a stage-play, and a solemn sight; to the end that men's eyes should be fed with nothing else but with mad gazings, and foolish gauds.[48]

What challenges do these vibrant histories pose for the theater that replaced the para-sacramental cycle plays as the largest, if much less enduring, mass theatrical phenomenon in England in the Reformation period—that of Elizabethan and Jacobean London? I close this chapter by looking to anti-performativity in early modern anti-theatrical tracts, before turning in Chapter 14 to the ways in which plays themselves responded to evangelical horror of performativity.

The Mass was like theater, but was theater like the Mass? Alison Shell focuses our attention on the question by pointing to a paradox: that the London of Shakespeare's theater was "one of the most antitheatrical climates that England has ever known."[49] A rush of anti-theatrical tracts issued from the press within a decade of the opening of the London theaters, precisely from those key years around 1570, which witnessed the closing of the cycle plays, the opening of the London theaters, and the excommunication of the Queen. The following, for example, produced texts devoted to demolishing theaters culturally and closing them practically: Stephen Gosson (1582); Phil[l]ip Stubbes (1583); and William Rankins (1587).[50] These are all preludes to the behemoth of all anti-theatrical treatises, William Prynne's *Histriomastix*, published in 1633. Like Augustine (whose *City of God*, c. 413–426, they frequently cite on the matter), these mostly evangelical authors deplore the depravity of the theater and associate it, like Augustine, with the old and "unclean" spiritual order.[51]

As we saw in Chapter 12, evangelical objections to theater ranged across a number of different topics, but the more subtle of them included the semiosis of theater's relation with sacraments. In this they follow, unconsciously no doubt, the path established in the first English vernacular treatise written against plays, the *Treatise against Miracles Playing* (late fourteenth / early fifteenth century), which attacks cycle plays by arguing that they "reverse" Christ in many ways. The proto-Protestant Lollard author imagines an opponent, who argues that the plays should be criticized only insofar as they are contrary to belief. The author responds by saying that they can be countenanced only if they are grounded *explicitly* in Christ's sayings. They are not so grounded: they only play at miracles, whereas Christ's were true; they joke about God; they detract from the serious business of penance; they add to or subtract from Christ's words; they encourage expense that would be better spent on the poor. Most damagingly, they are idolatrous: they move in reverse from the New Testament, constituting "a very going backward from deeds of the spirit to only signs don after [according to] lusts of the flesh"—to the mere flesh, that is, of the Old Testament.[52]

The charge of immorality is universal among these authors. But the immorality has a historical, ecclesiological twist, since it derives from the devil, who invented playing, and represents idolatry. William Prynne's vast *Histriomastix* best exemplifies the ecclesiological line of attack on

> profane, and poisonous STAGE-PLAYES; the common idol, and prevailing evil of our dissolute, and degenerous Age: which though they had their rise from Hell; yea, their birth, and pedigree from the very Devil himself.[53]

Prynne, like his predecessor Stephen Gosson writing against the theater in 1582, sounds like he has been reading a good amount of Augustine and Tertullian (d. c. 240), an early Christian apologist whose vivid anti-theatrical writing is, like Augustine's, directly focused on pagan religious theater. In fact both Prynne and Gosson sound much more like dedicated readers of early Christian theology than well-informed patrons of London theater.

Prynne's massive text positively vibrates, however, with a sense of the religiosity of all theater, even if religiosity of a distorted and dangerous kind. He explicitly compares the offerings of the Eucharistic host to the offerings of stage plays to pagan gods, *"offered, or consecrated unto Idols, as these Stage-Plays were"*:

> The things which the Gentiles Sacrifice, they Sacrifice to Devils, and not to God: therefore those that participate of them, must needs have communion with the Devil: and I would not (saith the Apostle) that ye should have fellowship with Devils. Secondly, because Christians cannot drink the Cup of the Lord, and the Cup of Devils: they cannot be partakers of the Lords Table, and the Table of Devils.[54]

For these evangelical authors, the theater is the cultural expression of the sacramental system of the old order, the space where diabolic impersonation mimics liturgical, sacramental practice with lethal intent. Their attacks on theater are not only synchronous with, but exactly parallel conceptually, the attacks on old women labelled "witches."

The attack on black magic witchcraft is, then, a decisively early modern phenomenon. Statutes outlawing witches, anti-witch tracts, and massive persecution of witches all rise dramatically between 1542 and 1645. So concentrated is the phenomenon chronologically that we are obliged, I think, to say that the persecution of black magic witchcraft is effectively an early modern, and, in England, a Puritan reinvention (reinvented from late Antiquity). The attack on black magic sacramentalism had immediate and threatening consequences for theater, though threatening consequences for theater can also, of course, be wonderful opportunities for it. How did playwrights respond to the pressures and / or opportunities posed by the description of theater as poisoned, performative sacramentality? I address that question in Chapter 14.

14

Last Judgement: Stage Managing the Magic

HOW DID THEATER respond to the changed sacramental environment, in which the very meaning of theater as a cultural form had changed? And how did theater express that changed environment through the representation of magic on stage?

All successful theater, even more than most other arts, must appeal to the collective identity of an audience. For two hundred years, from at least the late fourteenth century, the cycle plays had appealed to a collective identity that was, very broadly, ecclesiological and urban. Audience identification with the plays depended on membership of a Church and the freedom of a city, even if the plays themselves are, as one might expect of workers' theater, very and vibrantly critical both of official ecclesiastical and labor practice.[1]

Appeal to ecclesiological forms of collective identity in Elizabethan England was, however, no longer an option for the professional theater (or for anyone else) from the late 1560s, when the professional London theaters opened. This is not because Elizabethan Londoners suddenly developed an exclusive interest in nonreligious, secular cultural forms, as triumphalist Whig theatrical history, in its secularist mode, had it for most of the twentieth century.[2] On the contrary, there were many powerful reasons why appeal to a collective ecclesiological identity (the most powerful form of identity in early modern Europe) was not available for English playwrights in the 1570s.

Most obviously, that collective ecclesiological identity no longer existed. After at least four, possibly five major swings of official ecclesiastical policy, with attendant judicial sanctions, since 1534;[3] after the excommunication of Queen Elizabeth in 1570; after the emergence of the nascent Puritan party in the 1560s with the Vestiarian controversy; after the much more vigorous pursuit of Catholic missionaries in England from 1570, including their torture, especially after 1580; and after the classification of Catholic priests as traitors in 1585: after all these events and developments, English theatrical culture faced a much more divided and, no doubt, ecclesiologically cautious audience. Evangelical plays, of which there survive a certain number up to the end of the sixteenth century, provide good examples of how a theater appealing to one exclusive audience of the elect, to the active exclusion of broader audiences, cannot long survive.[4]

There is one further, non-negligible reason why Elizabethan theater could not appeal to an ecclesiologically grounded collective identity: it was illegal to do so, religion having been formally banned as a theatrical subject in a proclamation of 1559.[5] So, far from it being the case that Elizabethans were uninterested in religion, religion had become too hot to handle on stage in Elizabethan England. There are some notable exceptions to this ban, to some of which we will look in the present chapter, but those few exceptions tend to confirm the rule that religion had become an extremely dangerous subject to treat on the English stage from the 1560s.

As a result of these powerful, different, but convergent cultural pressures, Elizabethan playwrights needed in the first instance to appeal to other, nonreligious forms of collective identity. They did this most obviously by appealing not to City or Church, but to political identities, focused especially on the nation, via English or British history, either relatively recent or ancient.

Insofar as great Elizabethan playwrights sought to contain, or express, specifically Calvinist hostility to theater, they did so either, as this chapter will demonstrate, by close and spectacular alignment of magic, sacramentality, and theater (Marlowe), or by preserving the indestructible pair of magic and theater for the most part clear of the sacrament (Shakespeare). Another solution—not treated in this chapter—was closet drama, which did treat religion, but did so under the camouflage of Islam, and did so well outside the labile circulations of public theater (Greville).[6]

The theater that broached witchcraft and sacramentality in the first phase of the English Reformation was irreverent and lively in its effrontery, produced as it was before the first, Henrician statute against witchcraft of 1542. Theater of the second phase of the English Reformation (1558–1625 or so) broached the same issues but was intense and dark, now conscious as it was of the life-and-death issues facing the theater itself.

These responses to the nexus of magic, theatricality, and sacramentality were, of course, finally too much for theater in the context of permanent evangelical revolution: after a prolonged and vigorous campaign against theater, theaters were closed between 1642 and 1660. They were reopened and reintroduced only on much reduced jurisdictional (Southwark to Drury Lane) and social terms (more court focused), ever closer to, and often harmlessly about the social class of, centers of power.

How did magic and performativity emerge after the English Revolution? By the end of the Reformation sesquicentennial in the 1680s, English culture had devised a manageable form of what was regarded as "charming."[7] Just as the idol took refuge in the micro-form of the "doll,"[8] so too was magic belittled; it took refuge and reformed itself in the momentarily captivating but fundamentally marginal territory of *abracadabra* party tricks for the young. That was the refuge of performativity where the magical was prepared to state its name.

I

Playwrights of the second phase of the English Reformation were faced with a much more dangerous, constrained environment for theater than was Bale in the first phase. The vigorous persecution of witchcraft was grounded in part on an identification of the Mass with magic, and that attack on malicious performativity targeted not only old women as witches, but also stage plays. The theater of Marlowe and Shakespeare could not ignore these contemporary phenomena, which had immediate implications for the "event" of theater, by which I mean principally the event on stage, but also the event of theater as a cultural institution.

So how did English playwrights of the years 1580–1625 or so respond to this set of pressures? In this and the following section I argue that they either confronted the nexus of theater and blasphemous, idolatrous black magic head on, or else they worked to preserve the theatrical conjuring, but to separate it from the sacramental. Marlowe exemplifies the first, brave option (brave in both the modern and the early modern senses); Shakespeare, the second.

Spenser (1552/3–1599) has it that lethal performative magic derives from the Catholic past and maliciously threatens the enlightened present with destruction. His near-exact contemporary, the playwright and poet Christopher Marlowe (1564–1593) sees the relation very differently. In *The Tragicall History of the Life and Death of Doctor Faustus* (written between 1588 and Marlowe's murder in 1593; published 1604 (A text) and 1616 (B text)), magic is a distinctively modern and distinctively Protestant phenomenon. Like two other figures expressive of European early modernity, and especially of early modern despair, Luther and Hamlet, Faustus has Wittenbergian connections. He is a distinctively early modern academic, specializing in "heavenly matters of theology" (Prologue, 19), and his dreams of world domination and slavery are distinctively early modern fantasies.[9] His is an intellectual culture that sees new possibilities of "power, honor and omnipotence" in what academics often refer to as the "real" world.

> Thus Faustus dreams of colonial dominion, having spirits
> . . . fly to India for gold,
> Ransack the ocean for orient pearl
> And search all corners of the new found world
> For pleasant fruits and princely delicates.
> (1.82–84)

He wants a perfect spy service to tell him the "secrets of foreign kings" (1.87) (which may have been of especial interest to Marlowe, who was himself likely a spy); he desires a perfect defense system, "to wall all Germany with brass" (1.88), and a bigger army; and he longs, not least, for that distinctively early modern commodity, a slave: he commands Mephistopheles to "wait upon me whilst I live, / To do whatever Faustus shall command" (3.36–37). For Marlowe, magic is about power in the sixteenth-century world: "A sound magician is a mighty god" (1.62). Magic does not come from the pre-modern Middle Ages; it is, instead, an authentically Wittenbergian, early modern production.

Dr Faustus represents Marlowe's modernity, but throughout the play time is running out for that modernity. Time is obviously running out for Faustus himself, who begs for it to slow down as he approaches the edge of hell: "Stand still, you ever moving spheres of heaven, / That time may cease, and midnight never come . . . / O *lente, lente, currite noctis equi*" (13.60–66). But time is also running out in this play both for blasphemous magic and for the theater itself.

Time has already run out for Catholic sacramentalism, since the seven deadly sins have now become, as they also become in Spenser's *Faerie Queene* (1:4), an occasion for lightweight processional theater, designed to entertain spectators with vice figures drawn to life, as in genre painting (5.285–340). In fact the stage director for this lightweight production turns out to be none other than Lucifer, who puts on the aesthetic show precisely in order to distract Faustus from any thought of repentance after his most anguished call to Christ (5.256–257).

The grand performance and performativity of Catholic forgiveness is here reduced to a theatrical, aesthetic experience stage-managed by Lucifer. This trivializing, Luciferian theater uses pre-Reformation, sacramental materials as a clue to the dead end facing both magic and theater itself in this spectacular but hollow play within a play. In response, theater brilliantly lights up for one final curtain call, heading fast toward total exhaustion. For if deep horror of performative sacramentalism produces the correlative fear of black magic, then black magic will lose its charisma the moment Catholic sacramentalism does. In this play within a play, Catholic sacramentalism has become a pleasing, theatrical distraction.

Does black magic lose its charisma in *Faustus* as a whole? Faustus is the very model of the learned magician, unlike the women illiterates who were persecuted in the early modern witchcraft trials. Nonetheless he, like those "witches," operates very much with the same sacramentally inverted, performative instruments: he uses anagrammized versions of holy words, Latin invocations, and "characters . . . by which the spirits are enforced to rise" (3.12–13). And like the illiterates (as presented by the prejudicial trial accounts), Faustus indulges in apparently compulsive, truculent, obscene blasphemy: screwing himself up to follow through on the reverse logic of despair, Faustus vows with regard to Beelzebub, "To him I'll build an altar and a church / And offer lukewarm blood of newborn babes" (5.13–14).

Faustus remains locked, then, within the logic and the performative practice of Catholic sacramentalism, as described by evangelicals. If, however, performative sacramentalism has become poor theater, then neither can there be any future for its opposite—black magic. If, that is to say, black magic generates its own diabolic energy only from the Catholic ritual, then once the ritual is evacuated, so too is black magic running on empty. As Jay Zysk has so perceptively said, "The books Faustus reads, the language he speaks, and the conjuring acts he performs all depend on the sacramental rituals he purportedly rejects."[10] Catholic sacramentalism has become a target, in a new theater that is nonetheless fuelled by Catholic sacramental persuasions. That, however, is a dangerous game, since by the time it's finished, one is empty handed. No sacramentalism, no black magic, just the ugly, gaping Hell mouth of medieval theater.

And so it is that, in this play, black magic is a terrible letdown. It can take Faustus as a tourist to Rome, but that is precisely what Faustus becomes: a Protestant tourist, mocking sacramental practice in the papal court, with wholly trivial effect. Faustus's performative invocation to take him to Rome sounds impressive enough ("Now by the kingdoms of infernal rule . . . I do long to see the monuments of bright-splendid Rome," 7.43–47), but once he's there, he has the debased experience of many a tourist to Rome. The sacrament Faustus intends to disrupt is not a sacrament at all, just a run-of-the-mill papal delicacy being consumed, and the papal exorcism does not itself work. The whole event hollows out *both* the Catholic sacrament and its diabolic parody. The enfeeblement of these grand cycles of ritual practice, both the orthodox and the blasphemous parody, are pathetic in the modern sense, as we observe a mighty invocation descend to a charm, descend to a trick, descend to an exorcism that does not work, and descend from there to theatrical fireworks (Scene 7).

The pre-Reformation *Croxton Play of the Sacrament* (1461) exploits the theatrical potential of the sacrament of the Host so relentlessly and so violently as finally to have us question the Real Presence.[11] In *Dr Faustus* there is never any question of any sacrament being efficacious. This play, already in the late 1580s, points to the fact that Catholicism is no longer the real enemy; it works rather and wholly within the dynamic logic of Calvinist despair. Time is certainly running out for Faustus, but it's also running out, then, for the twinned pair Catholic performative sacramentalism and its black magic look-alike.[12] The energy of both is draining as we watch. If that is true, then time is also running out for theater, since theater that depends on performativity is being drained of energy and reduced to trivial spectacle, even as we watch it. One model for Marlowe's astonishing theater might, indeed, be the empty shows (the Seven Deadly Sins Show, the Helen of Troy Show) that do in fact conform to the very thing that anti-theatricalists said about plays: that whereas the things of God operate "both in sign and in deed . . . miracles playing . . . ben [are] signs without deed."[13]

As Faustus says when his contract with the devil is signed and sealed, *"consummatum est"* (another last call, after all, by Christ before he dies), which is a fit comment on the fate of theater as presented by this play: it's over. As an audience member, Faustus responds to Lucifer's distracting theater of the Deadly Sins by expressing his aesthetic pleasure, "O this feeds my soul!" to which Lucifer replies that "in hell is all manner of delight" (5.331). But the delight is aesthetic and it's bounded by hell, like the delight of Milton's thoughtful fallen angels, who retire apart in Hell to listen, ravished, to heroic poetry as a distraction from the fact that they're damned (PL 2.451). Those angels are listening to Miltonic poetry, just as Faustus is an audience member at the last call of Marlovian theater, a theater resonating with the charisma of its diabolic director, but with nowhere to go. It's a brilliant, pyrotechnic explosion, but it uses up so much powder (*both* the Catholic sacramental system *and* its malicious look-alike) that one can only ask what's left. We are left with a hollowed-out theater, a theater conscious of operating alone, now that the sacraments have themselves been hollowed out, a distinctively early modern condition of theater to which Stephen Greenblatt points with such acuity.[14]

Consummatum est, then, would be the curtain call for theater itself in this play, were it aimed only at the Catholic Church, or at magic, or (as is in fact the case) at both. If this electric play only ran the electric system down, it would prophesy the lifeless kind of theater we find in later Jacobean anti-Catholic plays, or, indeed, in Marlowe's own *Massacre at Paris*, which reads like nothing so much as a paid put up job for English foreign policy in the 1580s (however justified its presentation of Catholic barbarity in the St Bartholomew's Day Massacre of 1572).[15]

There is, however, one residue of *Faustus* of which we have not yet made mention, which is Faustus's own existential isolation. The Latin of the conjuring invocations turns out to be empty; the Latin, however, that expresses Mephistopheles's own solitude and explains his profound desire to gain Faustus's "company" remains potent after all the fireworks have died: "Solamen miseris socios habuisse doloris" (5.42).[16] To have had a companion in misery is solace of a kind. Like Hamlet, for whom death is a "consummation devoutly to be wished," and whose unaccommodated existential isolation and anguish movingly survives play's end, so too does Faustus's unmet wish for anti-baptism, his Hamletian dying appeal to disappear altogether as water ("to be changed into little water drops, / And fall into the ocean, ne'er to be found," Epilogue, 108–109), stay with us.[17] It survives after everything else—the sacraments, the gross absurdity of magic, and theater—have all run beyond their time.

II

Theater was not, course, running on empty for some playwrights after Marlowe.

Shakespeare could not help but be conscious of the existential challenges posed to theater by the broad and intense evangelical opposition to performative sacramentality (of both the ecclesiastical and black magic varieties), and by the specific, targeted, evangelical opposition to theater itself. The evidence for that awareness is written deep into his oeuvre, but for Shakespeare's demonstrable knowledge of this set of challenges, we need look no further than Samuel Harsnett's *Declaration of egregious popish impostures* (1603). This text was written to discredit the activities of a Jesuit, William Weston, who in 1585–1586 had conducted exorcisms in Buckinghamshire. Harsnett (1561–1631) was evenhanded: he had already written *A Discovery of the Fraudulent Practises of John Darel* (1599) to discredit John Darrell, a Puritan exorcist who had conducted exorcisms between 1586 and 1597.[18] Harsnett's *Declaration* was known to Shakespeare, since the names of Edgar's fiends in *Lear* are drawn from Harsnett's text.[19]

However virulent his detestation of Catholicism, and however mockingly dismissive he is of the tortured and executed Jesuit missionary Edmund Campion (d. 1581), Harsnett cannot be described as an evangelical. From as early as 1581, he had preached against a narrow definition of predestination, and his later rise to the archbishopric of York in 1628 was

as a known conservative. Harsnett's position as a theological conservative is revealing for the fact that the anti-performative theatricalism of
evangelicals is shared across a much wider Anglican spectrum: Harsnett
categorized black magic in exactly the same way as evangelicals did—as
the perverted mirror of a perverted Catholic model.

Harsnett is not fussy about distinguishing exorcism and witchcraft. Both
performative practices derive from Rome, and he attacks exorcism via a
larger attack on Catholic sacramentalism: the "witching powers have many
years since combined and united themselves in the Pope of Rome and his
disciples," who "take upon them the sovereign power . . . to command unclean spirits, and to make them obey" (image 2). For Harsnett magic derives
from the past of the entire Catholic sacramental system, and behind that,
from pagan polytheism,[20] whereby

> the Pope, and his spirits he sendeth in here amongst you, do play
> Almighty God, his son, & Saints upon a stage, do make a pageant
> of the Church, the blessed Sacraments, the rites & ceremonies of re-
> ligion, do cog & coin devils, spirits, & souls departed this life.

Harsnett is also, as is clear from the last citation, on the evangelical side
with regard to the relation of Catholic performative sacramentalism and
theater: both liturgy and drama use the same instruments, and both put
on a show.

Where Harsnett differs from his evangelical contemporaries is in dismissing both the Catholic and the entire world of magic and faerie as
empty. Most late sixteenth-century writers who condemn witchcraft take
care to underline that witchcraft is not at all absurd, despite appearances,
since the Devil is behind the performance, and it really does kill its victims.
Harsnett, by contrast, retains a largely detached position of ridicule, whence
he attacks both Catholic idolatry and the theater. Thus the Eucharist is
treated as an idol on stage, but it deserves nothing but a mixture of laughter
for its silliness, and loathing for its imposture:

> This new molded mass-Idol, laughed at by some, loathed by many,
> detested of all pious, and ingenious spirits . . . must be brought upon
> our devil-stage, to be graced, honored, and confirmed from hell.
> And the same devil, that sainted *Campian*, and *Brian*, must with the

same black breath, and foul mouth, deify this bread-Idol, and make it a God. And that it may be a perfect *Chimaera,* compounded all of fiction, and fantastical imagination; the smoke, the fire, the stench, the roar, hell, and the devil must be cogged [fraudulently evoked], feigned, and played, to help out with this infernal, and diabolical fascination.[21] (image 68)

A full treatment of how Shakespeare responded to the challenges posed to theater in England across his career between 1589 and 1612 is obviously beyond the scope of the present chapter. Harsnett, however, provides a focus for Shakespeare's response, since on the one hand Harsnett underlines that a collective sacramental identity that generates theater had become quite impossible; on the other, in the wake of the model of all theater—that of Catholic sacramentalism—Harsnett dimisses theater per se as a cultural form: it's trivial and wholly without substance.

Faced with challenges of that kind, Shakespeare for the most part generates the first decade of his career by addressing and shaping an alternative, non-ecclesiological collective identity for his audience—that of the English nation—focused on its relatively recent fifteenth-century civil wars. Shakespeare draws hardly at all on the resources of Catholic or anti-Catholic sacramentalism.

Shakespeare does, however, broach the issue once, in *Henry VI, Part I* (1591). In that play Talbot describes Joan of Arc as a "witch, that damnèd sorceress," and La Pucelle does attempt to conjure spirits to the aid of France.[22] But the most striking scene is when the familiar spirits refuse to help, despite the fact that Joan "was wont," she says, "to feed you with my blood" (5.3.14). Shakespeare has it, that is, that Joan is indeed a witch, but he refuses to make theatrical capital of that. The fiends take leave of the stage, abandoning La Pucelle, whose "ancient incantations are too weak" (5.3.27).

Only in *Macbeth,* performed within three years of the accession of James I to the English throne in 1603, does Shakespeare present a full-scale "sacramental" scene of witchcraft (4.1). That scene might strike modern viewers as not a little absurd, but the absurdity is diminished in the context of the early seventeenth century, where the following phenomena surround the play: the extended Witchcraft Act of 1604; the attempted terrorism of the Gunpowder Plot of November 5, 1605; and James I's personal conviction, published in his *Daemonologie* (1597, thrice republished in 1603, once in Edinburgh, twice in London), that witches and their children must be executed.[23] The renewed urgency for witch persecution derived from the fact that, in the king's view, there are so many more witches about, on account of

> the great wickedness of the people on the one parte . . . And on the other part, the consummation of the world, and our deliverance drawing near, makes Satan to rage the more in his instruments, knowing his kingdom to be so near an end.[24]

If Shakespeare refuses much to exploit what I have called the radioactive half-life of theater in the way of Marlowe's *Dr Faustus*, he does, nonetheless, remake the magic of theater with old, non-sacramental materials, and is accurately conscious as he does so that certain forms of the theater, and perhaps theater itself, have a limited life ahead in the context of the attack on magic, or what we might call performativity.

I therefore turn to the two plays in which Shakespeare deploys magic most unabashedly, *A Midsummer Night's Dream* (?1595/96) and *The Tempest* (1611), both of which not only represent non-Catholic performative magic in action but also underline the consequences of magic for certain forms of theater. In both, the practice of theater's magic, and of represented magic, derives from very different sources—one rural, the other learned—but in both cases magic occurs under time's sentence; in both plays the magical knows that the end is coming for different kinds of theater. However resourcefully Shakespeare reaches beyond, beside, and below Calvinism for a restorative theatrical magic, the space gained stands under strict temporal limit.

In *A Midsummer Night's Dream*, theatrical magic is heading away from the late medieval city as theater, away from the encircled Elizabethan professional theater, and toward, finally, the beautiful microworld of the nursery. One way or another, the magic show is just about over, even as bedazzling Baroque architecture in Catholic Europe is about to theatricalize the sacrament as spectacularly as it can. In Protestant Europe, the show is, by contrast, coming to an end. Thus *The Tempest*'s Prospero, at play's end, performatively abjures his "so potent Art," or what he modestly calls "this rough Magicke," on stage:

> . . . Ile break my staff,
> Bury it certain fathoms in the earth,
> And deeper than did ever plummet sound
> I'll drown my book.[25]

I turn first to the way this cultural logic works its way out in *A Midsummer Night's Dream* (1596).

III

Bishop John Jewel delivered a sermon before the Queen sometime between 1563 and 1571. He takes time off from his principal theme of defending the Calvinist status quo to focus on just how many people are looking terrible these days: "Your graces subjects pine away even unto the death, their color fadeth, their flesh rotteth, their speech is benumbed, their senses are bereft." And why? The answer is simple: "Witches, & sorcerers, within these few last years, are marvelously increased within this your graces realm."[26] Jewel implores the Queen to apply laws (he is presumably referring to the 1563 Act, specifying hanging for second offences of witchcraft), since "the school of them is great, their doings horrible, their malice intolerable, the examples most miserable."[27]

Five or so years after his representation of La Pucelle as a witch, Shakespeare returned in *A Midsummer Night's Dream* to the issue of magic on stage in an ailing natural world. Here, however, the magic is, however naughty, profoundly restorative; it serves finally to restore good health to psyche, polis, and cosmos. Dissention within the faerie microworld has produced the ecological disaster of climate change and human illness: "the human mortals want their winter here"; the moon, "pale in her anger, washes all the air, / That rheumatic diseases do abound" (2.1.104–105). Jewel has it that the general malaise is the product of malicious witchcraft, and requires the therapeutic application of the law. Shakespeare's diagnosis and therapy is, by contrast, drawn from the pharmacopoeia of romance, the ecological genre par excellence, designed to produce sustainable social structures in

which psyche, polis, and cosmos operate in synergy, "the complete consort dancing together." That therapy needs magic spells.

A Midsummer Night's Dream works wholly within the structural dynamics
of romance, whereby societies move from integration to disintegration to
reintegration.[28] This narrative structure moves within binary oppositions,
such as old and young, new and old, city and forest, reason and desire,
nurture and nature. The interaction of those opposed states generates romance narrative structures: before the rational order can establish its equilibrium, it must have commerce with all that threatens it. The top-down
operations of armed force and law are absent from such narratives, since
the state of equilibrium can be reestablished only from the bottom up,
through the dynamic, provisionally destabilizing interactions of the wild
and the civilized. The deepest and therapeutic wisdom of such infinitely
flexible, evergreen narrative structures is that civilization is not a unitary
entity; instead, it maintains its equilibrium cybernetically, which is to
say through self-governance, by recognizing that the rational order can
be renewed only by commerce with all that would apparently destabilize
and sicken it.

I need not belabor the way in which *A Midsummer Night's Dream* works
within this ancient structure: the rational order of the city, governed by the
old, cannot contain the forces of youth and desire, which must move to the
generative uncertainties of the forest.[29] That move is, however, insufficient
to restore the civilized order. This play recognizes the need for interspe-
cies interactions and translations—man becoming beast, faerie falling in
love with animal—before the consort of psyche, polis, and cosmos is again
possible. And those transformations, to and fro, are only possible through
the performative work of that alternate to the rational order, which is the
realm of the magical, the charm, the spell.

Playful Puck inhabits and animates this ancient world. Puck—otherwise
known as Robin Goodfellow—is both responsible for minor rural mayhem
(drinks spilled on laps, old crones falling harmlessly off stools) and also at
the service of deeper, restorative, cosmic synergies.

Both evangelicals and more mainline Calvinist Anglicans had been attacking, not so say demonizing, poor Puck for at least sixty years before
Shakespeare reintroduced him to the stage. In the late 1530s, John Bale had
identified Idolatry with Puck's standard operations and spells.[30] And sixty

years later, in the late 1590s, the "conservative" figure Samuel Harsnett had effectively rehearsed the same theme. The benighted folk who are fooled by the stage play of exorcisms are the same who believe in "Robin Good-fellow," who naughtily curdles the cream, and the world of "the man in the oak, helwain, the fire-drake, the puckle, Tom thumb, hobgoblin, Tom-tumbler, Boneless, and the rest."[31] For Harsnett this world is in no way therapeutic; as for Bale sixty years earlier, this is all a reflex of Papal per-formative sacramentalism, and of the paganism behind the Catholic Church. What "heathenish dreams," Harsnett declares in his tract written against the Puritan exorcist John Darrell,

> what a world of hell-work, devil-work, and Elf-work, had we walking amongst us here in England, what time that popish mist had be-fogged the eyes of our poor people?

In *A Midsummer Night's Dream* Shakespeare takes care to dissociate the re-storative spell-casting and the magic-making altogether from Catholicism; he seeks instead to return to an ancient conjuring rural world, without whose ministrations the world of the city will wither. Robin Goodfellow remains in place, restored to his own restorative function ("And Robin shall restore amends," 5.1.424).

Romances are restorative, and they draw on deep pasts to stabilize re-cent pasts. That said, they also isolate and expel waste, that which can no longer be contained in the newly synergized, recycled civilized order. Shakespeare understands the profound connection between magic and theater. But even if *A Midsummer Night's Dream* restores that connection in such a way as to bypass the early modern evangelical horror of performa-tivity, Shakespeare does nonetheless isolate one element that can have no further place in this restored world.

Shakespeare draws on the pre-Reformation world in this play, with debts both to Chaucer and to plays like the *Second Shepherds' Play*, which also per-forms spells on the sleeping, with inter-species stage hilarity.[32] But Shake-speare's connection of magic and theater must come at the expense of the vast and mightily ambitious sacramental workers' theater of late medieval cities. The professional, metropolitan, enclosed, paying theater of Shake-speare, for all its wide and deep embrace, cannot include the theater of "rude mechanicals," the theater of Bottom the weaver and Snug the joiner.

Weaving and joining might suggest artisanal coherence, but Shakespeare, for all his kindly sympathy toward these players, gently points out their *lack* of coherence, their world of badly built walls. However much Bottom comically refuses to die, Shakespeare's gently insistent time calls toward the end of the play ("her passion ends the play," 5.1.304; "'tis almost fairy time," 5.1.350) signal the passing of an old theatrical order for which there can be no place in this newly conceived theatrical dispensation. The artisans' lack of fit with the new social and theatrical order, in which theater will serve aristocrats in enclosed spaces, with non-sacramental, humanist narratives, is multiply evident, but nowhere more so than in the insistently non-performative, anti-theatrical, non-magical action of the rude mechanicals while playing. The inanimate world is animate, but only so as to underline its non-magical, purely denotative fabrication:

> *Wall*
> In this same interlude it doth befall
> That I, one Snout by name, present a wall;
> And such a wall, as I would have you think,
> That had in it a crannied hole or chink.
> (5.1.154–157)

In this worker's theater, no artisan can play God so as to bring light through his voice alone to the entire world on a summer's morning. Without that grand performative and sacramental claim, artisanal theater looks plain ridiculous.

In this respect, then, Shakespeare agrees with Samuel Harsnett, who refers to the cycle drama in saying that absurd exorcisms are "like the day of judgement acted on a stage," which, though "feigned in it self, yet procured reverence and fear in the simpler and looser sort." The cycle drama is hereby dismissed by Harsnett, along with the performativity of exorcisms, as "a singular foundation to uphold the Pope his play-house, and to make religion a pageant of Puppets."[33]

Like the theatrically well-informed Harsnett (b. 1561), it is not impossible that in Coventry Shakespeare (b. 1564) witnessed the sacramental theater of the cycle plays before their closure at some point in the 1570s.[34] *A Midsummer Night's Dream*, for all its restorative power, and for all its restoration of magical charm to the stage, simultaneously completes the closure of the mystery cycles and points to the future location of the faerie spell in the nursery.

We can peer with delight into this miniature world of asylum in Herrick's touching poem "Oberon's Chappell" (written sometime between 1620 and 1646, but published in 1648, in exceptionally inauspicious circumstances of civil war in which the anti-evangelical Herrick, bap. 1591–1674, was on the losing side). Here we peer into a microworld of the doll's house, to see Oberon's

> . . . Temple of Idolatry,
> Where he of *godheads* has such store,
> As *Rome's Pantheon* had not more.
> His house of *Rimmon,* this he calls,
> Girt with small bones instead of walls.
> First, in a *Neech,* more black than jet,
> His Idol-Cricket there is set.[35]

IV

In the final phase of his career, Shakespeare returned insistently to the therapeutic restorations of romance, in *A Winter's Tale* (1610–1611) and *The Tempest* especially (1610–1611). Each of these plays, not coincidentally, involves scenes of theatricality and magic. And each takes care to distinguish the performativity from Catholic sacramentalism. We have already had occasion to see how closely Shakespeare sails to the wind of magical practice in *A Winter's Tale,* and how careful he is to distinguish this performative action from anything blasphemous, even as he holds daringly by the word "spell": "Her actions shall be as holy as / You hear my spell is lawful" (5.3.104–105). Leontes reworks the word magic and its lexical partner "conjure" to denote the "miracle" of effective penitence: "O royal piece," he exclaims, "There's magic in thy majesty, which has / My evils conjured to remembrance" (5.3.38–40).

In what seems to be his last solo-written play, *The Tempest,* Shakespeare returns for one last time to the space he has opened from within the conjuncture of magic, evangelical religion, and theatricality that we have considered across these chapters. The very opening of the play—nay, the very gerundive name of his own daughter, "Miranda"—announces the amazing effect, the effect that demands admiration, that a theatrical magic can still command. This magic is, like the restorative magic of *A Winter's Tale,* safe. The opening moment of the play insists on the fact that this is not lethal, soul-killing magic. On the contrary, the shipwreck we have just witnessed is a mirage, in which there is, Prospero assures Miranda, "No not so much perdition as an hair / Betid to any creature in the vessel" (1.2.30–31).

Before we learn that, however, we are also warned ahead of time that the show is going to end: Prospero begins the play as he ends it, by asking for hands to help remove his magic powers. To Miranda at play's opening he asks for help in removing the costume: "Lend thy hand / And pluck my magic garment from me" (1.2.23–24). At play's end he addresses the audience, again asking for hands to help doff the burdens of magical priesthood. The forgiveness of this secular sacrament is now complete, but Prospero needs help from the audience: "With the help of your good hands," and with the audience's prayer, Prospero asks for a kind of audience manumission so as to lay down his magic and yet avoid despair (Epilogue, 10). The profound theatrical magic, which has come as close to sacramental power as the times permit, is now over:

> . . . Now I want
> Spirits to enforce: Art to enchant,
> And my ending is despair,
> Unless I be relieved by prayer
> Which pierces so, that it assaults
> Mercy it self, and frees all faults.
> As you from crimes would pardoned be,
> Let your indulgence set me free.
>   (Epilogue, 10–20)

Slavery and magic are deeply intertwined in the action of the play: Ariel's celestial music is impossible without recognition of his derivation from the foul and malicious Algerian witch Sycorax. Ariel derives his power from Sycorax, and has become Prospero's slave, even if he was "a Spirit too delicate / To act her earthy and abhorred commands" (1.2.272–273). We cannot profit from the secular sacrament of theater without acknowledging this shameful and enthralling genealogy, but now, at play's end, with the work of forgiveness complete, the magic is renounced, repeatedly: "My Charms I'll break, their sences I'll restore, / And they shall be themselves" (5.1.31–32), as Prospero says to Ariel with regard to the aristocrats under his power.

As the play and Shakespeare's career end, so too does the magic: "this rough Magic / I here abjure" (5.1.50–51). The end of the play, as "revels now are ended," is a farewell no less to theater than to charming magic, the spirit actors, along with all that theater can conjure, even "the great globe itself": all "Are melted into air, into thin air" (4.1.150–153). Shakespeare would seem to recognize here that the genealogy of theater and magic is mixed, that the effort to open up a secular "sacramental" theatrical space was time sensitive, but that it's time has now ended. It's the sixth hour, "at which time, my Lord / You said our work should cease" (5.1.4–5). Prospero would seem to speak for Shakespeare, renouncing magic and theater:

> Now my charmes are all o'erthrown,
> And what strength I have's mine owne.
> Which is most faint.
>   (Epilogue, 321–323)

Does, however, the magic drain completely out of the system? The instruments of magical power are, to be sure, about to be damaged, but they are not utterly destroyed. Instead they are to be broken, and then buried as future archaeological finds; they are to be buried deep, or cast deep full fathom five, to be discovered by some archaeologist at a later time: "I'll break my staff, / Bury it certain fathoms in the earth, / And deeper than did ever plummet sound / I'll drown my book" (5.1.54–57).

Consummatum est. Or so it would seem; in fact, however, the play's last moments make a wonderful move: like any great artist, Prospero courteously recognizes the immense, not to say magical, power of the audience. He will remain "confined," like Caliban, on the island unless the audience, by its applause, "by your spell," "release me from my bands" (Epilogue, 8–9). Restorative magical power is quietly transferred here from magician to his refreshed public.

V

The Tempest points in at least two ways to what was to become of theatrical magic in the final stages of the English Reformation. Prospero's instructive masques point to future aristocratic control and management of theatrical magic. And the play's penultimate moment, when Prospero abjures theatricality—the Great Globe itself—points to the end of theater.

I end this chapter by briefly pointing to the ways in which these two developments play out, in turn. Jonson's *Masque of Queens* was performed in Whitehall in 1609. It allows as its fictional premise that witches exist, but in every other respect it has them entirely under control, just as theater itself is tightly controlled by aristocratic governance. Jonson's humanist learning and the personification allegory thoroughly disenchant the witches well before their conjuration fails, but fail it does. The sequence of Hecate's invocations comes, happily, to naught at the arrival of Heroic Virtue: "All our charms do nothing win / Upon the night; our labor dies! / Our magic feature will not rise" (ll. 268–270). The total control of scene management of the masque expresses a royal governance of both witchcraft and theater, such that the entire scene vanishes in a trice, with the arrival of Heroic Virtue. That worthy figure heralds the processional arrival of the separate famous and virtuous women, each played by a noble woman of court, starting with the Queen herself, as "not only the Hags themselves, but the hell, into which they ran, quite vanished."[36]

In every respect, then, Jonson's play takes up but closes down the theatrical possibilities of *The Tempest*. It takes up the learned magic, but it closes down the possibilities of that magic, both its enchanting beauty and its power to produce both love and forgiveness. Jonson's masque withdraws from the performative possibilities of theater to privilege pre-scripted text. It curtails the invocational power of magic in the service of royal performance, royal location, royal spectatorship, and royal governance. Performativity plays its death throws before the spectacle of royal performance.

Effectively the same can be said of Milton's *Comus*, properly known as *A maske presented at Ludlow Castle, 1634 on Michaelmasse night.*[37] The masque was first performed on September 29, 1633, as part of the celebrations for the installment of John, first Earl of Bridgewater, as Lord Lieutenant of various counties of Western England and Wales. The earl's children were the actors, playing themselves. The play enacts the powerlessness of the malicious enchanter Comus over the virtue of the daughter of the house, who is lost in the forest on a summer's night. Here all is under control, with the transfer and diminution of various powers. The power of theater is transferred to and diminished by that of the masque; of popular audiences, theaters, and players to aristocrats, aristocratic theatrical spaces, and aristocratic actors; of magic to the charm of young feminine virtue and male philosophy; and of old malicious women to young and virtuous women.

This winding down of theatrical performativity and witchcraft, along with the move to much more socially restricted spaces, audiences, and performers for theater in the reign of Charles I, might suggest that English drama had found a manageable accommodation with the radioactivity of public charming. The evangelicals would seem effectively to have broken the nexus of sacramentality, performativity, and theater.

To read the situation thus would, however, fail to appreciate the logic of permanent revolution. As we saw with regard to images, the revolutionary moment of Presbyterian control of Parliament from August 1642 gave occasion for a final, massive push to "reform the Reformation." Just as an ordinance was issued in August 1643 ordering the destruction of all religious images, so too, less than a month after the effective outbreak of civil war in the summer of 1642, did Parliament order the closure of all public theaters. Thus on 2 September, Parliament issued an ordinance whereby it declared that "Public Stage plays" do not "agree well" with "seasons of humiliation," since they are "spectacles of pleasure"; it is therefore "thought fit" that, as long as the difficulty of the times continues, "Public Stage Plays shall cease, and be forlorn."[38] These prohibitions were renewed in 1647 and 1648. The public theaters were not to reopen until 1660, by royal command and under royal patronage and supervision of King Charles II and his brother the Duke of York.

Some scholars have argued that Parliamentary closure of theaters did not imply anti-theatricality. David Kastan, for example, conforms with a tradition of English theatrical scholarship by arguing that various kinds of English theater were closed not on account of evangelical pressure.[39] The massive *Histriomastix* of William Prynne, published in 1633, was, Kastan unpersuasively declares, "an anachronism," given the fact that the spate of evangelical anti-theatrical writing ended before 1600 (even though Kastan concedes that "there were a number of anti-theatrical tracts in the 1620s").[40] It's true that Prynne himself is a more complex figure than can be described by the word "Puritan," but 1,006 pages is a long anachronism.[41] Kastan argues that Paul's Cross sermons published between 1630 and 1642 do not attack theater, unlike the high incidence of such attacks in the late 1570s. That may be true, but there is no shortage of attacks on "stage plays" between 1630 and 1642.[42] Kastan's abbreviated reference to the 1648 Act rebukes his own argument, since this act speaks explicitly in the voice of the anti-theatricalists, and it bans stage plays forever. Thus it says that "stage plays, interludes and common plays," having been condemned by "ancient heathens," are "much less to be tolerated among Professors of the Christian Religion." Such entertainments tend to "the high displeasure of God's wrath and displeasure, which lies heavy on this kingdom." All actors are to be punished as vagabonds, and all theaters are to be "pulled down and demolished."

In sum, when Parliament closed theaters in 1642, it aimed to close theatricality. The period of Presbyterian control of Parliament not only produced the closure of theaters between 1642 and 1660; that same period also witnessed the high point of witch persecution in England: between 1645 and 1647, as noted in Chapter 13, upward of a hundred people, mostly women, were executed in Essex. In Scotland an Act was passed in 1649 that extended the 1563 Witchcraft Act. The coincidence of theater closure and witch persecution, by the argument of this chapter, are both expressive of evangelical horror at performativity. Only in 1735 was a further Act of Parliament passed, which redefined witchcraft as a fraudulent claim.[43] Of course the permanent revolution remained active in America, where the Salem witch trials of 1692–1693, which resulted in twenty executions, mostly of women, were the presage of further American "witch hunts" that took other, political forms.

Between the late fourteenth and the late seventeenth centuries, English theater traversed a vast arc, toward ever more controlled forms of play. It moved from workers' to aristocratic theater; from religious to secular theater; from amateur to professional theater; from street theater to proscenium arch theater, closely within the purview of royal patronage; from sacramental theater to, finally, the theater of upper class social comedy. Above all, or so the thesis of these three chapters would have it, we witness, via the representation of stage conjuration, a long, agonized, and finally successful effort to banish sacral performativity from the stage. The scars of this struggle are long visible; the asylums of magic—"spelling," in the microworld of the nursery, young adult fiction, edgy-scary-ugly Halloween fun—are symptoms of that long struggle.

Theater was by no means destroyed by permanent revolution, but it was, despite the astonishing brilliance of certain theatrical projects within this long arc, ever more tightly limited and constrained. Hostility to idolatrous theater also survived. We see it in blind Milton's last imagined push, as the blind suicide terrorist Samson pushes against the pillars of the theater, which looks very much like Shakespeare's Globe, the

> . . . . spacious Theatre
> Half round on two main Pillars vaulted high,
> With seats where all the Lords and each degree
> Of sort, might sit in order to behold,
> The other side was op'n, where the throng
> On banks and scaffolds under Skie might stand.[44]

Samson Agonistes (published in 1671, and very probably revolutionary Milton's last work) climaxes in a scene now grievously familiar to our own times, as terrorist Samson brings the theater down upon the innocent spectators.[45] Parliament ordered the demolition of theaters in 1648; although new theaters had been constructed after 1660 under royal protection, in the later 1660s Milton was still committed to the task of permanent revolution, imagining the terroristic demolition of the theater and death to its audience:

> He tugg'd, he shook, till down they came and drew
> The whole roof after them, with burst of thunder
> Upon the heads of all who sate beneath,
> Lords, Ladies, Captains, Councellors, or Priests,
> Their choice nobility and flower, not only
> Of this but each *Philistian* City round
> Of dire necessity.
>   (ll. 1650–1656)

Was, as one recent scholar has asked, Milton better than Shakespeare? According to Milton, the answer is most decidedly "yes."

PART 6

Managing Scripture

15

Scripture: Institutions, Interpretation, and Violence

ASK ANY EDUCATED PERSON in the Anglophone street to specify the greatest gain of the Reformation and the answer is likely to include, near the top of the list, freedom to interpret the Bible. Bump into a scholar, even a great scholar, in that same street, pose the same question, and the answer is sometimes the same. Ask, for example, Alistair McGrath, who, after stressing Lutheran "democratization of the faith," answers by underlining the great and indisputable gain of interpretative freedom: "Luther insisted that all believers have the right to read the Bible in a language they can understand and to interpret its meaning for themselves."[1] This right to interpret feeds directly, by McGrath's upbeat account, into a calm, deliberative process of ecclesiastical reform: "Luther insisted that every Christian has the right to interpret the Bible and to raise concerns about any aspect of the Church's teaching or practice that appears to be inconsistent with the Bible."[2]

The title of McGrath's book, published in 2007, is *Christianity's Dangerous Idea: The Protestant Revolution—A History from the Sixteenth Century to the Twenty First*. Given the triumphalist argument of this long book, one can only assume that, for McGrath, the "danger" of his title is an example of free indirect discourse: the revolutionary Protestant idea is "dangerous," that is, only to those with vested interests and who stand to lose by it. The title implicitly proclaims, that is, both the desirability of the "dangerous" revolution, and its ongoing force (from the sixteenth to the twenty-first centuries).

It will be clear from the theme of the current book thus far that I agree entirely with McGrath about Protestantism's revolutionary, dangerous, and kinetic nature. I disagree, however, with his triumphalism. The free indirect discourse of McGrath's title implies that the revolution was insufficiently dangerous; I hope the evidence of the current book so far might suggest that the inevitable passage to early European modernization was quite dangerous enough.

There is much to take issue with in McGrath's book, which is a classic and undiluted example of Protestant triumphalism. It looks to the proto-liberal end of the Reformation and reads that proto-liberalism directly back into the violent century and a half before 1688 (in England). One might mount an extended critique of the book by starting with phrases such as "raise concerns," in the quotation above, with regard to interpretive freedom ("right to interpret the Bible and to raise concerns about any aspect of the Church's teaching"): such phrases are the staple of Bible reading groups of the contemporary liberal university; they do not come from the sixteenth or seventeenth centuries. When we look to Lutheran and Calvinist reading practice, we certainly do find Bible translations, and we do find an intense reading culture. But we do not find "concerns raised"; we do not see practices that possibly "appear" to be at variance with the Bible. Neither do we see individual interpretive freedom.

On the contrary, we see a definition of institutional belonging and demand so extreme as to impose a punishing interpretative régime. We also see, instead of "concerns being raised," unending, uncompromising, physical, cultural, and psychic violence grounded on an entirely new and revolutionary understanding of divine textuality. By accepting accounts of the kind offered by McGrath (and he is far from being alone), the liberal tradition ends up praising the genealogy of fundamentalism and ignoring a much more persuasive claimant to a liberal genealogy—the variegated but rich tradition of anti-literalism that runs from the late fourteenth to the mid-seventeenth centuries and beyond. Although I do not have space precisely to delineate each point in that vernacular anti-literalist tradition in these three chapters, we should at least note the major contributions: Reginald Pecock (d. ?1460), Thomas More (d. 1535), Richard Hooker

(d. 1600), William Shakespeare (d. 1616), and, one way or another, John Milton (d. 1674).

Like most revolutions, the Reformation had its book and its reading practice. The book was the Bible, and the reading practice was literalism. Revolutions all usher in a new textual canon in their train, and they all, of necessity, locate interpretative truth in the literal sense. They must do that, since the revolution, by definition, constitutes a radical break with the past; the new society is determined by a document, either freshly written or rediscovered. The reading protocols for that document must be open and incontrovertible in the present; and the truth claim of any such document must not make appeal to a past reading community, with historically shaped interpretive practices. To recognize any historical determination of meaning would compromise the revolution's claim to have started afresh, without reliance on any practice of the ancien régime. The society brought into being by the revolution, whether in 1517, 1688, 1776, or 1789, is brought into being by the document, not the other way around. The document must therefore be self-generating; must posit literalism as the hermeneutic default position; and must itself lay claim to literalist status. Its understanding of textuality is nearly the opposite of, say, English common law, and of English constitutionalism, both of which depend wholly on precedent, so much so in the case of English constitutionalism as to abjure any single codified, written document whatsoever.[3]

Like all revolutions, the Reformation certainly had its new textual canon and its literalist hermeneutics. Unlike other revolutions, however, the Reformation was fundamentally *about* reading practice.

This may derive from the fact that early modern Europe experienced an information-technology revolution whose profound effects perhaps only we, who are experiencing our own information-technology revolution, are in a position remotely to appreciate.[4] It might be the case, that is, that the information technology of movable type, from its introduction to Europe in 1456 (to England in 1476), transformed the substance of religion as deeply as it utterly transformed almost every other aspect of European culture.[5] That the first product of Johannes Gutenberg (c. 1400–1468) was a Bible (1456) is expressive of a new technology in which nothing, including salvation itself, will escape the demand of textual legitimation.

The new technology, it could be argued, came so to mesmerize spirits that every aspect of the salutary process, including eternal salvation itself, needed to make its sacrifice at the altar of that new technology: to be legitimate, a practice had to be authorized by what was written; to be saved, one had to read. Certainly every aspect of Reformation practice can be traced, directly or indirectly, to a Scriptural foundation.

The imponderable transformation of the early modern information technology revolution happened to coincide with, and subtend, another transformative process, hardly less momentous in its consequences. Early modern state centralization exacerbated already existing divisive tensions, if not produced outright breaks, between European nation-states and the competing jurisdiction of the Papacy throughout the sixteenth and seventeenth centuries.[6]

The introduction of printing into this labile environment had both centrifugal and centripetal effects within nascent national polities. Print produced books in vastly greater numbers and at vastly reduced prices; it was most obviously, therefore, a centrifugal force. Print also created centrifugal international reading circles, as we can see in the circulation of learned discourse, such as of Thomas More's *Utopia* (1516).[7]

Centrifugalism should not, however, occlude the ways in which printing also contributed powerfully in the opposite direction—to modernity's fundamental narrative of centralization. Thus in England, for example, the language itself was centralized and, as it were, nationalized by one linguistic standard produced by the new medium of print from London.[8] The capital's dialect and its book commerce replaced a much more linguistically variegated and geographically dispersed network of literary production in the pre-Reformation period. The destruction of monasteries, their libraries, and their scriptoria in the latter 1530s also had the effect of centralizing book production and trade in London, and book storage in London, Oxford, and Cambridge.[9] The centralized printing of books both enabled and necessitated much tighter national regulation and censorship both of book and theater production.[10]

Above all, the newly centralizing states of early modern Europe needed one book in particular (i.e. the Bible) in their own vernacular language, by way of contributing to the independence and cultural authority of the newly affirmed, modernizing state.[11]

The effects of new information technologies, and new nationalisms, are profound yet elusive. They create new interiorities, new communities, and new forms of trust (and distrust). These are huge and complex topics, as much anthropological as technological, which, for want both of space and expertise, I cannot broach here. For the new information technologies of later medieval and early modern England, I direct the reader to pioneering scholarship that has investigated the history of late medieval literacy; later medieval writing and trust; early modern literacy; early modern print practice and Protestantism; and early modern history of the material book.[12] Much of this scholarship operates under the aegis of the evergreen, monumental, visionary work of Elizabeth Eisenstein, *The Printing Press as an Agent of Change* (1979).[13] For the cultural centralizations of sixteenth-century English nationalism, I direct the reader to superb books by Richard Helgerson and Cathy Shrank.[14]

The chapters to follow pursue less the material history of the book than the history of reading and community formation (and fracture). They pursue, to put it another way, the relation of textual interpretation and violence. The evidential materials I use are less material books than, on the one hand, Reformation discourse about how scriptural writing legitimates or delegitimates institutional practice and spiritual status; and, on the other hand, Reformation literary texts that express, and sometimes seek to neutralize, the violence of early modern revolutionary Biblical reading.

The violence unleashed by Lutheran and Calvinist reading programs was in the first instance directed, as a torpedo, at the Catholic Church. The overall scale of its institutional consequences was unlike any previous textual phenomenon in European history. It was of even greater scale than the passage from polytheism to Christianity, with its new textualities, in late Antiquity.[15] The hard-hitting, categorical impact of the early modern Scriptural was, as we shall see, felt with mighty force upon Catholic practice (no "raising concerns" here!) from the first stage of the Reformation.

Like other phenomena of Reformation revolutionary culture, however, the new reading régime quickly became a practice of permanent revolution, dividing Protestantism from itself much more vigorously than it divided Protestantism from Catholicism. The modernizing literalist power of the Biblical textual claim remained undiminished across the entire Reformation period and beyond.

The substance of the present chapter will be focused on the textual schisms largely internal to the English Protestant experience in England, and largely restricted to the first phase of the Reformation in England, up to the Elizabethan Settlement of 1559. The issues that determined action in that period continued to exert powerful influence up to the end of the seventeenth century (and beyond). The substance of Chapters 16 and 17 will be grounded in the evidence of literary texts. There we will find ourselves looking more to the ways in which this reading culture divided readers exhaustingly from themselves, with some extraordinary examples of attempts to move out from under the crushing heel of this reading régime.

McGrath is correct to locate interpretive freedom as one of the indisputable gains of the Protestant Reformation. That freedom only came, however, at terrible cost, with concerted repudiation of evangelical reading practice, and after fierce struggles within the Protestant movement. Its end point was indeed a renewed and sharpened sense of the profound value of individual reading and interpretive freedom. Indeed, the freedom to read and interpret remains close to the doctrine of "salvation" for secular liberalism (precisely given its Reformation genealogy). That liberal interpretative freedom is, to be sure, the achievement of Reformation's end, but it emerges from a diametrically opposed reading culture at the Reformation's start.

Not to put too fine a point on the matter, European modernity's initial, and enduring, fundamentalist reading culture produced 150 years of revolutionary violence. The true Church imposed intense institutional demands on interpretive practice and application. Those demands were of such exactingly high and nonnegotiable quality as inevitably to fracture nations, communities, and psyches.

Scripture alone is the arbiter of the present. Only elect members of the True Church are true readers of Scripture. In these two statements hang all the energy and all the violent fracture. The narrative genre of this reading lesson, from the dark Reformation beginning to its provisional and brighter end, is tragedy marked by historical irony. It was tragic because it swept entire communities up into violence beyond the imaginings of most participants. Its historical irony consists in this fact: the proto-liberal, provisional end point of the long and painful reading lesson was nearly the opposite of that intended by its initial illiberal, literalist teachers.

I

The history of the late medieval, early modern English vernacular Bible and its interpretation brings into view what may be a plausible, if hidden, period, or para-period in English cultural history.[16] We might name this para-period by using the principal headline of evangelicals themselves, "The Age of Biblical Literalism." The "period" would run from the late fourteenth century to the mid-seventeenth century, from Lollardy to the Civil War, a cultural unit with many other connecting strands (e.g. iconoclasm, hypocrisy, despair, anti-theatricality, fear of performativity), all of which are hidden from view by the standard periodic persuasions of Anglophone culture and its disciplines (i.e. medieval versus early modern, or pre- versus post-Reformation).

The main narrative of this cultural historical "period" as regards the Bible would be driven by the momentous interpretive struggle between two competing cultural formations. In the one corner, we would have what might be called originalists (for whom only the application of the original meaning in the present matters). Facing them, we see those who mount powerful cases for Scripture as a living document, to be interpreted afresh within new historical circumstances, with non-textual interpretative tools (e.g. charity and reason), and often within conciliar determinations. There would be plenty of stories of the huge impact of Biblical reading on individuals across this period, but no story of the right of individual interpretive freedom, outside a Church, until the latter half of the seventeenth century.

The main material for the delineation of this para-period would be twofold: on the one hand, the history of Bible translations into the vernacular, and, on the other, the history of competing interpretative positions and their immense historical impact. Of course our imagined new para-period would have long prehistories in England, from the especially rich set of Anglo-Saxon Biblical materials up to the eleventh century, and the Anglo-Norman Biblical materials in the thirteenth and fourteenth centuries.[17] For the English vernacular, however, the story both of Biblical translations and of interpretive contest and impact runs from the late fourteenth to the mid-seventeenth century. We will have occasion to observe some of the interpretative contests in this and the following chapters. For the moment, I briefly sketch the high points of the story of formal Biblical translation into the English vernacular in early modernizing England.

From 1380, upwards of 250 copies of part of, or in 21 instances the whole of, the Bible in English (translated from Jerome's late fourth-century Vulgate) survive. They do so in two distinct but consecutive versions, the second an improvement on the first in the crucial matter of stylistic accessibility.[18] This remarkable textual product met with fierce official opposition. Thus the seventh article of the *Constitutions* of Archbishop Arundel of 1407 specifies the punishment for translating Scripture as the punishment set aside for heresy (i.e. burning). The burning of those convicted of heresy was a new penal tool for English authorities, first instituted by statute in 1401, even if little used in the following century.[19]

In Henrician England the first Herculean effort at translation by William Tyndale also met with fierce official repression. The story of Tyndale's translations has been told by David Daniell.[20] We will not pause to recount it again here, beyond signalling these events: Tyndale's first, interrupted New Testament of 1525, produced in Cologne (of which only one set of sheets up to Matthew 22 survives), was followed by his first complete translation, the first translation of the Greek New Testament into English, in 1526, in Worms.[21] This was smuggled into England and Scotland in the face of active official resistance. Tyndale's 1525 text is supplied with Lutheran marginalia.[22]

Tyndale learned Hebrew in exile, and by 1530 he had translated and published the Pentateuch and supplied each of the five books with a prologue.[23] This is the first translation of the scriptures from Hebrew into English. Possibly a year later he published his translation of the Book of Jonah.[24] Before his likely translation, though not publication, of Joshua to 2Chronicles by 1535, Tyndale had published the second, revised edition of his 1526 New Testament, in 1534.[25] In August 1536, after having been captured by trickery in exile in Antwerp, Tyndale was convicted of heresy under imperial jurisdiction, and in October of that same year he was strangled prior to being burned.

From this wholly underground operation, the situation in England rapidly changed to one of official approval of the vernacular Bible. A year before Tyndale's execution, a full English Bible had been produced in 1535, in exile, by Miles Coverdale (1488–1569), using Tyndale for the Pentateuch and the New Testament, with the rest being supplied by Coverdale's own translations from Latin and German texts.[26] Only two years after this, Coverdale's version had been drawn on by John Rogers in Antwerp for the Matthew Bible of 1537, now using all the Tyndale material used by Coverdale, but also using Tyndale's translation from the Hebrew of Joshua to 2Chronicles.[27] All this, however, came before the really decisive event, the Great Bible of 1539, which was promoted by the full force of the state.[28] The Injunctions of Thomas Cromwell (Henry's Vicar-General from 1535) of 1538 enjoin every parish priest as follows:

> Ye shall provide . . . one book of the whole Bible of the largest volume in English, the same set up in some convenient place within the said church that ye have cure of [responsibility for], whereas your parishioners may most commodiously resort to the same, and read it.[29]

Biblical sales figures, even before 1539, underline the intense desire of the reading public for the vernacular Bible. Before a vernacular Bible became official in 1538, as many as fifty thousand copies of Tyndale's and of Coverdale's translations of scripture had been produced, each copy bought in danger.[30] Before his death in 1546, Luther's German Bible had gone through over four hundred total or partial printings.[31] In England, a total of 280 separate editions of the full Bible were published between 1520 and 1640, with a steep spike in production between 1610 and 1640.[32]

The pattern of unofficial vernacular Bible translation followed by officially approved versions was far from exhausted with the sanctioned dissemination of the Great Bible of 1539. A further official vernacular translation was produced in 1568, the so-called Bishops' Bible.[33] The next two main vernacular translations were both published unofficially, from abroad, by opposing confessional groups.

Thus Marian Protestant Genevan exiles (exiled both from England and then from Frankfurt), produced the Geneva Bible (1557 New Testament and 1560 Bible), which was licensed though not "actively endorsed by English authorities."[34] This staggeringly successful and influential book made the Biblical text much more accessible by its quarto and octavo formats, its use of roman font, its division not only of the text into chapters but also of chapters into numbered verses for the first time, and its apparatus of maps.[35] It also supplied the reader, counter to the 1542 prohibition on marginal commentary (of which more below), with abundant commentary in the outer margins of every page, both philological and theological (in this case Calvinist).[36] This Calvinist Bible can fairly claim to being the most influential Bible of our newly baptized "Age of Literalism," with 140 editions and "at least half a million copies sold."[37]

The second of these exilic translations was produced from the English Catholic, recusant college in Douai, and published in Rheims (New Testament 1582) and Douai (Old Testament, in two volumes, 1609–10).[38] These texts translate Jerome's late fourth-century Vulgate Latin, though promise to compare the text with the Greek and Hebrew. They are beautifully produced in roman font, with chapter and verse numbers. They also supply abundant marginal commentary that points to the liturgical placement of Scriptural text, and to Catholic theology. Their plentiful discursive marginalia manifest indubitable awareness of Protestant attack, as they defend, for example, pilgrimage, penance, Purgatory, and meritorious works.[39]

The last of the great early modernizing translations is the King James Bible of 1611.[40] This Bible is deliberately archaic, in both style and black-letter font. It is also minimalist in its marginalia, avoiding theology and restricting itself to small points of philology.

All these texts demonstrate a rule of inverse relation between proximity to power and density and quality of marginal annotations. The further, that is, the edition is from official status, the more dense and polemical the annotations. The clearest examples are the exilic translations, both Calvinist and Catholic, all of which nail confessional affiliation consistently to their marginal masts.

That same rule is confirmed when we look to officially sanctioned translations, where official sanction militates against marginalia (thus the low key and brief marginalia to the Bishops' Bible, 1568). King James is reported to have dismissed the Geneva Bible precisely on account of its marginal annotation: "he gave this caveat ... that no marginal notes should be added [to the King James Bible], having found in them, which are annexed to the Geneva translation ... some notes very partial, untrue, seditious, and savoring too much, of dangerous, and traitorous conceits."[41]

II

The previous section supplies a bare narrative of only the high points of Reformation English vernacular scriptural *translation*. That story runs from 1380 or so to 1611. The story of the *interpretation* of these texts runs for very much longer than up to 1611. That story uses, as its material, precisely the translations just listed. The fight for the scriptures in the vernacular was always a foregone conclusion, which even conservatives conceded early on.[42] The fierce fight for interpretive protocols for Scripture is not in the least foregone, even by 1688 (even, in the United States, by 2017). It began, again in the late fourteenth century, with the beginning of the characteristically early modern hermeneutics of literalism.[43] The rest of this chapter delineates the early and decisive phases of early modern debates about Biblical interpretation.

Luther's Ninety-Five Theses of 1517 are for the most part a brilliantly courageous, playful, and offensive polemical attack on the sale of indulgences. Buried within the document at Thesis 62 there lies, however, a simple statement aimed less at a particular practice of the Church and more at its very foundations: "The true treasury of the Church is the Holy Gospel [given by] the glory and grace of God."[44] *Scriptura sola* will quickly become the essential weapon of Lutheranism in its attack on the Catholic Church. It is a polemical textual weapon: Scripture is so much the treasure of the Church that it will quickly come to determine the Church.

In each of his three polemical works of 1520 (i.e. *The Babylonian Captivity of the Church, To the Christian Nobility of the German Nation,* and *The Liberty of a Christian Man*), Luther had clearly understood the mighty scriptural power at his disposal. In his address *To the Christian Nobility,* for example, Scripture is imagined as a battering ram that will break through one of the three illicit walls that the Roman Church has built around itself, the wall of the Church's jurisdiction over Scriptural interpretation:

> The Romanists want to be the only masters of Holy Scripture, although they never learn a thing from the Bible all their life long. They assume the sole authority for themselves, and, quite unashamed, they play about with words before our very eyes.[45]

A year later, Luther's convictions about Scripture's power are expressed in existential, psychic terms. Thus in his celebrated speech at Worms before the Emperor in April 1521, Luther summarizes the irresistibility of Scripture's power over him. In his peroration, he stands famously fast by effectively reordering the power relations between Scripture and the Church. He presents himself as Scripture's helpless prisoner, unable to recognize any but Scriptural authority. His conscience is captured by the Word of God: "I am defeated, the scriptures having been adduced by me, and, with my conscience captured by the words of God, I am unable to retreat." Compelled by that authority, he's helpless: "Ich kan nicht anders, hier stehe ich, Got helff mir, Amen" ("I cannot do otherwise; here I stand, may God help me").[46] Even if this reported speech is apocryphal, modernity of a powerful and post-human kind is born in this moment of defeat and imprisonment by text.[47]

The reassignment of power relations among Scripture and the Church effected by Luther in these years is momentous. The question at the heart of this reassignment is as follows: which has priority, Scripture or the Church, text or textual community? Does Scripture determine the Church, or does the Church determine Scripture?[48] The entire shape and activity of the Church will depend on one's answer. If one believes that Scripture determines the Church, as Luther and the entire evangelical tradition after him did, then Scripture's authority must eject everything without scriptural authorization—mere human "traditions"—from the Church. As William Tyndale (d. 1536) says, it is as difficult to answer the question as to which came first, Scripture or Church, as to answer the question which came first, father or son:

> For the whole scripture and all believing hearts testify that we are
> begotten through the Word. Wherefore if the Word is the begetter
> of the congregation . . . then is the gospel before the church.[49]

If, by contrast, one believes that the institution (what more recent literary theory has called "the interpretive community") determines Scripture and its authority, then Scripture falls into place as one authority among others in determining ecclesiastical structure and practice. One will in that case readily admit "traditions" not explicitly authorized by Scripture.

The breathtaking scale of the change necessitated by this new valuation of Scripture, and the violence required to effect it, was visible both to Catholics and to evangelicals from the beginning of the English Reformation.

On the Catholic side, it was not coincidentally a lawyer, Thomas More (d. 1535), who quickly pressed the case for the Church's priority over Scripture with greatest argumentative force and hermeneutic acumen. I have delineated these positions elsewhere.[50] In essence, More articulates a lawyer's, and in some ways a pre-modern, account of textuality, in which writing does not exclude all other forms of authority; in which writing is recognized as subject to historical contingency; in which the literal sense is elusive; and in which all writing requires prior agreement about how it will be interpreted. No writing can be expected to transmit a full package of a written interpretative key to its own understanding, since that interpretive key will require its own key, and so on ad infinitum. At some point we need to trust, and we need to trust representative institutions to shepherd canonical texts on which institutional structures and practices depend. For More (who is a conciliarist and not a proponent of Papal absolutism), those representative institutions are the General Councils of the Church.[51]

On the evangelical side, Thomas Cranmer's *A Confutation of Unwritten Verities* (first published 1556) might exemplify the evangelical position. It argues, in summary, that the Word of God, as written in Scripture, is both true and wholly sufficient for our salvation; that without written Scriptural authority, the writings of the fathers are without force; that without written Scriptural authority, Church Councils are insufficient to formulate articles of faith; that words reported by angelic visitation (and visitation of the dead) are worthless; that neither miracles nor custom are of any value in "proving a religion"; and that visions are worthless.[52]

Anyone proposing such upheaval is clearly prepared to countenance significant violence. Already by 1521 Luther looked at that violence in the face and accepted it, not only as inevitable, but as a positive sign that the Gospel was being preached. His grounds for such confidence were, of course, themselves Scriptural. Even if bearing witness to Scripture should cause upheaval, he declares in his speech to the Emperor, so be it. After all, Christ himself came to provoke internal dissention: "Think not, that I am come to send peace into the earth. I came not to send peace, but a sword. For I am come to set a man at variance against his father" (Matthew 10:34).[53] By 1525, in his *Bondage of the Will* (1525), Luther exclaims that the Word must be proclaimed whole, regardless of the tumult it causes. In fact the tumult is a sign that the Word is being truly preached. "For myself," he says, "if I did not see these tumults I should say that the Word of God was not in the world; but now, when I do see them, I heartily rejoice."[54]

By 1525 Germany had experienced very significant violence, indirectly associated with Lutheran influence. The Peasants' War of 1524–1525 saw between one and three hundred thousand peasants slaughtered by their rulers. By Luther's account, the peasants were inspired by their own mistaken reading of Scripture ("they cloak this terrible and horrible sin with the gospel").[55] Luther exhorted those repressing the revolt "to smite, slay and stab, secretly or openly, remembering that nothing can be more poisonous, hurtful or devilish than a rebel. It is just as when one must kill a mad dog" (p. 50). If a man is in open rebellion, "everyone is both his judge and his executioner"(p. 50). In this first test of readers "raising concerns" about Biblical meaning (to use McGrath's polite phrase), Luther adopts the killing-of-mad-dogs response over the recognition of readerly freedom.[56] This is consonant with what Luther stated as doctrine in 1523, just prior to his treatment of the bad peasant readers:

> This is not Christian teaching, when I bring an opinion to Scripture
> and compel Scripture to follow it, but rather, on the contrary, when
> I first have got straight to what Scripture teaches, and then compel
> my opinion to accord with it.[57]

In England the scale of change demanded by the evangelical reading protocol was dramatic. Already within the first fifty or so years of the Reformation, the following had fallen victim, at differing speeds, to the new régime of the scriptural written, and only the scriptural written: almost the entire sacramental system (including Purgatory and pilgrimage) of the Catholic Church; all its institutions of the regular life, including institutions of the contemplative life, between 1536–1541; its entire iconic apparatus (every religious image); and its tradition of the saints.[58] Theatrical performances, and visionary traditions that operated within, and sometimes outside, the ambit of ecclesiastical structures, were also proscribed.[59] In

England, only the Catholic Church's governance structure had effectively survived intact, in the form of a Caesaro-Papal monarch and bishops, even if that structure would also be temporarily abolished in the 1640s and 1650s. Each of these issues of practice or governance generated specific traditions of polemic, but the essential principle underlying them all is articulated by Richard Hooker: "that nothing should be placed in the Church but what God in his word hath commanded."[60]

III

When Luther in Germany and Tyndale in England recognized the violence inherent in their scriptural project, they imagined it to be turned against the Catholic Church. For the first sequence of the Reformation in England, up to the end of the reign of Edward VI in 1553, that front had in England been advanced, despite some reversals, with stunning success: in twenty or so years, from the Act of Supremacy of 1534, upwards of a thousand years of accreted institutional practice and structure had been dismantled (in many cases physically dismantled). England now had a Protestant Church, which, once Catholic Queen Mary had died in 1558, was confirmed with striking Calvinist clarity in the Elizabethan Settlement of 1559 and the Thirty-Nine Articles formulated in 1563 and ratified in 1571. The sixth of those articles declared that Scripture was to be the rule of doctrine: "whatsoever is not read therein, nor may be proved thereby, is not to be required of any man, that it should be believed as an article of the Faith."[61]

In the Prologue to the 1535 Bible, addressed to lay readers, Coverdale imagines the vernacular Bible being gratefully received by a calm and meditative public. He runs down a list of figures from different social levels and with different functions; and he encourages each in turn to apply the scriptural text to their respective positions in the world. Magistrates, preachers, parents as they teach their children: all are enjoined to consult, promulgate, and apply Biblical reading. The new Biblical society will be endowed with calm, and the new Biblical reader, with a wholly new and deeply pleasurable perception of the world: "Thou shalt find sweetness therein, and spy wondrous things, to thy understanding, to the avoiding of all seditious sects, to the abhorring of thy old sinful life, & to the stablishing of thy godly conversation."[62] The profound and wholly constructive transformation of society will have taken place through a redistribution of reading skill and practice.

Coverdale adumbrates the ideal and wide distribution of Biblical reading that would produce this obedient and coherent society when he wishes, in another Biblical prologue also published in 1535, that

> our minstrels had none other thing to play upon, neither our car-
> ters and ploughmen other thing to whistle upon, save psalms,
> hymns, and such godly songs as David is occupied withal! And if
> women, sitting at their rocks, or spinning at the wheels had none
> other songs to pass their time withal, than such as Moses sister, Gle-
> hana's wife, Debora, and Mary the mother.[63]

No modern reader can fail to be moved by Coverdale's imagination of profound reading experience descending the social scale, and moving across gender lines. Was it likely, however, that free distribution of a society's canonical text, on which the key institutional structures, both ecclesiastical and political, rested, would be effected with the kind of so-cial and doctrinal cohesion, "to the avoiding of all seditious sects," so readily imagined by Coverdale? Societies govern interpretation canonical texts on which public institutions rest with great care, since not to do so is to invite anarchy. Everyone is, for example, permitted to interpret the Constitution of the United States, to be sure, but not everyone is permitted to put their personal interpretations into practice.

How was interpretive power over Scripture distributed in early Refor-mation England? A given society's system of authority is like a hydraulic system: repress power in one place, and it will surface in another. Once the textual authority of the Catholic Church had been repressed, alternative claims of authority to govern Biblical meaning quickly resurfaced else-where within newly "Protestant" England. These resurfacings were signs of inevitably schismatic divisions that would continue to divide English so-ciety for more than a century, until more stable reading protocols had been recovered, and until new relations between political and ecclesiastical power had been established.

Luther breezily asserts that interpretative authority resides in Scripture, since Scripture handily interprets itself: Scripture, he declares in 1520, is "en-tirely secure, easy, and open through itself; it interprets itself (sui ipsius interpres), testing, judging and illuminating everything."[64] That solution will not survive in real interpretive contests. I briefly articulate the positions of two further claimants to interpretive authority - philology, and royal power - and the fractures produced by each, in the contest for control of Scriptural meaning in the first stage of the English Reformation. The claim of philology quickly surfaced already in the 1530s, while royal power made its persuasive bid for control in the immediate aftermath of the Great Bible of 1539.

If one simultaneously holds that the literal sense is all, and that there is no institution mediating dispute about the literal sense, then one's first claim for the authority of one's own reading will be based on philological expertise. Philological dispute immediately and inevitably broke out among evangelicals themselves in the 1530s. A moment's reflection by any textual scholar will confirm that the literal sense is a very fragile entity. Any interpretive movement premised on nonnegotiable commitment to the coherent literal sense will inevitably be a schismatic movement. This is especially true when the canonical texts were internally conflicted, and written at different times between 2,100 and 1,400 years ago (the temporal gap between the composition of Biblical texts and anyone living in the sixteenth century).

The most spectacular immediate philological dispute surfaced visibly at the Marburg Colloquy in 1529 over the literal sense of the word "is" (always a rhetorically tricky word!). A Zwinglian interpretation of "This is my body" (e.g. Matt 26:26) ran against the Lutheran view: for Zwingli the word "is" means "signifies," while for Luther it meant "is." This philological issue led directly to profound differences of sacramental understanding (or vice versa), which split the Protestant world from the beginning.[65]

This fissure immediately penetrated Lutheran England, and was part of the reason why England was so briefly Lutheran, before becoming briefly Zwinglian, before becoming enduringly if dividedly Calvinist. Thus England's premier evangelical philologist, William Tyndale (c. 1494–1536), published his *Brief Declaration on the Sacraments* between July 1533 and his imprisonment in May 1535. Tyndale adopted the Zwinglian position, which had enormous consequences for the future definition of the sacrament of the Eucharist in both English theology and in English memory systems.[66]

Accurate translation of single Biblical words was crucial for doctrine. Tyndale had provoked Thomas More's wrath by translating key words such as "*penitentia*," "*ecclesia*," "*caritas*," and "*presbyter*" as, respectively, "repentance," "congregation," "love," and "elder" instead of "penitence," "Church," "charity," and "priest."[67] These translational choices were, in More's view, tendentious, since they were made so as to destabilize key structural and doctrinal supports of the Catholic Church.[68]

Control over such words was authorized by a claim to philological expertise. Listen, for example, to Tyndale in the Prologue to his 1534 New Testament. In the very first paragraph Tyndale explains what the reader should do if differences are found between the Greek and this text:

> Let the finder of the fault consider the Hebrew phrase or manner of speech left in the Greek words. Whose preterperfect tense and present tense is oft both one, and the future tense the optative mode also.[69]

New forms of precise, grammatically informed, philological argument about the literal sense were being shaped as part of modernity's new textual culture. Matters of life and death hung on single letters, as Tyndale himself knew only too well. Thus in the Prologue to his Pentateuch of 1530, Tyndale says that his enemies have "so narrowly looked on my translation, that there is not so much as one i therein if it lack a tittle over his head, but they have noted it, and number it unto the ignorant people for an heresy."[70] If the sixteenth century marks the high point of philological influence in European history, it also, correlatively, marks the high point of danger for philologists. By John Foxe's account, Tyndale had declared to his detractors that he had translated Scripture with "faithful dealing and sincere conscience," never altering "one syllable of God's word against my conscience."[71] Every syllable counted in the discursive world of Henry VIII's England, a life-or-death pressure that also applied to readers, since, as Tyndale encourages his reader, think "that every syllable pertaineth to thine owne self."[72]

Disputes over the translational choices of individual words were not at all, then, minor philological quibbles, since major institutional issues of Church governance and practice, not to speak of charges of heresy for mistranslations, depended on their accuracy. Such issues most readily and obviously divided Catholics from Protestants (e.g. More versus Tyndale). But fierce divisions also immediately opened up within the evangelical camp in the 1530s and 1540s.[73] Such intra-Protestant interpretative divisions are prophetic of the fissile nature of evangelical culture, as long as evangelicals insisted that the literal sense of Scripture was the only acceptable sufficient basis for doctrine.

The second, abiding source of struggle for power over Scripture within Protestant polities, including England, derived from princely interest in the interpretation of Scripture. Frontispieces to Henrician and Edwardian Bibles make a point about reading and power visually: the Bible is now in the hands, literally, of the monarch. By 1542 it was clear that that interpretative power over Scripture would remain in the king's hands, and that the prison was to be enlisted in the reading program. In that year Parliament passed a statute, "An Act for the Advancement of True Religion," which addressed the disruptive interpretation of Scripture. Many "seditious" and "arrogant" people have interpreted the Bible, creating schism "of their perverse forward and malicious minds wills and intents intending to subvert the very true and perfect exposition . . . of the said Scripture, after their perverse fantasies."[74] They have taught Scripture "contrary to the very [i.e. true], sincere and godly meaning of the same," provoking "opinions, sayings, variances, arguments, tumults, and schisms."[75]

The legislative response to this hermeneutic anarchy was carefully to delimit the spaces in which, and the social classes by which, vernacular Bible reading was to be permitted. Above all, the statute disallowed Biblical interpretation. Tyndale's translation is proscribed. All "annotations and preambles" to other translated Bibles must be excised. Moral songs and plays are permitted, as long as they avoid interpretations of Scripture. No women below noblewomen and gentlewomen may read the Bible, and they may only read it to themselves, alone. No other women, and no men below the class of merchant, may read it. Noblemen may read or have it read by their families and servants in their houses or gardens. Merchants may read it privately. Arguing about scripture is prohibited: no one shall "take upon him openly to dispute or argue, to debate or discuss or expound Holy Scripture or any part thereof . . . upon the pains of one month's imprisonment."[76] Any priest who preaches anything contrary to the king's determination of doctrine shall, on the third conviction, be burned as a heretic.[77]

The king's power and responsibility to govern the dissemination and interpretation of Scripture had, by the time of this statute, already been theorized in the vernacular. Very soon after the Act of Supremacy, Christopher St German (d. 1540/41) had argued in his *Answer to a Letter* (1535) that the king had not assumed any new powers that he did not already possess by the Act of 1534.[78] These already-possessed powers include control of Scripture. St German argues that many passages of Scripture are in any case plain, but that where expert opinion is required, this should be the preserve of the king. A theoretical defense of royal hermeneutic supremacy of this kind underlies the strictures in the Act of 1542–1543.

IV

From the beginning, then, of the Protestant Reformation in England, issues of Biblical control, which were, in everyone's view, also issues of Church definition, set English Protestants against other English Protestants. How were disputes about Scriptural meaning to be resolved? Luther had his solution (i.e. Scripture interprets itself). Philologists had theirs (e.g. knowledge of what grammarians call "aspect" for the pluperfect tense in Hebrew). The king had his own answer to that pressing question (i.e. prison and fire).

Horizontal disputes remained, however, unresolved. The fantastic notion that Scripture interprets itself was not going to last more than ten seconds in any actual interpretive dispute, which left philology and royal power as claimants to settling the crucial but treacherous matter of establishing the meaning of ancient texts.

There was, however, a fourth potential claimant to settling the matter of meaning. Short of Scripture interpreting itself; short of philological victory; and short of authoritarian institutional resolution by the secular authority, the only way to conclude (not to resolve) a dispute about the crucial matter of the literal meaning of the Scriptural text was to claim personal conviction.

Tyndale fully recognized the inevitability of the appeal to what he called "feeling faith" (i.e. inner certainty) in claiming interpretive certainty.[79] This claim is not quite as crude as saying, "It's true because I believe it's true." It is, however, as crude as saying, "I'm right on account of the superior understanding I enjoy as a result of my election by God." This move compromises the evangelical principle that Scripture precedes the Church. For "feeling faith" is implicitly a claim to be an elect member of the True Church. This is how Tyndale puts the matter in his *Answer to More's Dialogue* (1531). Just as we believe, Tyndale says, that the fire is hot through experience, so too do the elect have the law of God written in their hearts, and they know it because it's hot. The elect know the truth of the text because they are members of the True Church (i.e. elect):

> Now, therefore, when they ask us how we know it is the scripture of God; ask them how John the Baptist knew, and other prophets, when God stirred up in all such times as the scripture was in like captivity under hypocrites? . . . Who taught the eagles to spy out their prey? Even so the children of God spy out their Father; and Christ's elect spy out their Lord, and trace out the paths of his feet, and follow; yea, though he go upon the plain and liquid water, which will receive no step, and yet there they will find out his foot: his elect know him, but the world knoweth him not.[80]

This is a fascinating moment, since it belies at least two fundamental claims of evangelicals. One fundamental claim is that Scripture precedes the Church. This argument effectively says the opposite: that the True Church precedes Scripture. One can only read properly if one is elect, which is to say a member of the True Church.[81] The doubleness of this inherently unstable claim, on which matters of such profound moment and potential violence rested, will continue to destabilize the evangelical "tradition" for 150 or so years after Tyndale made it.

The second fundamental claim undone by Tyndale's passionate defense of feeling faith in the matter of Biblical interpretation is the one with which we began: that everyone has, in Alistair McGrath's words, the "right to read the Bible in a language they can understand and to interpret its meaning for themselves." If only the elect can read Scripture aright, then that immediately cuts out both Jews and Catholics, as Tyndale himself says:

> Jews which thought themselves within, were yet so locked out, and are to this day that they can understand no sentence of the scripture unto their salvation, though they can rehearse the texts everywhere and dispute thereof as subtly as the popish doctors of dunce's dark learning, with their sophistry, served us.[82]

The ungodly are not the only ones to be excluded. We have already seen how the godly can suffer terrible anguish in the face of their own election. If only the elect can read properly, and if one tests one's election by one's experience of reading Scripture, then reading will obviously become an extremely fraught experience. For confident evangelicals the certainty of assurance permits them to remodel the entire visible Church on the basis of such certainty. For less confident, anguished souls, whose number was legion by the evidence of John Stachniewski's work, the existential question relentlessly posed by reading experience was whether or not they had been saved. All works were useless, and reading was itself a work. But it was, by Luther's account, the only thing to go by. This is not the cool and deliberative world of "rights" and "raising concerns." It is a good deal hotter and nonnegotiably fractious than McGrath's sentimental notion would have us believe.

I turn to the existential experience of those less assured selves, as expressed through the evidence of literary texts, in Chapter 16.

16

Private Scriptural Anguish

CHAPTER 15 FOCUSED ON THE inevitability of institutional schism and violence emerging from evangelical hermeneutics. We saw that early modernizing spiritual institutions, both of Church and State, could not avoid the implications of the new, categorical, literalist interpretation of Scripture. In the sixteenth century those implications were unavoidable and convulsive. Every aspect of Church doctrine, governance, and practice was potentially vulnerable to being rejected as idolatrous if it did not find justification in a set of texts at least 1,400 years old. That nonnegotiable situation, applying a very heterogeneous and ancient set of texts exactly to entirely different historical and cultural circumstances, was certain to produce pain and violence. Evangelical readers often read with a Bible in one hand and a hammer in the other.

In the first and most obvious place, that reading protocol would produce violence between Catholics and Protestants. It was also, however, certain to produce longer-lasting, multiple fissures between Protestants themselves, since, as expert evangelical readers quickly discovered, the grounds for establishing the incontrovertible literal sense, and, therefore, the institutional structures of the Church, were not themselves remotely incontrovertible. Neither was the limit of the literal sense at all clear: were all the Hebrew Scriptures to be applied in the present, or only the laws, or only some of the laws? Were the ceremonial specifications of the Hebrew Scriptures shadows of things to come (and so to be preserved), or mere fleshly law that had now been superseded by the spirit (and so to be wholly rejected)? English Calvinists disagreed spectacularly over these questions regarding the status and limits of the literal sense. Whatever the disputes over the meaning and applicability of the literal sense, everything in the Church that was not judged to be explicitly authorized by Scripture had to go. This persuasion would be the source of permanent revolution, or "scope creep" of the kind that forever extends the range of vulnerable practices whose Scriptural authorization was not iron fast.

The application of sixteenth- and seventeenth-century evangelical reading practice was not, however, restricted to the institution of the Church. It was also directed at individuals, who needed to feel assurance with regard to their own salvation. They therefore tended obsessively to read their own situation into Scripture, or, more often than not, the other way around. As one scholar has said about proto-Protestant Wycliffite readers from the late fourteenth century, "Jesus is always preaching about the Wycliffites rather than the other way around."[1] So too for Reformation evangelicals: Scripture is always about them, either their Church or their own salvation.

The existential experience of Biblical reading for sensitive evangelical readers was readily an experience not only of institutional self-division but also, often, of personal despair. Despair derived from the plain, incontrovertible literal sense. If the Scriptures were to be read literally, as evangelical experts never tired of saying, then the literal news from Scripture was bad: no one is righteous ("As it is written, There is none righteous no not one," Romans 3:10). The first text that Marlowe's Faustus hits upon as he turns to the Vulgate Bible is Romans 6:23 ("For the wages of sin is death"); of course Faustus fails to read the end of the same verse ("but the gift of God *is* eternal life, through Jesus Christ our Lord"), but Faustus's bad reading is precisely Marlowe's point: if one is a literalist, the memory seizes upon that text.[2] And Scriptural ethical injunction was not intended to improve matters, either: Biblical injunctions to good action, or works, in the world, were not at all intended to produce such action, as we shall see; on the contrary, by the evangelical account such injunctions were designed only to underline how *incapable* Biblical readers were of fulfilling them. The aim of the injunctions was not better action; they were instead designed to produce the reader's despairing humiliation.

The only way an evangelical reader could be saved by reading (and s / he could only be saved through the Word) was via grace; and one's assurance of grace was a matter of belonging to the True Church. One had to belong to the True Church before one could read properly, not the other way around. Reading became itself a sign of the one event that subsumes all human agency: God's decision before the creation of the world as to one's salvation or damnation.

Evangelical Scriptural reading was an experience of existential anguish. In this chapter we will look to two such writers from either end of the Reformation period in England, and from either end of the social scale—England's preeminent aristocrat, Henry Howard, Earl of Surrey, in the 1540s, and the Bedfordshire tinker John Bunyan in the 1660s. Both represent literalist Scriptural reading as an experience of anguish: for Surrey, anguished fury; for Bunyan, anguished terror.

I

Evangelical Biblical culture is driven by an inexhaustible textual paradox, caught between an economy of verbal parsimony and verbal excess. The emotional bust and boom economy of evangelical spirituality had its verbal equivalent.

On the one hand, this is a culture that insists on verbal parsimony: nothing must be added, and nothing subtracted, from the text of Scripture. Deuteronomy 4:2 is decisive on this cardinal point, without which evangelical hostility to all those added "traditions" would be without Scriptural backing: "Ye shall put nothing unto the word which I command you, neither do ought therefrom."

On the other hand, evangelical Reformation culture is indisputably a culture of words, words, words. Despite the Deuteronomic prohibition on adding anything to Scripture, in fact evangelical culture turns out to operate under a very different textual economy of verbal boom, if not monstrous excess. As Montaigne wrote in 1588, from within the unspeakable violence of the French Wars of Religion, "Tout fourmille de commentaires ... nostre contestation est verbale" ("Commentaries are multiplying rapidly ... our differences are verbal").[3]

The Deuteronomic prohibition on adding to Scripture should not in theory have worried evangelicals, who declared that Scripture was plain and simple. Their practice, however, betrays anxiety that Scripture is not at all plain or simple. The post-human reading practice that absolutely rejected the value of works in favor of God's grace, or gift, and that insisted on the sole virtue of belief, or faith, was new and extreme. No one except Luther was going to come to it without some serious guidance. Readers had to be trained into it, with abundant words.

So far from observing the stricture of not adding to Scripture, then, evangelical pastoral texts are themselves often, instead, very long.[4] Readers were supplied with abundant prologues; commentaries; marginalia (in unofficial editions of the Bible); catechisms; and interpretative keys that unlock the whole of Scripture.[5] Readers needed to be trained in the key terminology of Lutheran, and then Calvinist, theology. They needed to learn, for example, that "Law" and "Gospel," plus "New Testament," did not refer to historical periods or to certain sections of the Biblical canon. "Law" on the one side, with "Gospel," and "New Testament" on the other, were not consecutive historical sequences for evangelicals.[6] Evangelical readers also needed to learn, over and again, Luther's own fundamental reading lesson: that "justice" meant not human justice, but God's (impenetrable) justice.

Evangelical translators clearly felt uneasy about needing to add their own words. Thus in his Prologue to the New Testament of 1522, Luther explains why he adds words to a completely self-sufficient text:

> It would be right and proper for this book to go forth without any prefaces or extraneous names attached and simply have its own say under its own name. However, many unfounded interpretations and prefaces have scattered the thought of Christians to a point where no one any longer knows what is gospel or law, New Testament or Old. Necessity demands, therefore, that there should be a notice or preface, by which the ordinary man can be rescued from his former delusions, [and] set on the right track.[7]

The literal sense cannot do its work alone, because misunderstandings pre-exist and determine the literal sense.

Tyndale also liberally supplements Scripture. Translating from Luther's Preface to Romans, he also declares that the epistle to Romans is "the principal and most excellent part of the new testament, and most pure evangelion." Tyndale isolates the letter to Romans as, in fact, the key buried within Scripture to unlock what was ostensibly an open text: Romans is "also a light and a way in unto the whole scripture."[8] Tyndale's 1534 New Testament Prologue to the letters of Paul ends up, however, being as long as the letters themselves.[9] Like Luther, Tyndale recognizes that Paul's meaning, however blindingly clear, might have been obscured: although Romans, he says, has been "darkened with glosses and wonderful dreams of sophisters, [so] that no man could spy out the intent and meaning of it," in fact that meaning is "a bright light and sufficient to give light unto all scripture."[10] The text, in short, needs absolutely no accompaniment, except the vast accompaniment that it receives from evangelical theologians. "Tout fourmille de commentaires."

In pre-Reformation England, poets and dramatists were not saddled by the impropriety of "writing scripture," or supplementing Scripture. The pre-Reformation English Church was clearly very anxious about the vernacular Scriptures themselves, from 1407, as we saw in Chapter 15. Precisely because, however, the pre-Reformation Church understood Scripture as a living document that had to be received and renewed in the present, through tradition, it was broadly at ease with literary and dramatic receptions of Scripture. Fourteenth- and fifteenth-century English literary writing has many examples of Scripture being adapted in the present by represented readers who either find themselves in a Scriptural landscape (e.g. Will in *Piers Plowman,* or the narrator of *Pearl,* both written in the last two decades of the fourteenth century), or who bring Scriptural figures into a distinctly English landscape (e.g. the fifteenth-century *Second Shepherds' Play*).[11] To dismiss these transpositions as anachronistic is entirely to misunderstand the fundamental project of these works: bringing Scripture to England and England to Scripture is the entire point.

For post-Reformation evangelicals, on the contrary, writing Scripture, or writing about Scripture, was a peculiarly fraught activity. It was simultaneously otiose and absolutely necessary, as well as being potentially idolatrous, by virtue of adding the human word to the divine Word. Sensitive evangelical authors were themselves despairingly subject to the uselessness of their own textual projects. Thus even God is, as we saw in Chapter 5, incapable of fixing the ground of the *Slough of Despond*: for more than 1,600 years, God has, by the account of Christian's companion Help, sent his surveyors to shore up the spongy ground; despite their pouring "at least twenty thousand cart-loads; yea millions of wholesome instructions" into the slough, and despite the fact that those instructions were "the best materials to make good ground of the place," that ground remains fundamentally boggy and dangerous.[12]

Let us turn to two early modern reader-writers, at either end of the Reformation period, and either end of the social scale. They both confronted the stubbornly boggy verbal terrain of the Slough of Despond, reflecting on whether or not to add one more word to the inviolate text of Scripture, and reflecting on whether or not to make their talkative reading companions, Angst and Self-Doubt, part of the story. I begin with the predicament of Henry Howard, Earl of Surrey, as he awaited execution in late 1546, early 1547.

II

Henry Howard, Earl of Surrey (1516/17–1547), was imprisoned three times: in 1537, in Windsor Castle (rather than have his hand amputated); in 1542, in the Fleet; and finally, in December 1546, in the Tower, on charges of treason. It was there that Surrey was, in early January 1547, beheaded at the age of thirty-one, nine days before the death of the king. While under arrest, Surrey was abandoned by friends and family. This great poet—the accomplished inventor of blank verse in English, no less—was executed, in the chilling words of a recent historian, "as a precaution."[13]

As he awaited execution, Surrey wrote Psalm paraphrases. He had probably already written paraphrases of Psalms 30 and 50, but while in prison under imminent sentence of death across 1546–1547, certainly did write paraphrases of Psalms 55, 73, and 88.[14]

The psalms are routinely considered to be sources of comfort and occasions of thanksgiving. Take, for example, Matthew Parker's Preface to the Psalter, published in 1567:

> And certainly though a man were never so furiously raging in ire
> and wrath, yet as soon as he hears the sweet tunes of the Psalms,

straight way is he assuaged of his fury, and must depart more quiet in mind by reason of the melody. The psalm is the rest of the soul, the rod of peace, it stilleth and pacifieth the raging bellows of the mind ... it maketh amity, where was discord, it knitteth friends together, it returneth enemies to an unity again.[15]

Throughout the medieval and early modern periods, the Psalms were understood to emerge from, and to represent, the treacherous courtly worlds of Saul, David, and Jonathan in ancient Israel, as recounted most graphically in the extraordinary books of Samuel. They frequently present states of encirclement by hostile forces, whether national, legal, or personal.[16] They were, accordingly, perfect texts of choice for sixteenth-century courtiers in trouble.

Does the Psalter provide a resource that "stilleth and pacifieth the raging bellows of the mind" for Surrey and other imprisoned Tudor courtiers? The answer is consistently and simply "no." So far from supplying what sixteenth-century readers called "comfortable words," and so far from pacifying the "raging bellows of the mind," these psalm translations inflame authorial pain.[17] The treacherous courtly and evangelical textual conditions of their composition actively deprive these authors of any consolation. They deprive authors even of the consolations derived from expressing the desire for vengeance, despite the frequency with which these texts call vengeance down upon the heads of enemies.

Surrey rightly considered himself surrounded by treacherous enemies as he lay in prison between December 2, 1546, and January 1547, awaiting execution. (He was beheaded for treason on January 19, 1547, nine days before the death of Henry VIII, on 28 January.)[18] The main thrust of Surrey's psalm translations is to call down upon enemies and false friends, the psalm translations' ostensible addressees, the most terrible divine vengeance. Thus Psalm 55 (also translated by Thomas Smith and John Dudley) begins by expressing the fundamental position of the psalmist, surrounded by enemies and melting for fear were it not for his single, divine source of succor:

Give ear to my suit, Lord! fromward hide not thy face. [away
   from me]
Behold, harking in grief, lamenting how I pray.
My foos they bray so loud, and eke threpe on so fast, [also; press]

Buckled to do me scathe, so is their malice bent. [harm]
Care pierceth my entrails, and travaileth my spirit;
The grisly fear of death environeth my breast.
      (Ps 55, 1–6)[19]

The state of being persecuted is frequently expressed within evangelical culture, but this psalmic accent is especially pertinent to courtiers, who frequently find themselves thrown from the "slipper top / Of court's estates."[20] Thus the anonymous edition of the Psalms printed in Geneva in 1559 and dedicated to Queen Elizabeth, for example, begins its dedication by underlining that the work of translation was undertaken in the context of persecution of English evangelicals themselves, by the "cruel rage and horrible tyranny of the Papists." Yet, the author goes on in his address to the Queen, when the evangelicals heard that God had

> miraculously preserved you to that excellent dignity . . . from the
> fury as such as sought your blood, with most joyful minds and great
> diligence we endeavored ourselves to set forth and dedicate this
> most excellent book of the Psalms unto your grace.[21]

Here the Queen will behold

> the state of the Church and of all God's children continually perse-
> cuted by the wicked, slandered and brought to the pit's brink, yea, to
> slaughter: and yet miraculously preserved, defended, delivered, and
> their blood revenged by God's mighty power and justice.[22]

The early modern Psalms, in fact, explicitly advertise themselves as useful tools to attack persecutors—less ways of "still[ing] and pacif[ing] the raging bellows of the mind," than ways of expressing "ire and wrath." Indeed, a treatise on the Psalms by the fourth-century Eastern Doctor of the Church Athanasius (c. 296–373) regularly prefaced Elizabethan editions of the Psalms.[23] This text underlines the intimate way in which the psalms speak to, and as from, the voice of every reader: "It is easy therefore for every man to find out in the Psalms, the motion and state of his own soul, and by that means, his own figure and proper erudition."[24] The "motion and state of . . . soul" to which the Psalms appeal is not, however, that of assuaged and calm serenity. The state of mind Athanasius suggests for Psalm 55 (translated by Surrey, Smith, and the younger Dudley) is as follows:

> If any persecute thee & quarrel, willing [i.e. desiring] to betray the,
> like as the Pharisees did Christ, and strangers David, abash not thy
> self, but with trust in the Lorde, sing the 54. Psalm, and the 56.[25]

In sum, these courtiers' psalm translations expose a powerful and striking theme of the Psalter, that of the encircled, utterly threatened and exposed, dying voice, a voice betrayed in greatest need by his most intimate friends and coreligionists.

Surrey's own encirclement is without respite. So far from supplying succor, friends have become enemies. An intimate and evangelical friend has betrayed the speaker, whom I call "Surrey":

> Myne old fere and dear friend, my guide that trapped me;
>   [companion]
> Where I was wont to fetch the cure of all my care, [worry]
> And in his bosom hide my secret zeal to God.
>   (Ps 55 (Vulgate 54), 24–26)

As is often the case in the Psalms, the voice and body of the speaker are diminished and viscerally enfeebled in the context of unrelenting threat: in Psalm 55 (Vulgate 54), "Care pierceth my entrails and travaileth my spirit . . . A trembling cold of dread environeth my breast" (ll. 5–7). This is a body and a voice on the very edge, about to go under; all sources of human solidarity have vanished, and God alone is the source of aid; to God alone can Surrey address himself in the first place. The post-human, legally corrupt conditions of this situation produce unmistakable evangelical phraseology.

In stark contrast to the human relations of menacing opacity, spiritual relations are described as energizing in distinctively, and, in my view, un-mistakably evangelical language, such as "the lively faith and pure," the "sweet return to grace," "Whereby each feeble hart with faith might so be fed / That in the mouth of thy elect thy mercies might be spread," words that in the 1540s radiated high evangelical temperature.[26] In this social world, suspended between "hope and despair," the psalmist appeals to God as his only source of comfort. Surrey makes his appeal, via David's voice, as one of the "elect," appealing to the "lively name" of God with a "lively voice."

This very appeal is made, however, only by way of signalling its profound *lack* of felt success. Why, the psalmist begs, does God *refuse* to appear in defense of his own?

> To show such tokens of thy power, in sight of Adams line,
>   Whereby each feeble hart with faith might so be fed
> That in the mouth of thy elect thy mercies might be spread?
>   The flesh that feedeth worms can not thy love declare,
> Nor such set forth thy faith as dwell in the land of despair.
>   In blind endured hearts, light of thy lively name
> Can not appear, as can not judge the brightness of the same.
>   (Surrey, Ps 88 (Vulgate 87), ll. 20–26)

God's silence simply underlines the menace of the human voices threatening the speaker who, inevitably, inhabits "the land of despair" (Ps. 88 (Vulgate 87), l. 24). The ostensibly divinely inspired text falls away from dialogue with the divine into a voicing of solitary suffering. The experience of painful and wholly isolated persecution is itself the only imaginable consolation on offer, since it is a very sign of election. The human voice that expresses that intense suffering performs, however, its own demise, in the moment of its utterance, by voicing the "raging bellows of the mind." Surrey's paraphrases present the bare text, and nothing but the bare and unforgiving text, except to add expressions of Surrey's fury at having been betrayed.

III

New-found literalism left England's premier aristocrat high, dry, and raging in the 1540s. How does literalism look and feel more than a century later, as experienced by another great writer, the Bedfordshire tinker John Bunyan (1626–1688)? In three words: high and dry. In more than three words: Bunyan's *Grace Abounding* (1666, published in four further editions up to 1680) narrates a history of literalist reading that leaves the author/reader crushed and subject to agonized, splintered, chronic depression. Literalism actively hunts Bunyan as its helpless prey.

Luther insisted that salvation came from, and only from, the Word.[27] The Word alone, however, frequently pointed to damnation. Luther's *Freedom of a Christian Man* (1520) states the matter unequivocally, in a formulation that would receive many thousand agonized reformulations in the 150 years to come:

> Therefore the moment you begin to have faith you learn that all things in you are altogether blameworthy, sinful and damnable, as the Apostle says . . . "There is none righteous, no not one . . . they are all gone out of the way, they are all made unprofitable." (Rom. 3:10–12, citing Psalm 14:1–3)[28]

So the law as stated in Scripture was, frequently, unequivocal in its negative judgement. The frequent ethical injunctions of Scripture were, one might have thought, a bulwark against the threat of damnation, but evangelical reading protocols firmly blocked that possibility. A very long-standing tradition in Western pedagogic culture has it that reading serves ethics: we become better people through our reading of canonical texts.[29] Because Luther effectively repudiated ethical improvement as a means to persuade God, he also vigorously repudiated that long pedagogic tradition, and closed the door on that source of readerly comfort and encouragement. One can measure the sheer extremity of the wholly new, early modern evangelical reading protocols by statements of this kind, again from the *Freedom of a Christian Man* (1520):

> Although the commandments teach things that are good, the things taught are not done as soon as they are taught, for the commandments show us what we ought to do, but do not give us the power to do it. They are intended to teach man to know himself, that through them he may recognize his *inability* to do good and may despair of his own ability.[30]

The Biblical text gives us plenty of ethical injunctions, but it does so, by this frankly Kafkaesque account, only by way of insisting on our incapacity to fulfill them. Only through the transcendent portal of grace does the Biblical reader receive readerly comfort. To arrive at that distant portal is, however, an arduous passage, which involves not attempting to open two firmly closed doors, the doors marked "Encouragement to Works" and

"Works." Election preceded lection; one had to keep walking by those closed doors, not trying them, along the dark and long intervening corridor of despair, in order to reach the only open door, the portal of Grace.

The only exit from this reading culture is to persuade oneself that one is, by the Lutheran formula, *simul iustus et peccator*, simultaneously justified and a sinner. One has to be persuaded of one's already effected salvation before one can read with satisfaction. In the evangelical reading experience, Scripture is, therefore, effectively *about* one's own salvation. The Biblical injunction, by this account, says one thing ("Do it"), but that obvious meaning must be subject to crushing humiliation ("You can't do it"). Only that crushing humiliation in the face of a Biblical injunction's obvious meaning is the guarantor of being among the elect, and that humiliation derives from one's Scriptural reading. The primary and specific meaning of the words recedes into a vortex of a single question, "Have I been saved?"

The co-ordinates of this reading culture were established in the 1520s; almost 150 years later, they continued to debase and torture readers. One of the few named objects in *Grace Abounding* (1666) is "a book of Martin Luther" (Luther's commentary on Galatians), "so old that it was ready to fall to piece from piece, if I did but turn it over"; for Bunyan, however, it reads as if it were freshly published, and wholly about him: "I found my condition in his experience, so largely and profoundly handled, as if his book had been written out of my heart."[31] Nothing has changed since the early sixteenth century.

Nothing has changed, either, with regard to the punishing textual economy of evangelical spirituality. In his reading of Luther, Bunyan spectacularly breaks the rules of that textual economy of not adding one word to, or subtracting one word from, Scripture, since he immediately prefers Luther's commentary "before all the Books I had ever seen," except, he quickly adds, "the Holy Bible" (p. 38). That modification of the evangelical textual economy (adding Luther's prose to Scripture) also models Bunyan's own prose, in which he adds liberally to Scripture, even as he is always writing about reading Scripture. In Bunyan's texts, Angst and Self-Doubt are constant reading companions, even if they fail to offer comfort. They are garrulous in their production of words, words, words, none of them comforting for long, all of them predatory.

Grace Abounding to the Chief of Sinners was published for the first time in 1666, the year in which Bunyan was briefly freed from his imprisonment on account of unlicensed preaching. Apart from this brief liberation, the imprisonment lasted in all from January 1661 to March 1672, and was followed by a further period of imprisonment between December 1676 and June 1677. Bunyan's life story is one of being persecuted (he died in 1688, less than a year before the Toleration Act of 1689, having spent nearly ten years in prison since 1661). The official persecution of Bunyan was certainly savage, as related in *A Relation of the Imprisonment of Mr John Bunyan* (written 1660, first published 1765).[32] It pales by comparison, however, with the way in which the Biblical text persecutes Bunyan as reader.

Bunyan is routinely placed at a point of origin for the novel in English. In this text his spirituality, however, undoes all the resources of the novel. Despair, that is, leaves the Christian so mightily exposed that everything around and within him dissolves: narrative shapes; layers of narration; society. Bunyan presents the text as a "relation" of "the merciful working of God" upon his soul (p. 6). The word "relation" might suggest sequential, auto-biographical spiritual narrative. The introduction promises as much, with metaphors of journeying "from Egypt to the Land of Canaan" (p. 4). We are also promised empirical narrative detail, "the Close, the Milk-house, the Stable, the Barn . . . where God did visit your soul" (p. 5).

The Pilgrim's Progress (Book 1, published 1678), does deliver shaped narrative, even if that shape is subject to attrition from guerrilla attacks by Despair, who goes under different disguises, and who always threatens to put the narrative gears into neutral.[33] *The Pilgrim's Progress* also offers abundant narrative detail.

Grace Abounding, by contrast, struggles to narrate. It "relates" a history of reading; such a "relation" has, however, no narrative to speak of. The entire text manifests instead repetitive cycles of chronic despair ("even for some years together," p. 26) momentarily relieved, but in fact also triggered by, very short-lived flashes of conviction.[34] Such narrative details as the text offers (a person, a place, a body) evanesce in the face of appalling anguish.

All narrative impulse, all beginnings, middles, and ends, collapse back into an expression of existential anguish, a state of being so "overcome with despair of life and heaven" that Bunyan finds himself in a torture-chamber cosmos, in which all accretive narrative impulse collapses into repetitive expression of how he simply wishes to escape being human. Trying to understand decisive sequence in this chapter-less book (small sequences are numbered) is unsatisfying work. The closest we get to periodic definitions are with two possible periods of conversion: the first is fake and evanescent (p. 13), and the second strangely unspecified. We hear about it in retrospect: Bunyan tells us that he had "made profession of the glorious Gospel of Christ a long time, and preached the same about five year" (p. 87). This vague temporal reference is as close as we get to precision.

Apart from that fuzzy moment, all other temporal precision and sequence buckles under the pressure of personal suffering. We never learn when or what that moment of decisive "profession" to which Bunyan refers was, since all narrative articulations of this text are constantly undone by the experience of being repeatedly "assaulted with fresh doubts about my future happiness, especially with such as these, Whether I was elected; but how if the day of grace should now be passed?" (p. 19). These very sentences undo future hope even as they contemplate it; they are characteristic of the failure of *Grace Abounding*'s "relation" ever to attain accretive temporal definition and shape.

Neither does Bunyan have any protective layer, or mask, or narrative persona that mediates between him and his reader, so as to gain any distance or protection from the onslaught of despair. Any such layer as he assumes is quickly stripped, as when, for example, he begins by relating a brief period of "some outward Reformation." The word "outward" gives the game away, since this state is quickly dismissed as "play," only a pathetic distraction deployed by a "poor painted Hypocrite" (p. 13). Such outward show must and will be quickly and painfully stripped by the corrosive of unremitting despair, leaving Bunyan "afflicted and tossed about by my sad condition" (p. 27). All spaces of psychic asylum demolished, he is left with a single choice: either to inflict or to endure extreme pain: Bunyan thus finds himself wishing that he were a devil, since he imagines that devils "were only tormentors," and that if "indeed I went thither [i.e. to Hell], I might be rather a tormentor, than tormented myself" (p. 7). All we can see is Bunyan tortured and longing for post-humanity.

Neither does he have any friend or social resources that mediate between him and the predations of his despair: he is "alone, and above the most men unblest" (p. 27). Other people have but a shadowy existence in *Grace Abounding*; we hear nothing of community, only of occasional, almost always nameless, figures who give, or fail to give, some crumb of spiritual comfort ("I fell in company with one poor man," p. 12; "my neighbors were amazed," p. 13; "three or four poor old women," p. 14; "these poor people at Bedford," p. 18; "I heard one preach," p. 27; "an Antient Christian," p. 51).[35] The closest we get to some kind of socially generated moment of conversion is when Bunyan overhears the anonymous, undescribed "three or four poor old women" (p. 14) in Bedford, who talk of "new birth, the work of God on their hearts" (p. 14). The resources of narrative briefly spring up around this moment: the women are "sitting at a door in the sun" (p. 14)—a place, with weather! But narrative and its attendant detail can get no further. Bunyan remains distant and alone, drawing near only to overhear the group, and then to leave the women, alone. He even describes the women as alone: he sees them as "people that dwelt alone, and were not to be reckoned among their neighbors" (p. 14). Bunyan writes *Grace Abounding* with the avowed intent of helping others, but the very intensity of his experience undoes the possibility of exemplarity: Bunyan himself says that he "never endeavored to, nor durst make use of other men's lives" (p. 80), because his own experience out-scales and dwarves the force of exemplary narratives about others.[36]

Bunyan's predicament swallows the world. The first person plural pronoun appears thirty-eight times in *Grace Abounding*, as against 1,380 appearances of the singular form.[37] Christ's love, insofar as it is imaginable, is never imagined in universalist or communitarian terms. It is only ever for Bunyan, or only ever denied to Bunyan, alone: "If now I should have burned at a stake, I could not believe that Christ had love for me" (p. 24). So insistently does the cycle of brief grace and long despair recur to Bunyan that he becomes "both a burden and a terror to myself, nor did I ever so know, as now, what it was to be weary of my life" (p. 42). He loses mental grip on any solid details: "My mind would be so strangely snatched away . . . that I have neither known, nor regarded, nor remembered so much as the sentence that but now I have read" (p. 32). The sum of this self-sickness is an intense desire for annihilation; he wants to undo his most fundamental existential condition, since "I was now sorry that God made me a man" (p. 27). There is hardly a single moment of concerted institutional support sought or received; such as there are, provoke deeper and renewed feelings of despair,[38] unable as Bunyan is to focus on anything but his own agony of "racked upon the Wheel" (p. 42).

It is difficult not to read *Grace Abounding* diagnostically, as being about Bunyan, since Bunyan so clearly manifests the symptoms of chronic depression. After all, Bunyan himself frequently uses the term "condition" about himself, by which he means a pathological condition. ("Sometimes I would tell my condition to the people of God; which when they heard, they would pity me, and would tell me of the Promises," p. 25.) Of course one will always hesitate to make a definitive symptomatic judgment of this kind; as Bunyan himself says, "The Philistians understand me not" (p. 3), but the text gives us little choice, since everything else it might be about sinks and fades so quickly from precise apprehension.

Beyond being "about Bunyan," the text could also be read as being "about" the structure of relations that produces an interiority so magnified as to consume the world. That structure is in fact simple: faced with absolute power, the self becomes self-conscious and magnified. Bunyan is faced by a predestining God, and his selfhood responds to that absolutism in predictably pathological ways. Bunyan's is a characteristically early modern interiority, whose absolute demands arise in the face of absolute power.

But *Grace Abounding* is not simply "about" chronic depression, either that of Bunyan or that of the early modern evangelical subject. It is about the chronic, debilitating depression of a reader of Scripture.[39] If people, places, times, and narratives all fade or collapse in *Grace Abounding,* there is one set of actors who remain vivid and precise, and in the foreground. These are the animated texts of Scripture.[40] As he reads, Bunyan finds that Scripture is so "fresh, and with such strength and comfort on my spirit, that I was as if it talked with me" (p. 21). Bunyan's truly appalling experience is that of the committed Calvinist who believes the following package: predestination; that God communicates only through Scripture; and that Scripture must be read literally. "How," asks Bunyan, "can you tell you are elected? And what if you should not? What then?" (p. 20). The answer is reading, and the package of persuasions produces the early modern drama of reading. But the drama is one of extreme pain and predation.

Consider the ways the text of Scripture takes on agency in *Grace Abounding.* Different passages of scripture, always in the form of single categorical statements of promise or threat, rush in upon Bunyan suddenly, taking him unawares and wholly capturing, not to say imprisoning, his spirit.

Sometimes, though very rarely, the Word gives encouragement: Joel 3.21 "came in upon me" (p. 24) after months of doubt; after "several months together" of despair, "suddenly this sentence bolted in upon me" (p. 40), and "this word took hold upon me" (p. 40); "that Scripture came home upon me, *Mercy rejoyceth against Judgment* [Jas. 2.13]." For the most part, however, Scriptural texts are like random pieces of debris in a hurricane, appearing out of nowhere to hit Bunyan hard.[41]

Even encouraging texts are read negatively, as Bunyan "feared [with regard to 1Cor. 12] it shut me out of all the blessings" (p. 17). Most texts are plain threatening: with regard to Heb 9.22, "that Scripture lay much upon me" (p. 26); "I was much followed by this Scripture" (p. 28); regarding Esau (a key text for predestinarians, and one that especially tortures Bunyan):[42] "that Scripture did seize upon my soul" (p. 40), or "these words were like Fetters of Brass of my legs" (p. 40); every page of the book of Francis Spira was "as Knives and Daggers in my soul" (p. 45); "then did that Scripture seize upon my soul" (p. 51). Scripture is alive and dangerous.

Bunyan never questions the Calvinist reading package, and therefore labors under the impossible challenge of literalism in Scripture, which offers so many texts of both encouragement and threat. He feels himself either cut out from grace, or too late to take advantage of it, or, even worse, as having actively participated in its denial, of having compulsively repeated "sell him [i.e. Christ], sell him, sell him, sell him" (p. 40). The entire reading experience keeps offering to give the literal truth, but the words are all uninterpretable without assurance of salvation, which can only be gained by reading the words. Bunyan therefore finds himself an unprotected victim of the words, unmediated by any interpretive guide but literalism, and unmediated by any institutional protocols. Very occasionally it occurs to him that prayer is useless, since the Calvinist God has made his decisions already: it was "meer folly . . . to persuade with him to alter, yea, to disanul the whole way of salvation" (p. 51). That recognition, however, casts him again before the predations of Scripture: "that saying" (a threatening one) "rent my soul asunder" (p. 51).

Finally, Bunyan does achieve a measure of control over Scripture. After his (strangely unspecified) conversion he begins to approach those texts that he had almost wished "out of the Bible, for I thought they would destroy me" (p. 63). Having considered their "scope and tendence" (p. 63), he finds their "visage changed; for they looked not so grimly on me as before" (p. 63).[43] Bunyan runs through all the texts that had so terrified and rereads them, seeing that they can be read differently, and with qualification, in context (pp. 64–65). If there is any clear narrative shape to *Grace Abounding*, it turns on the real subject of the work, which is Bunyan's reading practice.

Bunyan cannot, however, be said to have broken free of literalism. Like Milton, if in wholly different ways, Bunyan begins to discover that the literal sense is never, as Luther had so confidently declared, "entirely secure, easy, and open through itself; it interprets itself, testing, judging and illuminating everything." On the contrary, it must always be subject to deeper, preexisting persuasions, at some of which one arrives through interpretation. In Bunyan's case, however, the preexisting conviction that gives him some defense against the predations of literalism is his persuasion that he is a member of the True Church. The authentic certificate of that certified membership is the published text we read. That persuasion must also logically involve the fact that most readers of Scripture are cut out from proper Gospel understanding.

The terrible drama of Bunyan's reading lesson is wholly unreasonable, not to say vicious. The textual and theological understandings that produced it are of such extremity as to be without parallel; we must look to Kafka before finding anything remotely comparable. But Bunyan himself never questions the viciousness, the "unthought of imaginations, frights, fears, and terrors . . . and yielding to desparation" (p. 53); instead he submits to its terrible discipline, "cutting himself with stones" (p. 53); the path of utter humiliation and despair is the only route to the Delectable Mountains or the Enchanted Ground of reading Gospel. But resistance to this wholly early modern revolutionary discipline is useless: "Heaven and Earth shall pass away before one jot or tittle of the Word and Law of Grace shall fail or be removed" (p. 53). The textual plenty of *Grace Abounding* itself is but a mirage that will evanesce under the relentless and pitiless sun of a reaffirmed literalism.

17

Escaping Literalism's Trap

FOR EACH OF THE TOPICS so far treated by this book, I have discerned roughly three sequences for the 150 years of the Reformation period: appropriation of powers and carnivalesque, revolutionary energy (c. 1520–1547); revolutionary grief (c. 1547–1625); and escaping revolutionary disciplines (c. 1603–1688). That model does not quite apply to the practice of reading. The evangelical claim to literalist simplicity runs throughout and beyond the entire period; the grief is felt very soon (Surrey was writing before 1547); and the escape routes from aggressive literalism are actively being planned from the moment the Presbyterian movement manifests it-self from within English Calvinism in the 1560s. We could trace that resis-tance to literalism by looking to theological disputes (e.g. Whitgift resisting Cartwright in the 1570s, or Hooker responding to Calvinist literalists in the 1590s), but in this chapter I look to great literary authors, writing between Surrey and Bunyan, as they seek humane escape routes from literalism.

Shakespeare and Milton seek, for different reasons, to step outside the kind of evangelical Scriptural predicament that crushes Surrey and Bunyan and to reformulate manageable, nonviolent reading protocols. Only legis-lation, in the form of the Toleration Act of 1689, was finally powerful enough to contain the revolutionary force of literalist evangelical reading practice. Before that decisive legislative act, however, literary writers explored the grounds of an alternative treatment of Scripture as a living document,

299

thereby contributing to a long anti-literalist tradition. Shakespeare and Milton worked out from the anguish of Scripture's relentless pressure.

I

Shakespeare's *Merchant of Venice* (performed soon before 1600) underlines the intense (not to say literal) personal and social pain of literalism. That same text also brilliantly devises a civilized response to literalism. The play is the first of Shakespeare's works to broach a major Reformation issue almost explicitly, which turns out to be the biggest Reformation issue, that of literalism and its society-corroding effects.[1]

How was the Bible read in the many new translations available in sixteenth-century England? It was certainly not read from a primarily historicist perspective, as a way to discover the theology of ancient or Roman-occupied Israel (despite the supply of helpful learning aids with regard to ancient Israel, such as maps, in evangelical Bibles).[2] Neither, despite the repeated protestations of evangelical exegetes themselves, was the Bible in fact read literally in any simple sense of literalism: they absorbed allegorical senses under the rubric of the "literal": that was what the text "really" meant.

Evangelicals, that is, absolutely needed to make the claim that they were reading the literal sense, since not to do so would, as we have seen, be to abandon the claim that text precedes institution. In practice, however, no reading culture except institutions devoted to the Higher Criticism (i.e., in our own time, modern academic departments) can or wants to stick to the literal sense literally defined. Sixteenth- and seventeenth-century evangelicals certainly didn't, since they needed to make the Scriptural text relevant, and literalism threatens the irrelevance of the ancient text to the present. So evangelicals freely practiced what they elsewhere derisively dismissed as "chopology," which is to say they practiced the fourfold system of Biblical exegesis that had been flexibly applied to the Biblical text since late Antiquity.[3] Evangelicals frequently, that is, deployed typological allegory (seeing the shadows of the Hebrew Scriptures fulfilled in Christ); tropology (seeing moral, or ethical application of the Biblical text to the European present); and anagogy (seeing the promise of future fulfilment at the end of time embedded in the Biblical text).[4]

The first of two real interpretive differences between evangelicals and a pre-Reformation Scriptural reading practice was that evangelicals *claimed* only to be reading the literal sense, by which they meant that they understood what the ancient text was really saying, its (redefined) "literal meaning." Their claim to literalism was in fact wholly rhetorical, since it did not involve any profoundly different interpretive approach from that of pre-Reformation exegesis. The second real difference was not in interpretation, but in *application*: if it was not "in" Scripture, it had to go from the Church; and if it was "in" Scripture, then it had to be applied, both to the Church and to individuals.[5] When Tyndale insisted in 1530 that Scripture "hath but one simple, literal sense, whose light the owls cannot abide," we should be cautious in accepting his claim as a statement of new practice, but we should prepare for radically new applications.[6]

The application of the literal text was, for individual readers, designedly bodily and painful. Luther, for example, declares that God's word "must be in us like a ... brand mark, burned in, not touching the heart lightly, as foam on water or spittle on the tongue which we want to spit out, but pressed onto the heart to remain there as a distinguishing sign which no one can remove from us."[7] Tyndale elaborates this Scriptural inner organ-branding. The true text is written not with ink, he says, and not engraved in tables of Mosaic stone: following Paul (2Corinthians 3:3) the true text of the life-giving literal sense is, rather, written "in the fleshly tables of the heart,"

> as who should say, we write not a dead law with ink and parchment, nor grave that which damned you in tables of stone: but preach you that which bringeth the spirit unto your breasts, which spirit writeth and graveth the law of love in your hearts and giveth you lust to do the will of God.[8]

Indeed, as the *Book of Homilies* (1547) puts it, "that thing which by the perpetual use of reading Holy Scripture ... is deeply printed and graven in the heart at length turneth almost into nature."[9]

In the 1560s and 1570s, harder line, proto-Presbyterian Calvinists were exploiting the penal possibilities of this painful heart writing, as they defined the capital punishments for those who weren't prepared to go under the Scriptural pen-knife. Thus in their dedicatory letter to Queen Elizabeth the translators of the hugely influential Geneva Bible hold up the excellent example King Asa of Israel that "whosoever would not seek the Lord God of Israel, should be slain, whether he were small or great, man or woman." They take care to establish their own authority as arbiters of who is following the law or not:

> And for the establishing hereof and performance of this solemn oath, as well Priests as Judges were appointed and placed through all the cities of Judah to instruct the people in the true knowledge and fear of God, and to minister justice according to the word, knowing that, except God by his word did reign in the hearts and souls, all man's diligence and endeavors were of none effect: for without this word we can not discern between justice, and injury, protection and oppression, wisdom and foolishness, knowledge and ignorance, good and evil.[10]

We have already seen in Chapter 2 how Thomas Cartwright wore his hard-line literalism as a badge of Puritan pride in the 1570s. By the letter of the law, proto-Presbyterian Cartwright affirms, with revolutionary relish, that the "stubborn Idolater, blasphemer, murderer, incestuous person, and such like should be put to death."[11] Cartwright also actively promoted the death sentence for adultery, on the grounds that Scripture demanded capital treatment for that offence:

> And when the Lord did afterward give testimony unto this punishment by the express words of his law: it is manifest that the law which God hath written in the table of the hearts of all men pronounceth the sentence of death against adulterers . . . it followeth that the punishment of death against adulterers . . . standeth in as full force now as ever it did before the coming of our Savior Christ.[12]

Challenged if he really would put those who failed thus to death (as a statute of 1650 did in fact legislate), Cartwright replied unequivocally: "If this be bloody, and extreme, I am content to be so counted with the holy ghost."[13]

In his *Merchant of Venice* Shakespeare puts literalism of this incisive kind to the test. The play has an extremely simple structure—the structure of a rigorously devised intellectual test. Of course its subject matter— anti-Semitism—is unavoidably preoccupying. Here, however, I treat the issue of anti-Semitism as secondary, and consider instead the play's primary issue to be the application of literalism. I do so for a number of reasons, not least because that issue has such high profile in the play; and because it is such a roiling issue for Shakespeare's England (much more dramatically pressing than anti-Semitism in the late sixteenth century); and, not least, because the play becomes much simpler, if more forceful, considered thus.

The play treats the application of literalism rigorously, as a self-contained problem. Shakespeare takes care not to introduce any crime into the plot; no playgoer could imagine that Antonio deserved the exaction of the law literally applied. Neither can anyone deny—the Duke of Venice does not (4.1)—that Shylock's position is not, on the face of it, legally compelling.

Shakespeare thus carefully delimits and exposes the hardest edges of the dominating question at hand: can we accept literalism itself? Because, of course, literalism is so profoundly associated with Judaism in the history of Christian hermeneutics, literalism always evokes issues of Christian-Jewish relations, which do demand to be confronted. But they are best confronted, I suggest, via the prime issue, which is the play's reading lesson with regard to the application of the literal sense. From that angle, Shylock is less recognizable as a Jew and more recognizable as a Puritan.

Throughout his corpus, Shakespeare plays with a distinctively early modern form of wit, whereby the forward motion of a dialogue is neutralized by play with verbal ambiguity. In each instance, Shakespeare is making a point about literalism, in a society in which literalism had rocketed in profile. "To see this age!," says *Twelfth Night*'s brilliant and melancholy Feste, "a sentence is but a chev'rel glove to a good wit. How quickly the wrong side may be turned outward."[14] After his verbal play, he makes an observation with melancholy implications for a professional wit: "But indeed, words are very rascals since bonds disgraced them" (3.1.18–19). The word "bonds" is ambiguous here: it means both legal contracts (as it is used forty-one times in *The Merchant of Venice*), and fetters. Use a word improperly in this contractual age, Feste implies, and you'll end up in chains.

The Merchant of Venice works through different economies, which are rationalized into a single system: even if Shylock repeatedly loses in a strictly monetary economy, he regards himself as a winner in the emotional economy of Christian-Jewish relations: he might, that is, lose his servant, his daughter, his jewels and then his 3,000 ducats, but by his own lights, he's still winning, since he wishes only to exact revenge on Antonio, by slicing out his precise pound of flesh.

The single mechanism that guarantees his win is the bond, around whose terrible power all appeals to common humanity, to psychic explanation, to apparent financial interest, and finally to mercy, fall away. Shylock's oft-cited speech about common humanity is, shockingly, spoken in the context of justifying revenge: "If you prick us do we not bleed? If you tickle us do we not laugh? If you poison us do we not die?" (3.1.53–55). These moving claims lead, however, to a unmoving conclusion regarding common humanity: "And if you wrong us shall we not revenge?" The force of the bond supervenes.

At least, the Duke of Venice asks, explain yourself, give us some inkling of what could justify such inhuman cruelty: Shylock stands by the voice of the bond, and refuses to go beyond a statement of simple hatred backed by that bond: "So can I give no reason, nor I will not, / More than a lodged hate, and a certain loathing / I bear Antonio" (4.1.59–61).

Then at least, his appalled debtors reply, take double what is owed. If Shylock were offered 216,000 ducats for his 3, he'd stick by the terms of bond (4.1.85). The visceral economy of hatred promises to repay liberally, with one pound of flesh.

None of the standard human appeals gains any traction, that is, against the single voice of the literally written law, however grotesque and senseless, however arbitrary that horrid law increasingly appears. Venice is, paradoxically, absolutely committed to uphold that arbitrary law, since failure to do so would compromise its reputation for justice among and between strangers (essential for any mercantile society), "since," as Antonio astutely says, "the trade and profit of the city / Consisteth of all Nations" (3.4.30–31). To maintain a reputation for justice, a polity must observe what every spectator will regard as injustice.

After all the standard human appeals have fallen silent, Portia appeals to a nonhuman source of resolution, in the most beautiful and persuasive speech of the play. As we approach the portal of damnation in a wholly senseless world, we cannot help but protest at the insane and pitiless logic of legal literalism.

And so it is that we hear the disguised Portia's wonderful speech about mercy and its nonhuman, divine source (4.1.182–203), about its paradoxical interest-bearing logic for both giver and receiver, about its superiority to law and likeness to divinity. "In the course of justice none of us / Should see salvation" (4.1.197–198), she declares in a society where evangelical literalists were insisting on the punishing letter of the law.

The result? "I crave the law / The penalty and forfeit of my bond" (4.1.204–205). Like Shylock's memorable speech about common humanity, Portia's speech about human access to divinity should win the day. Shakespeare takes care to have both speeches lose the day, by way of thrusting the apparently immutable logic of literalism at us. Two of the most rhetorically powerful and socially constructive speeches in the entire canon are, astonishingly, presented dramatically as rhetorical failures. Fidelity to an inhuman law must trump every other source of humane, pragmatic, or theological resource. Portia's prolonged and relentless insistence on ineluctable obeisance to that wholly inhuman law (4.1.215–302) underlines how rigorous and appalling its logic is.

How does Shakespeare manage this utterly legal march to socially destructive viciousness, under the aegis of strict literalism? In this book we have had occasion to observe how Shakespeare manages the destructive energies of Puritan culture: instead of confronting those destructive energies head-on, and instead of writing satire (something Shakespeare never does as generic choice), he dramatically doubles down on the Puritan practice. Thus in *Measure for Measure,* he manages hypocrisy by having the Duke act as a hypocrite—act, indeed, like *penetrans dom(um),* the very archetype of the Scriptural hypocrite. In *A Winter's Tale* he subtly broaches Puritan fears of moving images by having Hermione be . . . a moving image. And in *A Midsummer Night's Dream* and *The Tempest,* he tackles the issue of Puritan fears of magic and performativity by carefully carving out restorative spaces for precisely magical performativity, even if he also bids it a provisional farewell in the later play.

In *The Merchant of Venice,* too, Shakespeare adopts the doubling down approach. So, far from confronting literalism, he reveals how literalism is ironclad against all comers. The only way to beat literalism is to play it at its own inhumane, inhuman game: "Tarry a little. There is something else. / This bond doth give thee here no jot of blood . . ." (4.1.303–304). And so the play runs to its cruel but symmetrical resolution, exacting on Shylock the same precise logic of literalism that he stood ready to exact from Antonio. What we had all assumed was the unbendable literal sense turns out to be wholly unworkable as a way of dealing with the world; the lawyer's response, not the theologian's, wins the day, by revealing that "a sentence is but a chev'rel glove to a good wit."

Anti-Semitism is built into Christian hermeneutics. By being called the "Old Testament," the Hebrew Scriptures forever pose the question in Christian exegesis as to how the Old should be treated by the "New": either subject to rejection by supercessionism, or rather seen as a foreshadowing of the Christian dispensation. This second approach certainly regards Judaism with condescension, as the old particularist shadow that produced the new, universalist daylight of Christianity. It is also, however, a means of incorporating the old into a single historical process of salvation history. The position of both Luther and his follower Tyndale with regard to what they called Old Testament law was, however, supercessionist; it was applicable only to Jews, and it was to be surpassed by Christians.[15] Thus like Luther, who encourages his readers to love Moses for the Law and to stone Moses for hatred of the Law, Tyndale loves and distrusts the Old Testament.[16] He distrusts Hebraic observance. In, for example, his *Brief Declaration of the Sacraments* (published ?1548), he begins by noting the remarkable similarities between Hebraic and Christian events and "sacraments." Passover was

> a very prophecy of the passion of Christ, describing the very manner and fashion of his death, and the effect and virtue [strength] thereof also. In whose stead is the sacrament of the body and blood of Christ come as baptism in the room or stead of the circumcision.[17]

Once Christ came, however, Passover ended, since "in the room [function] thereof (concerning that spiritual signification) came the sign of the sacrament of the body and blood of our Savior Christ. As baptism came in stead of circumcision" (image 12). That decisive break asserted, persistence in the Old Law (not adding to or subtracting from it) amounts to hatred of Christ: these observances are "clean unprofitable": "And as the circumcision in the flesh, their [Jews'] hearts still uncircumcised. But hating the Law of God and believing in their own imaginations: [Jews] were circumcised unto their great damnation" (image 14). These same anti-Semitic positions are readily visible in the marginalia to the Geneva Bible, leaning as they do to total rejection of the ceremonial law of the Hebrew Scriptures.[18]

We can conclude by recognizing that these hermeneutic traditions are visible in *The Merchant of Venice*: the world of the play cannot operate without Shylock, but Shylock is the element to be expelled from this comedic ending. The play is decisively not racist in its anti-Semitism, since Shylock's daughter Jessica is absorbed into Christian society. Neither is it insensitive to the way in which Shylock's hatred of Christians is the result of his having been humiliated by Christians. But even if Shakespeare seems to participate in the ancient hermeneutic tradition of identifying literalism and Jewish law, he is also, in my view, tackling a profound source of social dislocation in his world by having Shylock resemble no one so much as contemporary Puritan divines, in their eager readiness to inflict the arbitrary, inhuman literal sense on their fellow Christians. And he joins a great tradition of anti-literalism with a novel solution to the post-human insanity of literalism (i.e. take literalism to the logical end of its own commitment to semantic precision, and see how utterly unworkable it is).

II

Evangelicals, as we have seen, in principle (if not at all in practice) favor their Scripture whole and self-sufficient, prior to and determinative of any institution or interpreter. Bacon's *New Atlantis* (first published 1627) offers a perfect example. *New Atlantis* is primarily about the institutions of scientific discovery, but those institutions are unthinkable, for Bacon, without an entire set of Scriptures preceding them. The ancient inhabitants of Atlantis are drawn to the pillar of cloud that hovers on the ocean around the island. One of the searchers is permitted to approach the pillar, there to find the text of Scripture miraculously gifted in its entirety, even before it has been completely written. They find the book of the Scriptures and a letter,

> both written in fine parchment, and wrapped in sindons [fine cloths] of linen. The book contained all the canonical books of the Old and New Testament, according as you have them (for we know well what the churches with you receive), and the Apocalypse itself; and some other books of the New Testament, which were not at that time written, were nevertheless in the book.[19]

The wholly self-sufficient book of the Scriptures, written before they are written, produces a further miracle: it is not only legible, but also salutary, as if by miracle, to whoever tries to read it:

> There was also in both these writings, as well the book as the letter, wrought a great miracle, conform to that of the apostles, in the original gift of tongues. For there being at that time in this land Hebrews, Persians, and Indians, besides the natives, everyone read upon the book and letter, as if they had been written in his own language. And thus was this land saved from infidelity.[20]

Bacon's scientific utopia is underwritten, that is, by a textual disclosure which is itself utopian, whereby the text is untouched by the mess and dispute of history, whether in shaping (the canon is somehow established), delivery (an error-free text) or reception (anyone can read it, and anyone who does so is saved). As we have seen, it was precisely this utopian textual model, designed to short-circuit the mess and dispute of history, that produced 150 years of European violence.

As utopian revolutionary, Milton is drawn to models of this kind: to wholly self-sufficient, prior states of complete perfection that require and ideally produce no supplements of any kind. The prelapsarian states of both heaven and earth are where Milton begins conceptually in, say, *Paradise Lost*, and from whose utopian bounds he is drawn only with the deepest resistance. That revolutionary commitment to wholly self-sufficient, ideal states also characterizes Milton's approach to Scripture, long before he began writing *Paradise Lost*, in 1658 or so.

As for all evangelicals, the Reformation was, for early Milton, in the first instance, a textual phenomenon: the "blissful *Reformation* (by Divine Power) struck through the black and settled Night of *Ignorance* and *Antichristian Tyranny*," by virtue of "the sweet Odor of the returning *Gospell* . . . Then was the Sacred BIBLE sought out of the dusty corners where profane Falsehood and Neglect had thrown it."[21] Thus Milton in his *Of Reformation* of 1641, the first of his five anti-prelatical tracts, all written in 1641–1642.

Written in Milton's Presbyterian phase, the text of Scripture here imposes a categorical textual economy. Like all other Presbyterians, Milton declares that Christians need no other text, and that all books of what he derisively dismisses as "Antiquity" are valueless (even if Milton knows these works very well indeed). The Fathers of the Church and the deliberations of the Councils of the Church are wholly otiose, not to say obfuscating: the "rabbis" (Milton's word, p. 569) who prefer Scriptural supplements that reveal the historical reception of Scripture

> fear the plain field of the Scriptures; the chase is too hot; they seek the dark, the bushy, the tangled Forrest, they would imbosk [hide]: they feel themselves struck in the transparent streams of divine Truth, they would plunge, and tumble, and think to lie hid in the foul weeds, and muddy waters, where no plummet can reach the bottom. (p. 569)

Why, Milton asks, waste time with those who dote on "immeasurable, innumerable, and therefore unnecessary, and unmerciful volumes," when there's so much more efficient and effective a way to understand the divine mind: "Wherefore should they not urge only the Gospel, and hold it ever in their faces like a mirror of Diamond, till it dazzle, and pierce their misty eye balls, maintaining it the honor of its absolute sufficiency, and supremacy inviolable" (pp. 567–568).

In fact the verbal economy is even more efficient, since Milton, in keeping with Puritan hermeneutics, makes a distinction within Scripture, whereby "Old Testament" moral law is given primacy over what Milton calls its superseded "political" law (by which I take him to mean ceremonial law), and the New Testament is given primacy over the Old Testament. Thus in *The Reason of Church Government Urged against Prelaty* (1642), he explains that

> the whole Judaick law is either political, and to take pattern by that, no Christian nation ever thought it self obliged in conscience; or moral, which contains in it the observation of whatsoever is substantially, and perpetually true and good, either in religion, or course of life. That which is thus moral, besides what we fetch from those unwritten laws and Ideas which nature hath ingraven in us, the Gospel, as stands with her dignity most, lectures to us from her own authentic hand-writing and command, not copies out from the borrowed manuscript of a subservient scrow [scroll], by way of imitating. (p. 764)

At this stage of his career, Milton's hermeneutics, it will be clear, are driven by a kinetic logic that produces an ever simpler economy: Scripture is superior to custom and historical authority; the moral law is superior to the ceremonial or "political" law; the Gospel's moral law is superior to that of the Hebrew Scriptures. In this Presbyterian phase, the textual winnowing machine even finally winnows the error of human reason itself from the luminous clarity and authority of the Gospel: let, Milton says, "the mighty weakness of the Gospel throw down the weak mightiness of man's reasoning" (p. 827). This kinetic, ever forward moving logic leads Milton, along with many other Presbyterians in the early 1640s, to millenarian fervor in expectation of the imminent second coming of Christ. "Thy Kingdom is now at hand," he fervently declares in the astonishing and royalist peroration of the *Animadversions* (1641). "Come forth out of thy Royall Chambers, O Prince of all kings of the earth, and put on the robes of thy imperial majesty . . . for now the voice of thy Bride calls thee, and all creatures sigh to be renewed" (p. 707).

Above all, Scripture is totally clear: "Let others therefore dread and shun the Scriptures for their darkness, I shall wish I may deserve to be reckon'd among those who admire and dwell upon them for their clearness."[22] Scripture, in a by now long tradition of evangelical hermeneutics, interprets itself; its arguments, in Milton's words, "easily imply themselves."[23]

Or they do until Milton comes up hard against the inhuman clarity of the Scriptures, which he did in 1643. If Milton's ultimate textual moment was imagined in marital terms in 1641, with the Bride of Christ longing to welcome her returned spouse, in 1643 it was the disaster of Milton's actual marriage that provoked a deep shift in his reception of Scripture. This is the moment that Scripture becomes difficult; requires interpretation; and must not be read literally. It is also, not coincidentally, the moment when Milton seems to abandon his Presbyterian allies and become an Independent. And, finally, it is the prelude to Milton writing Scripture of a kind himself, in *Paradise Lost,* as another married couple walk mournfully out of Eden: "They hand in hand with wandering steps and slow, / Through Eden took their solitary way."[24]

Matthew 19 would seem pretty clear about divorce. The Pharisees tempt Christ to make a statement against the permission given in the Hebrew scriptures to a husband to divorce his wife, "if so be she find no favor in his eyes, because he hath espied some filthiness in her" (Deuteronomy 24:1). "Is it lawful," the Pharisees ask Christ, "for a man to put away his wife upon every occasion?" (Matthew 19:3). Christ is clearly not a literalist, since he does not follow the letter of the law; instead, he is more restrictive in the reasons for which a husband may divorce a wife (no one in the Scriptures speaks about wives divorcing husbands). His answer argues that, given the uniting of flesh of a married couple, that couple cannot be separated: "Wherefore they are no more twain, but one flesh. Let not man therefore put asunder that, which God hath coupled together" (Matthew 19:6). Christ would seem to be protecting the wife from arbitrary divorce, but the Pharisees push back to the letter of the Deuteronomic law: "Why did then Moses command to give a bill of divorcement, and to put her away?" (Matthew 19:7). In reply, Christ gives his definitive resolution: before the law of Moses, "in the beginning," it was not so. Therefore "whosoever shall put away his wife, except it be for whoredom, and marry another, commiteth adultery" (Matthew 19:9).

In 1642, these texts posed challenges for Milton, since his seventeen-year-old wife, Mary Powell, had in that year walked out on thirty-four-year-old Milton after only a few weeks of married life. Milton wanted a divorce, but to get one, he had to petition to have the law changed. He therefore set to writing four tracts in favor of divorce between August 1643 and March 1645, the first three of which are addressed to Parliament.[25] Here I discuss the interpretive tactics of the second, enlarged edition of the first of these tracts, *The Doctrine and Discipline of Divorce* (published in separate editions in 1643 and 1644, the second of which was also addressed to the Presbyterian Westminster Assembly).[26]

Itemized summation of the tract's extended argument is unnecessary. The essence of Milton's strategy is to read Christ's words for their intention and their context. The essence of his strategy, that is, is to read Christ's words rhetorically, by looking to style in context (psychological, social, and historical) for the true meaning of Christ's words. "All such places of Scripture wherein just reason of doubt arises from the letter, are to be expounded by considering upon what occasion every thing is set down; and by comparing other texts" (p. 282). Any such reading leads immediately away from literalism, what Milton calls "precious literalism" (p. 334), where the word "precious" is pejorative and where "literalism" is, by the *OED*'s account, the first such usage in English.

Christ's refusal to accept Deuteronomic law is plausibly attributed to Christ's own charity, but that model of charitable reading urges us to read Christ's own words charitably, whereby we should not be "more severe in paraphrasing the considerate and tender Gospel, than he was in expounding the rigid and peremptory law" (p. 281). Christ was arguing with "extravagant" opponents, and so needed to give a "sharp and vehement answer" (p. 282). Christ did not intend his words to be taken "word for word," but he spoke rather like a doctor, "administering one excess against another to reduce us to a perfect mean" (pp. 282–283). He spoke thus to the Pharisees "to dazzle them, and not to bind us" (p. 308).

When Christ refers to couples whom God has joined, he cannot, so Milton argues, be referring to ill-matched couples. So God joins couples whose parties are suited to each other, when minds "are fitly disposed, and enabled to maintain a cheerful conversation, to the solace and love of each other, according as God intended from the first foundation of matrimony," when God made a "help meet" for Adam (p. 328). In marriage, says 1 Corinthians 7:15, "God hath called us to peace." When Christ allowed "fornication" as sufficient cause of divorce, he did not mean by "fornication" only illicit sexuality; the word "fornication" is used with wide application in Scripture, so as to cover "such a continual headstrong behavior, as tends to plain contempt of the husband" (p. 335).

I need not go on: Milton will of course seem to engage in special pleading in some of these arguments, but his strategy is clear. He states it himself: "There is scarce any one saying in the Gospel, but must be read with limitations and distinctions, to be rightly understood" (p. 338). Should readers not apply that contextual and intentionalist attention, Scripture will frequently appear hard, as "strange and repugnant riddles" (p. 338). Barbara Lewalski has given a beautifully lucid list of Milton's anti-literalist interpretive maneuvers. They are as follows: the "internal scripture of the Holy Spirit"; reason; recognition of accommodation (i.e. God's descending to our capacities of comprehension); charity; and experience.[27] This is not Presbyterian reading, from any angle. On the contrary, it puts Milton in a long tradition of anti-literalism, a tradition that opposes, to use Milton's own coinage, the "extreme literalist" (p. 340).

The entire tradition of fourfold interpretation that dominated Christian Biblical reading for the millennium prior to the Reformation was not constrained by the literal sense. That tradition escaped the violent trap of literalism by folding the literal sense back into a sequence of interpretive operations that together treated Scripture as a living document. The literal sense was treated with respect, but it was never held to have any exclusive claim on the present.[28] Specifically, explicitly anti-literalist arguments arose only in response to exclusivist claims for the literal sense. So specifically anti-literalist positions arose in England, predictably, only in our "Age of Literalism," between 1380 and 1640 or so (i.e. the period, from Lollardy to the Civil War, when literalism makes its most forceful, non-negotiable claim).

The "tradition" of such anti-literalists would, in England, include figures with whom Milton would not wish to associate at all, such as William Woodford, Reginald Pecock, Thomas More, John Whitgift, and Richard Hooker.[29] It also includes, precisely as Milton is writing, figures with whom Milton might feel more comfortable, such as the remarkable William Walwyn.[30] Immediately outside the English tradition, it would include, most famously, Desiderius Erasmus.[31] Further outside the English tradition, it includes Augustine of Hippo.[32] The list of anti-literalist literary artists would of course be coincident with the list of literary artists, but one would wish to underline at least William Langland, Geoffrey Chaucer, and William Shakespeare as three especially self-conscious anti-literalists.[33] Such writers knew literalism from the inside, and knew that literalism posed an existential threat to the liberating powers of literary discourse.

Of course Miltonic interpretive practice differs from that of most of the anti-literalists mentioned, since it involves no institution (even if it does compact an echo of an institution, by including the illumination of the Holy Spirit).[34] But the chronological length of the list of English anti-literalists, going at least as far back as the late fourteenth century, underlines that Milton's hermeneutics recovered, without him ever saying so (perhaps without him knowing so), pre-Reformation traditions of interpretation. Any account of Milton's hermeneutics will stress his anti-literalism; such a story needs also, however, to set that anti-literalism in the larger historical context of Milton's own career, which began as a literalist, and the larger story of anti-literalism, which begins, in England, from the late fourteenth century. As in *Paradise Lost*, Milton is pulled from literalism by "experience," one of his own rules for charitable and rational reading. He is pulled by the "repugnant riddles" of experience from what he had earlier called the simple, dazzling, "absolute sufficiency" of the Gospel. Like Adam and Eve themselves, in their marital predicament, Milton as Biblical reader is forced by experience from enclosed, utopian, wholly self-sufficient places out into the real world of humane interpretation.

Milton's expulsion from the Gospel Eden was also, however, a liberation. Not only did that expulsion possibly produce his break with Presbyterianism, and not only did it produce, in response to Parliamentary attempts to repress Milton's divorce tracts, *Areopagitica* (1644), Milton's qualified argument against print censorship. A break with literalism also in some sense produced *Paradise Lost*. Arguments have been persuasively made that the narrative of *Paradise Lost* embeds reading lessons, which effectively model Milton's post-Presbyterian interpretive insights.[35] Such persuasive arguments might distract us from what is hidden in plain sight: that the entirety of *Paradise Lost* itself is a reading lesson. *Paradise Lost,* that is, breaks entirely from the textual economy of evangelical textuality.

That textual economy, as we have seen, demands either not a word added to or subtracted from scripture, or, if words are added, demands that they be single-mindedly focused on elucidation of Scripture. *Paradise Lost* will have nothing to do with that economy. It is a vast rewriting and reordering of Scripture, thus recovering a pre-Reformation literary practice of remaking Scripture in works of literature. And it does so via the recovery of performative literary language, from its first mighty, single-sentence, performative invocation (ll. 1–26). So completely does it rewrite Scripture so as to produce "things unattempted yet in prose or rhyme" (and so unattempted even by Moses), that it is immediately treated like Scripture. Now, according to Marvell's introductory poem (1674) to *Paradise Lost,* Milton's poem has created its own economy, "so that no room is here for writers left, / But to detect their ignorance or theft."[36] Milton's treatment of "things divine" preserves both them "and thee, inviolate" (l. 34).[37] Out of his battle in the interpretation of Scripture, and out of a battle with an evangelical textual economy, Milton creates a distinctively modern notion of literary discourse as a new, sublime Scripture.

PART 7

Liberty and Liberties

18

Liberty Taking Liberties

REVOLUTIONARIES OFTEN DEVISE thematic names for themselves and their children. Ioseb Jughashvili, for example, became "Joseph Stalin" ("Joseph Steel"). Bolsheviks also apparently gave their children names like "Vsemir," an abbreviation of "Worldwide Revolution," just as Puritans also named thematically, as satirized in Ben Jonson's *Bartholomew Fair* ("Zeal of-the-Land Busy," "Win-the-Fight").[1] Giving names like that to one's children may not be such a great idea, but the naming practice makes sense for people who consider individual agency to be wholly subsumed by an animated historical force.

In 1517, one Martin Luder decided to make a similar move, changing his name at first to Martin Eleutherius and then to Martin Luther, thereby thematizing his name, for the learned at least, as "Martin Freed" (from Greek *eleutheros,* freed, liberated, not a slave).[2] The change was a brilliant stroke. It prepared the way for Martin Liberated's own publication, *Von der Freiheit eines Christenmenschen* (*Concerning the Freedom of a Christian*) (published in Latin as *De libertate christiana, Concerning Christian Liberty*) of 1520, and capturing early modernity's mesmerisation with liberty. So powerful was the force of Luther's name change that, five hundred years later, the thematized name stood for the entire Reformation movement. Thus, for example, the German Government's official website for its five hundred year celebration of the Lutheran Reformation, which focuses on freedom:

> In 1520 Luther reacted against the Papal ban imposed upon him . . . Under the title *Concerning the Freedom of a Christian* he merged his reforming concepts of belief and demands for religious freedom. Luther's message, according to which a Christian should not permit his or her freedom to be restricted by ecclesiastically determined, formal duties, but should rather believe freely in the here and now, struck powerful resistance.[3]

If Luther as freedom fighter has been crucial in German cultural history, the same is true for English reception of English Reformation movers between 1520 and 1660. Thus in what Blair Worden calls the "Whig Era of English history" (1688–1914), Whig historians dissolved two wholly distinct early modern traditions of liberty, the religious and the political. They either downplayed the religious, or redescribed the religious input into the English revolution as primarily devoted to political, constitutional liberty.[4] "In the Victorian age," for example, "it became a commonplace that the parliamentarians [of the 1640s] had fought for 'civil and religious liberty.'"[5] Historiography of this kind, in both British and American traditions, endured long into the twentieth century.[6] Thus Glenn Burgess makes very much the same argument as Worden, summarizing thus:

> The religious dimensions of the English Revolution were, then, diminished very early and very successfully, to long-lasting effect. . . . the cunning of history had made Puritans the servants of *political* liberty, whether they wanted to be so or not. Twentieth-century historians would add economic freedom and social egalitarianism . . . to the good causes fostered by the Puritan Revolution . . . The master narrative of the English Revolution lay in its advancement of political and civil liberty.[7]

In this chapter I distinguish the main traditions of liberty in the sixteenth and seventeenth centuries. Two are of especial importance: evangelical liberty and the so-called Neo-Roman theory of liberty, traditions that are, evidently, wholly heterogeneous in content. I will not parse which of these traditions was the principal force in the English Revolution (a task outside my competence in any case). Instead, I look first to the ways in which these wholly heterogeneous traditions in fact *share* formal properties in their understanding of Liberty as singular and animated.

We have seen other singularizations of early modernity in this book already—notably the singularization of subjectivity into its early modern sincere, authentic form. In this chapter I look to the singularization of liberty. My argument will be that liberty goes singular in response to a singularization of power; as it does so, it assumes the same despotic force of the power it resists. Liberty becomes, paradoxically, an early modern absolutist. As with other punishing features of early modernity, however, England finally escaped the worst excesses of an absolutist Liberty by reinvoking a third, pre-modern tradition of liberty, the concept of plural liberties. Promoters of this common law tradition refused to have resistance to absolutist power mirror that power.

Of course the absolutist, singular Liberty survives in high-profile and vibrant form into our own times, in different revolutionary cultures. It survives, for example, in the motto of the French state. In the United States, it survives among those often erroneously called "conservatives": in, for example, the evangelical right, or in especially destructive, government-hostile libertarian forms. That, however, is another story.

In sum, this final chapter aims to work out when liberties (plural) became Liberty (singular). I'll also attempt to elucidate what the stakes of that change were. The essence of my argument is that singular Liberty is a product of early modernity: it comes into re-existence as a response to the theological and political centralizations—singularizations, if you will—of early modernizing Europe. Above all, it comes into existence as the response to two distinctively early-modern neoclassical resurgences: those of political absolutism on the one hand, and of theological absolutism on the other.

Our enquiry is a matter of intellectual history, both political and theological. We therefore turn to law and politics for the first time in the book, since the dominant discourse of the Reformation period (theology) so desperately needed a solution from outside theology—which is to say a primarily political and legal solution—from at least the 1650s onwards. But we also need to look to literature, beyond political and legal theory. Only works of literature reveal, through their own logic, the emergent need for resources outside theology, and outside Liberty singular.

In order, therefore, to address the history of the concepts of "liberties," and "Liberty" we'll move up the disciplinary ladder. I'll start with lexicography. In Section II, I parse our words, "liberties" and "Liberty," conceptually. Intellectual history elucidates traditions of singular liberty, both theological and political, in the third section. Finally, I turn to the queen of the sciences, literary criticism, where, inevitably, Milton must command our attention.

I pose the question of liberty's genealogy as the fit conclusion to this entire book, since liberty, as we have seen, is the master-code of the Whig tradition. I am persuaded, as will be obvious throughout every chapter, that the Whig / liberal tradition is profoundly confused, not to say plain wrong, about its own account of the genealogy of liberty. In addition to completing the book with this inevitable chapter, so as to underline that cardinal error, I have two further, experiential reasons for ending the book with a reflection on the singularization of Liberty. My experience as a scholar and my experience as a citizen have both turned me skeptically toward singular Liberty.

As a scholar, in 2002 I drafted the following sentence in the introduction to a literary history that traced the movement from late medieval to early modern culture in England: "If literary history and criticism is, as I believe it should be, ancillary to the complex history of freedom, then this is a narrative of diminishing liberty." Even as I drafted the sentence, however, I realized that it wasn't accurate. For my history of late medieval to early modern in England had traced a movement from a complex, divided, decentered set of literary jurisdictions, or liberties, to a single jurisdiction with a king who could be plausibly described as tyrannical at its center.[8] For the late medieval period, I was talking about plural liberties. For the early modern period of the first half of the sixteenth century, I was instead conscious of a singular liberty, defined in relation to a single, newly centralized source of power. So the singular concept of "liberty" was itself, I suddenly understood, part of my story.

I therefore rewrote the sentence thus: "If literary history and criticism is, as I believe it should be, ancillary to the complex history of freedoms, then this is a narrative of diminishing liberties."[9] The change appeared minor (the same concept changed twice from singular to plural), but it turns out to be momentous. In this final chapter, therefore, I want to understand and explicate the momentous consequences of that minute grammatical alteration. In particular, I want to explicate ways in which the diminution of late medieval, plural liberties also produced the claim to early modern, singular Liberty.

Any citizen of the United States also needs to think about singular Liberty. Pursuit of Liberty is the motor of American political discourse. Both political parties, Republican and Democrat, appeal to liberty, whether it be principally economic liberty (Republicans) or principally liberty of social choice (Democrats). Other political groupings, such as libertarians, proclaim individual liberty even more stridently, in both the economic and the social realms. Or the religious right, both evangelicals and, with greater historical paradox, Catholics, bundle their claims as one claim, for religious "Freedom." The pursuit of Liberty is, in sum, the one unchallengeable appeal of the entire political spectrum in the United States, except, perhaps, for recently resurgent white nationalism. And how, after all, could we not be inspired by Liberty's statue? This gift of France to the United States (in 1886) not only represents liberty, but was itself made possible by a long iconoclastic struggle for liberty against enslaving idols, in both the Reformation and in late eighteenth-century France.[10] We are inspired by her promise of liberty to "your tired, your poor / Your huddled masses yearning to breathe free," and by the extraordinary museum at Ellis Island beside her, which underlines the delivery of freedom to those escaping Europe's "damned shadow," to use Hawthorne's phrase.[11]

But is Liberty working for the United States right now? Many features of American life would suggest not. Let us settle for this single paradox (there are very many more): the nation that is most consistently persuaded that it is the "home of the free" is also the nation with by far the world's highest gross and per capita prison population.[12] Has Liberty become an idol, demanding, as idols habitually do, human sacrifice?

Let us, then, return our unblinking gaze to the Statue of Liberty, and ask about her singularity. For that singularity masks a richer narrative of liberty. The richer narrative begins in early European modernity, as we notice the crucial shift from plural, lowercase "liberties" to singular, uppercase "Liberty."

The key articulations of this longer narrative occur in the Reformations of the sixteenth and seventeenth centuries. The key driver of this change in early modernity is as follows: as power centralizes and singularizes, so too does resistance to power centralize and singularize. As power claims absolutist prerogative, so too does resistance to power. The subjects of absolute power describe their condition as one of slavery. The past is described as the period of enslavement, enslavement either to the tyranny of the Roman Church, or to absolutist, or to potentially absolutist monarchical power. In response to those enslavements, singular, revolutionary, absolutist Liberty commands attention. The pattern also works in reverse: in response to a notion of singular Liberty defined negatively, as a savage state of nature, theorists such as Hobbes turn to the attractions of singularized, absolute Power.[13] Promoters either of Liberty, or of absolutist monarchy, work within distinctively early modern singularizations of both liberty and power. Singularization of one produces a mirroring response in the other.

In returning to the sixteenth and seventeenth centuries for the genealogy of liberty, we can do no better than to return to Milton. For in the political *prose* of this great champion of Liberty, we can also clearly see the shift to singular, personified Liberty. By contrast, the gymnasium of Milton's *poetry* presents an alternative, nonrevolutionary concept of liberties. God and Satan certainly mirror each other in their absolutist claims; out of the condition of their war emerges a third, non-absolutist model of human flourishing, in the solidarities of fallen Adam and Eve. The sanctuary spaces—or "liberties"—of poetry turn out, as is often the case, to be the places where alternative truths, truths not subject to the crushing utopian singularities of centralized power, emerge.

I broach the topic with lexicography, and so start, as I have said, with the word "liberty," plural and singular.

I

We begin with a plural and then a singular example of "liberty." Herewith the earlier, plural example, from Magna Carta in 1215, though translated into English in 1534: "We have granted also and given to all the freemen of our realm for us and our heirs, for evermore, these liberties [Latin, *libertates*] underwritten."[14] And herewith a singular example, from Milton, 445 years later, in 1660: "Liberty of conscience," Milton declares in the *Ready and Easy Way*, is "above all other things to be to all men dearest and most precious."

So precious is it that it justifies emergency powers. Milton argued that it was more just, "if it come to force," that the

> less number compel a greater to retain . . . their liberty, than that a greater number, for the pleasure of their baseness, compel a less most injuriously to be their fellow slaves. They who seek nothing but their own just liberty have always right to win it and to keep it whenever they have power, be the voices never so numerous that oppose it.[15]

Both these statements are remarkable in different ways: the first as marking the beginnings of explicitly constitutional practice in England, in the name of liberties won; the second as declaring an unconstitutional revolutionary practice, in the name of liberty demanded. I will return later to the force and fire of this second, Miltonic statement; for the moment I focus simply on the plural form of the word "liberty" versus the singular.

Does the shift from plural to singular reveal a shift in consciousness? Lexicography, with the help of the *OED*, will be our first resource in answering this question.

There are many definitions of "liberty": I abbreviate the lexicographical state of play by highlighting the difference between the plural and the singular.

Plural "liberties" is primarily a legal word. Thus the *OED*'s sense II 6a: "Chiefly in *pl.* A privilege, immunity, or right enjoyed by prescription or grant . . . Now chiefly *hist.*"[16] The example given is from the Rolls of Parliament in 1399: "Al other castles, manors, lordships, possessions, franchises, and liberties that they had of the king's gift at that same day." The fundamental source of this notion of liberty is the late medieval political order, in which the king's jurisdiction did not extend evenly across his realm. On the contrary, faced with powerful ecclesiastical jurisdictions, lordships, and cities, the medieval English king was obliged to recognize certain jurisdictions where his writ did not have authority. These extensive jurisdictions were called "liberties."[17] The word comes to be applied to many sorts of exemption enjoyed by separate secular and ecclesiastical groupings.

Singular "liberty," by contrast, is found in many discursive areas. The *OED*'s sense 2a runs as follows: "The condition of being able to act or function without hindrance or restraint; faculty or power to do as one likes." Examples from that sense range from theological, legal, marital, psychological, poetic, political, medical, and so on. Thus, as the example, Chaucer's *Clerk's Tale* (1390s): "I me rejoysed of my libertee, / That selde tyme is founde in mariage."

Does the distinction between a plural, legal sense and a singular sense of liberty, used in many discursive fields, have any *historical* significance?

Some forms of the plural, and some forms of the singular, are indeed historically distinctive. Sense 2 (a) shows up frequently, mainly in political discourse, from the seventeenth century forward. That sense is: "The condition of being able to act or function without hindrance or restraint; faculty or power to do as one likes." Likewise, the expression "liberty of conscience" is also historically specific: it appears for the first time in evangelical discourse in 1555: "They redeemed liberty of conscience with the bondage of the body."[18] Sense II 6a ("Chiefly in *pl.* A privilege, immunity, or right enjoyed by prescription or grant . . .") is "Now chiefly *hist[orical]*." This sense of the word, capable of being pluralised, derives from pre-modernity.

Lexicography tells us, in short, that plural *liberties* will be more characteristic of legal discourse, in pre-modern jurisdictions, while singular *liberty* will be found in some distinctive formulations from early modernity forwards. Only an early modern would make Milton's claim for liberty of conscience as the supreme human value.[19] And only an early modern would personify Liberty. Thus Milton begins his *Second Defence of the English People* by assuming the task of "publically defending . . . the cause of the English people and thus of Liberty herself."[20] Milton wrote this text, published in Latin in 1654, as part of his job for the Cromwellian military junta as "Secretary for Foreign Tongues." (His other duties at this time, in fact from 1649, included inspection and censorship of books.)[21] In the *Second Defence*, Milton imagines himself thus: "I seem," he says, "to be leading home again everywhere in the world, after a vast space of time, Liberty herself, so long expelled and exiled." His followers in this captive train are imagined as "conquered at last by the Truth," who "acknowledge themselves my captives."[22] In crucial ways, then, early modern liberty has gone singular, just as Milton himself, as the sole hero of the battle for Liberty, has also gone spectacularly singular. Liberty's throng of captives, by Milton's own paradoxical account, grows as she returns.

II

Lexicography, then, does suggest historical distinctions: pre-modern liberties (plural) and early modern evangelical and political Liberty (singular, personified, animated). What's at stake in that shift? Our lexicographical examples prompt us to parse these two notions of liberty conceptually, so as to arrive at a more nuanced set of contrasts between them. For the examples we have so far observed also encode profoundly different conceptions of liberty. Above all, the plural, legal sense of liberty acknowledges the force and validity of the past, while the singular sense wishes only to repudiate the past. Let's look again at our examples and see how they embed different postures with regard to history.

Our first example from Magna Carta read thus: "We have granted also and given to all the freemen of our realm for us and our heirs, for evermore, these liberties [Latin, *libertates*] underwritten." In this single sentence, I isolate four aspects of the notion of plural liberties thus implied.

First, the word "grant" implies a certain *narrative* of liberties: these liberties are granted by the king, and thereby imply an institutional authority *prior to* the granting of separate liberties.

Second, the word "grant" also implies prerogative: if the king grants these liberties, he is implicitly able not to grant them. Liberties granted imply the prerogative of an institution prior to the existence of the particular liberty. It's the prerogative that brings the liberty into existence, rather than the liberty that brings the prerogative into existence. The granting of a liberty is an act of grace.[23]

Third, one liberty granted among others applies to a certain segment of the population, not to everyone. This set of liberties applies only to "all the freemen of our realm." The privilege or immunity enjoyed by one segment of a population will not necessarily be enjoyed by all. The actual liberties granted by Magna Carta include grants to separate bodies.

Fourth, and finally, these liberties are *distinct,* and *plural.* Magna Carta has sixty-three clauses, almost each making a separate concession. Each is a liberty.

In sum, liberties are granted by prerogative; not universally applicable; partitive; and therefore plural.

Let us now turn to an example of the early modern, singular form of liberty, which highlights two of *its* distinctive aspects. Milton, we remember, declared that liberty of conscience is "above all other things to be to all men dearest and most precious." So precious is it that it justifies emergency powers whereby the "less number should compel a greater to retain ... their liberty." Two conclusions might be drawn from this concept of liberty: (i) life without such liberty is regarded as a state of slavery not worth living; liberty is an animating, indispensable principle informing the desirable life; and (ii) Milton's Liberty justifies emergency action, by minorities, without precedent. Such a concept of liberty derives its legitimacy from the *dictates* of conscience, not necessarily from any already established precedent or convention. Milton's Liberty is therefore prospective, categorical in its demand, and potentially revolutionary.

We are now in a position to summarize and tabulate a much more nuanced set of conceptual distinctions that flow from the distinction between plural and singular liberty. Herewith, then, a tabulated set of differences:

Table 1 *Liberties versus Liberty*

Liberties	Liberty
One particular liberty, implying others (plural)	Liberty (singular)
Recognizes normative, constraining history prior to change; retrospective	Proclaims a future possibility against a repudiated past; prospective
Applies to particular, specified segment of a jurisdiction	Applies universally to a jurisdiction
Recognition that the prerogative to grant liberties rests with another body	Recognition only of those dignified by true understanding of Liberty are fit to grant Liberty
Given by grace or negotiated agreement	Demanded by right
A liberty not necessarily life changing (e.g. remission from tax; exemption from a rule)	An animating principle without which life is seriously diminished
Antonym: uniformity	Antonym: slavery
Grounded in positive law	Grounded in natural law

III

We have parsed our two notions of liberty lexicographically and conceptually. We have also suggested that one form, the plural, is principally pre-
modern, while the other, singularized form is characteristic of early
modernity.

We should now turn to religious, political, and legal history to understand why, and roughly when, the Anglo-American tradition shifted from
the plural to the singular concept. The key events, and the key traditions
produced by those events, occur in the sixteenth and seventeenth centuries, bounded by the Reformation initiated in 1517 and the Bill of Rights of
1689. When we look across this period, we see one conception of plural liberties, and at least two very different conceptions of singular liberty. The
plural, pre-modern form appears frequently in legal discourse that became
political discourse, as used by constitutionalist promoters of the common
law in the seventeenth century. The singular forms are respectively evangelical and political, and distinctively early modern. The plural form is
legal, and is a pre-modern survivor in early modern England (if not elsewhere in Europe).

The common lawyers who shaped understanding of what they called the
"Ancient Constitution" preserved and promoted the plural version of lib-
erties.[24] Let us listen to Sir John Davies (1569–1626) in the Preface to his *Irish
Reports* of 1612:

> Neither could any one man ever vaunt, that, like Minos, Solon or
> Lycurgus, he was the first lawgiver to our Nation, for neither did the
> King make his own prerogative, nor the Judges make the Rules or
> Maxims of the Law, nor the common subject prescribe and limit the
> Liberties which he enjoyeth by the law. But, as it is said of every art
> or science which is brought to perfection, *Per varios usus Artem expe-*
> *rientia fecit* ["through wide usage, experience made the art"], so may
> it properly be said *Per varios usus Legem experientia fecit* ["through wide
> usage, experience made the Law"]. Long experience, and many trials of
> what was best for the common good, did make the Common Law.[25]

Many features of the notion of plural liberties are compacted in this crisp
formulation: (i) liberties are plural; (ii) they derive from distinct historical

moments; (iii) they derive from a specific national history; (iv) each one has a long, not to say immemorial, history arrived at through experiential trial and error; (v) no one can claim propriety over, or to be the originator of, liberties; and (vi) they depend on prerogative, but the king did not make that prerogative (a key difference between Davies and the Magna Carta example). In the same report, Davies underlines that common law is not written.[26]

The concept that Davies limns here is given fullest expression and influence (until, that is, Edmund Burke's formulation of it, above all in his *Reflections on the Revolution in France*, 1790), by Sir Edward Coke (1552–1634), in his *Reports* (1600–1615) and in his *Institutes of the Laws of England* (1628–1644).[27] In practical politics, common law defense of liberties was most influentially expressed in the Petition of Right of late May 1628, ratified by Charles I in June 1628.[28] As is characteristic of revolutionary emergency (one thinks of the Girondins in the French Revolution), promoters of democratic reform are swept aside by revolutionary impatience with constitutional form. Thus by 1643 texts such as *The Privileges of Parliament* were arguing that the ancient constitution should give way before parliamentary supremacy.[29] By 1659, the very word "parliament" and its ancient liberties was anathema to Milton: "The name of parliament . . . is a Norman or French word, a monument of our Ancient Servitude."[30]

I turn now to the singular, distinctively early modern evangelical and political conceptions. These conceptions of Liberty have entirely different premises, but they derive from the same historical moment (i.e. the first century CE), and share a conception of power (i.e. absolutism).

The evangelical conception seeks liberty to submit to an absolutist God—it seeks, that is, as both J. C. Davis and Blair Worden have argued, to preserve *God's* liberty.[31] It also seeks liberty from the enslaving regime of free will's works and the tyranny of the Catholic Church, which is what Luther means with his celebrated title *The Freedom of a Christian Man* (1520). Evangelical, singular liberty is a purely theological concept, with first-century Gospel sources, particularly the letters of Paul (e.g. Romans 8.21: "the glorious liberty of the sons of God"; 2 Corinthians 3.17: "Now the Lord is the Spirit, and where the Spirit of the Lord *is*, [there is] liberty"; and above all Galatians 5.1: "Stand fast therefore in the liberty wherewith Christ hath made us free"). In each of these cases the Geneva Bible's "liberty" translates *eleutheria.* Liberty of this kind is paradoxically grounded in inescapable recognition of human enslavement to sin, and nonnegotiable acceptance of God's absolutist prerogative.[32]

We have examined these two sides (i.e. human enslavement to sin and divine absolutism) of the same early modern evangelical coin very frequently in this book, but especially in Chapters 3–5. When evangelical parliamentarians referred to "Liberty" in the 1640s, they referred to this evangelical concept. They referred, that is, to a concept of "liberty" premised on slavery and absolutism as the fundamental, inescapable default position of humans with regard to God. In the face of that absolutism, liberty (the "freedom" of a Christian man) is, paradoxically, "liberty" from the "tyranny" of free will and works, and "liberty" fully to accept the posthuman condition of total submission to God via his Word.

The second, political conception, the so-called "neo-Roman theory of liberty," is purely humanist and secular, however frequently its proponents cite Scripture in its defense.[33] It seeks liberty from tyrannical, arbitrary political rule, acceptance of which is described as slavery (imaginably actual slavery, but always, in the early modern English context, metaphorical slavery). The neo-Roman theory, freshly recovered in the seventeenth century, is republican, drawn principally from commentary on Roman civil law, reading of Roman history, and reading of newly translated Machiavelli.[34] The essence of this theory, which initially applied to the liberty, or independence, of states, is the notion of liberty as nondependence: to be in any way dependent on the arbitrary will of another is to be a slave. So life under arbitrary rule, even benign arbitrary rule, is described as a condition of slavery. I rely on Quentin Skinner to state the essence of the conception, as applied by certain parliamentary debates from the late 1620s to 1640s: "The very existence of the royal prerogative . . . has the effect of making everyone dependent for the maintenance of their liberties upon the goodwill of the king, and this condition of dependence lowers their status from free-men to that of slaves."[35] For the neo-Roman writers, the "essence of what it means to be a slave, and hence to lack personal liberty, is thus to be *in potestate*, within the power of someone else."[36]

Despite the very big differences in the content of these early modern theories of singular liberty, Whig scholarship has been very happy to elide them seamlessly. Thus an influential text of 1942 states that, with the Putney Debates of 1647,

> the priesthood of all believers became the natural equality of all men: Christian liberty, the natural liberty and right of every individual to consent to and share in the government under which he lives; God's law, the law of nature expressed in the fundamental laws of the constitution according to which the executive governs by the authority received from the people or its representatives.[37]

Despite their profound differences, both evangelical and humanist conceptions of liberty also share histories, and both share cardinal formal orientations. I isolate one shared history and three shared formal orientations.

The shared history: both the concept of evangelical liberty and the neo-Roman theory of liberty derive from the slave society of the first-century Roman Empire, appealing to different classes in that imperial society (i.e., respectively, slaves and citizen-intellectuals).[38] Both emerge from a confrontation with arbitrary power, either that confronted by every slave, or that confronted by republican citizens who feel they have become imperial subjects. In both cases these first-century conceptions of liberty, whether Christian or political, presuppose the slavery of Roman society. Both models of singular liberty take shape historically in response to a singularization of power, whether the power be that of a freshly available monotheistic God or of a freshly installed Roman emperor. Singularizations and simplifications of power also characterize sixteenth- and seventeenth-century Europe; it is perhaps no accident that these two first-century notions of liberty should offer themselves up for fresh reaffirmation in the European period we know as Reformation and Renaissance.

The two conceptions of liberty, the evangelical and the political, also share formal orientations with regard to power. The first such shared orientation between the evangelical and the neo-Roman conception of liberty concerns their hostility to the older notion of "liberties." Both the evangelical and the political conceptions I have sketched are explicitly opposed to the partitive distribution of liberties. Jurisdictional extension and simplification, with more widely applicable bureaucratic instruments (aka centralization), is in my view, as I argued in Chapter 1, the fundamental story of European modernity. So particular jurisdictions, granted the right to enjoy particular liberties, franchises, and privileges, will always be the target of what Weber calls the "rationalization" of early modernity.[39]

This is as true of sixteenth-century evangelical Protestants as it is of seventeenth-century Protestant political revolutionaries. So for both camps, plural "liberties" will be deeply offensive. Take, for example, Tyndale's *Obedience of a Christian Man* (1528): "What good conscience can there be among our spirituality [i.e. church officers]," he asks, "to gather so great treasure together . . . and yet not therewith content but with all craft and wiliness to purchase so great *liberties and exemptions* from all manner bearing with their brethren, seeking in Christ no thing but lucre?"[40] Jurisdictional uniformity will repudiate one liberty granted here but not there.

Seventeenth-century promoters of Liberty also make dismissive references to liberties and secular prerogative to grant them. Thus Milton says about a bishop who excommunicates that he "may eat his dainties, drink his wine, use his delights, enjoy his Lands, and liberties, not the least skin raised, not the least hair misplaced for all that excommunication has done."[41] Milton's larger position is in fact more subtle, since he frequently uses the word "liberties" with approbation (as long as they are the people's liberties), and he makes clear that liberties (or what he calls "prerogatives") are produced by liberty.[42]

A second, shared formal orientation between the sixteenth-century evangelical Protestant and the seventeenth-century revolutionary Protestant conception of liberty focuses on slavery: both conceive of a condition short of absolute liberty as utterly servile. Gospel accounts of liberty (especially Galatians 5:1), vitally renewed in the sixteenth century, are, as I have just argued, drawn from a slave society of the first century. Classical slavery is now used as the figure for Catholic domination. The *entire* Church has been overtaken by slave-master Antichrist; the *whole* face of the institution is the face of malicious, diabolical, enslaving hypocrisy. In 1550 Thomas Becon described the situation in Germany as having fallen into servitude: whereas Germany had been "a sure sanctuary for godly-learned men to flee unto from antichrist's tyranny . . . O how lamentable a thing is it, so noble, free, and famous a country to be brought into slavery."[43]

Slavery is also the condition used by Milton and many of his revolutionary fellows as they draw on a new republican theory of liberty. Milton deploys the word "slavery" very liberally indeed, in ways that suggest he knows little about the actual institution of slavery. (We nowhere hear about violently enforced, unpaid work.) In 1649, for example, in the wake of the execution of the king, Milton declares that people who habituate themselves to royal governance are "slaves"; and that those who are overthrown by political revolution will defend themselves by appeal to privileges (what would have been called "liberties"), and to law, which is in fact nothing but a sign of slavery: "Some contesting for Privileges, customs, forms, and that old entanglement of iniquity, their gibberish Laws, though the badge of their ancient slavery."[44]

Third, in both traditions liberty once perceived necessitates pursuit. We have seen this in Milton already, in his justification of the lesser number forcing liberty on the larger number, a quotation with which we began: the "less number should compel a greater to retain . . . their liberty, than that a greater number, for the pleasure of their baseness, compel a less most injuriously to be their fellow slaves."[45] We can also see the same sense of compulsion deriving from evangelical liberty of the gospel in sixteenth-century evangelical polemic, with the correlative charge that those who fail to pursue liberty are merely hypocrites. Thus an anonymous text of 1538 declares that true Christians must be

> doers of the word & not hearers only, deceiving your own selves
> with Sophistry. For if any hear the word & do it not, he is like unto
> a man that beholdeth his bodily face in a glass, for as soon as he hath
> looked on him self, he goeth his way, & hath immediately forgotten
> what his fashion was. But whosoever looketh in the parfite law of
> liberty and continueth therein (if he be not a forgetful hearer but a
> doer of the word) he shall be happy in his deed.[46]

Across the sixteenth and seventeenth centuries, then, we see two discourses, theology and politics, both claiming singular "Liberty" for themselves. Three motives in particular, I have suggested, drive this lexical and conceptual triumph of a singular liberty: (i) hostility to plural liberties; (ii) a distinctively early modern conviction that power is tyrannical and enslaving; and (iii) a new placement of liberty as the overriding, ineluctable, compelling ideal of life worth living, whose demands must be obeyed.

Of course there are also stark dissonances between the two traditions of liberty. Counter to popular perception, Luther and his immediate followers promoted absolute political obedience, even to absolutist rulers.[47] Sixteenth-century mainline evangelicals would concentrate all secular powers in the hands of the prince. Listen, for example, to the English Lutheran William Tyndale, in his significantly titled *Obedience of a Christian Man* of 1528, citing Romans 13:1–2: "He that judgeth the king judgeth God; and he that layeth hands on the king layeth hand on God; and he that resisteth the king resisteth God, and damneth God's law and ordinance."[48] The duty of obedience extends to tyrants, since the tyrant has been appointed by God. Christians should submit to tyrants humbly, and not act like a rebellious child, who, "as long as he seeketh to avenge himself upon the rod, hath an evil heart." On the contrary, Tyndale enjoins submission: "If we . . . meekly knowledge our sins for which we are scourged, and kiss the rod, and amend our living: then will God take the rod away, that is, he will give the rulers a better heart."[49]

That politically submissive view came under pressure in evangelical culture already in Marian England (marriages of politics, which must negotiate, and religion, which often can't, always end badly).[50] The submissive view contrasts most obviously, though, with mid-seventeenth-century Protestant political views (even if evangelical statements of divine right absolutism are also made then).[51] To look no further than Milton writing in 1649, in the immediate aftermath of the regicide, for example, we find active promotion of potentially permanent revolution against rulers judged to be tyrannical. Indeed, the people may remove *any* king, tyrant or no tyrant. Since the king "holds his authority of the people," then "may the people, as oft as they shall judge it for the best . . . retain or depose him, though no tyrant, merely by the liberty and right of free-born men to be governed as seems to them best."[52] The evangelical and political traditions here exactly mirror each other in opposition: the sixteenth-century evangelical accepts the tyranny of the king, while the seventeenth-century political activist promotes what looks like the tyranny of the people. Both positions are, however, expressions of a singular "Liberty." And both singular notions are born of, and themselves prompt, emergency. Whenever singular Liberty is challenged, the intolerable life of the slave presents itself as the necessary consequence. Unlike the more moderate temperature of plural "liberties," singular Liberty is always in a febrile state, forever threatened with slavery as it feels itself to be.

These stark differences between two traditions of liberty, evangelical and political, should not, however, blind us to deeper similarities: both are revolutionary, both pose slavery as their antonym, and both posit pursuit of liberty as a categorical moral necessity. Liberty gives one no choice. Both express these compacted convictions through an apparently tiny grammatical and rhetorical shift, by singularizing and personifying Liberty. In all these respects, both traditions of singular liberty are contrastive with the common law, pre-modern, constitutionalist tradition of plural liberties.

IV

Seventeenth-century Europe can be fitly dubbed the Age of Absolutism.[53] France is the most obvious case, but England offers many defenses of absolutist politics across the century, from James VI and I's defenses of the divine right of kings in his *The true lawe of free monarchies* (1598) and in *Basilikon Doron* (1603); to Robert Filmer's defense of monarchical absolutism on social, patriarchal grounds, as in his *The anarchy of a limited or mixed monarchy* (1648), *The necessity of the absolute power of all kings* (1648), and his *Patriarcha* (1680); and to Thomas Hobbes's philosophical defense of a people's willed monarchical absolutism in *Leviathan* (1651).[54] Calvinist theological absolutism, which holds by God's "independent and illimited Prerogative over all Kingdoms and Nations to build them, or destroy them as he pleaseth," continues unabated across the century.[55]

The early modern phenomenon of absolutism is difficult for scholars of different traditions to see clearly, given their mistaken persuasion that the history of European political power from medieval, to early modern, to modern is a history of continually progressivist, wider, increasingly democratic distribution of power. Such an illusion has the effect of retrojecting absolutism back onto the Middle Ages, as the default position of medieval kingship. Thus, for example, Terry Eagleton's formulation "feudal absolutism" betrays basic ignorance of the logic of feudalism as a decentered political structure in which power is necessarily distributed.[56]

That same view of ever-widening distribution of power in the practice of politics, shared by both progressivist (though not Burkean) liberals and Marxists, also tends to block understanding of the history of political theory. In particular, it blocks recognition that, in Quentin Skinner's words, "it was in late-medieval conciliarism and in the natural-law theories of the second scholastic that the fundamental concepts of modern constitutionalism were originally forged."[57] Some late-medieval scholastics did produce theories of Papal absolutism, but such theories were minority currents beside the major current of late medieval conciliar and constitutionalist theory, which also found forceful expression (and practice) in fifteenth-century England.[58]

In the context of this chapter, as I turn to Milton, I suggest that we enrich our list of seventeenth-century English absolutists by adding a separate category of absolutist opponents of absolutism. The name Oliver Cromwell will head the list, but "John Milton" will also figure near its top. Milton himself understood the logic whereby the opponents of absolutism become absolutists ("New *Presbyter* is but old *Priest* writ large"),[59] and here I apply Milton's own logic to himself. Determination to see Milton as a consistent lover of liberty,[60] and the conviction that a defender of liberty is by definition anti-absolutist, have tended to obscure recognition of Milton's consistently anti-democratic, oligarchic politics. His frequent, savage dismissals of the "people" as, for example, "slaves,"[61] have tended to produce a good deal of special pleading to explain away Milton's active participation in, and support of, an anti-parliamentary military dictatorship in the 1650s.[62] Charles I was not the only one to treat parliament with contempt in the mid-seventeenth century.

The portrait of Milton as anti-absolutist absolutist is easy to draw from his prose writings from 1649 (*The Tenure of Kings and Magistrates*) to 1660 (*The Ready and Easy Way to Establish a Free Commonwealth*). We look, however, for political history in the wrong places if we restrict ourselves to texts of political theory. Literary discourse and literary genres are liberties in the older sense: spaces of exemption where the normal rules do not apply. To give substance to my perhaps surprising claim that Milton is an absolutist of sorts, I turn to Milton's writing, both prose, but also the poetry. The prose tells the story of Milton as one kind of absolutist, and the poetry a more interesting one, of Milton recognizing the need to move out from singular, Liberty-driven purity.

I begin with the prose, by focusing on what strikes me as the hubris and instability of Milton's formulation of republicanism in his prose works after 1649. *The Tenure of Kings and Magistrates* was written during the trial of Charles I in early January 1649, and published in mid-February of the same year, two weeks after the execution of the king. Despite Milton's later denials, the tract was intended to inflect the outcome of that trial.[63] The trial of the king was conducted under the auspices of a parliament that had been purged by the Army in December 1648 of those parliamentarians in favor of restoring the king with curtailed prerogative. The king was the captive of the Army, which insisted that he be brought to trial.

Milton's opening sets the co-ordinates of his absolutist anti-absolutism:

> If Men within themselves would be govern'd by reason, and not gen-
> erally give up their understanding to a double tyrannie, of custome
> from without, and blind affections within, they would discerne
> better what it is to favour and uphold the Tyrant of a Nation. But
> being slaves within doores, no wonder that they strive so much to
> have the public State conformably govern'd to the inward vitious
> rule, by which they govern themselves. For indeed none can love
> freedom heartilie, but good men; the rest love not freedom, but li-
> cence; which never hath more scope or more indulgence then under
> Tyrants.[64]

The king's putative tyranny produces slavery, and so must be met by the governance of reason. What Milton here dismisses as "custom," and what he dismisses within two pages as "the old entanglement of . . . gibberish Laws," should in no way determine how the king must be treated.[65] Those who resist the governance of reason are "bad men." Those who accept reason's governance are "good men." The bad men are "slaves," who love not liberty but libertinism. Scripture points in only one way in the case, and should not be used to "transform the sacred verity of God to an idol with two faces."[66]

The "people" play two roles in Milton's tracts of this period. They are either the noble source of liberty, who have delegated or removed power to the king, or they are licentious fools. As long as the said people play the rhetorical role of the sources of freedom, they have the right to depose kings at will, as we have seen already in this chapter: "The people, as oft as they shall judge it for the best . . . [may] retain or depose him [the king], though no tyrant, merely by the liberty and right of free-born men to be governed as seems to them best."[67] These are the "people" of theory; the actual people who do not wish to put the king to trial on a capital offense, express the "vulgar folly of men to desert their own reason," who shut their own eyes "to think they see best with other men's."[68]

The upshot of this double attitude to the people, simultaneously the source of political salvation and its stubborn obstacle, is, by Milton's account in the second edition of his later *The Readie and Easie Way to Establish a Free Commonwealth* (1660), at least twofold. On the one hand, the people need some forcing to come to the right decision: it is, as we have seen, fitter that the "less number should compel a greater to retain . . . their liberty, than that a greater number, for the pleasure of their baseness, compel a less most injuriously to be their fellow slaves."[69] On the other, Milton's plan for actual governance keeps the compelled people at a good distance from decision making and well away from democratic consultation. He proposes a government whose sovereignty resides with a ("although it may seem strange at first hearing") perpetual "Grand Council" whose members shall themselves elect a "Councel of State."[70]

Milton's authoritarianism and distrust of actual "people," despite his frequent and moving appeals to "the people," cannot be explained by the special pleading of claiming that he was writing under emergency. He routinely dismisses the "vulgar folly of men," or, to cite another characteristic formulation from 1649, the "worthless approbation of an inconstant, irrational, and image-doting rabble," who is "like a credulous and hapless herd, begotten to servility, and enchanted to these popular institutes of Tyranny."[71] (These are the same "English people," just five years later in 1654, whose "purity of life and . . . blameless character . . . showed them the one direct road to true liberty, and it was the most righteous defense of law and religion that of necessity gave them arms."[72]) Milton's plans for oligarchic government are not for an emergency, but "perpetual." His singularized Liberty has gained captives who march behind her, and actively relishes the prospect of compelling more into her train. Milton's resistance to what he sees as tyranny produces something that looks very much like a recipe for tyranny.

V

My skepticism about Milton as champion of Liberty will be clear. Were that skepticism merely mine, it would have a certain, but limited, interest. Such skepticism about singular Liberty is not, however, merely mine, so much as Milton's, which makes my case, and the case of Milton, much more interesting.

Paradise Lost was begun in 1658 or so, by which time the imminent failure of the republic was clear. Its very verse form is an expression "of ancient liberty recovered . . . from the troublesome and modern bondage of rhyming."[73] The profile of Liberty in the poem's action is, however, more equivocal. The word "liberty" is used twelve times within *Paradise Lost*—ten times by an angel, once by Sin, and once by Milton as narrator. (Only angels, Sin, and Milton discuss liberty.)[74] Some angelic usages are approbative, especially as buttressed by adjectives ("rational liberty"). Many instances (5/12) are, however, putatively negative, spoken as they are by fallen angels, especially Satan (3/12), or Sin. The word "liberties" does not appear in *Paradise Lost*.

That Milton at least opens the door onto potentially negative valences of singular liberty is also suggested by that fact that, in a poem whose stated theme is disobedience, there are two great disobeyers, Satan and Eve. Both, by Milton's account, disobey precisely in the name of Liberty. Both Eve and Satan disobey a royal decree in whose making they had no part, and both dismiss that prior condition of their very being as an unjustified, enslaving restraint on their liberty. In this they are good test cases for Miltonic Neo-Roman republican theory, which demands that free humans have a part in any rule to which they are subject. Furthermore, both Eve and Satan disobey not because they suffer indignity or oppression, but rather because they *might* suffer oppression. In this, too, they are good test cases of Miltonic republican theory, which has it that rebellion is justified if non-conceded prerogative exists, regardless as to whether that prerogative is being exercised.

For Milton the question of liberty is clearly the main issue, since it's the issue that troubles ostensibly ideal, utopian states: *before* the fall of Lucifer in Paradise, and *before* the fall of Eve in Eden, there's trouble brewing: bad dreams, flushed faces, and grumbling—all producing revolution against God, and all produced by claims to singular liberty.

I begin with Satan. The mirroring effect of singular absolutism producing an absolutist claim to singular Liberty is readily visible in the political relations between God and Satan. God is evidently an absolutist, who foresees, foreplans, and sees all with utterly self-assured, unassailable prerogative and impregnable power. The premise of that kind of power produces a mirroring response in Satan, who consistently calls not for liberties but for Liberty. *Paradise Lost* imagines a distinctively early modern revolutionary confrontation.

In Book 5 Satan, astonishingly, incites his fellow angelic conspirators against God in very much the terms, and the very words, of English revolutionaries in the 1640s. He repudiates "knee-tribute" as "prostration vile" (5.782) and plants the thought of insurrection from this indignity: "But what if better counsels might erect / Our minds and teach us to cast off this yoke?" (5.785–786). All this prepares for the most resounding call to arms, made in the name of liberty:

> Will ye submit your necks and choose to bend
> The supple knee? Ye will not if I trust
> To know ye right or if ye know yourselves
> Natives and sons of Heav'n possessed before
> By none, and if not equal all, yet free,
> Equally free, for orders and degrees
> Jar not with liberty but well consist.
> (5.787–793)

This speech is made prior to any fall, but it also provokes an argument about liberty. This debate is initiated by the sole voice against Satan's rousing call to liberty against tyranny, that of the angel Abdiel. Obedient but courageous Abdiel speaks in much the accents, fascinatingly, of defenders of royal prerogative. Satan, Abdiel declares, has no right to condemn the "just decree of God pronounced and sworn" that all in heaven shall confess Christ "rightful king" (5.814–818). Milton's lonely hero Abdiel has no time whatsoever for neo-Roman theories of liberty:

> Shalt thou give law to God, shalt thou dispute
> With Him the points of liberty who made
> Thee what thou art and formed the pow'rs of Heav'n
> Such as He pleased and circumscribed their being?
> Yet by experience taught we know how good
> And of our good and of our dignity
> How provident He is.
>   (5.822–828)

Abdiel, in short, favors a pre-modern "liberties" model of liberty, liberties granted by a legitimate, prior jurisdiction. He does this on the grounds that what I have called the singular "liberty" model is fundamentally hubristic. That model of liberty involves arrogation of divine prerogative by claiming to be fully formed and fully autonomous regardless of one's condition as a historical being. It strenuously rejects the notion that one might be necessarily constrained and subject in ways beyond one's ken.

Satan's response takes especial umbrage at the assertion of any constraint posed by history itself. Against what Abdiel says about having been formed by God in ways he cannot know, libertarian Satan vehemently thrusts an assertion of being wholly self-made, in the present of one's own creation. "Who saw," he derisively responds,

> When his Creation was? Remember'st thou
> Thy making while the Maker gave thee being?
> We know no time when we were not as now,
> Know none before us, self-begot, self-raised
> By our own quick'ning power.
>   (5.857–861)

In this confrontation, then, we can see that Milton is fully capable of delineating and promoting a pre-modern model of liberties: he represents a situation in which freedom is granted; in which prior conditions exist, beyond the judgment of the free; and in which the poem's great failure Satan fails precisely by promoting the republican theory of liberty to which Milton himself subscribed, and was subscribing to even as *Paradise Lost* was being written.

Eve's is a similar case. When Eve wishes to work alone in the garden of Eden, before the Fall, Adam and Eve have what very nearly amounts to an argument, again about liberty. Adam warns Eve that "God left free the will," but argues that trial shall come unsought. Troubled by the thought of a theoretical constraint, however, Adam relents and agrees that Eve should go alone: "For if thou think trial unsought may find / Us both securer than thus warned thou seem'st, / Go, for thy stay, not free, absents thee more" (9.370–373). Adam, that is, underlines that Eve's freedom is not infringed in any way except in being *thought* infringed, which thought of potential infringement suffices to initiate liberating action. In this concession, Adam recognizes the force of the neo-Roman theory, even if he also exercises a prerogative by granting Eve's singular liberty.

After Satan has tempted Eve, she argues herself into seeking another theoretical good, this one produced by God's very prohibition: the prohibition against eating the apple itself argues the desirability of the apple; and a "good unknown sure is not had, or had / And yet unknown is as not had at all" (9.756–757). If, that is, the good is not known, then it cannot be enjoyed; or if it is enjoyed without being known as such, then neither can it be said to be enjoyed. Eve, that is, must both enjoy everything desirable, and simultaneously know it as desirable. In Milton's theological universe, Eve arrogates to herself divine prerogatives, in the name of liberty. In Milton's political universe, Eve acts like Milton.

In the poem, this is original sin. The result of that sin is, however, persuasively beautiful. Adam and Eve confess their mutual solidarity, precisely given a preexisting condition that Adam is powerless to avoid. Adam and Eve both make speeches of humble solidarity to each other:

> However I with thee have fixed my lot,
> Certain to undergo like doom, if death
> Consort with thee, death is to me as life:
> So forcible within my heart I feel
> The bond of nature draw me to my own,
> My own in thee, for what thou art is mine;
> Our state cannot be severed, we are one,
> One flesh; to lose thee were to lose myself.
> (9.952–959)

Thus Adam; and Eve:

> Were it I thought death menaced would ensue
> This my attempt, I would sustain alone
> The worst, and not persuade thee rather die
> Pernicious to thy peace, chiefly assured
> Remarkably so late of thy so true,
> So faithful love unequalled.
>   (9.977–983)

In a poem where instances of self- and self-conscious invention, with their bristling, proudly arrogant rhetorical expression, are so much the norm, these speeches of mutually generous solidarity in the face of overpowering and threatening historical conditions, which constrain liberty, offer tender contrast.

Above all, this encounter shapes the grounds of a politics that recognizes prior constraint. *Paradise Lost* as a whole is, after all, structured (like classical epics) so as to underline the conditions of history as beyond any single consciousness: in *Paradise Lost* we start in the middle of things, with the Fall and Satan's voyage to Eden (Books 1–4); move backwards in time to the failed revolution in heaven (Books 5–8); and only then return to the present and point outward to the future (Books 9–12). The very poem, that is, whose main players seek to inhabit an eternal present of their own making, and who deny their place in a preexisting historical structure that might constrain their liberty, is structured so as to underline the conditions of historicity. The poem's own narrative structure therefore concedes preexisting historical condition.

So too does the narrative of Adam and Eve begin here, in beautiful speeches of solidarity at the moment of joint original sin. Adam and Eve knowingly enter a space of demanding historical condition (both original sin and their love for each other), and as they do so they grant prerogative to each other. Milton as narrator immediately condemns them for licentiousness (9.996–1016), but he has been, we have been, surprised by sin as the moment when history begins. This is the moment in which actors break out of the logic of singular Absolutism / Liberty, in which singular, absolute Liberty is no longer possible, and from which time there will only be separate, hard-won liberties to be gained. This is the condition of submitting to "those wise restraints that make us free."[75]

Milton's poetry (as opposed to his contemporaneous prose) tells us that seventeenth-century revolutionary republican theory of liberty is an ahistorical theory; that it is born of, and can produce, the emergency of slavery. Always to identify history's constraint as a state of slavery is a very unstable ground of the civilized order. Slavery, of course, did and does exist; it must always be vigorously resisted. But not every constraint of one's environment or one's history can properly be described as slavery. Milton was, we might say remembering Blake, of America's party, without knowing it; but would he have promoted Liberty or some version of liberties? By his prose, he promotes Liberty; by his poetry, he sometimes promotes liberties.

Conclusion

IF LITERARY HISTORY and criticism is, as I believe it should be, ancillary to the complex history of freedoms, then this is a narrative of both newly forged and partially recovered liberties.

Early modernization in England imposed, through its principal cultural vehicle (evangelical theology), astonishingly demanding disciplines upon every English subject. I approach that phenomenon from the outside, either as a cultural historian of the late medieval period, or as a twenty-first century liberal. As a scholar of late medieval pre-modernity, I approach early English modernization from the past coming forward; as a liberal, I consider the same phenomenon from the present looking backward. Either way, what strikes the eye is both arresting and illuminating: although by no means promoted only by state sponsors, one sees state-sponsored cultural extremity of a singular, soul-crushing and violence-producing kind. I conclude this book by summarizing the thousand natural shocks and illuminations delivered to an outsider by the period 1517–1688 in England, and by categorizing them thus: those of the late-medievalist; those of the liberal.

The late medievalist sees so sharp a cultural convulsion as s/he enters early English modernity that no word short of "revolution" will answer to the experience. Once that word is introduced, a range of cultural practices (e.g. predestination and denial of free will; models of singular personal authenticity; image destruction; persecution of "witches"; suppression of drama; literalist reading practice; and absolutist politics) come into view as characteristic of revolutions, and as starkly contrastive with the preceding cultural dispensation. They also present themselves as a template of later revolutionary movements in both Europe and Asia.

In addition, one observes the revolutionary regime's cultural mechanisms, of both rejection and retrojection, with regard to the immediate past: violence against the immediate past is legitimated by trashing it on the one hand; and, on the other, the early modern regime retrojects its own embarrassments (e.g. spiritual slavery, hypocrisy, obscurantist magic, absolutism) onto the repudiated past. These mechanisms are prosecuted with such vigor as to open the deepest cultural crevasse in Anglo-American cultural history, that between the medieval and the early modern.

Revolutions do not like narrative for various reasons. Revolutions claim to start history afresh, and narrative of the pre-revolutionary period threatens the freshness of that start. Further, revolutions also claim to deliver the entire revolutionary package in a single, swift intervention that is immune from the predations of future tradition and change. For both these reasons, I resist revolutionary historiography's temperamental inclination to treat history in hermetically sealed units. I have tried, that is, not only to give some idea of the pre-revolutionary story, but also, in greater detail, to tell the story of the revolution itself. That story is, I suggest, best narrated as the unfolding of a historical logic within the revolutionary movement. I have called that logic "permanent revolution." Telling that story points us less to the Catholic / Protestant conflict and more to the much more dynamic energies within Protestantism, that push Protestant movements to reject prior versions of themselves.

All of the above might suggest that I have mounted an ethical case against the Reformation. It is true that, when an outsider looks at evangelical theological practice, s/he cannot help but be struck, to the point of being repelled, by the singularity and crushing, virtue-parading extremity of the movement (notably in the matter of denying the value of human agency). Neither can s/he contemplate with complete equanimity a hugely influential historiographical tradition (in this case, still vibrant Whig historiography) that describes this crushing culture in triumphalist terms. And one cannot help focusing on the arrogant absolutisms of certain big voices (here notably William Perkins and John Milton); neither can one help praise the heroes who resist the cultural regime from within (here notably William Shakespeare).

Those reactions to the culture, its players, and its mistaken historiographical reception produce a certain heat, I concede, in the outsider. That heat should not, however, be taken to suggest that I object to the Reformation. The Reformation is a mighty historical phenomenon, so mighty that I have sometimes felt, in writing this book, that we have hardly begun to understand it. It happened. Objecting to it is entirely otiose. The most intelligent way of responding to the event is to understand it as the expression of modernization, no less than the so-called Counter Reformation is another such expression of modernization's story.

Once we describe the Reformation as part of the story of modernization, then we understand the continuing magnetism of evangelical religion, in both the West and elsewhere: evangelical religion is a key expression of modernity, a non-reformist, non-conservative revolutionary form of modernization in every respect, including its current antinomianism. As long as liberals do not understand this, they remain utterly bewildered by evangelical culture, dismissing it, with 180 degree inaccuracy, as "conservative." It is unquestionably, and objectionably, illiberal and regressive, but it is also, as I say, by far the most powerful expression of early European revolutionary modernity, which is one of the reasons it remains powerful in the United States.

By understanding evangelical religion as a key form of modernizing Europe, we also understand Liberalism better, at which point I turn to my second view point on the Reformation, that of a committed liberal. By looking at the process of permanent revolution across the 150-year period of the Reformation, we see that nascent Liberalism is itself one of the forms taken by Protestantism, as it repudiates prior forms of itself. As a form of modernization Liberalism is, however (unlike evangelical religion), a stabilizing form. Each of the following characteristics of the liberal tradition serves to stabilize the force field that is evangelical religion: its insistences on democracy; on division of powers; on separation of church and state; on free will; on equality before the law; on toleration for (not necessarily tolerance of) minorities; on respect for liberty and privacy of conscience; on artistic liberties; and on liberty of textual interpretation.

That Liberalism is derived from evangelical religion is, I need not underline, a standard position of the Whig tradition. In this book I actually support that long-standing tradition. My support is, however, differently grounded: so far from it being the case that Liberalism is derived from evangelical religion in any straightforward fashion, I have argued here that proto-Liberalism defines itself in opposition to the dominant forms of Reformation Protestantism. It does so in order to stabilize cultures after 150 years of psychic and social violence, and to shape the conditions for cultural flourishing in reaction to the crushing disciples of modernization. I cite Herbert Butterfield again, who said it better than I can: the Whig tradition, he said in 1931, "likes to imagine religious liberty issuing beautifully out of Protestantism when in reality it emerges painfully and grudgingly out of something quite different, out of the tragedy of the post-Reformation world."[1]

Whereas evangelical religion aspires to one key form of modernity (rationalization, centralization, and collapse of separate jurisdictions), Liberalism expresses the reactive, decentralizing countermovement of modernization (i.e. a balance between rationalization on the one hand and preservation of decentralized jurisdictions and individual rights on the other). Insofar as this is true, nascent Liberalism can fairly be said to forge some new liberties, notably equality before the law, toleration (if not always tolerance) of minorities, respect for liberty and privacy of conscience, and artistic and interpretive liberties. Some of the chapters here point less to the formation of new liberties, and more to liberties recovered from late medieval, pre-Reformation culture, notably modified free will, anti-literalist interpretation, space for the image, and the very idea of plural liberties themselves.

This revised genealogy of Liberalism points us not only to the preciousness of the liberal tradition but also to its weaknesses. I sketch three such weaknesses.

First, contemporary Liberalism looks unpersuasive in its account of its own history. When many liberal early modernist scholars go back to the sixteenth century, they focus on the following (for example) with approval: liberty, equality, free will, consent, the individual conscience, interiority and individuality, division of powers, rationality, toleration, reading, work, revolution. They focus on the following (for example) with disapproval:

absolutism, predestination, hypocrisy, iconoclasm, anti-theatricality. "Protestantism" tends to be a code for the terms of approval, whereas "Catholic"
encodes many of the terms of disapproval.

If, then, in this book I finally promote the liberal tradition, I do so only
having first subjected it to a salutary embarrassment. Liberalism is so
much more interesting than its dutiful, tolerationist, consistentist, almost-
history-free self-presentation would have us believe. It is, in fact, just as
interesting as its older sibling Calvinism. The sum effect of *Permanent Revolution* will therefore, I hope, be to re-evaluate the coding of these terms
("Protestant" and "Catholic" are impossibly blunt), and to redistribute the
terms of approval and disapproval between opposed traditions *within* the
Protestant tradition. Each of these terms will now look different, differently distributed across the formations of the evangelical Reformation
and proto-Liberalism.

Second, Liberalism has not escaped the influence of its older sibling,
evangelical religion. The reader will have noticed that in my chapters I
consistently say that anti-evangelical movements "almost," "nearly," or
"partially" succeeded in neutralizing the forces of permanent evangelical
revolution. These qualifications are crucial, even if they cannot be fully
substantiated within the bounds of the present book. If a revolution is truly
permanent, then it leaves its scars on even the most resourceful alternative cultural forms that seek to neutralize and survive its punishing regime.
For good or ill, liberals continue automatically to distrust institutions; over-
work; calibrate agency with minute attention; fear inauthenticity; enjoy
visual art in aesthetic conditions that remain partially iconoclastic; remain
appalled at various forms of idolatry, even if the idolaters are now consumers; read to save themselves. Above all, many of us remain historical
secessionists, vigilantly insisting on the legitimacy of the modern age, even
as we find ourselves forever rowing against the current. We liberals remain children of our permanent revolutions, both energized and scarred
by them.

The continuing influence of evangelical religion on contemporary
Liberalism can also take much more aggressive and damaging forms. Liberalism is, by the account of this book, the always younger sibling to modernization's elder child (i.e. evangelical religion). Liberalism therefore stands
in danger of reproducing the logic of permanent revolution in militant

forms. Liberalism, that is, carries the DNA of a crushing revolutionary movement within itself. Contemporary Liberalism looks especially unpersuasive when it mimics, as it not infrequently does, the intolerant, exclusivist, identitarian politics characteristic of the non-democratic, anti-meritocratic, virtue-parading, evangelical True Church. When liberals act like the elect, they betray their tradition.

Third, and finally, progressivist liberals stand in danger of damaging the good of Liberalism by claiming impossibly excellent standards for Liberalism. Liberals regard Liberalism as a worldview, or what Germans would call a *Weltanschauung*. A worldview proper implies claims about the process of history and the makeup of human being. A worldview claims to understand the historical process and to deliver humans from history, so as to liberate full human being. Christianity and Marxism are, for example, worldviews, with their separate salvation histories and anthropologies.

Liberalism is not a worlview. It claims no scheme of salvation history, or *Heilsgeschichte,* and has no developed anthropology. It does not offer itself as a category to sit beside a religious or political Weltanschauung. When those with a proper Weltanschauung (what might be called a first-order belief system), either religious or secularist, dismiss Liberalism as "hollow" (as they frequently do), they are missing the point. Liberalism is *meant* to be hollow. Liberalism is a *second-order belief system,* a tool for managing first-order belief systems. It is derivative (as its historical appearance would suggest), and secondary to first-order belief systems. It promises only to manage and mediate those first-order systems. The clash of first-order belief systems leads to violence; Liberalism promises to manage the violence. Liberalism is a tool, an instrument designed to govern first-order belief systems that tend not to negotiate. For this reason, Liberalism stands always in an asymmetrical rhetorical position with regard to first-order belief systems, looking cool and detached against its hot and committed first-order competitors.

When progressivist liberals treat Liberalism itself as a first-order belief system, they produce what look like hollowed-out versions of first-order belief systems. Liberalism's minimalist anthropology; the abstract, universalist legal principles that flow from that anthropology; its lack of a salvation history; its default positions of institutional distrust; its often impoverished conception of singular Liberty: each make Liberalism look weak as long as liberals claim that Liberalism is a worldview rather than a tool for governing worldviews.

One can, that is, be a liberal and a modified Catholic, or a liberal and a modified Socialist, where the modification points to acceptance of state mechanisms (notably constitutional democracy) for managing ideological conflict. Liberalism becomes vulnerable the moment it claims to be a first-order belief system—when it lays claim, that is, to reshape the world on what are shallow grounds (e.g. abstract, universalist human rights (however precious) and tolerance as an absolute virtue). All the liberal within a given constitutionalist democracy need commit to, as liberal, is the following: pressure to ensure that the constitution answers to its mediating responsibilities; defense and promotion of division of powers, separation of church and state, equality before the law, toleration of minorities, freedom of association, respect for liberty and privacy of conscience, artistic liberties, and liberty of textual interpretation; and, of course, acceptance of the democratic judgment of the majority. Once the liberal signs on to those mediating mechanisms, s/he is free to adopt any other first-order belief system. The only voice the liberal must strenuously reject is that of the figure who refuses to accept the wise constitutional restraints, derived from the liberal tradition, that make us freer.

Note on Texts and Citations

The spelling of all citations from prose texts in English cited from *EEBO* has been modernized. The original spelling adds nothing to the sense of these texts for the arguments of this book, which are not dependent on strictly philological evidence; their modernization renders them easier of access. Citation of titles from *EEBO* preserves original spelling. Whenever a citation is made in the form of a reference to an "image," the reader should assume that the source text is consulted via *EEBO*. Citations from the Bible will, unless otherwise stated, be from the Geneva Bible (*The Bible and Holy Scriptures conteyned in the Olde and Newe Testament*, Geneva, 1561, RSTC 2095). All translations throughout the book are mine unless otherwise stated.

Abbreviations

CPWJM   John Milton, *Complete Prose Works of John Milton*, ed. Don M. Wolfe, rev. ed., 8 vols. (New Haven, CT: Yale University Press, 1953–1982)

CWSTM   *The Yale Edition of the Complete Works of St Thomas More*, 21 vols. (New Haven, CT: Yale University Press, 1963–1997)

DLCPT   Digital Library of Classic Protestant Texts

EEBO   Early English Books Online

EETS   Early English Text Society

JMEMS   *Journal of Medieval and Early Modern Studies*

NLH   *New Literary History*

ODNB   *Oxford Dictionary of National Biography*, consulted online

OED   *Oxford English Dictionary*, consulted online

PMLA   *Publications of the Modern Language Association of America*

RSTC   *A Short-Title Catalogue of Books Printed in England, Scotland and Ireland and of English Books Printed Abroad 1475–1640*, ed. A. W. Pollard and G. R. Redgrave, 2nd ed. rev. W. A. Jackson et al., 3 vols. (Bibliographical Society, 1976–1991)

SR   *Statutes of the Realm*, ed. T. E. Tomlins et al., 11 vols. (Dawsons, 1810–1828; repr. 1963)

SAC   *Studies in the Age of Chaucer*

TRP   *Tudor Royal Proclamations*, ed. Paul L. Hughes and James F. Larkin, 3 vols. (New Haven, CT: Yale University Press, 1964–1969)

YLS   *Yearbook of Langland Studies*

Notes

Preface

1. "If her [Truth's] waters flow not in a perpetual progression, they sicken into a muddy pool of conformity and tradition. A man may be a heretic in the truth; and if he believe things only because his pastor says so, or the Assembly so determines, without knowing other reason, though his belief be true, yet the very truth he holds, becomes his heresy." John Milton, *Areopagitica*, in *CPWJM*, 2:486–570 (at p. 543).

Introduction

1. For Whig historiography of the Reformation, and especially for the influence of J. A. Froude's *History of England from the Fall of Wolsey to the defeat of the Spanish Armada*, 12 vols. (1856–1870), see J. W. Burrow, *A Liberal Descent: Victorian Historians and the English Past* (Cambridge, UK: Cambridge University Press, 1983), chap. 9. See also Rosemary O'Day, *The Debate on the English Reformation* (London: Methuen, 1986), pp. 91–95.
2. For the profile of "liberty" in Reformation discourse, see Chapter 18 below. For the function of liberty in the historiography of the English Revolution especially, see Glenn Burgess, "Introduction: Religion and the Historiography of the English Civil War," in *England's Wars of Religion, Revisited*, ed. Charles W. A. Prior and Glenn Burgess (Farnham, Surrey: Ashgate, 2011), pp. 1–25.
3. Herbert Butterfield, *The Whig Interpretation of History* (London: Bell and Sons, 1931), p. 88.
4. For an exceptionally careful account of historiographical perils in dealing with the Reformation, see Alexandra Walsham, "Migrations of the Holy: Explaining

Religious Change in Medieval and Early Modern Europe," *JMEMS* 44 (2014), 241–280.

5. The historiographical situation I am describing has its parallel in this, as in many other cardinal respects, with the historiography of the French Revolution. See François Furet, *Penser la Révolution Française* (Paris: Gallimard, 1978). Constitutional government: Geoffrey Elton, *England under the Tudors* (London: Methuen, 1955) (and repeated in many later studies by Elton), for whom the Reformation in England is fundamentally and positively a constitutional break. English moderation: A. G. Dickens, *The English Reformation,* 2nd ed. (London: Batsford, 1989; first pub. 1964), for whom the English Reformation was a moderate and popular movement, expressive of English moderation and popular will (e.g. pp. 205–206). Working-class values: Christopher Hill, *Society and Puritanism in Pre-Revolutionary England* (New York: Schocken Books, 1964), in which Puritanism is taken to be the liberating religion of the working class. Rationality: Keith Thomas, *Religion and the Decline of Magic: Studies in Popular Beliefs in Sixteenth and Seventeenth Century England* (New York: Oxford University Press, 1971), for whom the Reformation is expressive of the rational disenchantment of the world against the deceptive magical operations of the pre-Reformation Catholic Church.

6. See James Simpson, "Trans-Reformation English Literary History," in *Forms of Time: Temporal Thinking, Periodization, and the Making of Early Modern English History and Literature,"* ed. Kristen Poole and Owen Williams (Philadelphia: University of Pennsylvania Press, forthcoming).

7. Religious: see Alister E. McGrath, *Christianity's Dangerous Idea: The Protestant Revolution—A History from the Sixteenth Century to the Twenty-First* (New York: Harper, 2007). See also, for a pure example of a direct channel between early modern Calvinism and liberal, democratic values and practices, John Witte Jr, *The Reformation of Rights: Law, Religion and Human Rights in Early Modern Calvinism* (Cambridge, UK: Cambridge University Press, 2007). I am grateful to Stefan-Ludwig Hoffmann for this reference. Secularist and republican: see e.g. David Norbrook, *Writing the English Republic: Poetry, Rhetoric, and Politics, 1627–1660* (Cambridge, UK: Cambridge University Press, 1999), and Annabel M. Patterson, *Early Modern Liberalism* (Cambridge, UK: Cambridge University Press, 1997).

8. E.g., see especially the essays by Christopher Haigh in *The English Reformation Revised,* ed. Christopher Haigh (Cambridge, UK: Cambridge University Press, 1987), Introduction, and chaps. 1 and 3; Eamon Duffy, *The Stripping of the Altars: Traditional Religion in England, c. 1400–c. 1580* (New Haven, CT: Yale University Press, 1992); and Brad S. Gregory, *The Unintended Reformation: How a Religious Revolution Secularized Society* (Cambridge, UK: Cambridge University Press, 2012). For critiques of Duffy and Gregory respectively, see David Aers, "Altars of Power: Reflections on Eamon Duffy's *The Stripping of the Altars," Literature and History,* third series, 3 (1994), 90–105, and James Simpson, "Brad Gregory's Unintended Revelations," *JMEMS* 46 (2016), 545–554 (and other essays in this

volume of *JMEMS*). For a broad and recent review of Reformation historiography, see Walsham, "Migrations of the Holy."

9. For exceptions see e.g. the work of the following post-Duffy and post-Collinson ecclesiastical and social historians: Ethan H. Shagan, *Popular Politics and the English Reformation* (Cambridge, UK: Cambridge University Press, 2003); Peter Marshall, *Reformation England, 1480–1642,* 2nd ed. (London: Bloomsbury Academic, 2012); Alexandra Walsham, *Charitable Hatred: Tolerance and Intolerance in England, 1500–1700* (Manchester, UK: Manchester University Press, 2006); and Karl Gunther, *Reformation Unbound: Protestant Visions of Reform in England, 1525–1590* (Cambridge, UK: Cambridge University Press, 2014).

10. See especially Alison Shell, *Catholicism, Controversy, and the English Literary Imagination, 1558–1660* (Cambridge, UK: Cambridge University Press, 1999).

11. See Simpson, "Trans-Reformation English Literary History."

12. For a subtle and penetrating account of the medieval / early modern periodic divide in Anglophone cultural history, and its relevant scholarship, see Andrew James Johnston, *Performing the Middle Ages from* Beowulf *to* Othello (Turnhout: Brepols, 2008), pp. 1–17.

13. See especially the brilliant and seminal critique by David Aers, "A Whisper in the Ear of the Early Modernists, or Reflections on Literary Critics Writing the 'History of the Subject'," in *Culture and History 1350–1600: Essays on English Communities, Identities and Writing,* ed. David Aers (London: Harvester Wheatsheaf, 1992), pp. 177–202. For a wide-ranging attempt to begin to remedy that situation, see *Cultural Reformations: Medieval and Renaissance in Literary History,* ed. Brian Cummings and James Simpson (Oxford: Oxford University Press, 2010).

14. For exceptions see e.g. Sarah Beckwith, *Shakespeare and the Grammar of Forgiveness* (Ithaca, NY: Cornell University Press, 2011); Helen Cooper, *The English Romance in Time: Transforming Motifs from Geoffrey of Monmouth to the Death of Shakespeare* (Oxford: Oxford University Press, 2004); and Katherine Little, *Transforming Work: Early Modern Pastoral and Medieval Poetry* (Notre Dame, IN: University of Notre Dame Press, 2013).

15. For the history of English doctrinal intolerance, see David Loewenstein, *Treacherous Faith: The Specter of Heresy in Early Modern English Literature and Culture* (Oxford: Oxford University Press, 2013). On equality, see McGrath, *Christianity's Dangerous Idea,* p. 52, where it is stated that Luther set out "one of the greatest themes of the Reformation—the democratization of faith," articulated through the idea of the priesthood of all believers. For recent examples on rights of interpretation, see McGrath, *Christianity's Dangerous Idea,* p. 53, discussed in Chapter 15 below, and David Daniell, *The Bible in English: Its History and Influence* (New Haven, CT: Yale University Press, 2003), pp. 126, 130. For many examples on rationality, and a measured critique thereof, see Alexandra Walsham, "The Reformation and 'The Disenchantment of the World'," *The Historical Journal* 51 (2008), 497–528. For excellent histories and measured critiques of toleration, see Jeffrey R. Collins, "Redeeming the Enlightenment: New Histories of Religious

Toleration," *The Journal of Modern History* 81 (2009), 607–636, and Walsham, *Charitable Hatred*, pp. 6–13. The history of individuality, or, more recently, subjectivity, in the West, is routinely part of a progressivist narrative, consistently dated to early modernity, and grounded in either secular and / or religious developments. The seminal work is Jacob Burckhardt, *The Civilization of the Renaissance in Italy*, trans. S. G. C. Middlemore (New York: Harper, 1958; first pub. in German, 1860), pt. 2, "The Development of the Individual." The more recent history of the concept in literary studies derives from an influential article by Thomas M. Greene, "The Flexibility of the Self in Renaissance Literature," in *The Disciplines of Criticism: Essays in Literary Theory, Interpretation and History*, ed. Peter Demetz, Thomas Greene, and Lowry Nelson Jnr. (New Haven, CT: Yale University Press, 1968), pp. 241–264. For a recent example, which conflates both secular and religious sources for the newly dignified individual of early modernity, see McGrath, *Christianity's Dangerous Idea*, pp. 34–36.

16. See Louis Montrose, "New Historicisms," in *Redrawing the Boundaries: The Transformation of English and American Literary Studies*, ed. Stephen Greenblatt and Giles Gunn (New York: Modern Language Association of America, 1992), pp. 392–418. For some great exceptions to cursory treatment, or no treatment at all, of English literary history between 1520 and 1580, see John N. King, *English Reformation Literature: The Tudor Origins of the Protestant Tradition* (Princeton, NJ: Princeton University Press, 1982); Stephen Greenblatt, *Renaissance Self-Fashioning from More to Shakespeare* (Chicago, IL: University of Chicago Press, 1980); and *The Oxford Handbook to Tudor Literature, 1485–1603*, ed. Mike Pincombe and Cathy Shrank (Oxford: Oxford University Press, 2009). For the recent scholarly turn to religion, and its background, see Ken Jackson and Arthur F. Marotti, "The Turn to Religion in Early Modern English Studies," *Criticism* 46 (2004), 167–190. For exemplary forerunners and / or instances of that turn, see King, *English Reformation Literature*; Brian Cummings, *The Literary Culture of the Reformation: Grammar and Grace* (Oxford: Oxford University Press, 2002), and Alison Shell, *Catholicism, Controversy, and the English Literary Imagination, 1558–1660* (Cambridge, UK: Cambridge University Press, 1999); for reflections on the need for that turn, see Brian Cummings, *Mortal Thoughts: Religion, Secularity, & Identity in Shakespeare and Early Modern Culture* (Oxford: Oxford University Press, 2013), and Simpson, "Trans-Reformation English Literary History."

17. For these grander narratives see e.g. Margaret Aston, *England's Iconoclasts*, vol. 1, *Laws against Images* (Oxford: Clarendon Press, 1988); Margaret Aston, *Broken Idols of the English Reformation* (Cambridge, UK: Cambridge University Press, 2016); Duffy, *Stripping of the Altars*; Diarmaid MacCulloch, *Reformation: Europe's House Divided* (London: Allen Lane, 2003); Marshall, *Reformation England, 1480–1642*. For the short-termism of Reformation historiography that pertained until the 1990s, see Nicholas Tyacke, "Introduction: Rethinking the 'English Reformation'," in *England's Long Reformation, 1500–1800*, ed. Nicholas Tyacke (London: UCL Press, 1998), pp. 1–32 (at p. 1), and, in a wide-ranging,

generous survey of English ecclesiastical Reformation historiography, Peter Marshall, "(Re)Defining the English Reformation," *Journal of British Studies* 48 (2009), 564–586 (at pp. 567–569 for longer chronologies). Marshall dates calls to lengthen the English "Reformation" to as recently as Patrick Collinson's call in 1986 to extend the Reformation to the end of the reign of James I (p. 56).

18. The great exceptions, until the strong periodic breakthrough from late medieval to early modern in the 1990s, being C. S. Lewis, *The Allegory of Love* (Oxford: Oxford University Press, 1936; repr. 1972), and Helen Cooper, *Pastoral: Mediaeval to Renaissance* (Ipswich: Brewer, 1977).

19. For institutional history, the key work is Duffy, *Stripping of the Altars;* for English literary history, see James Simpson, *Reform and Cultural Revolution, 1350–1547* (Oxford: Oxford University Press, 2002).

20. For the routine retrojection of iconoclasm onto the Middle Ages, see James Simpson, *Under the Hammer: Iconoclasm in the Anglo-American Tradition* (Oxford: Oxford University Press, 2010), Introduction. For an immensely influential literary example of the retrojection of slavery onto the entire medieval period, see Mark Twain (aka Samuel Clemens), *A Connecticut Yankee in King Arthur's Court*, ed. Allison R. Ensor (New York: Norton, 1982). More's *Utopia* (1516) marks the recovery of the classical tradition of slavery, which, so far as my knowledge extends, has no representation in English writing (or ground in English law) between the eleventh and the late fifteenth century. For the persecution of witches as simultaneously an early modern phenomenon, and retrojected back onto the Middle Ages, see Chapters 12–14 of the present book. On judicial torture in England, see especially John H. Langbein, *Torture and the Law of Proof: Europe and England in the Ancien Régime* (Chicago, IL: University of Chicago Press, 2006; first pub. 1977), and James Simpson, "No Brainer: The Early Modern Tragedy of Torture," *Religion and Literature* 43 (2011), 1–23. For the phenomenon of Biblical literalism, which begins in early modernity, see James Simpson, *Burning to Read: English Fundamentalism and Its Reformation Opponents* (Cambridge, MA: The Belknap Press of Harvard University Press, 2007). Royal absolutism is an early modern phenomenon, the predictable product of powerfully centralized modernizing states. See the great book by Michael Wilks, *The Problem of Sovereignty in the Later Middle Ages: The Papal Monarchy with Augustinus Triumphus and the Publicists* (Cambridge, UK: Cambridge University Press, 1963). For scholastic theories of republican liberty, and the fact of divine right absolutism as an early modern phenomenon, see Quentin Skinner, *The Foundations of Modern Political Thought* (Cambridge, UK: Cambridge University Press, 1970), 1:53–65 and 2:3–65 respectively.

21. From the available records, the number of people burned for heresy between 1401 (the date of the first statute authorizing such punishment in England) and 1521 is a possibly underestimated minimum of forty. See John A. F. Thompson, *The Later Lollards, 1414–1520* (Oxford: Oxford University Press, 1965), pp. 237–238. This figure is widely divergent from the groundless claim by David Daniell that

"many hundreds of Lollards [were] burned." Daniell, *Bible in English*, p. 130. I thank Anne Hudson for help on this point. The Devonshire rebellion of people resistant to the 1549 Protestant edition of *The Book of Common Prayer* in 1549 saw between four and five thousand victims. Anthony Fletcher and Diarmaid MacCulloch, *Tudor Rebellions*, rev. 5th ed. (Harlow, England: Pearson Longman, 2008), p. 57. In the reign of Queen Mary (1553–1558), upwards of three hundred Protestants were burned, "numbers unprecedented in England." MacCulloch, *Reformation*, p. 285. Between 1581 and 1590, under Elizabeth (r. 1558–1603), 78 priests and 25 laypeople were executed for religious reasons, with 53 priests and 35 laypeople executed for the same reason between 1590 and 1603 (a total of 191). Figures and comment are cited from MacCulloch, *Reformation*, p. 392. For Civil War deaths between 1642 and 1649, a recent scholarly estimate is 62,000 deaths in war, and a further 100,000 from disease. M. J. Braddick, *God's Fury, England's Fire: A New History of the English Civil Wars* (London: Allen Lane, 2008), pp. 389, 395. Although Cromwell denied that he had tried to extirpate the Catholic religion from Ireland in 1650, by 1652 he supported the "Act of Settlement of 1652 that envisaged up to 100,000 executions, mass emigration, and ethnic cleansing on a scale unknown in western European history" (cited from *ODNB*, "Oliver Cromwell," under "Cromwell in Ireland 1649–1650"). For a somber narrative of sixteenth- and seventeenth-century confessional persecutions in England, see Walsham, *Charitable Hatred*, pp. 106–159.

22. For which see Michael Walzer, *The Paradox of Liberation: Secular Revolutions and Religious Counterrevolutions* (New Haven, CT: Yale University Press, 2015), treating the rise of populist religious forces in the formally secularist states of India, Algeria, and Israel. To these one should now add Turkey.

23. For a call to much longer term, larger scale historiography, see Jo Guldi and David Armitage, *The History Manifesto* (Cambridge, UK: Cambridge University Press, 2014). For a critique of short chronologies, or "synchronic historicism," in English literary history, see Simpson, "Not Yet: Chaucer and Anagogy," *Studies in the Age of Chaucer* 37 (2015), 31–54.

24. See e.g. William Haller, for whom the "rise of Puritanism" was equivalent to "the way to the New Jerusalem as set forth in pulpit and press from Thomas Cartwright to John Lilburne and John Milton." Cited in Lake, "Historiography of Puritanism," p. 347, where Lake outlines the broader ideological liberal investment in puritanism. For contemporary statements of the same account of a direct relation between Reformation religion and the liberal order, see e.g. McGrath, *Christianity's Dangerous Idea*, and Witte, *Reformation of Rights*.

25. For a surgical demolition of the secularization thesis, see Cummings, *Mortal Thoughts*, Introduction. See also Peter L. Berger "The Desecularization of the World: A Global Overview," in *The Desecularization of the World: Resurgent Religion and World Politics*, ed. Peter L. Berger (Washington, D.C.: Ethics and Public Policy Center; W. B. Eerdmans, 1999), pp. 1–18. For a historiographical survey of the operation of the secularization thesis in English Reformation historiog-

raphy, see Alexandra Walsham, "The Reformation and the Disenchantment of the World." For an instance of the repudiation of religious culture, see Jonathan Israel, *Enlightenment Contested: Philosophy, Modernity, and the Emancipation of Man, 1670–1752* (Oxford: Oxford University Press, 2006). Thus on p. 5 we learn that the modern revolution of the radical Enlightenment is "a massive intellectual break with the past"; on p. 9 that revolution (in the modern sense) was "inconceivable in the West until the late seventeenth century." The "past" for Israel is always very easily summarized as "trust in and acceptance of social hierarchy and kings, bishops, and aristocracy" (p. 9). Israel repeats these absurdly superficial positions in a number of books, some of them very long. See also, for example, his *A Revolution of the Mind: Radical Enlightenment and the Intellectual Origins of Modern Democracy* (Princeton, NJ: Princeton University Press, 2010).

26. Alexis de Tocqueville, *The Old Régime and the French Revolution,* trans. Stuart Gilbert (New York: Doubleday, 1955), p. 5, first pub. as *L'ancien régime et la révolution* (Paris: Lévy, 1856).

27. Though the Chinese premier took an even longer view (if we credit the interview report). Asked in 1972 if the French Revolution had been a success, his response was, apparently, that it was "too early to say." Even if we do not credit the report, the remark is *ben trovato.*

28. In one powerful respect, I am clearly in the tradition of Max Weber's *The Protestant Ethic and the Spirit of Capitalism,* trans. Talcott Parsons (New York: Scribner, 1948; first pub. as *Die Protestantische Ethik und Der Geist Des Kapitalismus,* 1905). Even if Weber is a crucial contributor to the secularization, or "disenchantment" thesis, he can in no way be charged with practicing supercessionist history. One aspect of his brilliance lies precisely in his perception that the seismic charge of religious changes continues to reverberate in new, ostensibly nonreligious cultures. I am also in the tradition of Karl Löwith, *Meaning in History* (1949), since Löwith understands that religious forms produce secularized forms of themselves. For a brief but pregnant account of secularity as a religious term, see Charles Taylor, *A Secular Age* (Cambridge, MA: The Belknap Press of Harvard University Press, 2007), pp. 264–267.

29. The word "supercessionism" is drawn from theological discourse. *OED*: "The belief that the New Testament covenant supersedes the Mosaic covenant of the Hebrew Bible, and that the Christian Church has displaced Israel as God's chosen people." Applied to cultural historiography, the word designates the practice whereby one period is felt completely to replace its predecessor. For the larger tradition, see the excellent book by Anthony Kemp, *The Estrangement of the Past: A Study of the Origins of Modern Historical Consciousness* (New York: Oxford University Press, 1991).

30. Simpson, "Trans-Reformation English Literary History."

31. I am not of course the first to see the relation between the beginnings and the effects of the Reformation as a relation of historical irony. See e.g. David Hume,

who, in his *History of England* (1754–1761) "was aware that, while religious zealots brought about a process both necessary and lamentable, the real story to tell was of the unintended development of political liberty that arose from the clash of parties." Cited from Glenn Burgess, "Introduction: Religion and the Historiography of the English Civil War," p. 4.

1. Revolutionary Religion

1. For religious intolerance in the later medieval period (from the early eleventh century), see R. I. Moore, *The Formation of a Persecuting Society: Power and Deviance in Western Europe, 950–1250* (Oxford: Blackwell, 1987).
2. In my care to use the words "modernizing" and "modernization," not "modernity," I follow both Michael Walzer, *The Revolution of the Saints: A Study in the Origins of Radical Politics* (Cambridge, MA: Harvard University Press, 1965), p. 18, and Steven C. A. Pincus, *1688: The First Modern Revolution* (New Haven, CT: Yale University Press, 2011), p. 9.
3. For centralization and bureaucratization as the key markers of "modernization," see Pincus, *1688*, pp. 9–10.
4. Thus, for a representative example, Jonathan Israel, *Enlightenment Contested: Philosophy, Modernity, and the Emancipation of Man, 1670–1752* (Oxford: Oxford University Press, 2006), p. 11.
5. Weber uses the word "rationalization" in different senses, but his principal usage does not designate a process of becoming more "rational." "Rationalization" for Weber instead primarily designates a process of uniform bureaucratization. See Max Weber, "The Nature, Conditions and Development of Bureaucratic *Herrschaft*," in *Weber's Rationalism and Modern Society*, ed. and trans. Tony Waters and Dagmar Waters (New York: Palgrave Macmillan, 2015) pp. 73–127.
6. The French Revolution is the most obvious case. For this paradox as it works itself out in the English Reformation, see Ethan H. Shagan, *The Rule of Moderation: Violence, Religion and the Politics of Restraint in Early Modern England* (Cambridge, UK: Cambridge University Press, 2011): "The rule of moderation may be near the heart of a central paradox of English modernity: the contradiction between a developing liberal ideology that insisted upon the limitation of government and the expansion of that government's authority upon its own subjects and the world" (p. 186).
7. *SR*, 26 Henry VIII, ch. 1, 3:492.
8. For liturgical practice see Ramie Targoff, *Common Prayer: The Language of Devotion in Early Modern England* (Chicago, IL: University of Chicago Press, 2001), ch. 1; Timothy Rosendale, *Liturgy and Literature in the Making of Protestant England* (Cambridge, UK: Cambridge University Press, 2007), pp. 6–7; and *The Book of Common Prayer: The Texts of 1549, 1559, and 1662*, ed. Brian Cummings (Oxford: Oxford University Press, 2011), pp. xviii–xix. For law see e.g. *SR*, 27 Henry VIII,

ch. 26, 3:563–569. This statute abolishes differences of law and language between England and Wales by incorporating Wales wholly within the jurisdiction of England. For Church property see *SR*, 27 Henry VIII, ch. 27, 3:569–574, which establishes the Court of Augmentations in order to administer the nationalized properties of the monasteries. For library localization see C. E. Wright, "The Dispersal of the Libraries in the Sixteenth Century," in *The English Library before 1700*, ed. F. Wormald and C. E. Wright (London: Athlone, 1958), 148–175, and James P. Carley, *The Libraries of King Henry VIII* (London: The British Library in association with the British Academy, 2000). For the early modern centralization of literary language in England, see N. F. Blake, "The Literary Language," in *The Cambridge History of the English Language*, ed. N. F. Blake (Cambridge, UK: Cambridge University Press, 1992), pp. 500–541 (at p. 501).

9. Mervyn James, "English Politics and the Concept of Honour 1485–1642," in Mervyn James, *Society, Politics and Culture: Studies in Early Modern England* (Cambridge, UK: Cambridge University Press, 1986), pp. 308–415.

10. An Act of 1545 (*SR*, 37 Henry VIII, ch. 4, 3:988–993) suppressed a huge network of communal institutions, "Chantries, Hospitalles, Fraternityes, Brotherheddes, Guyldes." See also *SR*, 1 Edward VI, ch. 14, art. 1 (4.1:24), which restates and embellishes Henry's statute of 1545.

11. See Elizabeth L. Eisenstein, *The Printing Press as an Agent of Change: Communications and Cultural Transformation in Early-Modern Europe*, 2 vols. (Cambridge, UK: Cambridge University Press, 1979), Vol. 1, pp. 117–118, for the way in which the printing press contributed to Erastian, nationalizing tendencies, both linguistic and legal; and Ian Green, *Print and Protestantism in Early Modern England* (Oxford: Oxford University Press, 2000), pp. 12–24.

12. In England, this was initially a matter of controlling heterodox theological matter, from 1530. See *TRP*, 1:193–197, no. 129 (1530), which prohibited the printing of "any books in the English tongue concerning Holy Scripture"; 1:270–276, no. 186 (1538), which prohibited the unlicensed printing of Scripture and required all licensed books to print *cum privilegio regali ad imprimendum solum* on the title page; *SR* 34/35 Henry VIII, c. 1,2 (1543), 3:895, which for the first time specified penalties for printers of illicit matter; and *TRP*, 1:373–376, no. 272 (1546), which required the printer to identify himself, the author of the book, and the date of publication. Each of these pieces of legislation specifies theological matter as the source of danger. For a conspectus of censorship and legislation concerning printing, see D. M. Loades, *Politics, Censorship, and the English Reformation* (London: Pinter, 1991), chs. 8 and 9.

13. For the ongoing operations of centralizing state formation in Tudor England, see Steve Hindle, *The State and Social Change in Early Modern England, c. 1550–1640* (Basingstoke: Macmillan, 2000), esp. pp. 1–34.

14. For ordained and absolute powers in late medieval theology, see Heiko Augustinus Oberman, *The Harvest of Medieval Theology: Gabriel Biel and Late Medieval Nominalism* (Cambridge, MA: Harvard University Press, 1963). For late medieval

promoters of the late Augustinian, absolutist theology that was later to dominate Protestant theology, see Gordon Leff, *Bradwardine and the Pelagians: A Study of His "De Causa Dei" and Its Opponents* (Cambridge, UK: Cambridge University Press, 1957).

15. The citation is from Edmund Calamy, *Englands looking-glasse* (London, 1642), image 6. See Chapter 2 for fuller discussion of this sermon.

16. For the doctrine of predestination across the long Reformation, see Dewey D. Wallace, *Puritans and Predestination: Grace in English Protestant Theology, 1525–1695* (Chapel Hill: University of North Carolina Press, 1982). For its psychological effects, see John Stachniewski, *The Persecutory Imagination: English Puritanism and the Literature of Religious Despair* (Oxford: Clarendon, 1991).

17. See n. 10 above.

18. For the clerical and internationalist quality of English Puritanism, see Walzer, *Revolution of the Saints*, pp. 114–148. The doctrine of the "priesthood of all believers" is already stated by Luther in 1520; see e.g. Martin Luther, *To the Christian Nobility of the German Nation*, in *Luther's Works*, vol. 44, *The Christian in Society*, 1, ed. James Atkinson (Philadelphia, PA: Fortress Press, 1966), pp. 123–217: "The pope or bishop anoints, shaves heads, ordains, consecrates, and prescribes garb different from the laity, but he can never make a man into a Christian or a spiritual man by so doing . . . We are all consecrated as priests through baptism, as St. Peter says in 1 Peter 2:9: 'Ye are a royal priesthood, a priestly realm'" (p. 127).

19. The Johannine topos of being born again (John 3) and the Pauline topos of putting on the new man (e.g. Colossians 3) are both carried over into institutional models. See Chapter 2.

20. See e.g. Mary Morrissey, "Confessionalism and Conversion," in *Oxford Handbooks Online, Literature* (www.oxfordhandbooks.com), pp. 1–19; and Alec Ryrie, *Being Protestant in Reformation Britain* (Oxford: Oxford University Press, 2013), pp. 35–38, 42–43, and further references. For an example of how Calvinist conversion works in a specific text, see David Aers, "Conversion in Arthur Dent's *The Plain Man's Pathway to Heaven*" (unpublished manuscript).

21. See Chapters 6 and 7.

22. See Eamon Duffy, *The Stripping of the Altars: Traditional Religion in England, c. 1400–c. 1580* (New Haven, CT: Yale University Press, 1992), ch. 5, for the pre-Reformation cult of saints, and, for the dismantlement of the cult of saints from 1538, pp. 407, 443. For the main and immensely influential exemplar of a new martyrology, see John Foxe, *Actes and Monuments of the English Martyrs*, in *The Unabridged Acts and Monuments Online* or *TAMO* (HRI Online Publications, Sheffield, 2011; 1st ed. pub. 1563). Available from: www.johnfoxe.org. See also Alice Dailey, *The English Martyr from Reformation to Revolution* (Notre Dame, IN: University of Notre Dame Press, 2012).

23. James Simpson, *Burning to Read: English Fundamentalism and Its Reformation Opponents* (Cambridge, MA: The Belknap Press of Harvard University Press, 2007).

24. For iconoclasm, see esp. Margaret Aston, *England's Iconoclasts: Laws against Images* (Oxford: Clarendon, 1988), and Margaret Aston, *Broken Idols of the English Reformation* (Cambridge, UK: Cambridge University Press, 2016). See also James Simpson, *Under the Hammer: Iconoclasm in the Anglo-American Tradition* (Oxford: Oxford University Press, 2010). For anti-theatricality, see Jonas A. Barish, *The Antitheatrical Prejudice* (Berkeley: University of California Press, 1981). See also Chapters 12–14 and further references.

25. See Alexandra Walsham, *The Reformation of the Landscape: Religion, Identity, and Memory in Early Modern Britain and Ireland* (Oxford: Oxford University Press, 2011), and James Simpson, "Place," in *Cultural Reformations: Medieval and Renaissance in Literary History,* ed. Brian Cummings and James Simpson (Oxford: Oxford University Press, 2010), pp. 95–112.

26. G. R. Elton, *Policy and the Police: The Enforcement of the Reformation in the Age of Thomas Cromwell* (Cambridge, UK: Cambridge University Press, 1972). For the Elizabethan intelligence operation, see "Francis Walsingham," in *ODNB,* and further references.

27. Simpson, *Burning to Read,* ch. 6.

28. See Susan Brigden, "Youth and the English Reformation," in *Rebellion, Popular Protest, and the Social Order in Early Modern England,* ed. Paul Slack (Cambridge, UK: Cambridge University Press, 1984), pp. 77–107.

29. See n. 8 above. The appropriation of monastic lands was the largest transfer of property in England since the Norman Conquest. See R. H. Fritze, "'Truth hath lacked witnesse, tyme wanted light': The Dispersal of the English Monastic Libraries and Protestant Efforts at Preservation, ca. 1535–1625," *Journal of Library History* 18 (1983), 274–291.

30. This is most clearly signalled by changes to the Edwardian Prayer Book. In the first edition (1549), the dead person is addressed by the priest: "I commend thy soul to God the father almighty, and thy body to the ground." In the second, revised edition of 1552, the priest addresses not the dead person but the bystanders around the grave: "We therefore commit his body to the ground." See *Book of Common Prayer,* ed. Cummings, pp. 82 and 172 (for the 1559 edition, in this respect identical to 1552); and, for discussion, Stephen Greenblatt, *Hamlet in Purgatory* (Princeton, NJ: Princeton University Press, 2001), pp. 244–245.

31. For explicit evangelical promotion of violence, see Karl Gunther, *Reformation Unbound: Protestant Visions of Reform in England, 1525–1590* (Cambridge, UK: Cambridge University Press, 2014), pp. 75–96.

32. For the main approaches, see Jack A. Goldstone, "Introduction: The Comparative and Historical Study of Revolutions," in *Revolutions: Theoretical Comparative and Historical Studies,* ed. Jack Goldstone, 3rd ed. (Belmont, CA: Thompson, 2003), pp. 1–21. For examples of the major contemporary scholarly positions, see Jack A. Goldstone, *Revolution and Rebellion in the Early Modern World* (Berkeley: University of California Press, 1991), and Theda Skocpol, *Social Revolutions in the Modern World* (Cambridge, UK: Cambridge University Press, 1994). These works

368 Notes to Pages 23–24

focus on the analysis of the conditions of actual revolutions; they do not consider religion as a revolutionary force. For a survey and critique of these and further theorizations of revolutions in history, see Pincus, *1688*, ch. 2. I thank Niklas Frykman for help with this scholarship.

33. *OED*, s.v. 1a and b "circular movement," and s.v. 1b ". . . an orbital period." For the larger European picture, see "Revolution," in *Geschichtliche Grundbegriffe: Historisches Lexikon Zur Politisch-Sozialen Sprache in Deutschland*, gen. ed. Reinhart Koselleck, 8 vols. (Stuttgart: E. Klett, 1972–1997), vol. 5. For the original astronomical sense, see 5:670.

34. *OED*, s.v. 3b, ". . . a completed cycle . . . a circuit."

35. "To return to an original state." The example is drawn from William Langland, *The Vision of Piers Plowman: A Critical Edition of the B-Text*, ed. A. V. C. Schmidt, 2nd ed. (London: Dent, 1995), B.10.320. *"Pristinus status"* has a long political genealogy, for which see Gerhart Ladner, "Terms and Ideas of Renewal," in *Renaissance and Renewal in the Twelfth Century*, ed. Robert L. Benson and Giles Constable (Cambridge, MA: Harvard University Press, 1982), pp. 1–33 (at p. 18).

36. See Giles Constable, "Renewal and Reform in Religious Life: Concepts and Realities," in *Renaissance and Renewal in the Twelfth Century*, ed. Benson and Constable, pp. 37–67. See also Alexandra Walsham, "Migrations of the Holy: Explaining Religious Change in Medieval and Early Modern Europe," *JMEMS* 44 (2014), 241–280 (at pp. 244–245).

37. See David Norbrook, *Writing the English Republic: Poetry, Rhetoric, and Politics, 1627–1660* (Cambridge, UK: Cambridge University Press, 1999), under "reduction, return to first principles" in the index. See also *OED*, s.v. 2a, "The action of bringing someone or something back *to* (also *from*) a particular state, condition, belief, etc."

38. John Milton, *Reason of Church Government*, in *CPWJM*, 1:853.

39. Thomas Case, *Two sermons lately preached at Westminster* (London, 1642), images 19 and 21. Further citations will be made by image number in the body of the text. Cited also in Walzer, *Revolution of the Saints*, pp. 10–11.

40. "by the perpetual rotation of all things in a circle," in Marchamont Nedham, *The Case of the Common-wealth of England Stated* (London, 1650), image 5. Further references will be made by image number in the body of the text.

41. David Wootton argues that, while the concept of "revolution," in the modern sense, was available in the English Revolution, the word was not. See his "Leveller Democracy and the Puritan Revolution," in *The Cambridge History of Political Thought, 1450–1700*, ed. J. H Burns and Mark Goldie (Cambridge, UK: Cambridge University Press, 1991), 412–440 (at pp. 420–421).

42. See "Nedham, Marchamont," in *ODNB*.

43. Marchamont Nedham, *The Excellencie of a Free-State* (London, 1656), image 19.

44. Glenn Burgess, "Introduction: Religion and the Historiography of the English Civil War," in *England's Wars of Religion, Revisited*, ed. Charles W. A. Prior and Glenn Burgess (Farnham, Surrey: Ashgate, 2011), pp. 1–25 (at pp. 8–10). See also

Daniel Schönpflug, "La faute à Voltaire? Secularizations and the Origins of the French Revolution," in *Redefining the Sacred: Religion in the French and Russian Revolutions*, ed. Daniel Schönpflug and Martin Schulze Wessel (Frankfurt am Main: Peter Lang, 2012), pp. 25–50, for the historiography of treating the French Revolution as a religious movement.

45. For the different, anti-Puritan, anti-revolutionary traditions of the eighteenth century as expressed by Hume and Burke (and for the nineteenth-century survival of anti-Puritanism), see John Netland, "Of Philistines and Puritans: Matthew Arnold's Construction of Puritanism," in *Puritanism and Its Discontents*, ed. Laura Lunger Knoppers (Newark: University of Delaware Press, 2003), pp. 67–84.

46. For this historiographical tradition, see Burgess, "Introduction: Religion and the Historiography of the English Civil War," s. 2: "The Marginalisation of Religion in the Historiography of the English Revolution" (pp. 2–8); Catherine Gimelli Martin, *Milton among the Puritans: The Case for Historical Revisionism* (Farnham, Surrey: Ashgate, 2010), pp. 8–16; and Blair Worden, "Oliver Cromwell and the Cause of Civil and Religious Liberty," in *England's Wars of Religion, Revisited*, ed. Charles W. A. Prior and Glenn Burgess, pp. 231–251.

47. François Guizot, *The History of Civilization in Europe*, trans. William Hazlitt, ed. Larry Siedentop (London, 1977), p. 217. Cited in Burgess, "Introduction: Religion and the Historiography of the English Civil War," p. 10.

48. Most explicitly Christopher Hill, in e.g. *Society and Puritanism in Pre-Revolutionary England* (New York: Schocken, 1964). For other examples and the broader historiographical tradition, see also Peter Lake, "The Historiography of Puritanism," in *The Cambridge Companion to Puritanism*, ed. J. Coffey and P. Lim (Cambridge, UK: Cambridge University Press, 2008), pp, 346–371 (at p. 357).

49. Walzer, *Revolution of the Saints*, p. vii.

50. See Art. 17 of "The Thirty-Nine Articles of Religion" (ratified 1571), in *Book of Common Prayer*, ed. Cummings, pp. 674–685 (at p. 678). For a rich survey of the breadth and depth of predestination as a Reformation doctrine in England, see Wallace, *Puritans and Predestination*.

51. See esp. J. G. A. Pocock, *The Ancient Constitution and the Feudal Law: A Study of English Historical Thought in the Seventeenth Century* (Cambridge, UK: Cambridge University Press, 1957), and, for the situation on the ground, Hindle, *State and Social Change*, pp. 1–34.

52. Act of Uniformity, 1558: SR, 1 Eliz c 2, 4.1:355–358. See also *TRP*, 2:122–123; SR, 13 Eliz c.12, 4.1:546–547; SR, 35 Eliz c 1, 4.2:841–843. Protestant ecclesiology is most influentially conceived in John Foxe, *Acts and Monuments* (1563, 1570, 1576, 1583), which sees the Reformation in England as a typological fulfilment of the history of the early Church. On nationality, see Richard Helgerson, *Forms of Nationhood: The Elizabethan Writing of England* (Chicago, IL: University of Chicago Press, 1992), and Cathy Shrank, *Writing the Nation in Reformation England, 1530–1580* (Oxford: Oxford University Press, 2004). Subjective identity is a huge

topic, but for one penetrating account of the individual, subjective experience of Calvinism, see John Stachniewski, *The Persecutory Imagination: English Puritanism and the Literature of Religious Despair* (Oxford: Clarendon, 1991). For national and intra-national conflict, see Diarmaid MacCulloch, *Reformation: Europe's House Divided, 1490–1700* (London: Allen Lane, 2003). On media consumption, see Green, *Print and Protestantism*, pp. 13–14 for "divinity" as the largest single category of books produced in early modern England; and John Coffey, "Religion," in *The Oxford Handbook of Literature and the English Revolution*, ed. Laura Knoppers (Oxford: Oxford University Press, 2012), pp. 98–117 (at p. 99). For the comparative printing figures, for which, e.g., the Puritan Perkins vastly outsells Shakespeare up to 1640, see Kari Konkola and Diarmaid McCulloch, "People of the Book: Success in the English Reformation," *History Today* 53 (2003), 23–29.

53. Most crisply argued by Nicholas Tyacke, *Anti-Calvinists: The Rise of English Arminianism, c. 1590–1640* (Oxford: Clarendon, 1987).

54. A claim that, according to Alexandra Walsham, began with Richard Hooker's publication of *The Laws of Ecclesiastical Polity* between 1593 and 1604; see Alexandra Walsham, *Charitable Hatred: Tolerance and Intolerance in England, 1500–1700* (Manchester: Manchester University Press, 2006), p. 253. For a penetrating account of the entire history of the Anglican Church as "moderate" and as pursuing a via media, see Shagan, *Rule of Moderation*. For yet more recent examples of the tradition, see Gunther, *Reformation Unbound*, p. 4, including a representative citation from A. G. Dickens, *The English Reformation*, 2nd ed (University Park: Pennsylvania State University Press, 1989). The Church of England was, by Dickens's account, born out of "a Reformation of compromise and detachment, partly because the attitudes come naturally to the English temperament, partly as in consequence of a patriotic distrust for foreign models." Dickens, *English Reformation*, pp. 204–205. For the structure of thought that produced this result, see also Lake, "Historiography of Puritanism," p. 350.

55. George Herbert, "The Temple (1)," in *The Complete English Poems*, ed. John Tobin (London: Penguin, 1991), 1.22.

56. For which see Wallace, *Puritans and Predestination*, ch. 3.

57. John Morrill, "The Religious Context of the English Civil War," in *The English Civil War*, ed. Richard Cust and Ann Hughes (London: Arnold, 1997; first pub. 1984), pp. 155–178 (at p. 176).

2. Permanently Revolutionary Religion

1. "Kings will be tyrants from policy when subjects are rebels from principle." Edmund Burke, *Reflections on the Revolution in France*, ed. Frank M. Turner (New Haven, CT: Yale University Press, 2003), p. 67. "But the religion most prevalent in our Northern colonies is a refinement on the principle of resistance; it is the

dissidence of dissent; and the protestantism of the Protestant religion." Edmund Burke, "Speech on Conciliation with the Colonies," 22 Mar. 1775 (London: Dodsley, 1778), p. 28. I thank Eric Nelson for this reference.

2. Cited from *The Norton Anthology of English Literature*, gen. ed. Stephen Greenblatt, 10th ed. (New York: W. W. Norton, 2017), vol. C, ll. 200–202, p. 121.

3. e.g. Christopher Jones, "The Cleansing of Mosul" (blog post), *Gatesofnineveh* .*wordpress.com*, 6 June 2016, https://gatesofnineveh.wordpress.com/2016/06/06 /the-cleansing-of-mosul/. I thank Joe Greene for this reference.

4. Cited in *Geschichtliche Grundbegriffe: Historisches Lexikon Zur Politisch-Sozialen Sprache in Deutschland,* gen. ed. Reinhart Koselleck (Stuttgart: E. Klett, 1972– 1997), 5:761.

5. See "Permanent Revolution," in *Geschichtliche Grundbegriffe*, gen. ed. Koselleck, 5:761–766, on which I am dependent for the history of the term "permanent revolution." Further references to this volume of *Geschichtliche Grundbegriffe*, gen. ed. Koselleck, will be made in the body of the text.

6. "Ist es unser Interesse und unsere Aufgabe, die Revolution permanent zu machen, so lange, bis alle mehr oder weniger besitzenden Klassen von der Herrschaft verdrängt sind, die Staatsgewalt vom Proletariat erobert . . . ist." Cited in "Permanent Revolution," in *Geschichtliche Grundbegriffe*, gen. ed. Koselleck, 5:763.

7. "Ihr Schlachtruf muss sein: Die Revolution in Permanentz." Cited in "Permanent Revolution," in *Geschichtliche Grundbegriffe*, gen. ed. Koselleck, 5:763.

8. For persecution as a felt necessity by evangelicals in the English Reformation, see Karl Gunther, *Reformation Unbound: Protestant Visions of Reform in England, 1525–1590* (Cambridge, UK: Cambridge University Press, 2014), pp. 68–96.

9. For Bale's biography, see *ODNB*, and Peter Happé, *John Bale* (New York: Twayne, 1996).

10. John Bale, *The Image of Both Churches* (London, 1570) (first pub. 1545), image 121.

11. Bale, *Image of Both Churches*, image 307.

12. Gunther, *Reformation Unbound*, pp. 68, 76.

13. Cited in Patrick Collinson, *The Elizabethan Puritan Movement* (London: Methuen, 1967), p. 33.

14. Thomas Cranmer, *Speech at the Coronation of Edward VI*, in Thomas Cranmer, *Miscellaneous Writings and Letters of Thomas Cranmer*, ed. John E. Cox (Cambridge, UK: Cambridge University Press, 1846), pp. 126–127 (at p. 127). For the common mid-sixteenth-century comparison between Edward VI and Josiah, see Margaret Aston, *The King's Bedpost: Reformation Iconography in a Tudor Group Portrait* (Cambridge, UK: Cambridge University Press, 1993), pp. 26–36; and Diarmaid MacCulloch, *Tudor Church Militant: Edward VI and the Protestant Reformation* (London: Allen Lane, 1999), pp. 57–104.

15. *SR*, 37 Henry VIII, c. 4 (3:988–993). This statute was restated and embellished in the first Edwardian parliament: *SR*, 1 Edward VI, c. 14, art. 1 (4.1:24).

16. *SR*, 3 and 4 Edward VI, c. 10 (4:110–111).

17. *The Book of Common Prayer: The Texts of 1549, 1559, and 1662*, ed. Brian Cummings (Oxford: Oxford University Press, 2011), pp. xxxiv, and 727 (which describes the changes to Communion in the 1552 Prayer Book as "a revolution in ritual as dramatic as the initial introduction of the vernacular service in 1549"). For the broader operation of the Edwardian Church, see MacCulloch, *Tudor Church Militant*.

18. For a nuanced narrative of the formation of English Puritanism in Elizabethan England, see Collinson, *Elizabethan Puritan Movement*. See also Peter Marshall, "Confessionalization, Confessionalism and Confusion in the English Reformation," in *Reforming Reformation*, ed. Thomas F Mayer and Ronald F. Thiemann (Farnham, Surrey: Ashgate, 2012), pp. 43–64.

19. *ODNB*.

20. Thomas Becon, *David's Harp*, in Thomas Becon, *The Early Works*, ed. John Ayre (Cambridge, UK: Cambridge University Press, 1843), p. 274.

21. For the experiences and divisions among Marian exiles who returned to England under Elizabeth, see Gunther, *Reformation Unbound*, ch. 5.

22. *A Second Admonition to the Parliament*, in *Puritan Manifestos: A Study of the Origin of the Puritan Revolt with a Reprint of the Admonition to the Parliament and Kindred Documents, 1572*, ed. Walter Howard Frere, Charles Edward Douglas, and C. E. Douglas (New York: B. Franklin, 1972; first pub. 1907), pp. 80–133 (at p. 81). Further citations of this text will be made by page number in the body of the text.

23. For figures of 62,000 deaths from war between 1642 and 1646 and 100,000 deaths from disease for the same period, see M. J. Braddick, *God's Fury, England's Fire: A New History of the English Civil Wars* (London: Allen Lane, 2008), pp. 389 and 395 respectively.

24. For the intensity of official, Elizabethan persecution of Catholics, see, e.g., Peter Lake and Michael Questier, "Puritans, Papists, and the '"Public Sphere"' in Early Modern England: The Edmund Campion Affair in Context," *The Journal of Modern History*, 72 (2000), 587–627, and Peter Lake, "Anti-Popery: The Structure of a Prejudice," in *The English Civil War*, ed. Richard Cust and Ann Hughes (London: Arnold, 1997), pp. 179–205. Also see Diarmaid MacCulloch, *Reformation: Europe's House Divided* (London: Allen Lane, 2003), p. 392.

25. John A. F. Thompson, *The Later Lollards, 1414–1520* (Oxford: Oxford University Press, 1965), pp. 237–238. *SR*, 2 Henry IV, c. 15 (2: 125–128) of 1401 (*De Haeretico Comburendo*) marks the first statute in England specifying burning as the punishment for heresy.

26. See John H. Langbein, *Torture and the Law of Proof: Europe and England in the Ancien Régime*, repr. with a new preface (Chicago, IL: University of Chicago Press, 2006; first pub. 1977), pt. 2, pp. 73–139. See also James Simpson, "No Brainer: The Early Modern Tragedy of Torture," *Religion and Literature* 43 (2011), 1–23.

27. Collinson, *Elizabethan Puritan Movement*, pp. 60–61.

28. John Field and Thomas Wilcox, *An Admonition to the Parliament*, in *Puritan Manifestos*, ed. Frere and Douglas; Thomas Cartwright, *A Second Admonition to the Parliament*, in *Puritan Manifestos*, ed. Frere and Douglas, pp. 80–133.

29. See Donald Joseph McGinn, *The Admonition Controversy* (New Brunswick: Rutgers University Press, 1949), pp. 26–27, for the evident novelty of the contested word "puritan" in these texts.

30. Thomas Cartwright, *A replye to an answere made of M. Doctor Whitgifte against the admonition to the Parliament* (Hemel Hempstead, 1573), image 15.

31. Braddick, *God's Fury, England's Fire*, p. 199.

32. For the same phenomenon in the Dutch Republic in the early seventeenth century, see Freya Sierhuis, *The Literature of the Arminian Controversy: Religion, Politics and Stage in the Dutch Republic* (Oxford: Oxford University Press, 2015), p. 41.

33. For the fact that Richard Hooker's "single minded target was Puritanism," not Catholics, see Patrick Collinson, "Hooker and the Elizabethan Establishment," in *Richard Hooker and the Construction of Christian Community*, ed. Arthur Stephen McGrade (Tempe, AZ: Medieval & Renaissance Texts & Studies, 1997), pp. 148–181 (at p. 171).

34. Thomas Cartwright, *The second replie of Thomas Cartwright: agaynst Maister Doctor Whitgiftes second answer, touching the Churche discipline* (London, 1575), image 64. See Margaret Aston, *England's Iconoclasts; Laws against Images* (Oxford: Clarendon Press, 1988), 1:472–473, for discussion of Cartwright's call for the death sentence for idolatry.

35. Cartwright, *Second replie of Thomas Cartwright*, image 74.

36. Field and Wilcox, *Admonition to the Parliament*, in Frere and Douglas, *Puritan Manifestos*, p. 19.

37. See Collinson, *Elizabethan Puritan Movement*, pp. 273–287, for the confrontations between Whitgift and the Puritans in the parliament of 1583–1584, for example.

38. For the Reformation evangelical need to provoke aggression, see Ethan H. Shagan, *The Rule of Moderation: Violence, Religion and the Politics of Restraint in Early Modern England* (Cambridge, UK: Cambridge University Press, 2011), p. 160.

39. In using the phrase "radical edge," I avoid the prejudicial but frequently found language of "left" and "progressive" used in this historiography. Whenever I use the word "radical," I simply denote the etymological force of the word (i.e. going to roots). My use of the word carries no evaluation in itself. In using the word "edge," I simply denote distance from the mainline position. I do not mean to imply that the mainline position is "moderate." For Gifford's biography, see *ODNB*. For Gifford's career against separatists, see David Loewenstein, *Treacherous Faith: The Specter of Heresy in Early Modern English Literature and Culture* (Oxford: Oxford University Press, 2013), pp. 165–166, and Shagan, *Rule of Moderation*, pp. 164–167. For Barrow and Greenwood's place within the larger context of English ecclesiological radicals in Elizabethan England, see David Como, "Radical Puritanism, c. 1558–1660," in *The Cambridge Companion*

to Puritanism, ed. John Coffey and Paul C. H. Lim (Cambridge, UK: Cambridge University Press, 2008), pp. 241–258.

40. George Gifford, *A briefe discourse . . . which may bee termed the countrie diuinitie* (London, 1582), image 8 (further references will be made in the body of the text). I am very grateful to Joanna Picciotto for pointing me to this text.

41. Arthur Golding, *The Psalmes of David and others. With M. John Calvins Commentaries* (London, 1571), Ep. Ded. sig. *.iii: "The Atheistes which say . . . there is no God."

42. Arthur Dent, *The Plaine mans Path-way to Heauen* (London, 1607), a text that profoundly influenced Bunyan's *The Pilgrim's Progress*—for which see John Bunyan, *Grace Abounding with Other Spiritual Autobiographies*, ed. John Stachniewski (Oxford: Oxford University Press, 1998), p. 9. For Dent's *Plaine mans Pathway to Heaven*, see David Aers, "Conversion in Arthur Dent's *The Plain Man's Pathway to Heaven*," (unpublished manuscript); Alexandra Walsham, *Church Papists: Catholicism, Conformity, and Confessional Polemic in Early Modern England* (London: Royal Historical Society, Boydell Press, 1993), pp. 1–2.

43. Dent, *Plaine mans path-way to heauen,* image 76.

44. Henry Barrow and John Greenwood, "The True and the False Church," in *The Writings of John Greenwood, 1587–1590: Together with the Joint Writings of Henry Barrow and John Greenwood, 1587–1590* (London: Published for the Sir Halley Stewart Trust by G. Allen and Unwin, 1962), pp. 97–102 (at p. 98). The text was written in 1588 by John Greenwood (1560–1593), possibly with Henry Barrow (1550–1593). Both Barrow and Greenwood were executed in 1593. For both figures, see *ODNB*.

45. See e.g. Presbyterian opposition to Brownist separatism in 1588, in Shagan, *Rule of Moderation*, pp. 159–164.

46. Shagan, *Rule of Moderation*, pp. 174–175.

47. John Whitgift, *An answere to a certen libel intituled, An admonition to the Parliament* (London, 1572), image 17.

48. The French Wars of Religion claimed between two million and four million victims between 1562 and 1629, including the St Bartholomew Day's massacre on August 18, 1572 (c. five thousand victims), for which see R. J. Knecht, *The French Wars of Religion*, 3rd ed. (London: Longman, 2010), p. 96.

49. Books 6 and 8 published 1648, and Book 7 1660; Fulke Greville, *Mustapha*, in *Selected Writings of Fulke Greville*, ed. Joan Reese (London: Athlone, 1973), p. 124, l. 18.

50. Richard Hooker, *Works*, gen. ed. W. Speed Hill, 7 vols. (Cambridge: Belknap Press, 1977–1998), Vol. 1, *Of the Laws of Ecclesiastical Polity*, Preface, Books 1–4, ed. George Edelen (Cambridge: Belknap Press, 1977), p. 4.

51. For Calamy's biography, see *ODNB*.

52. *Constitutions and canons ecclesiasticall* (London, 1640), image 17.

53. "Roots and Branches Petition, 1640," in *Religion and Society in Early Modern England: A Sourcebook*, ed. David Cressy and Lori Anne Ferrell (London: Routledge, 1996), pp. 174–179.

54. Edmund Calamy, *Englands looking-glasse* (London, 1642). Further references will be cited in the body of the text.

55. Julie Spraggon, *Puritan Iconoclasm during the English Civil War* (Woodbridge, Suffolk: Boydell, 2003), Appendix I. For the novelty of this legislation, extending as it did from religious imagery in churches to religious images in any public place, see Margaret Aston, *Broken Idols of the English Reformation* (Cambridge, UK: Cambridge University Press, 2016), p. 846.

56. For the Westminster Assembly, the account of William Haller, *Liberty and Reformation in the Puritan Revolution* (New York: Columbia University Press, 1955) remains excellent (pp. 103–110). See also John Coffey, "Religion," in *The Oxford Handbook of Literature and the English Revolution*, ed. Laura Lunger Knoppers (Oxford: Oxford University Press, 2012), pp. 98–117 (at pp. 103–104).

57. John Milton, *Of Reformation Touching Church-Discipline in England and the Causes that hitherto have Hindred it*, ed. Dan Wolfe, in *CPWJM*, 1:519–617. Further references will be made in the body of the text, by volume and page number. For the biographical context and the content of this work, see Barbara K. Lewalski, *The Life of John Milton: A Critical Biography* (Oxford: Blackwell, 2000), pp. 129–130, and 141–145.

58. See Gunther, *Reformation Unbound*, ch. 7, for the broader tradition within English Protestantism of attacking the Edwardian Church and questioning the place of Marian martyrs.

59. Thus, for example: "Oxford burnt up the right reverend fathers Cranmer, Ridley, and Latimer, the noble witnesses of the clear light of the Gospel." John Foxe, *Actes and Monuments of the* (London 1563), 5:1634, consulted www.johnfoxe.org/index.php.

60. For Milton's striking refusal ever to critique himself, see e.g. Stephen M. Fallon, *Milton's Peculiar Grace: Self-Representation and Authority* (Ithaca, NY: Cornell University Press, 2007), pp. 37, 91. For Milton's version of personal election, see pp. 196–202.

61. In *The Reason of Church Government* (1641) Milton recalls that, until dissuaded otherwise by the compromises required, he had intended to enter the Church of England (*CPW* 1:822–823). See also *De Doctrina Christiana*, ed. John K. Hale and J. Donald Cullington, 2 vols, in *The Complete Works of John Milton*, gen. ed. Gordon Campbell and Thomas N. Corns, 11 vols. (Oxford: Oxford University Press, 2008–2012), 8:3. For the theological heterogeneity and individuality of Milton's final phase, as expressed by his *De Doctrina Christiana* (?1658–1674), see Lewalski, *Life of John Milton*, pp. 415–441.

62. *Of Reformation*, in *The Works of John Milton*, ed. Frank Allen Patterson, 18 vols. (New York: Columbia University Press, 1931), 3.1:35.

63. See "Of the new forcers of conscience under the Long Parliament," in *John Milton, The Major Works*, ed. Stephen Orgel and Jonathan Goldberg (Oxford: Oxford University Press, 2003), l. 20, pp. 83–84.

64. Thus, for example, Abraham Cowley, James Harrington, Andrew Marvell, Thomas May, Marchamont Nedham, and Edmund Waller.

65. For an account of the way criticism reads Milton for consistency, see Peter C. Herman and Elizabeth Sauer, "Introduction: Paradigms Lost, Paradigms Found: The New Milton Criticism," in *The New Milton Criticism*, ed. Peter C. Herman and Elizabeth Sauer (Cambridge, UK: Cambridge University Press, 2012), pp. 1–22.

66. John Milton, *Areopagitica*, in *CPWJM*, 2:486–570 (at pp. 553–554; my emphasis).

67. For the Protestant emphasis on the elect few, with a correlative dismissal of parliaments or general councils, see James Simpson, *Burning to Read: English Fundamentalism and Its Reformation Opponents* (Cambridge, MA: The Belknap Press of Harvard University Press, 2007), ch. 6.

68. John Milton, *The Readie and Easie Way to Establish a Free Commonwealth*, 2nd ed. in *CPWJM*, 7:407–463 (at pp. 432–434); discussed in David Norbrook, *Writing the English Republic: Poetry, Rhetoric, and Politics, 1627–1660* (Cambridge, UK: Cambridge University Press, 1999), p. 409.

69. Milton, *Ready and Easy Way*, *CPWJM*, 7:455.

70. Thomas Edwards, *The first and second part of Gangraena* (London, 1646). Further citations will be made by image number in the body of the text. The text went through six editions, all in 1646. For Edwards's project, see Ann Hughes, *Gangraena and the Struggle for the English Revolution* (Oxford: Oxford University Press, 2004). Hughes describes *Gangraena* as "the most famous printed book in a revolutionary era in which printed texts played a crucial role," though she also stresses that its fame was short-lived (p. 2).

71. Thomas Edwards, *The third part of Gangraena* (London, 1646).

72. Calamy, *Englands looking-glasse*, image 25. For the broader context of Presbyterian heresy hunting in the 1640s, see Loewenstein, *Treacherous Faith*, ch. 5.

73. "What was distinctive about this period of religious warfare [the 1640s] was that the orthodox godly were not only furiously demonizing Papists but demonizing other Protestants, as they obsessed about the enemy within the fold." Loewenstein, *Treacherous Faith*, p. 192.

74. Richard Bancroft, *A sermon preached at Paules Crosse* (London, 1588), image 22. See also Bancroft's *Daungerous positions and proceedings* (London, 1593) for the same analysis. Bancroft later succeeded John Whitgift as Archbishop of Canterbury (1604–1610).

75. Joseph Hall, *An humble remonstrance to the High Court of Parliament* (London 1641), image 22.

76. Braddick, *God's Fury, England's Fire*, p. 445.

77. Braddick, *God's Fury, England's Fire*, p. 452.

3. Modernizing Despair

1. For the late medieval / early modern distinction with regard to despair, see Michael McDonald, "*The Fearefull Estate of Francis Spira*: Narrative, Emotion, and Identity in Early Modern England," *Journal of British Studies* 31 (1992), 32–61; and

Nicholas Watson, "Despair," in *Cultural Reformations: Medieval and Renaissance in Literary History*, ed. Brian Cummings and James Simpson (Oxford: Oxford University Press, 2010), pp. 342–360.

2. William Langland, *The Vision of Piers Plowman, A Critical Edition of the B-Text*, ed. A. V. C. Schmidt, 2nd ed. (London: Dent, 1995), X. 371–76a. See also James Simpson, *Piers Plowman: An Introduction to the B-Text*, 2nd, rev. ed. (Exeter: Exeter University Press, 2007), ch. 4, and Emily Rebekah Huber, "Langland's Confessional Dissonance: Wanhope in *Piers Plowman B*," *YLS* 27 (2013), 79–101. Geoffrey Chaucer, *Troilus and Criseyde*, in *The Riverside Chaucer*, gen. ed. Larry D. Benson, 3rd ed. (Oxford: Oxford University Press, 1987), 4.953–1084.

3. For the breadth and intensity of the experience of despair in early modern England, see John Stachniewski, *The Persecutory Imagination: English Puritanism and the Literature of Religious Despair* (Oxford: Clarendon Press, 1991).

4. See e.g. Giovanni Pico della Mirandola (1463–1494), *Oration on the Dignity of Man: A New Translation and Commentary*, ed. Francesco Borghesi, Michael Papio, and Massimo Riva (New York: Cambridge University Press, 2012).

5. For More's participation in this tradition see Alistair Fox, *Thomas More, History and Providence* (Oxford: Blackwell, 1982).

6. For a powerful expression of which, see Desiderius Erasmus, *De libero arbitrio*, trans. as *On the Freedom of the Will* in *On the Bondage of the Will*, in *Luther and Erasmus: Free Will and Salvation*, trans. E. Gordon Rupp, A. N. Marlow, Philip S. Watson, and B. Drewery (Philadelphia, PA: The Westminster Press, 1969), pp. 35–97. For an illuminating discussion of Erasmus's debate with Luther regarding free will, see Brian Cummings, *The Literary Culture of the Reformation: Grammar and Grace* (Oxford: Oxford University Press, 2002), pp. 144–183.

7. For the historiographical tradition of a progressivist "Renaissance," see Wallace K. Ferguson, *The Renaissance in Historical Thought* (Boston, MA: Houghton Mifflin, 1948). See James Simpson, *Reform and Cultural Revolution, 1350–1547* (Oxford: Oxford University Press, 2002), ch. 1 n. 28, for more detailed bibliography and discussion. The strained effort to harness both movements under the same progressivist yoke has a long history and remains active. For just two recent examples by influential scholars of the continuing life of this topos, see Alister E. McGrath, *Christianity's Dangerous Idea: The Protestant Revolution—A History from the Sixteenth Century to the Twenty-First* (New York: Harper, 2007), pp. 34–36; and Carlos M. N. Eire, *Reformations: The Early Modern World 1450–1650* (New Haven, CT: Yale University Press, 2016), pp. 64–113 (pp. 84–85 for a summary).

8. The Arminian exceptions will be considered in Chapter 5.

9. George Herbert, "The Holdfast," in *George Herbert: The Complete English Poems*, ed. John Tobin (London: Penguin, 1991), p. 134, l. 12.

10. The English text is available as *The Pathway into the Holy Scripture*, in William Tyndale, *Doctrinal Treatises and Introductions to Different Portions of the Holy Scriptures*, ed. Henry Walter (Cambridge, UK: Cambridge University Press, 1848), pp. 7–28.

The *Pathway* is a revision of Tyndale's 1525 New Testament Prologue. All further references to this text in this chapter will be made by page number in the body of the text. For further discussion, see James Simpson, *Burning to Read: English Fundamentalism and Its Reformation Opponents* (Cambridge, MA: The Belknap Press of Harvard University Press, 2007), ch. 3, and further references.

11. See Gordon Leff, *William of Ockham: The Metamorphosis of Scholastic Discourse* (Manchester, UK: Manchester University Press, 1975), pp. 455–527. For the clearest history of the terminology of *potentia absoluta* and *potentia ordinata*, see William J. Courtenay, *Capacity and Volition: A History of the Distinction between Absolute and Ordained Power* (Bergamo: Pierluigi Lubrina, 1990). For the key definitional changes from "power as considered in and of itself" to "applied, absolute power," first introduced by canon lawyers in discussion of papal power, which occurred between 1250 and 1275, see pp. 92–95. This changed definition was first taken up by a theologian and applied to God, with momentous consequences, by Duns Scotus (d. 1308) (see pp. 100–103).

12. For the late medieval "semi-Pelagianism" against which Luther reacted with such vehemence, see Heiko A. Oberman, *The Harvest of Medieval Theology: Gabriel Biel and Late Medieval Nominalism* (Cambridge, MA: Harvard University Press, 1963), esp. pp. 36–50; Robert Adams, "Piers's Pardon and Langland's Semi-Pelagianism," *Traditio* 39 (1983), pp. 367–418; and, for Christian soteriology more generally, Alister E. McGrath, *Iustitia Dei: A History of the Christian Doctrine of Justification*, 2 vols. (Cambridge: Cambridge University Press, 1986). For a searching account of how one great late medieval English poet, William Langland, himself takes issue with semi-Pelagianism, see David Aers, *Salvation and Sin: Augustine, Langland, and Fourteenth-Century Theology* (Notre Dame, IN: University of Notre Dame Press, 2009), ch. 4.

13. For examples of which, see Cindy L. Vitto, *The Virtuous Pagan in Middle English Literature* (Philadelphia, PA: American Philosophical Society, 1989).

14. The orthodox, predestinarian, Augustinian traditions are powerfully represented in late medieval England by e.g. Thomas Bradwardine (Archbishop of Canterbury, 1349), in his *De Causa Dei Contra Pelagium*. See Gordon Leff, *Bradwardine and the Pelagians: A Study of His "De Causa Dei" and Its Opponents* (Cambridge, UK: Cambridge University Press, 1957). For the broader context of late medieval Augustinian voluntarism, see Heiko Augustinus Oberman, *Masters of the Reformation: The Emergence of a New Intellectual Climate in Europe* (Cambridge, UK: Cambridge University Press, 1981), pp. 64–110. For the heterodox traditions of pre-Reformation predestinarian theology, see Anne Hudson, *The Premature Reformation: Wycliffite Texts and Lollard History* (Oxford: Clarendon Press, 1988), pp. 314–315, 389. For the deeper reach of predestination as an element of late orthodox medieval doctrine, see David Aers, "'Predestinaet' or 'prescit': Langland's Treatment of Election in *Piers Plowman* (C Version)" (forthcoming, Notre Dame University Press).

15. With regard to soteriology, I remain informed by Gordon Leff, *The Dissolution of the Medieval Outlook: An Essay on Intellectual and Spiritual Change in the Fourteenth Century* (New York: New York University Press, 1976).

16. For which see the extraordinary and underexploited work by Michael Wilks, *The Problem of Sovereignty in the Later Middle Ages: The Papal Monarchy with Augustinus Triumphus and the Publicists* (Cambridge, UK: Cambridge University Press, 1963), passim, but, for a succinct summary, p. 17: "The constitutional theories of the age [i.e. the thirteenth and fourteenth centuries] were no more than an expression in terms of government of all the discordant elements in contemporary philosophy ["theology" could be inserted here]."

17. For the place of Purgatory in late medieval spirituality, see Eamon Duffy, *The Stripping of the Altars: Traditional Religion in England, c. 1400–c. 1580* (New Haven, CT: Yale University Press, 1992), pp. 338–376.

18. For the sixteenth-century dismantlement of Purgatory as registered in English culture especially, see Duffy, *Stripping of the Altars*, pp. 393–394; Stephen Greenblatt, *Hamlet in Purgatory* (Princeton, NJ: Princeton University Press, 2001), and James Simpson, "Diachronic History and the Shortcomings of Medieval Studies," in *Reading the Medieval in Early Modern England*, ed. David Matthews and Gordon McMullan (Cambridge, UK: Cambridge University Press, 2007), pp. 17–30.

19. For crisp accounts of Luther's theology, see E. Gordon Rupp, *The Righteousness of God: Luther Studies* (London: Hodder and Stoughton, 1953), and Carl R. Trueman, *Salvation and English Reformers, 1525–1556* (Oxford: Clarendon Press, 1994), pp. 56–72. What Gordon Leff says about Thomas Bradwardine's theology is equally true of Luther's. Faced with the semi-Pelagian idea that human merit has some part to play in salvation, "Bradwardine's reply was to reassert God's grace to the exclusion of all merit. His intention was to win back for God all power which he considered to have been usurped by men. His whole system was designed to establish God as the senior partner in all that concerned his creatures. This allowed no independent freedom to them at all." Leff, *Bradwardine and the Pelagians*, p. 15.

20. See Simpson, *Burning to Read*, ch. 3.

21. For two other scholars who have arrived at formulations close to my "posthuman" for Lutheran and Calvinist theology, see Sarah Beckwith, *Shakespeare and the Grammar of Forgiveness* (Ithaca, NY: Cornell University Press, 2011), pp. 47–48 ("the eradication of the human in reformed discourse"); and Jennifer A. Herdt, *Putting on Virtue: The Legacy of the Splendid Vices* (Chicago, IL: University of Chicago Press, 2008), p. 175, for Luther's demand that the starting point for repentance must be the recognition of the utter bankruptcy of human agency. "Any attempt to earn God's favor," Herdt eloquently argues with regard to Luther's core theology, "is not only disobedient to God's law but is also a form of idolatry" (p. 176). See also the excellent discussion of

David R. Como, *Blown by the Spirit: Puritanism and the Emergence of an Antinomian Underground in Pre-Civil-War England* (Stanford, CA: Stanford University Press, 2004), ch. 4, pp. 104–137, whose interest in how late sixteenth-century practical Calvinist pastoral theology will produce antinomianism leads him directly to the crevasses lying in wait for the Calvinist believer.

22. I take the phrase "absolute givenness" from Cummings, *Literary Culture of the Reformation,* p. 320.

23. Ephesians 1:4: "As he hath chosen us in him, before the foundation of the world."

24. For Luther's commitment to predestination see e.g. his Preface to Romans, in Luther, "Preface to the Epistle of Paul to the Romans," in Martin Luther, *Prefaces to the New Testament,* in *Luther's Works* 35, *Word and Sacrament* 1, ed. Bachmann, p. 378. See also Rupp, *The Righteousness of God,* pp. 186–188, and, for predestinarianism generally before Calvin, see Dewey D. Wallace, *Puritans and Predestination: Grace in English Protestant Theology, 1525–1695* (Chapel Hill: University of North Carolina Press, 1982), pp. 5–6.

25. For which information, see *EEBO,* Jean Calvin, *The institution of Christian religion.*

26. Jean Calvin, *The institution of Christian religion* (London, 1561), image 322.

27. John Bunyan, *Grace Abounding with Other Spiritual Autobiographies,* ed. John Stachniewski (Oxford: Oxford University Press, 1998), p. 19.

28. Jean Calvin, *Institution of Christian religion* (London, 1561), image 322.

29. Stachniewski, *Persecutory Imagination,* p. 17.

30. *TRP,* 2:122.

31. *The Book of Common Prayer: The Texts of 1549, 1559, and 1662,* ed. Brian Cummings (Oxford: Oxford University Press, 2011), p. 678 (taken from the 1662 Prayer Book; the Thirty-Nine Articles were first published in 1563).

32. *Book of Common Prayer,* ed. Cummings, p. 678.

33. *SR,* 13 Eliz. 12, 4:546. Nicholas Tyacke further reports that "between 1579 and 1615 at least thirty-nine quarto editions of the Geneva Bible, all printed in England, had a predestinarian catechism bound with them [author's emphasis]." See Nicholas Tyacke, *Anti-Calvinists: The Rise of English Arminianism, c. 1590–1640* (Oxford: Clarendon Press, 1987), pp. 2–3.

34. *Book of Common Prayer,* ed. Cummings, p. 683.

35. See *Certain Sermons Or Homilies Appointed to be Read in Churches,* ed. Ronald B. Bond (Toronto: University of Toronto Press, 1987), pp. 57–58.

36. "A Fruitful Exhortation to the Readyng and Knowledge of Holy Scripture," in *Certain Sermons Or Homilies Appointed to be Read in Churches,* ed. Bond, pp. 61–69 (at p. 61).

37. *The seconde tome of homelyes* (London, 1563), images 89–90.

38. For the first provisional failure of the Puritan movement, in the late sixteenth century, see Patrick Collinson, *The Elizabethan Puritan Movement* (London: Methuen, 1967), pp. 448–467.

39. William Perkins, *A treatise tending vnto a declaration whether a man be in the estate of damnation or in the estate of grace* (London, 1590), image 4. Further citations of this text will be made in the body of the text by image number.

40. William Perkins, *A golden chaine* (London, 1591), image 159.

41. *Histoire Des Conciles d'Après Les Documents Originaux*, ed. Karl Joseph von Hefele, 5 vols. (Paris: Letouzey, 1907), Canon 21, 5.2:1349–1351.

42. *Religion and Society in Early Modern England: A Sourcebook*, ed. David Cressy and Lori Anne Ferrell (London: Routledge, 1996), pp. 18–20.

43. *Book of Common Prayer*, ed. Cummings, pp. 94–97, for the 1549 commination and general confession; p. 680, for Article 25 of the Thirty-Nine Articles (ratified 1571), specifically limiting the number of sacraments to two (Baptism and the Supper of our Lord).

44. For first-hand accounts of the destruction of saints' shrines in the late 1530s, see *Letters to Cromwell and Others on the Suppression of the Monasteries*, ed. G. H. Cook (London: John Baker, 1965). For chantry chapels, see Duffy, *Stripping of the Altars*, pp. 301–302. For the 1545 Henrician and the 1547 Edwardian statutes abolishing chantry chapels, see Duffy, *Stripping of the Altars*, pp. 454–456. For the destruction of "idolatrous" religious images, see Margaret Aston, *England's Iconoclasts: Laws against Images* (Oxford: Clarendon Press, 1988), pp. 222–246.

45. Stephen Gardiner, *A declaration of suche true articles as George Ioye hath gone about to confute as false* (London, 1546), image 86.

46. For the history and influential restatements, see Introduction, n. 15.

47. See Chapter 16.

48. A point brilliantly made by Max Weber in *The Protestant Work Ethic and the Spirit of Capitalism*, trans. Talcott Parsons (New York: Scribner's Sons, 1958; first pub. in German, 1904), p. 172.

4. Narrative and Lyric Entrapment

1. See e.g. the pages headed "Of Penance" in William Tyndale, *The Obedience of a Christian Man* [1528], ed. David Daniell (London: Penguin, 2000), pp. 115–116. Simon Fish, *Supplicacyon for the Beggers* available in Thomas More, *Letter to Bugenhagen; Supplication of Souls, Letter against Frith*, CWSTM, 7:412–422. *Letters to Cromwell and Others on the Suppression of the Monasteries*, ed. G. H. Cook (London: John Baker, 1965).

2. Edited in *The Poetical Works of John Skelton*, ed. Alexander Dyce (Cambridge, UK: Cambridge University Press, 1843), 2:413–447 (pp. 430–431).

3. None of the psalm paraphrases of either Thomas Wyatt or Henry Howard, Earl of Surrey, was published during their lifetimes. See e.g. Thomas Wyatt, *Certayne Psalmes chosen out of the psalter of David commonlye called the vii penitential psalms* (London, 1549) (composed c. 1534–1542); and Henry Howard, Early of Surrey, *Certayne chapters of the proverbs of Salomon* (London, 1549–1550) (composed 1546–1547). For a complete bibliographic conspectus of English independent

psalm versions 1530–1601, see Rivkah Zim, *English Metrical Psalms: Poetry as Praise and Prayer 1535–1601* (Cambridge, UK: Cambridge University Press, 1987), Appendix, pp. 211–259.

4. For scholarship on whether or not Wyatt's psalm paraphrases were written in prison, see Ruth Ahnert, *The Rise of Prison Literature in the Sixteenth Century* (Cambridge, UK: Cambridge University Press, 2013), p. 61 n. 56.

5. In *Sir Thomas Wyatt, The Complete Poems*, ed. R. A. Rebholz (Harmondsworth: Penguin, 1978), "Who list his wealth and ease retaine," ll. 16–19, p. 155. The epigraph to Wyatt's text is itself drawn from the Psalms (Ps 16.9): *"Circumdederunt me inimici mei"* ("My enemies surrounded me").

6. For which see Susan Brigden, *Thomas Wyatt: The Heart's Forest* (London: Faber and Faber, 2012), pp. 524–525.

7. See Eamon Duffy, *Marking the Hours: English People and Their Prayers, 1240–1570* (New Haven, CT: Yale University Press, 2006), pp. 5–10, and 53–64. For "the normative use of the Penitential Psalms as a devotional reading before or after confession," see Lynn Staley, "The Penitential Psalms: Conversion and the Limits of Lordship," *JMEMS* 37 (2007), 221–269 (at p. 244). For the larger story of the Penitential Psalms from late medieval into early modern England, see Clare Costley King'oo, *Miserere Mei: The Penitential Psalms in Late Medieval and Early Modern England* (Notre Dame, IN: University of Notre Dame Press, 2012).

8. Thomas Wyatt, *Paraphrase of the Penitential Psalms*, in *Sir Thomas Wyatt, The Complete Poems*, ed. Rebholz, ll. 99–100. All further citations of this text will be made by line number in the body of the text.

9. See further James Simpson, *Reform and Cultural Revolution, 1350–1547* (Oxford: Oxford University Press, 2002), pp. 322–329.

10. Thomas Wyatt, *The Life and Letters of Sir Thomas Wyatt*, ed. Kenneth Muir (Liverpool: University of Liverpool Press, 1963), p. 197.

11. *Life and Letters of Sir Thomas Wyatt*, ed. Muir, p. 210.

12. For the key events by which Catholics were defined with much greater precision as internal enemies from the late 1560s, see Diarmaid MacCulloch, *Reformation: Europe's House Divided, 1490–1700* (London: Allen Lane, 2003), pp. 332–334 and 369.

13. Edmund Spenser, *The Faerie Queene*, ed. Thomas P. Roche (London: Penguin, 1987). Further references to this poem will be made by book, canto, stanza, and line number in the body of the text.

14. For an articulate account of early modern and Romantic romance as characterized by endless dilation, see Patricia Parker, *Inescapable Romance: Studies in the Poetics of a Mode* (Princeton, NJ: Princeton University Press, 1979). For the broader tradition of romance, for which closure is the defining characteristic, see James Simpson, "Derek Brewer's Romance," in *A Modern Medievalist: Traditions and Innovations in the Study of Medieval Literature*, ed. Charlotte Brewer and Barry Windeatt (Cambridge, UK: Boydell and Brewer, 2013), pp. 154–172.

15. Christopher Marlowe, *Doctor Faustus*, in *Christopher Marlowe: The Complete Plays*, ed. Frank Romany and Robert Lindsey (London: Penguin, 2003), pp. 343–394, scene 7.

16. William Perkins, *A treatise tending vnto a declaration whether a man be in the estate of damnation or in the estate of grace* (London, 1590), image 29.

17. Harold Skulsky, "Spenser's Despair Episode and the Theology of Doubt," *Modern Philology* 78 (1981), 227–242: "The notorious truth . . . is that the result of insisting on assurance was to create a scandal for believers by making a duty out of an impossibility" (p. 235).

18. For Greville's biography, see R. A. Rebholz, *The Life of Fulke Greville, First Lord Brooke* (Oxford: Clarendon Press, 1971), and *ODNB*. For a review of his literary career, see Freya Sierhuis, "Politics, Imagination and Desire in the Work of Fulke Greville," in *Oxford Handbooks Online, Literature* (www.oxfordhandbooks .com).

19. For detailed arguments about the dating of Greville's works, on which I am dependent, see Rebholz, *Life of Fulke Greville*, Appendix I, pp. 325–340, with a summary on p. 340. Citations from *Caelica* will be drawn from *Poems and Dramas of Fulke Greville, First Lord Brooke*, ed. Geoffrey Bullough (Edinburgh: Oliver and Boyd, 1939), and will be made by lyric and line number in the body of the text.

20. Fulke Greville, *The tragedy of Mustapha* (London, 1609).

21. Rebholz, *Life of Fulke Greville*, Appendix I, pp. 325–340 (at pp. 328–331).

22. For which see both Sierhuis, "Politics, Imagination and Desire in the Work of Fulke Greville," and Debora Kuller Shuger, *Habits of Thought in the English Renaissance: Religion, Politics, and the Dominant Culture* (Toronto: University of Toronto Press, 1997), pp. 211–217.

23. For a penetrating analysis of the play's novelty, both generic and philosophical, and of its dark pessimism, see Russ Leo, "Natures freedome," the Art of Sovereignty and *Mustapha*'s Tragic Insolubility: Fulke Greville and Jean Bodin Among the Ottomans" (forthcoming). I am grateful to Professor Leo for sharing this essay.

24. This analysis is exactly coincident with that of Shuger, *Habits of Thought in the English Renaissance*, pp. 210–217.

25. Fulke Greville, *The remains of Sir Fulk Grevill Lord Brooke* (London, 1670). Citations from the text of Greville's *Treatise on Religion* are taken from *Fulke Greville. The Remains: Being Poems of Monarchy and Religion*, ed. G. A. Wilkes (Oxford: Oxford University Press, 1965), pp. 203–232. Further references will be made by stanza number in the body of the text.

26. Though, to my knowledge, Anne Locke deserves to be recognized for the first sonnet sequence in English, where the sonnets are turned to religious (Calvinist) expression. See Anne Locke, *Meditation of a Penitent Sinner*, appended to *Sermons of John Calvin, vpon the songe that Ezechias made* (London, 1560). I thank Brian Cummings for guidance on this point.

27. For revisionist readings of Petrarch as participating in early forms of absolutist culture, see David Wallace, *Chaucerian Polity: Absolutist Lineages and Associational Forms in England and Italy* (Stanford, CA: Stanford University Press, 1997), pp. 261–298, and James Simpson, "Breaking the Vacuum: Ricardian and Henrician Ovidianism," *JMEMS* 29 (1999), 325–355.

28. See Thomas M. Greene, *The Light in Troy: Imitation and Discovery in Renaissance Poetry* (New Haven, CT: Yale University Press, 1982), chs. 10–12.

29. For the way in which Chaucer's precocious translation of a Petrarchan sonnet is prophetic, see Paul Strohm, "Chaucer's *Troilus* as Temporal Archive," in his *Theory and the Premodern Text* (Minneapolis: University of Minnesota Press, 2000), pp. 80–96.

30. George Herbert, "The Pilgrimage," in *George Herbert: The Complete English Poems*, ed. John Tobin (London: Penguin, 1991), l. 4. All further citations from Herbert's poetry will be drawn from this edition, and cited by line number in the body of the text.

31. "Donne, John," in *ODNB*.

32. "Herbert, George," in *ODNB*.

33. For the interesting slowness of criticism to recognize Herbert's intense Calvinism, see Richard Strier, *Love Known: Theology and Experience in George Herbert's Poetry* (Chicago, IL: University of Chicago Press, 1983), pp. xv–xviii. The key breakthrough came with Barbara Kiefer Lewalski, *Protestant Poetics and the Seventeenth-Century Religious Lyric* (Princeton, NJ: Princeton University Press, 1979), ch. 9.

34. For an account of Donne's politics as absolutist no less than his theology, see Shuger, *Habits of Thought in the English Renaissance*, ch. 5 ("Absolutist Theology: The Sermons of John Donne"), esp. pp. 159–210.

35. For this neo-Platonic tradition as found in late fourteenth-century English vernacular texts, see A. J. Minnis, "The *Cloud of Unknowing* and Walter Hilton's *Scale of Perfection*," in *Middle English Prose: A Critical Guide to Major Authors and Genres*, ed. A. S. G. Edwards (New Brunswick, NJ: Rutgers University Press, 1984), pp. 61–81.

36. John Donne, *Poems* (London, 1633), image 23; Perkins, *A treatise tending vnto a declaration whether a man be in the estate of damnation or in the estate of grace*, image 27; John Donne, *Holy Sonnets*, in *John Donne's Poetry*, ed. Donald R. Dickson (New York: W. W. Norton, 2007), sonnet 10, ll. 1–4. Further references will be made to this edition by line number in the body of the text.

37. See e.g. John Calvin, *The institution of Christian religion* (London, 1561), image 14. The victim of Calvinist predestination is frequently represented as being driven to obscenity: see, for influential example, Marlowe, *Doctor Faustus* (?1592–1593): (Faustus speaking) "To him [Beelzebub] I'll build an altar and a church, / And offer lukewarm blood of new-born babes," in *Marlowe: The Complete Plays*, ed. Romany and Lindsey, scene 5, ll. 13–14; and, seventy-five years later, John Bunyan, *Grace Abounding* (1666): "One morning as I did lie in my bed, I was, as at

other times, most fiercely assaulted with this temptation, *to sell and part with Christ;* the wicked suggestion still running in my mind, *to sell him, sell him, sell him, sell him.*" See John Bunyan, *Grace Abounding,* ed. John Stachniewski with Anita Pacheco (Oxford: Oxford University Press, 1998), p. 40.

38. For the specifically Calvinist thematic of this poem, and its extremity, see Lewalski, *Protestant Poetics and the Seventeenth-Century Religious Lyric,* p. 265 and 271–272 respectively.

39. George Herbert, "Perirrhanterium," or "The Church Porch," in *George Herbert: The Complete English Poems,* ed. Tobin, pp. 6–22. For the dissonances between the three parts (i.e. Church Porch, The Church, Church Militant) of Herbert's *The Temple,* see Shuger, *Habits of Thought in the English Renaissance,* ch. 3, pp. 91–119, and Lewalski, *Protestant Poetics and the Seventeenth-Century Religious Lyric,* ch. 9, pp. 283–316.

40. For the use of euphemism in contemporary torture, see Elaine Scarry, *The Body in Pain: The Making and Unmaking of the World* (New York: Oxford University Press, 1985), p. 44, and, for early modern English torture euphemism, James Simpson, "No Brainer: The Early Modern Tragedy of Torture," *Religion and Literature* 43 (2011), 1–23 (at p. 5).

5. Modernizing Despair's Epic Non-Escape

1. Christopher Hill, *Society and Puritanism in Pre-Revolutionary England* (New York: Schocken Books, 1964), p. 128.

2. Hill, *Society and Puritanism,* p. 129.

3. Max Weber, *The Protestant Work Ethic and the Spirit of Capitalism,* trans. Talcott Parsons (New York: Scribner's Sons, 1958; first pub. in German, 1904), p. 172. See Chapter 3 of the present book for further elucidation of the paradox of Protestant work.

4. Weber, *Protestant Work Ethic,* p. 112.

5. For Arminius's recovery of thirteenth-century scholastic theology, in which the realms of grace and nature are reconnected, so constraining God's absolute power, see Freya Sierhuis, *The Literature of the Arminian Controversy: Religion, Politics and the Stage in the Dutch Republic* (Oxford: Oxford University Press, 2015), pp. 43–45.

6. In *Mustapha* (pub. 1609); see *Selected Writings of Fulke Greville,* ed. Joan Reese (London: Athlone, 1973), pp. 123–125 (see esp. p. 124, ll. 23–24). Greville also predicts civil war in his *Treatise on Religion* (probably written 1621–1628): *Fulke Greville. The Remains: Being Poems of Monarchy and Religion,* ed. G. A. Wilkes (Oxford: Oxford University Press, 1965), stanza 31. See Chapter 4 for discussion.

7. R. J. Knecht, *The French Wars of Religion,* 3rd ed. (London: Longman, 2010), p. 96; *OED* records instances of "massacre" in English only post, and almost immediately post, 1572. See also Diarmaid MacCulloch, *Reformation: Europe's House Divided* (London: Allen Lane, 2003), pp. 306–316.

8. MacCulloch, *Reformation*, p. 485.

9. Fulke Greville, *A Treatise on Religion*, in *The Remains: Being Poems of Monarchy and Religion*, ed. G. A. Wilkes (London: Oxford University Press, 1965), stanza 33, p. 211.

10. For the high profile of anti-Arminianism in the parliaments of 1625–1640, see Nicholas Tyacke, *Anti-Calvinists: The Rise of English Arminianism, c. 1590–1640* (Oxford: Clarendon Press, 1987), pp. 125–144; with regard to the 1629 Parliament, Tyacke says that "Arminianism soon emerged as an overriding concern of the Commons" (p. 160).

11. Hillel Schwartz, "Arminianism and the English Parliament, 1624–1629," *Journal of British Studies* 12 (1973), 41–68 (at p. 41). See also M. J. Braddick, *God's Fury, England's Fire: A New History of the English Civil Wars* (London: Allen Lane, 2008), p. 71.

12. See e.g. "Charles I, King of England," in *ODNB* for the narrative of the 1629 Parliament.

13. For an introduction to early seventeenth-century Puritan New England, see Francis J. Bremer, "The Puritan Experiment in New England, 1630–1660," in *The Cambridge Companion to Puritanism*, ed. John Coffey and Paul C. H. Lim (Cambridge, UK: Cambridge University Press, 2008), pp. 127–142, and David D. Hall, *A Reforming People: Puritanism and the Transformation of Public Life in New England* (New York: Alfred A. Knopf, 2011).

14. George Herbert, "The Church Militant," in *George Herbert: The Complete English Poems*, ed. John Tobin (London: Penguin, 1991), pp. 179–187, ll. 224–227. Further references to this text will be made from this edition by line number in the body of the text.

15. For English Antinomianism, which arises in precise tandem with the arrival of Arminianism in England, see David R. Como, *Blown by the Spirit: Puritanism and the Emergence of an Antinomian Underground in Pre-Civil-War England* (Stanford, CA: Stanford University Press, 2004), pp. 58–81.

16. For a lucid account of the theological and political fractures within the United Provinces across the Arminian controversy, and the larger context, see Sierhuis, *Literature of the Arminian Controversy*, pp. 18–52 (esp. pp. 36–52).

17. See Stephen M. Fallon, "Milton's Arminianism and the Authorship of *De doctrina Christiana*," *Texas Studies in Literature and Language* 41 (1999), 103–127.

18. For this narrative, see Sierhuis, *Literature of the Arminian Controversy*, pp. 164–175; for the figures, p. 169.

19. Tyacke, *Anti-Calvinists*, p. 100. For what looks like a later change of view by James with regard to predestination, see pp. 102–103.

20. See Tyacke, *Anti-Calvinists*, and Nicholas Tyacke, "Puritanism, Arminianism and Counter-Revolution," in *The Origins of the English Civil War*, ed. Conrad Russell (London: Macmillan, 1973), pp. 119–143.

21. Richard Montagu, *A gagg for the new Gospell? No: a new gagg for an old goose* (London, 1624). For the particular passage defending free will against Calvin-

ists, see *Religion in Early Stuart England, 1603–1638: An Anthology of Primary Sources,* ed. Deborah Shuger (Waco, TX: Baylor University Press, 2012), pp. 402–408.

22. "Montagu, Richard," in *ODNB.*

23. See n. 11 above.

24. Fallon, "Milton's Arminianism," and Barbara K. Lewalski, *The Life of John Milton* (Oxford: Blackwell, 2003), pp. 155, 214–215, and 420. Nigel Smith dates the change from anti- to pro-Arminianism in Milton to 1644. Nigel Smith, *Is Milton Better Than Shakespeare?* (Cambridge, MA: Harvard University Press, 2008), pp. 64–65.

25. John Milton, *Paradise Lost,* in *John Milton, The Major Works,* ed. Stephen Orgel and Jonathan Goldberg (Oxford: Oxford University Press, 2003), pp. 355–618, 5.524–534. Further references to this text will be drawn from this edition, and cited by book and line number in the body of the text.

26. For recent examples of the first, see David Norbrook, *Writing the English Republic: Poetry, Rhetoric, and Politics, 1627–1660* (Cambridge, UK: Cambridge University Press, 1999), pp. 433–491, and Smith, *Is Milton Better Than Shakespeare?* Of the second, see Lewalski, *Life of John Milton;* see p. xiii for a candid account of why Lewalksi admires Milton.

27. William Blake, *The Marriage of Heaven and Hell,* in *The Complete Poems of William Blake,* ed. Alicia Ostriker (Harmondsworth: Penguin, 1977), pp. 180–194 (at p. 182).

28. Thus, for grand example, "By demonstrating how there can be no possible parallel between earthly kings and divine kingship, he [Milton] flatly denies the familiar royalist analogies: God and King Charles, Satan and the Puritan rebels." Lewalski, *Life of John Milton,* p. 466. See also p. 466 for a handy survey of scholarship on this crucial question. The rules for the republican critic on the matter are clearly stated by Norbrook: "Obedience to such an entity [i.e. Milton's monarchical God] was fully compatible with the positive liberty demanded of the republican citizen." Norbrook, *Writing the English Republic,* p. 469. And, "It is simply invalid to make analogies between heavenly rule and earthly government." Norbrook, *Writing the English Republic,* p. 477. For a recent summation and critique of reading Milton as consistent, see Peter C. Herman and Elizabeth Sauer, "Introduction: Paradigms Lost, Paradigms Found: The New Milton Criticism," in *The New Milton Criticism,* ed. Peter C. Herman and Elizabeth Sauer (Cambridge, UK: Cambridge University Press, 2012), pp. 1–22.

29. For a bold attempt to unsettle what I am facetiously calling "consistentism" in Milton scholarship, see Peter C. Herman, *Destabilizing Milton:* Paradise Lost *and the Poetics of Incertitude* (New York: Palgrave, 2005).

30. For a penetrating account of the early modern sublime in English, see Patrick Cheney, *English Authorship and the Early Modern Sublime: Spenser, Marlowe, Shakespeare, Jonson* (Cambridge, UK: Cambridge University Press, forthcoming). I thank Patrick Cheney for discussion of this matter.

31. William Perkins, *A discourse of conscience* (London, 1596), image 80.

388   Notes to Pages 107–117

32. Here, as ever, I am inspired by John Stachniewski, *The Persecutory Imagination: English Puritanism and the Literature of Religious Despair* (Oxford: Clarendon Press, 1991): despite rejecting Calvinism, in Milton "human consciousness is still stalked by the Calvinist figments" (p. 332).

6. Pre-Modern and Henrician Hypocrisy

1. Edward Hall, *The union of the two noble and illustre famelies of Lancastre [and] Yorke* (London, 1548), images 637–638.
2. See Brian Cummings, *Mortal Thoughts: Religion, Secularity, & Identity in Shakespeare and Early Modern Culture* (Oxford: Oxford University Press, 2013), p. 96, in the context of a discussion of authenticity as a cardinal feature of modernity.
3. See Hannah Arendt, *On Revolution* (New York: Penguin Books, 2006; first pub. 1963).
4. Arendt, *On Revolution*, p. 89.
5. John Donne, *Holy Sonnets*, in *John Donne's Poetry*, ed. Donald R. Dickson (New York: W. W. Norton, 2007), sonnet 16, l. 8. Donne is lamenting the impossibility of escaping the charge of hypocrisy. See also Donne's reference to his "muse's white sincerity" in *La Corona*, 1.6.
6. Geoffrey Chaucer, *Canterbury Tales*, in *The Riverside Chaucer*, gen. ed. Larry D. Benson, 3rd ed. (Oxford: Oxford University Press, 1987), *Parson's Tale*, l. 394, p. 299.
7. Though the intra-ecclesiastical charge of hypocrisy predates the friars; for early twelfth-century charges of hypocrisy directed at monks, see Giles Constable, *The Reformation of the Twelfth Century* (Cambridge, UK: Cambridge University Press, 1996), pp. 34 and 122.
8. William of St Amour, *De Periculis Novissimorum Temporum*, ed. G. Geltner (Dudley, MA: Peeters Press, 2008). For the broad tradition, see Penn R. Szittya, *The Antifraternal Tradition in Medieval Literature* (Princeton, NJ: Princeton University Press, 1986).
9. William of St Amour, *De Periculis*, ed. Geltner, p. 58, derived from 2Tim 3:5. See also p. 62 for the claim that the hypocritical false teachers look like the elect. Further citations will be made by page number in the body of the text.
10. Wendy Scase, Piers Plowman *and the New Anticlericalism* (Cambridge, UK: Cambridge University Press, 1989), pp. 5, 14.
11. For orthodox attack on the friars, see Richard Fitzralph, *Defensio Curatorum*, in *Dialogus inter Militem et Clericum*, ed. Aaron Jenkins Perry, EETS, o.s. 167 (London: Oxford University Press), pp. 39–93. Fitzralph (d. 1360) was Bishop of Armagh, Ireland. For the heterodox attack on the friars, see, for a quasi-literary example, *Pierce Plowman's Crede* (c. 1393–1400), in *The Piers Plowman Tradition*, ed. Helen Barr

(London: Dent, 1993). For the larger phenomenon, see also Szittya, *Antifraternal Tradition*, passim, and Anne Hudson, *The Premature Reformation: Wycliffite Texts and Lollard History* (Oxford: Clarendon Press, 1988), pp. 348–351.

12. William Langland, *The Vision of Piers Plowman, A Critical Edition of the B-Text*, ed. A.V.C. Schmidt, second edition (London: Dent, 1995). For more extensive discussion, see James Simpson, *Piers Plowman: An Introduction to the B-Text*, second, revised edition (Exeter: Exeter University Press, 2007), Chapter 7.

13. Thus *Romance of the Rose*, trans. Dahlberg, l. 10931, and *Piers Plowman*, ed. Schmidt, B.20.354.

14. A very partial list would include John Heywood, *The Pardoner and the Frere* (1533); Thomas More's *Dialogue Concerning Heresies* (1529); Simon Birckbek, *The Protestants evidence taken out of good records* (London, 1635). See further Caroline F. E. Spurgeon, *Five Hundred Years of Chaucer Criticism and Allusion 1357–1900*, 3 vols. (Cambridge, UK: Cambridge University Press, 1925) for further allusions, and James Simpson, "Not Yet: Chaucer and Anagogy," *Studies in the Age of Chaucer* 37 (2015), 31–54.

15. Guillaume de Lorris and Jean de Meun, *The Romance of the Rose*, trans. Charles Dahlberg (Hanover, NH: Univ. Press of New England, 1983), lines 11163–11187.

16. William Roper, *The Life of Sir Thomas More*, in *Two Early Tudor Lives*, ed. Richard S. Sylvester and Davis P. Harding (New Haven, CT: Yale University Press, 1962). The text was finished in the reign of Queen Mary (i.e. pre-1558), but it was only published for the first time in 1626, in Paris, as *The mirrour of vertue in worldly greatnes*. For further discussion, see James Simpson, "Rhetoric, Conscience and the Playful Positions of Sir Thomas More," in *The Oxford Handbook to Tudor Literature, 1485–1603*, ed. Mike Pincombe and Cathy Shrank (Oxford: Oxford University Press, 2009), pp. 121–136.

17. Roper, *Life of Sir Thomas More*, p. 198. The story also appears in Nicholas Harpsfield's slightly later biography of More (1559, though not published until 1932), *The Life and Death of Sir Thomas Moore, Knight, Sometime Lord High Chancellor of England*, ed. Elsie Vaughan Hitchcock, EETS, 186 (London: Oxford University Press, 1932), pp. 10–11.

18. Thomas More, *Utopia*, ed. Edward Surtz and J. H. Hexter, CWSTM, 4:99. See also Erasmus, whose *Encomium Moriae* was begun while staying with More in 1509, and was published in 1549 in a translation into English by Thomas Chaloner: *The Praise of Folie, by Sir Thomas Chaloner*, ed. Clarence H. Miller, EETS, 257 (London: Oxford University Press, 1965), p. 38. For the theme of Folly in late medieval and early modern England, see Greg Walker, "Folly," in *Cultural Reformations: Medieval and Renaissance in Literary History*, ed. Brian Cummings and James Simpson (Oxford: Oxford University Press, 2010), pp. 321–341. For More's strategic playfulness, see Stephen Greenblatt, "At the Table of the Great: More's Self-Fashioning and Self-Cancellation," in *Renaissance Self-Fashioning, from More to Shakespeare* (Chicago, IL: University of Chicago Press, 1980), pp. 11–73.

19. Anthony Munday and others, *Sir Thomas More*, ed. Vittorio Gabrieli and Giorgio Melchiori (Manchester, UK: Manchester University Press, 1990), 3.3.274–77, p. 154.

20. *SR*, 2 H 4, c. 15, 2:125–128 (at 2:126).

21. *TRP*, 2:117–132 (at pp. 117–118).

22. *TRP*, 2:118.

23. William Tyndale, *An exposycyon vpon the v.vi.vii. chapters of Mathewe* (Antwerp, 1533). I cite by image number from the 1536 edition (London, 1536).

24. Thomas More, *The Confutation of Tyndale's Answer*, *CWSTM*, 8.2:879.

25. See further David Loewenstein, *Treacherous Faith: The Specter of Heresy in Early Modern English Literature and Culture* (Oxford: Oxford University Press, 2013), pp. 47–48.

26. More, *Confutation*, 8.2:879.

27. For a broader account of the closing down of fiction in the 1530s and 1540s, see Alistair Fox, *Politics and Literature in the Reigns of Henry VII and Henry VIII* (Oxford: Blackwell, 1989). Any such argument should of course also remember More's last work, the *Dialogue of Comfort against Tribulation*, written from the Tower awaiting execution between April 1534 and July 1535. In this work More assumes his subtle masks again.

28. *An Open Letter to Leo X*, in *Reformation Writings of Martin Luther*, trans. Bertram Lee Woolf (New York: Philosophical Library, 1953), 1:333–347 (at p. 337).

29. Erasmus Sarcerius, *Common places of Scripture* (London, 1538), image 199. See Karl Gunther, *Reformation Unbound: Protestant Visions of Reform in England, 1525–1590* (Cambridge, UK: Cambridge University Press, 2014), pp. 70–71.

30. William Tyndale, *The Parable of the Wicked Mammon*, in *Doctrinal Treatises and Introductions to Different Portions of The Holy Scriptures by William Tyndale*, ed. Henry Walter (Cambridge, UK: Cambridge University Press, 1848), p. 182.

31. William Tyndale, *The exposition of the fyrst epistle of seynt Jhon*, image 33.

32. William Tyndale, *An answere vnto Sir Thomas Mores dialoge made by Willyam Tindale* (Antwerp, 1531), image 6.

33. John Bale, *The image of both Churches* (London, 1570; first printed Antwerp, 1545), image 3. Further citations from this text will be made by image number, in the body of the text, to the 1570 edition.

34. William Tyndale, *An exposycyon vpon the v.vi.vii. chapters of Mathewe*, image 32.

7. The Revolutionary Hypocrite

1. For scholarship pointing to the nascent history of evangelical rudeness, see both Karl Gunther, *Reformation Unbound: Protestant Visions of Reform in England, 1525–1590* (Cambridge, UK: Cambridge University Press, 2014), pp. 70–71, and Ethan H. Shagan, *The Rule of Moderation: Violence, Religion and the Politics of Restraint in Early Modern England* (Cambridge, UK: Cambridge University Press, 2011), p. 160.

2. Edmund Burke, *Reflections on the Revolution in France*, ed. Frank M. Turner (New Haven, CT: Yale University Press, 2003), p. 67.

3. On the pre-Reformation concept and institutional organization of spiritual perfectionism, see Nicholas Watson, "Chaucer's Public Christianity," *Religion & Literature* 37 (2005), 99–114, and "*Piers Plowman*, Pastoral Theology, and Spiritual Perfectionism: Hawkyn's Coat and Patience's *Pater Noster*," *YLS* 21 (2007), 83–118.

4. John Bale, *The image of both Churches* (London, 1570; first printed Antwerp, 1545), image 86.

5. Peter Lake and Michael C. Questier, *The Anti-Christ's Lewd Hat: Protestants, Papists and Players in Post-Reformation England* (New Haven, CT: Yale University Press, 2002), pp. 528–530.

6. Richard Bancroft, *Dangerous positions* (London, 1593), image 28.

7. Arthur Dent, *The plaine mans path-way to heauen* (London, 1607), image 16.

8. Ben Jonson, *Bartholomew Fair*, in *Volpone and Other Plays*, ed. Michael Jamieson (London: Penguin, 2004), 1.3.115. Further references to this text will be made by act, scene, and line number in the body of the text.

9. Andrew Marvell, "The First Anniversary," in *The Poems of Andrew Marvell*, ed. Nigel Smith, rev. ed. (Harlow: Pearson Education, 2007), pp. 281–298, l. 317. The poem was first published anonymously in 1655.

10. For which see Andrew Pettegree, "Nicodemism and the English Reformation," in *Marian Protestantism: Six Studies* (Aldershot, Hampshire: Scolar, 1996), pp. 86–117, and Gunther, *Reformation Unbound*, ch. 5.

11. Gunther, *Reformation Unbound*, p. 100.

12. *SR*, 1 Eliz c 2, 4.1:355–358; see also *TRP*, 2:122–123.

13. Alexandra Walsham, *Church Papists: Catholicism, Conformity, and Confessional Polemic in Early Modern England* (London: Royal Historical Society, Boydell Press, 1993), p. 9.

14. *Proceedings in the Parliaments of Elizabeth I*, ed. T. E. Hartley (Wilmington, DE: Michael Glazier, 1981), p. 241.

15. *Proceedings in the Parliaments of Elizabeth I*, ed. Hartley, 1:240; Walsham, *Church Papists*, p. 12.

16. *A Second Admonition to the Parliament*, in *Puritan Manifestos: A Study of the Origin of the Puritan Revolt with a Reprint of the Admonition to the Parliament*, ed. Walter Howard Frere and Charles Edward Douglas (New York: B. Franklin, 1972; first pub. 1907), p. 92.

17. William Perkins, *A commentarie or exposition, vpon the fiue first chapters of the Epistle to the Galatians* (London, 1604), image 80.

18. e.g. John Calvin, *The institution of Christian religion, wrytten in Latine by maister Ihon Caluin, and translated into Englysh* (London, 1561), images 10, 13–14. Further references to this translation of Calvin's *Institutes* will be made by book, chapter and image number in the body of the text. Calvin, *The institution of Christian religion*.

19. See John H. Langbein, *Torture and the Law of Proof: Europe and England in the Ancien Régime*, repr. with a new preface (Chicago, IL: University of Chicago Press, 2006; first pub. 1977), pp. 103–107, and James Simpson, "No Brainer: The Early Modern Tragedy of Torture," *Religion and Literature* 43 (2011), 1–23.

20. Thomas Norton, *A declaration of the fauourable dealing of her Maiesties commissioners appointed for the examination of certain traitours and of tortures* (London, 1583). For authorship, see Langbein, *Torture and the Law of Proof*, pp. 191–192. For Norton's life, and his reputation as rack-master, see *ODNB*. See also Simpson, "No Brainer."

21. Norton, *Declaration*, image 5.

22. Robert Parsons [Persons], *An epistle of the persecution of Catholickes in Englande* (Douai, 1582), image 45.

23. See Calvin, *Institution of Christian religion*, 3.2, images 188–206.

24. William Perkins, *An exposition of the Symbole or Creed of the Apostles* (London, 1595), image 10. There were seven further independent editions of this work up to 1631. Further citations will be made by title and image number in the body of the text.

25. William Perkins, *A golden chaine* (London, 1592; orig. pub. 1591), image 159. This large work went through nine editions between 1591 and 1621. Further references to this text will be made by title and image number in the body of the text.

26. William Perkins, *A case of conscience* (London, 1592), image 16. This work went through four editions in 1592 alone, with one more in 1595.

27. *TRP*, 2:117.

28. John Donne, *Holy Sonnets*, in *John Donne's Poetry*, ed. Donald R. Dickson (New York: W. W. Norton, 2007), sonnet 16, l. 8.

29. Patrick Collinson, *The Birthpangs of Protestant England: Religious and Cultural Change in the Sixteenth and Seventeenth Centuries* (Basingstoke, Hampshire: Macmillan, 1988), p. 117, and Chapters 9–11 of the present book. For hostility to theater see Jonas A. Barish, *The Antitheatrical Prejudice* (Berkeley: University of California Press, 1981), and Chapters 12–14 of the present book.

30. William Prynne, *Histriomastix The players scourge* (London, 1633), image 98.

31. *TRP*, 2:122–123.

32. Nathaniel Woodes, *The Conflict of Conscience*, 1581 (facsimile, Oxford: Malone Society, 1952). The facsimile is taken from Nathaniel Woodes, *An excellent new commedie intituled, The conflict of conscience* (London, 1581). All further citations to this text will be made in the body of the text by act and scene numbers. For the source of the core narrative (the despair of Francis Speira), see Nicholas Watson, "Despair," in *Cultural Reformations: Medieval and Renaissance in Literary History*, ed. Brian Cummings and James Simpson (Oxford: Oxford University Press, 2010), pp. 342–360. For the possible influence of this play on Marlowe's *Doctor Faustus*, see David Bevington, "Christopher Marlowe's Doctor Faustus and Nathaniel Woodes's *The Conflict of Conscience*," in *The Oxford Handbook to*

Tudor Literature, 1485–1603, ed. Mike Pincombe and Cathy Shrank (Oxford: Oxford University Press, 2009), pp. 704–717.

33. For which see Huston Diehl, *Staging Reform, Reforming the Stage: Protestantism and Popular Theater in Early Modern England* (Ithaca, NY: Cornell University Press, 1997), pp. 24–25, 43–45. Foxe, it might also be mentioned, also wrote plays of sorts; see his turgid *Christus triumphans*, in John Foxe, *Two Latin Comedies: Titus Et Gesippus; Christus Triumphans*, ed. John Hazel Smith (Ithaca, NY: Cornell University Press, 1973).

34. Prynne, *Histriomastix*, image 429.

35. The classic study is David M. Bevington, *From Mankind to Marlowe: Growth of Structure in the Popular Drama of Tudor England* (Cambridge, MA: Harvard University Press, 1962); see also Paul Whitfield White, "Theater and Religious Culture," in *A New History of Early English Drama*, ed. John D. Cox and David Scott Kastan (New York: Columbia University Press, 1997), pp. 133–151.

36. See Paul Whitfield White, *Theatre and Reformation: Protestantism, Patronage and Playing in Tudor England* (Cambridge, UK: Cambridge University Press, 1993), and Adrian Streete, *Protestantism and Drama in Early Modern England* (Cambridge, UK: Cambridge University Press, 2009), p. 131 and further references.

37. In Bale's *King Johan* and *Three Laws* respectively, in *The Complete Plays of John Bale*, ed. Peter Happé, 2 vols. (Cambridge: D. S. Brewer, 1985).

8. Managing Hypocrisy?

1. I thank Penelope Buckley for this point, and for her exceptionally inward reading of the entire chapter.

2. Arthur Dent, *The plaine mans path-way to heauen* (London, 1607), image 16.

3. *Hamlet*, in *The Norton Shakespeare*, gen. ed. Stephen Greenblatt, 3rd ed. (New York: W. W. Norton, 2016), 2.3.17. All further citations from the works of Shakespeare are drawn from this edition and will be made by act, scene, and line number in the body of the text.

4. See also *Measure for Measure*, 3.1.92–95.

5. For the 1650 act making adultery a capital offence, see Keith Thomas, "The Puritans and Adultery: The 1650 Act Reconsidered," in *Puritans and Revolutionaries: Essays in Seventeenth-Century History Presented to Christopher Hill*, ed. Keith Thomas and D. H. Pennington (Oxford: Clarendon Press, 1982), pp. 257–282. For the earlier, pre-Shakespearean Puritan promotion of capital punishment for adultery, see pp. 264–267 and 271.

6. For the history of secular readings of Shakespeare, see Brian Cummings, *Mortal Thoughts: Religion, Secularity, & Identity in Shakespeare and Early Modern Culture* (Oxford: Oxford University Press, 2013), pp. 1–12. See also David Loewenstein and Michael Whitmore, "Introduction," in *Shakespeare and Early Modern Religion*, ed. David Loewenstein and Michael Whitmore (Cambridge, UK: Cambridge University Press, 2015), pp. 1–20.

7. Thus Calvin, in *Luther and Calvin: On Secular Authority*, ed. Harro Höpfl (Cambridge, UK: Cambridge University Press 1991), 4.20, pp. 47–86 (the very last chapter of the 1559 *Institutes*). For a summary of Calvin's understanding of the moral and doctrinal role of the magistracy, see Alister E. McGrath, *Reformation Thought: An Introduction*, 3rd ed. (Oxford: Blackwell, 1999), pp. 230–234

8. For the theory of monarchical supremacy in both State and Church in Tudor and Stuart England, see Alan Cromartie, *The Constitutionalist Revolution: An Essay on the History of England, 1450–1642* (Cambridge, UK: Cambridge University Press, 2006), esp. chs. 2 and 3.

9. See also "Pardon is still the nurse of second woe" (2.1.258), and all of 2.2.

10. Knowable by Shakespeare from Thomas Speght's 1598 edition of Chaucer that included the relevant *Romance of the Rose* translation: see *The workes of our antient and lerned English poet, Geffrey Chaucer, newly printed* (London, 1598), republished twice more in the same year; and *The vvorkes of our ancient and learned English poet, Geffrey Chaucer, newly printed* (London, 1602), reprinted once more in 1602.

11. John Bale, *The image of both Churches* (London, 1570; first printed Antwerp, 1545), image 86.

12. For the history of the topos of fraternal abuse of confession, see Penn R. Szittya, *The Antifraternal Tradition in Medieval Literature* (Princeton, NJ: Princeton University Press, 1986), p. 79.

13. See 5.1.20–131 for what is effectively a play within a play.

14. For the ways in which *Measure for Measure* measures the absence of the sacrament of penance, see Sarah Beckwith, *Shakespeare and the Grammar of Forgiveness* (Ithaca, NY: Cornell University Press, 2011), ch. 3, pp. 59–81.

15. For which see James Simpson, "Derek Brewer's Romance," in *A Modern Medievalist: Traditions and Innovations in the Study of Medieval Literature*, ed. Charlotte Brewer and Barry Windeatt (Cambridge, UK: Boydell and Brewer, 2013), pp. 154–172 (at p. 171).

16. For a learned and profound meditation on the function of the state in *Measure for Measure*, see Debora K. Shuger, *Political Theologies in Shakespeare's England: The Sacred and the State in Measure for Measure* (Basingstoke, Hampshire: Palgrave, 2001).

17. Fulke Greville, *A Treatise on religion*, in *Fulke Greville. The Remains: Being Poems of Monarchy and Religion*, ed. G. A. Wilkes (Oxford: Oxford University Press, 1965), stanza 18, p. 206. For discussion, see Adrian Streete, *Protestantism and Drama in Early Modern England* (Cambridge, UK: Cambridge University Press, 2009), p. 92.

18. Greville, *Treatise on religion*, stanza 39, p. 212.

19. Thomas Adams, *The white deuil, or The hypocrite vncased* (London, 1613). I thank John Gillies for pointing me to this text. Further references will be made by image number in the body of the text.

20. John Milton, *Of Reformation Touching Church-Discipline in England and the Causes that hitherto have Hindred it*, in *CPWJM*, 1:519–617 (at p. 590).

21. John Milton, *The Tenure of Kings and Magistrates*, in *CPWJM*, 3:190–258 (at p. 242).

22. As reported by the royalist *Mercurius Pragmaticus* (edited by Marchmont Needham, who would soon switch back to serving the Parliamentary newspaper), for January 4–11, 1648; see *Mercurius pragmaticus* Number 17, image 5.

23. Charles I, King of England, *ODNB*.

24. Statistics drawn from *EEBO*, John Milton, *Eikonoklastes*.

25. For further discussion of Milton as iconoclast, see James Simpson, *Under the Hammer: Iconoclasm in the Anglo-American Tradition* (Oxford: Oxford University Press, 2010), ch. 4, and Chapter 10 of the present volume. Citation from *Eikonoklastes* will be taken from *CPWJM*, 3:337–601; citations will be made by page number in the body of the text.

26. For a searching account of Bunyan's heroic effort to be authentic, see Jason Crawford, *Allegory and Enchantment: An Early Modern Poetics* (Oxford: Oxford University Press, 2017), pp. 175–201.

27. John Bunyan, *Grace Abounding with Other Spiritual Autobiographies*, ed. John Stachniewski (Oxford: Oxford University Press, 1998), p. 42.

28. Bunyan, *Grace Abounding*, p. 53.

29. John Bunyan, *The Pilgrim's Progress*, ed. David Hawkes (New York: Barnes and Noble, 2005), p. 30. All further references to this edition will be made by page number in the body of the text.

30. e.g. *Faerie Queene*, 1.1.14–26; 1.8.12–22; 1.8.35–36.

31. The best scholarship I have encountered on *Pilgrim's Progress* is by John Stachniewski, *The Persecutory Imagination: English Puritanism and the Literature of Religious Despair* (Oxford; New York: Clarendon Press; Oxford University Press, 1991), ch. 4.

32. For the late seventeenth- and eighteenth-century history of toleration, see the convenient bibliographical summary in Jeffrey R. Collins, "Redeeming the Enlightenment: New Histories of Religious Toleration," *The Journal of Modern History* 81 (2009), 607–636. For the English context, see Alexandra Walsham, *Church Papists: Catholicism, Conformity, and Confessional Polemic in Early Modern England* (Woodbridge, Suffolk: Boydell Press, 1993), pp. 1–10. From the mid-seventeenth-century, see especially the writings of John Goodwin and William Walwyn, discussed in detail in David Loewenstein, *Treacherous Faith: The Specter of Heresy in Early Modern English Literature and Culture* (Oxford: Oxford University Press, 2013), pp. 238–256. For Walwyn, see also the fascinating account in William Haller, *Liberty and Reformation in the Puritan Revolution* (New York: Columbia University Press, 1955), pp. 162–175.

33. *SR*, 1 William and Mary, ch. 18, 6:74–76.

34. Collins, "Redeeming the Enlightenment," p. 609.

35. Collins, "Redeeming the Enlightenment," p. 609–613.

36. For Locke's biography, I am dependent on *ODNB*.

37. John Locke, *Two Treatises of Government, and a Letter Concerning Toleration*, ed. Ian Shapiro (New Haven, CT: Yale University Press, 2003), pp. 225–226. All citations in this chapter are drawn from the second treatise (Locke, *Two Treatises of*

Government, ed. Shapiro, pp. 100–211), and will be cited by page number of the Shapiro edition in the body of the text.

38. For which see Jenny Davidson, *Hypocrisy and the Politics of Politeness: Manners and Morals from Locke to Austen* (Cambridge, UK: Cambridge University Press, 2004).

9. Liberating Iconoclasm

1. For surveys and more focused studies, see Stanley J. Idzerda, "Iconoclasm during the French Revolution," *The American Historical Review* 60 (1954), 13–26; Horst Bredekamp, *Kunst Als Medium Sozialer Konflikte: Bilderkämpfe von der Spätantike bis zum Hussitenrevolution* (Frankfurt am Main: Suhrkamp, 1975); Marie-France Auzépy, *L'Iconoclasme* (Paris: Presses Universitaires de France, 2006); Helen Saradi-Mendelovici, "Christian Attitudes toward Pagan Monuments in Late Antiquity," *Dumbarton Oaks Papers* 44 (1990), 47–61; Dario Gamboni, *The Destruction of Art: Iconoclasm and Vandalism since the French Revolution* (London: Reaktion Books, 1997); and James Noyes, *The Politics of Iconoclasm: Religion, Violence and the Culture of Image-Breaking in Christianity and Islam* (London: I. B. Tauris, 2013).

2. For the Anglo-American model of that larger, generative tradition of image breaking, see James Simpson, *Under the Hammer: Iconoclasm in the Anglo-American Tradition* (Oxford: Oxford University Press, 2010).

3. For a profound and indispensable philosophical reflection on Hebraic iconoclasm and its many uptakes, properly classified under "idolatry," see Moshe Halbertal and Avishai Margalit, *Idolatry* (Cambridge, MA: Harvard University Press, 1992).

4. See Alexandra Walsham, *The Reformation of the Landscape: Religion, Identity, and Memory in Early Modern Britain and Ireland* (Oxford: Oxford University Press, 2011), and James Simpson, "Place," in *Cultural Reformations: Medieval and Renaissance in Literary History*, ed. Brian Cummings and James Simpson (Oxford: Oxford University Press, 2010), pp. 95–112.

5. Simpson, *Under the Hammer*, Introduction.

6. James P Walsh, "Holy Time and Sacred Space in Puritan New England," *American Quarterly* 32.1 (1980), 79–95 (at p. 79). See also James F. White, "From Protestant to Catholic Plain Style," in *Seeing beyond the Word: Visual Arts and the Calvinist Tradition*, ed. Paul Corby Finney (Grand Rapids, MI: W. B. Eerdmans, 1999), pp. 457–477.

7. The citation is drawn from Margaret Aston's magnificent book, *Broken Idols of the English Reformation* (Cambridge, UK: Cambridge University Press, 2016), p. 172.

8. For the very long history of the image moving from being sacred to being Art, see Hans Belting, *Likeness and Presence: A History of the Image before the Era of Art*, trans. Edmund Jephcott (Chicago, IL: University of Chicago Press, 1994; first pub. in German, 1990). For instances of this passage of sacred images to Art and to the museum in the Anglo-American tradition, see Simpson, *Under the Hammer*, chs. 1 and 4.

9. Margaret Aston, *England's Iconoclasts; Laws against Images* (Oxford: Clarendon Press, 1988), 1:371–392.
10. On Gregory, see Celia M. Chazelle, "Pictures, Books and the Illiterate: Pope Gregory I's Letters to Serenus of Marseilles," *Word and Image* 6 (1990), 138–153. For the ever-present threat of idolatry inhabiting late medieval art, see Michael Camille, *The Gothic Idol: Ideology and Image-Making in Medieval Art* (Cambridge, UK: Cambridge University Press, 1989).
11. See e.g. Denise Despres, *Ghostly Sights: Visual Meditation in Late-Medieval Literature* (Norman, OK: Pilgrim Books, 1989). For the tradition's most widely disseminated text, the *Meditationes vitae Christi* (composed between 1336 and 1364), see Sarah McNamer, "The Origins of the *Meditationes vitae Christi*," *Speculum* 84 (2009), 905–955.
12. For Wyclif's own, moderate views on images, see John Wycliffe, *Tractatus de mandatis divinis*, ed. Johann Loserth and F. D. Matthew (London: C. K. Paul, 1922), ch. 15, esp. pp. 152–162. For a detailed account of Wyclif's position, see Aston, *England's Iconoclasts*, pp. 98–104.
13. *Selections from English Wycliffite Writings*, ed. Anne Hudson (Toronto: University of Toronto Press, 1997; first pub. 1978), p. 27.
14. James Simpson, "Orthodoxy's Image Trouble: Images in and after Arundel's Constitutions," in *After Arundel: Religious Writing in Fifteenth-Century England*, ed. Vincent Gillespie and Kantik Ghosh (Turnhout, Belgium: Brepols, 2011), pp. 91–113.
15. For excellent summaries of the Lollard positions on images, see W. R. Jones, "Lollards and Images: The Defense of Religious Art in Later Medieval England," *Journal of the History of Ideas* 34 (1973), 27–50; Aston, *England's Iconoclasts*, ch. 4; Anne Hudson, *The Premature Reformation: Wycliffite Texts and Lollard History* (Oxford: Clarendon Press, 1988), pp. 301–309; and Kathleen Kamerick, *Popular Piety and Art in the Late Middle Ages: Image Worship and Idolatry in England, 1350–1500* (New York: Palgrave, 2002), pp. 19–27. See also Simpson, *Under the Hammer*, ch. 2.
16. For the text of the *Constitutions* regarding images, see *Concilia Magnae Britanniae et Hiberniae*, ed. David Wilkins, 4 vols. (London: Bowyer, Richardson, Purser, 1737), article 9, 3:317–318. The translation is by Sarah James, to whom I am grateful.
17. For which see Simpson, "Orthodoxy's Image Trouble"; Shannon Gayk, *Image, Text, and Religious Reform in Fifteenth Century England* (Cambridge, UK: Cambridge University Press, 2010); and Nicholas Watson, "Et que est huius ydoli materia? Tuipse': Idols and Images in Walter Hilton," in *Images, Idolatry and Iconoclasm in Late Medieval England*, ed. Jeremy Dimmick, James Simpson, and Nicolette Zeeman (Oxford: Oxford University Press, 2002), pp. 95–111.
18. Thomas More competes with Pecock for the accolade just given Pecock. See Thomas More, *A Dialogue Concerning Heresies*, in *CWSTM*, Book 1, ch. 2 (1:40–51); Book 1, ch. 19 (1:110–113), and Book 4, ch. 2 (1:356–359). For discussion, see Aston, *England's Iconoclasts*, pp. 174–194.

19. For which see Wendy Scase, *Reginald Pecock* (Aldershot, Hampshire: Variorum, 1996).
20. Reginald Pecock, *The Repressor of Over Much Blaming of the Clergy*, ed. Churchill Babington, 2 vols. (London, Longman, Green, Longman: and Roberts, 1860), pt. 2, ch. 2, p. 136. Spelling has been modernized. All further citation will be made from this edition by part, chapter, and page number in the body of the text.
21. For the proliferation of the private image in the late Middle Ages, see Belting, *Likeness and Presence*, ch. 19. See also Camille, *Gothic Idol*, p. 219, where Camille discusses the effect of what he calls the "image explosion" of the later Middle Ages.
22. See, for striking example, John Capgrave's fascinating *Life of St Katharine of Alexandria* (c. 1445), in which Katherine the saint comes very close to agreeing with Lollards about images in her rejection of the pagan emperor's proposal that he erect an image of her. See James Simpson, *Reform and Cultural Revolution, 1350–1547* (Oxford: Oxford University Press, 2002), pp. 420–429.
23. The magisterial authority is Aston, *England's Iconoclasts*. For the 1538 legislation, see pp. 220–246. See also Simpson, *Under the Hammer*, Introduction.
24. *Visitation Articles and Injunctions of the Period of the Reformation*, ed. Walter Howard Frere and William McClure Kennedy (London: Longmans, Green, 1910), 1:38.
25. Thomas Cranmer, *Miscellaneous Writings and Letters of Thomas Cranmer*, ed. John E. Cox (Cambridge, UK: Cambridge University Press, 1846), pp. 509–511.
26. For further discussion on iconoclasm, see Aston, *England's Iconoclasts*, pp. 249–250; *SR*, 3 and 4 Edward VI, c. 10 (1551/52), 4:110–111.
27. On pilgrimage see Eamon Duffy, *The Stripping of the Altars: Traditional Religion in England, c. 1400–c. 1580* (New Haven, CT: Yale University Press, 1992), p. 407. For examples of shrines being destroyed, see *Letters to Cromwell and Others on the Suppression of the Monasteries*, ed. G. H. Cook (London: John Baker, 1965).
28. "An Homily Against Peril of Idolatry," in The Church of England, *The seconde tome of homelyes* (London, 1563). I cite from the 1687 edition for ease of reference: *Certain sermons or homilies appointed to be read in churches in the time of Queen Elizabeth* (London, 1687), images 94–147 (at image 123). Further references will be made by image number in the body of the text. I cite from the *EEBO* facsimile because the modern edition of the Homilies—*Certain Sermons Or Homilies Appointed to be Read in Churches (1547); and, A Homily Against Disobedience and Wilful Rebellion (1570)*, ed. Ronald B. Bond (Toronto: University of Toronto Press, 1987)—does not unfortunately publish this crucial homily from the second, 1563 edition.
29. *The Complete Plays of John Bale*, ed. Peter Happé (Woodbridge, Suffolk: Brewer, 1986), 2:1–33. *God's Promises* was printed, with three other plays by Bale, in Wesel in 1547; see *Complete Plays of John Bale*, ed. Happé, p. 6. Further citations will be made by line number in the body of the text. Spelling is modernized where possible.

30. See e.g. Sodomy and Idolatry as minions of Infidelity in Bale's *Three Laws* (*Complete Plays of John Bale*, ed. Happé, l. 425). For the first statute against sodomy, see *SR*, 25 Henry VIII, c. 6, 3:441.

31. For Bale's categorization of witchcraft with idolatry, see James Simpson, "John Bale's *Three Laws*," in *The Oxford Handbook to Tudor Drama*, ed. Greg Walker and Tom Betteridge (Oxford: Oxford University Press, 2012), pp. 109–122, and Chapter 11 of the present book.

32. Thomas Becon, *The displaying of the Popish masse* (London, 1637; first pub. 1559), image 8.

33. John Knox, *The Appellation of John Knox*, in *Works*, ed. David Laing (Edinburgh: Wodrow Society, 1846–1864), 4:504. Cited in Aston, *Broken Idols*, pp. 68–69.

34. Knox, *The Appellation of John Knox*, in *Works*, ed. Laing, p. 507. Knox was not alone in Tudor Britain in calling for the death sentence for idolaters; see also Thomas Cartwright, *The second replie of Thomas Cartwright: agaynst Maister Doctor Whitgiftes second answer, touching the Churche discipline* (London, 1575), image 64. For discussion, see Aston, *England's Iconoclasts*, pp. 472–473.

35. Henry Barrow, *Brief Discoverie of the False Church*, in *The Writings of John Greenwood, 1587–1590: Together with the Joint Writings of Henry Barrow and John Greenwood, 1587–1590*, ed. Leland H. Carlson (London: Allen and Unwin, 1962), p. 470. Cited in Aston, *Broken Idols*, pp. 85–86.

36. Henry Barrow, *Brief Discoverie of the False Church*, ed. Carlson, p. 468.

10. Saving Images and the Calvinist Hammer

1. Most recently and with astonishing tenacity and breadth, Margaret Aston, *Broken Idols of the English Reformation* (Cambridge, UK: Cambridge University Press, 2016). See also Julie Spraggon, *Puritan Iconoclasm during the English Civil War* (Woodbridge, Suffolk: Boydell, 2003); and Nicholas Tyacke and Kenneth Fincham, *Altars Restored: The Changing Face of English Religious Worship, 1547–c.1700* (Oxford: Oxford University Press, 2007).

2. Margaret Aston, *England's Iconoclasts: Laws against Images* (Oxford: Clarendon Press, 1988), pp. 452–466 ("Idols of the Mind").

3. For Bacon's account of idolatry, see Francis Bacon, *Novum Organum. English & Latin; the Instauratio Magna. Part 2, Novum Organum and Associated Texts*, ed. Graham Rees and Maria Wakely (Oxford: Oxford University Press, 2004), ss. 38–62, pp. 79–99 (at pp. 79–81).

4. For which, see Aston, *England's Iconoclasts*, pp. 280–283.

5. *Visitation Articles and Injunctions*, ed. Walter Howard Frere and William McClure Kennedy (London: Longmans, Green, 1910), 3:2. Discussed in Aston, *England's Iconoclasts*, pp. 300–301.

6. "An Homily against Peril of Idolatry," in The Church of England, *The seconde tome of homelyes* (London, 1563). I cite from the 1687 edition for ease of reference:

Certain sermons or homilies (London, 1687), images 94–147 (at image 116). Further references will be made by image number in the body of the text.

7. Cited here in *Commentary on Romans*, trans. J. Theodore Mueller (Grand Rapids, MI: Kregel, 1976; first pub. 1954). Further citations from this edition will be made by page number in the body of the text. For Lutheran understanding of idolatry, see Joseph Leo Koerner, *The Reformation of the Image* (Chicago, IL: University of Chicago Press, 2004), pp. 94–102.

8. Luther, *Commentary on Romans*, trans. Mueller, p. xiii. Further references will be made by page number to this translation.

9. John Calvin, *Institutes of the Christian Religion*, ed. John T. McNeill, trans. Ford Lewis Battles (Philadelphia: The Westminster Press, 1960), 1:5, p. 65. This is an edition of the 1536 edition of Calvin's *Institutio Christianae Religionis*. For discussion of Calvin's understanding of iconoclasm, see James Noyes, *The Politics of Iconoclasm: Religion, Violence and the Culture of Image-Breaking in Christianity and Islam* (London: I. B. Tauris, 2013), pp. 23–58.

10. John Calvin, *Institutes of the Christian Religion*, ed. John T. McNeill, trans. Ford Lewis Battles (Philadelphia, PA: The Westminster Press, 1975), 1:11.8, p. 108. I have altered the translation of "fabricam" to "workshop." This is an edition of the 1536 edition of Calvin's *Institutio Christianae Religionis*.

11. For which see Aston, *Broken Idols*, pp. 236–239, and 254–255 (for the inspection of private homes in the 1640s).

12. *Visitation Articles and Injunctions*, ed. Frere and McClure, 2:189; discussed by Aston, *England's Iconoclasts*, p. 301.

13. "Fateor me ex animo crucifixi imaginem detestari"; cited from Aston, *Broken Idols*, p. 709.

14. Laurence Humphrey, *De religionis Conservatione et Reformatione Vera* (Basel, 1559), translation by Janet Karen Kemp, "Laurence Humphrey, Elizabethan Puritan: His Life and Political Theories" (PhD, West Virginia University, 1978), pp. 178–179. Cited in Karl Gunther, *Reformation Unbound: Protestant Visions of Reform in England, 1525–1590* (Cambridge, UK: Cambridge University Press, 2014), p. 125.

15. Patrick Collinson, *The Birthpangs of Protestant England* (Basingstoke, Hampshire: Macmillan, 1988), esp. pp. 115–121 for iconoclasm and iconophobia.

16. Citations from *Caelica* will be drawn from *Poems and Dramas of Fulke Greville, First Lord Brooke*, ed. Geoffrey Bullough (Edinburgh: Oliver and Boyd, 1939), and will be made by lyric and line number in the body of the text.

17. I have modernized the spelling since such modernization does not damage meter.

18. Shakespeare, Sonnet 27 ("Weary with toil"), l. 10. Cited from *The Norton Shakespeare*, gen. ed. Stephen Greenblatt, 3rd ed. (New York: W. W. Norton, 2016), p. 2259.

19. Edmund Spenser, *The Faerie Queene*, ed. Thomas P. Roche (London: Penguin, 1987). Further references to this poem will be made by book, canto, stanza, and line number in the body of the text.

20. For the relevant Aristotelian faculty psychology, see E. Ruth Harvey, *The Inward Wits: Psychological Theory in the Middle Ages and Renaissance* (London: Warburg Institute, 1975).

21. See e.g. "Bower of Bliss," in *The Spenser Encyclopedia*, gen. ed. A. C. Hamilton (Toronto: University of Toronto Press, 1990).

22. For which see James Simpson, *Sciences and the Self in Medieval Poetry: Alan of Lille's "Anticlaudianus" and John Gower's "Confessio amantis"* (Cambridge, UK: Cambridge University Press, 1995), pp. 148–166.

23. For Laudian reforms, see Tyacke and Fincham, *Altars Restored*, pp. 226–273. For the texts of the iconoclastic legislation of 1641, 1643, and 1644 by the Long Parliament, see Julie Spraggon, *Puritan Iconoclasm during the English Civil War* (Woodbridge, Suffolk: Boydell, 2003), Appendix I, pp. 257–261.

24. All citation from *The Winter's Tale* is drawn from *The Norton Shakespeare*, gen. ed. Greenblatt, 3rd ed. Citations will be made by act, scene, and line number in the body of the text.

25. I thank Stephen Greenblatt for discussion of this point and for his generous reading of an earlier version of some of this chapter.

26. Collinson, *Birthpangs of Protestant England*, p. 117.

27. Aston, *Broken Idols*, p. 228.

28. For which see James Simpson, *Under the Hammer: Iconoclasm in the Anglo-American Tradition* (Oxford: Oxford University Press, 2010), ch. 4, and further references.

29. Simpson, *Under the Hammer*, ch. 4 and further references.

30. See Chapters 12–14 of the present book for investigation of performative magic and theater in early modern England.

31. For the liturgical resonance, see *Regularis Concordia* (970s), in M. Bradford Bedingfield, *The Dramatic Liturgy of Anglo-Saxon England* (Woodbridge, Suffolk: Boydell Press, 2002), pp. 160–161. For the continuation of this ritual right up to the Reformation, see Eamon Duffy, *The Stripping of the Altars: Traditional Religion in England, c. 1400–c. 1580* (New Haven, CT: Yale University Press, 1992), pp. 29–30.

32. See Chapter 12 of the present book for the documentation of this point.

33. For which see Sarah Beckwith, "Shakespeare's Resurrections," in *Shakespeare and the Middle Ages*, ed. Curtis Perry and John Watkins (Oxford: Oxford University Press, 2009), pp. 45–67.

11. One Last Iconoclastic Push?

1. Anon, *The Crosses case in Cheapside; whether its militia, the setting of it in a posture of defence, be according to law* (London, 1642), image 20. Further references will be cited in the body of the text, by image number.

2. Edmund Spenser, *The Faerie Queene*, ed. Thomas P. Roche (London: Penguin, 1987). Further references to this poem will be made by book, canto, stanza, and line number in the body of the text.

3. John Milton, *Eikonoklastes*, in *CPWJM*, 3:3:337–601 (at p. 343). Further references to this text will be made from this edition by page number in the body of the text.

4. See further James Simpson, *Under the Hammer: Iconoclasm in the Anglo-American Tradition* (Oxford: Oxford University Press, 2010), ch. 3.

5. For the text, see *Puritanism and Liberty: Being the Army Debates (1647–9) from the Clarke Manuscripts with Supplementary Documents*, ed. A. S. P. Woodhouse and William Clarke, 3rd ed. (London: Dent, 1986), pp. 166–168. Discussed in Margaret Aston, *England's Iconoclasts: Laws against Images* (Oxford: Clarendon Press, 1988), p. 473.

6. Voltaire, "Idol-Idolater-Idolatry," in *The philosophical dictionary for the pocket* (London, 1765; first pub. in French in 1764), pp. 183–200 (at p. 184).

7. *Puritanism and Liberty*, ed. Woodhouse and Clarke, pp. 167–168.

8. Julie Spraggon, *Puritan Iconoclasm during the English Civil War* (Woodbridge, Suffolk: Boydell, 2003), Appendix I, pp. 257–258 (at p. 257). See also Nicholas Tyacke and Kenneth Fincham, *Altars Restored: The Changing Face of English Religious Worship, 1547–c.1700* (Oxford: Oxford University Press, 2007).

9. Spraggon, *Puritan Iconoclasm*, Appendix I, p. 258.

10. Spraggon, *Puritan Iconoclasm*, Appendix I, p. 261. For further discussion, see Margaret Aston, *Broken Idols of the English Reformation* (Cambridge, UK: Cambridge University Press, 2016), pp. 605–614. For the novelty of destroying images in "open space," see pp. 350 and 842–843.

11. Spraggon, *Puritan Iconoclasm*, Appendix I, p. 261.

12. John Morrill, "William Dowsing and the Administration of Iconoclasm in the Puritan Revolution," in *The Journal of William Dowsing: Iconoclasm in East Anglia during the English Civil War*, ed. Trevor Cooper (Woodbridge, Suffolk: Boydell, 2001), pp. 1–28.

13. Robert Ram, *The souldiers catechisme: composed for the Parliaments Army* (London, 1644), image 12.

14. Cited in Aston, *England's Iconoclasts*, p. 73.

15. Joseph Hall, *The shaking of the Olive-tree . . . Together with his Hard Measure* (London, 1660), image 40. See Aston, *England's Iconoclasts*, pp. 63–74, and Spraggon, *Puritan Iconoclasm during the English Civil War*, ch. 6 (at p. 186–188).

16. See Jason Rosenblatt, "'Audacious Neighborhood': Idolatry in *Paradise Lost*, Book I," *Philological Quarterly* 54 (1975), 553–568, Barbara Lewalski, "Milton and Idolatry," *Studies in English Literature, 1500–1900* 43 (2003), 213–232, and, for a vigorously prosecuted but in my view unpersuasive case, Daniel Shore, "Why Milton Is Not an Iconoclast," *PMLA* 127 (2012), 22–37.

17. John Milton, *Samson Agonistes*, in *John Milton, The Major Works*, ed. Stephen Orgel and Jonathan Goldberg (Oxford: Oxford University Press, 2003), pp. 671–715 (at p. 671). Further references to *Samson Agonistes* will be to this edition, and made by line number in the body of the text.

18. For a clear summary of critical debate with regard to *Sampson Agonistes,* see Joseph Wittreich, *Interpreting* Samson Agonistes (Princeton, NJ: Princeton University Press, 1986), pp. 3–52, and further references.

19. The first to point to this disquieting possibility, to which the grievous history of contemporary terrorism alerts us, was John Carey, "A Work in Praise of Terrorism? September 11 and *Samson Agonistes,*" *Times Literary Supplement,* 6 September 2002, pp. 15–16.

20. John Bunyan, *The Pilgrim's Progress,* ed. David Hawkes (New York: Barnes and Noble, 2005), p. 102. Further references are to this edition, and made by page number in the body of the text.

21. *SR,* 14 Charles II, c. 4 (1662), 5:364–70. This Act required ministers to assent to use of the Book of Common Prayer (p. 365). John Bunyan, *I will pray with the spirit* (London, 1663), images 19–20. The text is a sermon preached by Bunyan while briefly at liberty in c. 1662. For Bunyan's 1661 arrest and imprisonment under an Act of 1593, see "John Bunyan," ODNB.

22. See David Hawkes, *Idols of the Marketplace: Idolatry and Commodity Fetishism in English Literature, 1580–1680* (New York: Palgrave, 2001).

23. See Max Weber, *The Protestant Work Ethic and the Spirit of Capitalism,* trans. Talcott Parsons (New York: Scribner's Sons, 1958; first pub. in German, 1904), p. 36. For the process of the monasticization of the laity, see the superb study by Amy Appleford, *Learning to Die in London, 1380–1540* (Philadelphia: University of Pennsylvania Press, 2015), pp. 98–136. For some post-Reformation, seventeenth-century examples of lay regular communities, see Suzanne Trill, "Lay Households," in *The Oxford Handbook of Early Modern English Literature and Religion,* ed. Andrew Hiscock and Helen Wilcox (Oxford: Oxford University Press, 2017), pp. 397–413.

24. See Simpson, *Under the Hammer,* ch. 4, and further references.

12. Religion, Dramicide, and the Rise of Magic

1. For an especially authoritative defense and active promotion of this practice, see James VI, *Daemonology* (Edinburgh, 1597), ch. 6. Cited in *The Witchcraft Sourcebook,* ed. Brian P. Levack, 2nd ed. (Abingdon, Oxon: Routledge, 2015), ch. 29, pp. 159–161 (at p. 161).

2. Alexandra Walsham, "The Reformation and the 'Disenchantment of the World' Reassessed," *The Historical Journal* 51 (2008), 497–528.

3. For Weber's secularization thesis, see "Science as a Vocation," trans. Michael John, in *Max Weber's "Science as a Vocation,"* ed. Peter Lassman, Irving Velody, and Herminio Martins (London: Hyman, 1989), pp. 3–31.

4. Walsham, "Reformation," p. 510.

5. Euan Cameron, *Enchanted Europe: Superstition, Reason, and Religion, 1250–1750* (Oxford: Oxford University Press, 2010).

6. For Augustine's repudiation of the practice of demonic intervention, see Augustine of Hippo, *Concerning the City of God against the Pagans,* trans. David Knowles (Harmondsworth: Penguin, 1972), Books 8 and 9. *The City of God* was written c. 413–426. For discussion, see Richard Kieckhefer, "The Specific Rationality of Medieval Magic," *The American Historical Review* 99 (1994), 813–836 (at p. 819).

7. Edmund Spenser, *The Faerie Queene,* ed. Thomas P. Roche (London: Penguin, 1987), 3.11.16.6–9.

8. *OED,* "hocus pocus," is skeptical of the "hoc est corpus meum" etymology for no persuasive reason given. For the earlier instance of what is clearly the same phrase, see Samuel Harsnett, *A declaration of egregious popish impostures* (London, 1603). Harsnett lists the tricks needed to perform persuasive conjurations: "to teach her role her eyes, wrie her mouth, gnash her teeth, . . . and can mutter out two or three words of gibridg, as obus bobus."

9. William Perkins, *A golden chaine* (London 1600; first pub. 1591), image 31.

10. James Simpson, *Burning to Read: English Fundamentalism and Its Reformation Opponents* (Cambridge, MA: The Belknap Press of Harvard University Press, 2007), ch. 6.

11. For some recent guides into a large area, see *Witchcraft Sourcebook,* ed. Levack; James Sharpe, *Witchcraft in Early Modern England* (Harlow: Longman, 2002); and Peter Elmer, *Witchcraft, Witch-Hunting, and Politics in Early Modern England* (Oxford: Oxford University Press, 2016).

12. For the performative issues of early modern Eucharistic liturgy, see Jay Zysk, *Shadow and Substance: Eucharistic Controversy and English Drama across the Reformation Divide* (Notre Dame, IN: University of Notre Dame Press, 2017).

13. I thank Rebecca Kastleman and Derek Miller for help on the issue of theatrical censorship.

14. I come to that number by a simple count of how many plays in the York Cycle feature Christ as actor. See also Sarah Beckwith, *Signifying God: Social Relation and Symbolic Act in the York Corpus Christi Plays* (Chicago, IL: University of Chicago Press, 2001), pp. 39 and 101.

15. For evangelical attitudes toward theater, see Huston Diehl, *Staging Reform, Reforming the Stage: Protestantism and Popular Theater in Early Modern England* (Ithaca, NY: Cornell University Press, 1997); Paul Whitfield White, "Theater and Religious Culture," in *A New History of Early English Drama,* ed. John D. Cox and David Scott Kastan (New York: Columbia University Press, 1997), pp. 133–151; and Adrian Streete, *Protestantism and Drama in Early Modern England* (Cambridge, UK: Cambridge University Press, 2009).

16. My understanding of linguistic performativity is directly indebted, it perhaps goes without saying, to J. L. Austin, *How to Do Things with Words* (Cambridge, MA: Harvard University Press, 1962).

17. Su-kyung Hwang, "From Priests' to Actors' Wardrobe: Controversial, Commercial and Costumized Vestments," *SP* 113 (2016), 282–305, and further refer-

ences. For one example and further references, see Margaret Aston, *Broken Idols of the English Reformation* (Cambridge, UK: Cambridge University Press, 2016), p. 179, and n. 214. For the "symbolic aggression" of this transference from liturgy to theater, see Stephen Greenblatt, "Shakespeare and the Exorcists," in *Shakespearean Negotiations: The Circulation of Social Energy in Renaissance England* (Berkeley: University of California Press, 1988), pp. 94–128 (at p. 113).

18. Greenblatt, "Shakespeare and the Exorcists."

19. For the simultaneity of "medieval" and early modern theater, see the seminal essay by Richard K. Emmerson, "Contextualizing Performance: The Reception of the Chester *Antichrist*," *JMEMS* 29 (1999), 89–119.

20. Karl Young, *Drama of the Medieval Church*, 2 vols. (Oxford: Oxford University Press, 1933), vol. 1, chaps. 9–13.

21. I use the word "evolved," which has a very contentious history within the criticism of medieval drama, with deliberation, following the brilliant intervention of John Parker, "Who's Afraid of Darwin? A Whisper in the Ear of (Some) Medievalists," *JMEMS* 40 (2010), 7–35. Chester assigned the Play of the Assumption of the Virgin to the "wyfus of the town," for which see David M. Bevington, *From Mankind to Marlowe: Growth of Structure in the Popular Drama of Tudor England* (Cambridge, MA: Harvard University Press, 1962), p. 79. For a broader discussion of the representation and participation of women in the Chester Cycle, see Nicole R. Rice and Margaret Aziza Pappano, *The Civic Cycles: Artisan Drama and Identity in Premodern England* (Notre Dame, IN: University of Notre Dame Press, 2015), ch. 4. "Mystery," derived from Latin "*ministerium*," here meaning occupation, trade, has nothing to do with "mystery." For which see Beckwith, *Signifying God*, chs. 2 and 3.

22. Beckwith, *Signifying God*, chs. 4–6.

23. Lee Palmer Wandel, *The Eucharist in the Reformation: Incarnation and Liturgy* (Cambridge, UK: Cambridge University Press, 2006), p. 146.

24. For the position of Ulrich Zwingli (1484–1531), see Palmer Wandel, *Eucharist in the Reformation*, p. 72. This anti-Lutheran view made ready inroads into English evangelical circles from as early as 1532, for which see James Simpson, "Tyndale as Promoter of Figural Allegory and Figurative Language: *A Brief Declaration of the Sacraments*," *Archiv für das Studium der Neueren Sprachen und Literaturen* 245 (2008), 37–55, and further references. The phrase "effectual sign" is drawn from the *Thirty-Nine Articles of Religion*, in *The Book of Common Prayer: The Texts of 1549, 1559, and 1662*, ed. Brian Cummings (Oxford: Oxford University Press, 2011), Article 25 (p. 680) (taken from the 1662 Prayer Book; the Thirty-Nine Articles were ratified in 1571). For an extended and careful account of Calvin's eucharistic theology, see Palmer Wandel, *Eucharist in the Reformation*, pp. 139–166.

25. William Prynne, *Histriomastix* (London, 1633), image 75. Further references to this text will be made to the facsimile of the 1633 edition available in *EEBO*, by image number, in the body of the text. I am indebted for this reference to

Kurt A. Schreyer, *Shakespeare's Medieval Craft: Remnants of the Mysteries on the London Stage* (Ithaca, NY: Cornell University Press, 2014), p. 45.

26. *The York Plays*, ed. Richard Beadle (London: Edward Arnold, 1982), 3.33–36. All further citations will be from this edition, and made by play and line number in the body of the text. For a summary of scholarship on this cycle, see Richard Beadle, "The York Cycle," in *The Cambridge Companion to Medieval English Theatre*, ed. Richard Beadle (Cambridge, UK: Cambridge University Press, 1994), pp. 85–108.

27. For an overview of Bale's career, see Peter Happé, *John Bale* (New York: Twayne, 1996).

28. John Bale, *Three Laws*, in *The Complete Plays of John Bale*, ed. Peter Happé, 2 vols. (Cambridge: Brewer, 1985), ll. 50–52. All citations of Bale's plays are drawn from this edition, and will be cited by line number. For discussion and further references, see James Simpson, "John Bale's *Three Laws*," in *The Oxford Handbook to Tudor Drama*, ed. Greg Walker and Tom Betteridge (Oxford: Oxford University Press, 2012), pp. 109–122.

29. The phrase "unwritten verities" is a shorthand for one key aspect of the Catholic position with regard to Biblical textuality, for which see George H. Tavard, *Holy Writ or Holy Church?* (London: Burns and Oates, 1959).

30. John Bale, *A comedy concernynge thre lawes* (Wesel, 1548), image 45.

31. For unpersuasive skepticism about centrally driven evangelical religion being responsible for the closing of the cycles, see Bing Duane Bills, "The 'Suppression Theory' and the English Corpus Christi Plays: A Re-evaluation," *Theatre Journal* 32 (1980), 157–168; Richard K. Emmerson, "Dramatic History: On the Diachronic and Synchronic in the Study of Early English Drama," *JMEMS* 35 (2005), 39–66 (at p. 43); and David Klausner, Helen Ostovitch, and Jessica Dell, "Introduction: The Chester Cycle in Context," in *The Chester Cycle in Context, 1555–1575: Religion, Drama and the Impact of Change*, ed. David Klausner, Helen Ostovitch, and Jessica Dell (Farnham, Surrey: Ashgate, 2012), pp. 1–10. For equally unpersuasive resistance to evangelical anti-theatricalism and the closing of the London theaters in 1642–1660, see David Scott Kastan, "Performances and Playbooks: The Closing of the Theaters and the Politics of Drama," in *Refiguring Revolutions: Aesthetics and Politics from the English Revolution to the Romantic Revolution*, ed. Kevin M. Sharpe and Steven N. Zwicker (Berkeley: University of California Press, 1998), pp. 167–184. The "suppression theory" refers to the thesis of Harold C. Gardiner that the cycle plays were closed by concerted government action. See his *Mysteries' End: An Investigation of the Last Days of the Medieval Religious Stage* (New Haven, CT: Yale University Press, 1946). For a set of documents relating to the regulation of early modern English professional theater and its opposition, see *English Professional Theatre, 1530–1660*, ed. Glynne Wickham, Herbert Berry, and William Ingram (Cambridge, UK: Cambridge University Press, 2000).

32. *A Tretise of Miraclis Pleyinge*, in *Selections from English Wycliffite Writings*, ed. Anne Hudson (Cambridge, UK: Cambridge University Press, 1978), pp. 97–104; Gardiner, *Mysteries' End;* Jonas A. Barish, *The Antitheatrical Prejudice* (Berkeley: University of California Press, 1981), ch. 4. For both the 1642 and 1647 ordinances closing public theaters down, see the documents reproduced in *English Professional Theatre, 1530–1660*, ed. Wickham, Berry, and Ingram, p. 132.

33. Stephen Gosson, *Playes confuted in fiue actions* (London, 1582), image 18. Further references to this text will be made to the facsimile of the 1633 edition available in *EEBO*, by image number, in the body of the text.

34. For examples, see Barish, *Antitheatrical Prejudice*, ch. 4.

35. *SR*, 25 Henry VIII (1534), c. 6, 3:441. See Donald N. Mager, "John Bale and Early Tudor Sodomy Discourse," in *Queering the Renaissance*, ed. Margaret Hunt (Durham, NC: Duke University Press, 1994), pp. 141–161.

36. This and the following two paragraphs are drawn from James Simpson, "John Bale's *Three Laws*," in *The Oxford Handbook to Tudor Drama*, ed. Greg Walker and Tom Betteridge (Oxford: Oxford University Press, 2012), pp. 109–122.

37. *Three Lawes*, in *The Complete Plays of John Bale*, ed. Happé, p. 121.

38. The relevant statutes are as follows, beginning in 1542: *SR*, 33 Henry VIII, c. 8 (1542), 3:837; 5 Elizabeth 1, c. 16 (1562–3), 4.1:446–447; and 1 James 1, c. 12 (1604), 5:1028–1029.

39. *Three Lawes*, in *The Complete Plays of John Bale*, ed. Happé, p. 121.

40. John Bale, *An expostulation or complaynte agaynste the blasphemyes of a franticke papyst of Hamshyre* (London, 1552), image 18.

41. *The Examinations of Anne Askew*, ed. Elaine V. Beilin (Oxford: Oxford University Press, 1996), p. 145.

42. Perkins, *A golden chaine*, image 31.

43. For which see Paul Whitfield White, "Reforming Mysteries' End: A New Look at Protestant Intervention in English Provincial Drama," *JMEMS* 29 (1999), 121–147.

44. For the argument that the "Wakefield Cycle" is not a cycle, and that the sixteenth-century manuscript is not from Wakefield, see Pamela M. King, "Manuscripts, Antiquarians, Editors and Critics: The Historiography of Reception," in *The Routledge Research Companion to Early Drama and Performance*, ed. Pamela M. King (London: Routledge, 2017), pp. 277–295 (at pp. 285–287).

45. See also *The York Plays*, ed. Beadle, 33.56.

46. For discussion of the cycle plays' presentation of interrogation scenes, see James Simpson, *Reform and Cultural Revolution, 1350–1547* (Oxford: Oxford University Press, 2002), pp. 506, 513–516

47. See e.g. Anne Askew: "Then he asked me, why I had so few words?" *The Examinations of Anne Askew*, ed. Beilin, p. 51. See Ritchie D. Kendall, *The Drama of Dissent: The Radical Poetics of Nonconformity, 1380–1590* (Chapel Hill: University of North Carolina Press, 1986).

13. Enemies of the Revolution

1. Of course the "garbage" was considered by many as still sacred, which accounts for the popular protests at Bale's drama. For Bale being chased out of Kilkenny, Ireland, see John Bale, *The Vocacyion of Johan Bale*, ed. Peter Happé and John N. King (Binghamton, NY: Medieval and Renaissance Texts and Studies, 1990), p. 59.

2. R. I. Moore, *The Formation of a Persecuting Society: Power and Deviance in Western Europe, 950–1250* (Oxford: Blackwell, 1987). figures for the execution of witches are drawn from *The Witchcraft Sourcebook*, ed. Brian P. Levack, 2nd ed. (Abingdon, Oxon: Routledge, 2015), p. 269.

3. For the first commercial theatre opening in 1567, and not 1576 as is usually stated, see Andrew Gurr, *Playgoing in Shakespeare's London*, 2nd ed. (Cambridge, UK: Cambridge University Press, 1996), p. 13.

4. For lucid introductions to the institutional and commercial shapes of Elizabethan theater, see Holger Schott Syme, "The Theater of Shakespeare's Time," in *The Norton Shakespeare*, gen. ed. Stephen Greenblatt, 3rd ed. (New York: W. W. Norton, 2016), pp. 93–118, and Gurr, *Playgoing in Shakespeare's London*, pp. 13–31.

5. See Gurr, *Playgoing in Shakespeare's London*, p. 14, for a helpful map of theater placements up to and beyond 1600; see also Schott Syme, "Theater of Shakespeare's Time," pp. 94–97.

6. For Blackfriars, see Christopher Highley, "Theatre, Church and Neighbourhood in the Early Modern Blackfriars,"in *The Oxford Handbook of the Age of Shakespeare*, ed. R. Malcolm Smuts (Oxford: Oxford University Press, 2016), pp. 616–632 (at p. 617). I am grateful to Chris Highley for help with this matter. See also Gurr, *Playgoing in Shakespeare's London*, p. 23.

7. Steven Mullaney, *The Place of the Stage: License, Play and Power in Renaissance England* (Chicago, IL: University of Chicago Press, 1988), p. 8.

8. Mullaney, *Place of the Stage*, p. 9.

9. See *The Cambridge Companion to Medieval English Theatre*, ed. Richard Beadle (Cambridge, UK: Cambridge University Press, 1994). Cycle drama was very far from being the only form of pre-Reformation theater; see Jessica Brantley, "Middle English Drama beyond the Cycle Plays," *Literature Compass* 10 (2013), 331–342.

10. *SR*, 34–35 Henry VIII, c. 1, 3:894–895.

11. *TRP*, 1:341–342.

12. *TRP*, 1:517. For discussion of script approval, see Paul Whitfield White, *Theatre and Reformation: Protestantism, Patronage and Playing in Tudor England* (Cambridge, UK: Cambridge University Press, 1993), p. 57. See also *TRP*, 2:5–8. For discussion of the Tudor regulation of printing dramatic texts, see Greg Walker, *The Politics of Performance* (Cambridge, UK: Cambridge University Press, 1998), Appendix 1.

13. *TRP*, 2:115.

14. For the text of the new and regulatory functions of the Master of the Revels, see *The Norton Shakespeare*, gen. ed. Greenblatt, p. 40.

15. Jonas A. Barish, *The Antitheatrical Prejudice* (Berkeley: University of California Press, 1981), p. 83.

16. For scholarship's reticence, see Chapter 12, n. 28. For the role of economic factors see John C. Coldewey, "Some Economic Aspects of the Late Medieval Drama," in *Contexts for Early English Drama*, ed. Marianne G. Briscoe and John C. Coldewey (Bloomington, IN: Indiana University Press, 1989), pp. 77–101. For the available documentation for governmental surveillance and control of theater see *English Professional Theatre, 1530–1660*, ed. Glynne Wickham, Herbert Berry, and William Ingram (Cambridge, UK: Cambridge University Press, 2000).

17. Harold C. Gardiner, *Mysteries' End: An Investigation of the Last Days of the Medieval Religious Stage* (New Haven, CT: Yale University Press, 1946), p. 61. For further discussion, see Michael O'Connell, *The Idolatrous Eye: Iconoclasm and Theater in Early-Modern England* (New York: Oxford University Press, 2000), pp. 20–27.

18. *English Professional Theatre, 1530–1660*, ed. Wickham, Berry, and Ingram, p. 33.

19. Gardiner, *Mysteries' End*, p. 78. See also *English Professional Theatre, 1530–1660*, ed. Wickham, Berry, and Ingram, p. 69.

20. *The York Plays*, ed. Richard Beadle (London: Edward Arnold, 1982), Bakers' Play of "The Last Supper," pp. 230–231.

21. *The Chester Mystery Cycle: Essays and Documents*, ed. R. M. Lumiansky and David Mills (Chapel Hill: University of North Carolina Press, 1983), pp. 206–220.

22. Gardiner, *Mysteries' End*, p. 73.

23. See Nicole R. Rice and Margaret Aziza Pappano, *The Civic Cycles: Artisan Drama and Identity in Premodern England* (Notre Dame, IN: University of Notre Dame Press, 2015), p. 203. For the closing of Chester, in the context of Elizabethan anti-theatricality, see also Kurt A. Schreyer, *Shakespeare's Medieval Craft: Remnants of the Mysteries on the London Stage* (Ithaca, NY: Cornell University Press, 2014), ch. 2.

24. See the Theatres Act of 1968, available at www.legislation.gov.uk/ukpga/1968/54/contents. I am extremely grateful to Rebecca Kastleman for guidance in this matter.

25. *OED*, "maleficium": "An act of witchcraft performed with the aim of causing damage or injury," first cited (?)1613.

26. John Philips, *The Examination and confession of certaine wytches at Chensforde* [sic] *in the countie of Essex* (London, 1566), images 13 and 16.

27. See Peter Elmer, *Witchcraft, Witch-Hunting, and Politics in Early Modern England* (Oxford: Oxford University Press, 2016), p. 2.

28. See *The Witchcraft Sourcebook*, ed. Levack, p. 273. For Hopkins, see *ODNB*.

29. *SR*, 5 Elizabeth c. 16 (1563), 4.1:446–447.

30. See Thomas D. Hill, "The *æcerbot* Charm and Its Christian User," *Anglo-Saxon England* 6 (1977), 213–221. For this subject, I am indebted to the excellent dissertation of Alexis Becker, "Practical Georgics: Managing the Land in Medieval Britain" (PhD diss., Harvard University, 2015).

31. For both cases, see Ralph A. Griffiths, "The Trial of Eleanor Cobham: An Episode in the Fall of Duke Humphrey of Gloucester," *Bulletin of the John Rylands Library* 51 (1968–1969), 381–399.

32. For the *Canon Episcopi*, and its skepticism about the existence of malicious witchcraft, see *The Witchcraft Sourcebook*, ed. Levack, pp. 36–37. For the fact that Aquinas (d. 1274) "said nothing about witchcraft as such," see p. 38.

33. For the generally accepted historical inability to distinguish between Protestant and Catholic witch persecution, see Stuart Clark, *Thinking with Demons: The Idea of Witchcraft in Early Modern Europe* (Oxford: Oxford University Press, 1997), ch. 35. My argument about Protestant fear of performativity does suggest a confessional difference of accent.

34. See *SR*, 33 Henry VIII, c. 8 (1542), 3:837; 5 Elizabeth 1, c. 16 (1562–3), 4.1:446–447; and 1 James 1, c. 12 (1604), 5:1028–1029.

35. Thus the early fifteenth-century dialogue *Dives and Pauper* (c. 1410), which, while not Lollard, voices Lollard views. See *Dives and Pauper*, ed. Priscilla Heath Barnum, 2 vols. in 3 parts, *EETS* O.S. 275, 280, and 323 (Oxford: Oxford University Press, 1976, 1980, and 2004), Commandment 1.34, vol. 1:158.

36. Phil[l]ip Stubbes, *The second part of the anatomie of abuses* (London, 1583), image 21. Stubbes was in many respects anti-Presbyterian (see *ODNB*). Henry Holland, *A treatise against vvitchcraft* (London, 1590). George Gifford, *A discourse of the subtill practises of deuilles by vvitches and sorcerers* (London, 1587), and *A dialogue concerning witches and witchcraftes* (London, 1593). James VI of Scotland (later James I of England), *Daemonologie* (Edinburgh, 1597). William Perkins, *A discourse of the damned art of witchcraft* (London, 1610). Alexander Roberts, *A treatise of witchcraft* (London, 1616).

37. James I of England, *Daemonologie* (London, 1603).

38. Elmer, *Witchcraft*, p. 2.

39. For the very high profile of performative language in early modern witchcraft persecution, see Clark, *Thinking with Demons*, ch. 18.

40. Phillips, *Examination and confession of certaine wytches*, image 5.

41. *The Witchcraft Sourcebook*, ed. Levack, p. 249, and Phillips, *Examination and confession of certaine wytches*, image 23.

42. *The Witchcraft Sourcebook*, ed. Levack, p. 267.

43. *The Witchcraft Sourcebook*, ed. Levack, p. 267.

44. William Perkins, *A discourse of the damned art of witchcraft* (London, 1610), image 82.

45. J. L. Austin, *How to Do Things with Words* (Cambridge, MA: Harvard University Press, 1962), pp. 15–16.

46. James VI of Scotland, *Daemonologie* (Edinburgh, 1597), image 15.

47. Reginald Scot, *Discovery of witchcraft* (London, 1584), images 10–11.

48. John Jewel, *An Apology in Defense of the Church of England* (1848, first pub. 1562), in DLCPT, p. 64.

49. Alison Shell, *Shakespeare and Religion* (London: Arden Shakespeare, 2010), p. 30.

50. Stephen Gosson, *The schoole of abuse* (London, 1579); and *Playes confuted in fiue actions* (London, 1582); Phil[l]ip Stubbes, *The anatomie of abuses* (London 1583), image 87 (even if it should be remembered that this text is a dialogue); William Rankins, *A mirrour of monsters* (London, 1587).

51. Augustine frequently expresses his disgust for Roman theater, insisting at every point that it derives from pagan religion and that the "unclean spirits" of the pagan gods are actively involved in the disgraceful performances. See e.g. Augustine, *City of God*, 2.26. See both Barish, *Antitheatrical Prejudice*, pp. 38–65, and John Parker, *The Aesthetics of Anti-Christ: From Christian Drama to Christopher Marlowe* (Ithaca, NY: Cornell University Press, 2007), pp. 10–11 and 72–74.

52. *A Tretise of Miraclis Pleyinge*, ed. Clifford Davidson (Kalamazoo, MI: Medieval Institute Publications, 1993), ll. 526–534. See Ruth Nissé, "Reversing Discipline: The *Tretise of Miraclis Pleyinge*, Lollard Exegesis, and the Failure of Representation," *YLS* 11 (1997), 163–194.

53. William Prynne, *Histriomastix The players scourge* (London, 1633), image 20.

54. Prynne, *Histriomastix*, image 35.

14. Last Judgement

1. For which see James Simpson, *Reform and Cultural Revolution, 1350–1547* (Oxford: Oxford University Press, 2002), ch. 10, and further references.

2. For a crisp and critical summation of which, see Brian Cummings, *Mortal Thoughts: Religion, Secularity, & Identity in Shakespeare and Early Modern Culture* (Oxford: Oxford University Press, 2013), pp. 1–15.

3. 1536, 1539, 1547–1549, 1552, 1558/59. For a lucid narrative of which, see Peter Marshall, *Reformation England, 1480–1642*, 2nd ed. (London: Bloomsbury, 2012).

4. See Paul Whitfield White, *Theatre and Reformation: Protestantism, Patronage and Playing in Tudor England* (Cambridge, UK: Cambridge University Press, 1993).

5. *TRP*, 2:115. See also the Jacobean ban of 1606, prohibiting the name of God from being spoken on stage: Adrian Streete, "Drama," in *The Oxford Handbook of Early Modern English Literature and Religion*, ed. Andrew Hiscock and Helen Wilcox (Oxford: Oxford University Press, 2017), pp. 166–184 (at p. 168). For a survey of Tudor and Stuart theatrical censorship, see Richard Dutton, "Censorship," in *A New History of Early English Drama*, ed. John D Cox and David Scott Kastan (New York: Columbia University Press, 1997), pp. 287–304.

6. Thus Fulke Greville, *Mustapha* (pub. 1609); see *Selected Writings of Fulke Greville*, ed. Joan Reese (London: Athlone, 1973).

7. See the fascinating essay by Herbert F. Tucker, "After Magic: Modern Charm in History, Theory and Practice," *NLH* 48 (2017), 103–122.

8. The *OED* does not suggest this etymology. For a historical example of former images being repurposed as nursery dolls, with the word "ydoll" being used for "doll," see Margaret Aston, *Broken Idols of the English Reformation* (Cambridge, UK: Cambridge University Press, 2016), p. 181.

9. Citations are from Christopher Marlowe, *Doctor Faustus,* in *The Norton Anthology of English Literature,* gen. ed. Stephen Greenblatt, 9th ed. (New York: W. W. Norton, 2012), 1023–1057 [this is the 1604 text], Prologue, l. 19. Further citations will be made from this edition, by scene and line number in the body of the text.

10. Jay Zysk, *Shadow and Substance: Eucharistic Controversy and English Drama across the Reformation Divide* (Notre Dame, IN: University of Notre Dame Press, 2017), p. 120.

11. See Ruth Nissé, *Defining Acts: Drama and the Politics of Interpretation in Late Medieval England* (Notre Dame, IN: University of Notre Dame Press, 2005), ch. 4.

12. For a parallel argument see John Parker, *The Aesthetics of Anti-Christ: From Christian Drama to Christopher Marlowe* (Ithaca, NY: Cornell University Press, 2007), p. 197 and further references.

13. *A Tretise of Miraclis Pleyinge,* ed. Clifford Davidson (Kalamazoo, MI: Medieval Institute Publications, 1993), ll. 202–207.

14. Stephen Greenblatt, "Shakespeare and the Exorcists," in *Shakespearean Negotiations: The Circulation of Social Energy in Renaissance England* (Berkeley: University of California Press, 1988), pp. 94–128.

15. For later Jacobean anti-Catholic plays see the excellent study by Alison Shell, *Catholicism, Controversy, and the English Literary Imagination, 1558–1660* (Cambridge, UK: Cambridge University Press, 1999); Christopher Marlowe, *The Massacre at Paris,* in *The Complete Plays,* ed. Frank Romany and Robert Lindsey (London: Penguin, 2003). For an excellent discussion of the play in context, see David Womersley, *Divinity and State* (Oxford: Oxford University Press, 2010), pp. 136–140.

16. "It is a solace to the despairing to have had fellows in despair" (my free translation, guided by its sense in this context).

17. Cf. Hamlet's desire that his flesh "melt, / Thaw, and resolve itself into a dew" (1.5.129–130).

18. For Harsnett's career, see the *ODNB.*

19. Samuel Harsnett, *A declaration of egregious popish impostures* (London 1603), image 64: "Campian, with the rest of the Martyrs, that had suffered at Tiburne, and by applying of their holy reliques, vnto the afflicted body: Frateretto, Fliberdigibet, Hoberdicut, Cocabatto, with fourtie assistants, were expelled." Further citations of this text will be made to the 1603 edition, and cited by image number in the body of the text. For discussion, see Greenblatt, "Shakespeare and the Exorcists"; see p. 94 and further references for the scholarly history of connecting Harsnett and Shakespeare.

20. Thus, the black magic from Catholic sacramentalism: Harsnett, *Declaration,* e.g. images 3, 36, 60. For this being derived from polytheism: e.g. images 64, 72.

21. "Campian and Brian" refer to the Catholic priests Edmund Campion and Alexander Briant, executed for treason, along with a third priest Ralph Sherwin, by being hanged, drawn, and quartered, on 1 December 1581.

22. William Shakespeare, 1 *Henry VI*, in *The Norton Shakespeare*, gen. ed. Stephen Greenblatt, 3rd ed. (New York: W. W. Norton, 2016), 3.2.37. Further references are to this edition, made by act, scene, and line number in the body of the text.

23. For the extended Witchcraft Act of 1604: 1 James 1, c. 12 (1604), 5:1028–1029.

24. James VI, *Daemonologie in forme of a dialogue* (Edinburgh, 1597), image 46.

25. William Shakespeare, *The Tempest*, in *The Norton Shakespeare*, gen. ed. Stephen Greenblatt, 3rd ed. (New York: W. W. Norton, 2016), 5.1.54–57. Further references are to this edition, made by act, scene, and line number in the body of the text.

26. John Jewel, *Certaine sermons preached before the Queenes Maiestie* (London, 1583), image 98.

27. Jewel, *Certaine sermons*, image 99.

28. The characterizations of the romance structure of *A Midsummer Night's Dream* to follow are all discussed at greater length in James Simpson, "Derek Brewer's Romance," in *A Modern Medievalist: Traditions and Innovations in the Study of Medieval Literature*, ed. Charlotte Brewer and Barry Windeatt (Cambridge, UK: Boydell and Brewer, 2013), pp. 154–172.

29. For the Greek models, see Elizabeth Archibald, "Ancient Romance," *A Companion to Romance from Classical to Contemporary*, ed. Corinne Saunders (Oxford: Blackwell, 2004), pp. 10–25.

30. John Bale, *Three Laws*, in *The Complete Plays of John Bale*, ed. Peter Happé, 2 vols. (Cambridge: Brewer, 1985), Vol. 2, ll. 441–449.

31. Harsnett, *Declaration*, image 72.

32. For debts to Chaucer see Ann Thompson, *Shakespeare's Chaucer: A Study in Literary Origins* (Liverpool: Liverpool University Press, 1978), pp. 88–94, and Misha Teramura, "Shakespeare and Chaucer: Influence and Authority on the Renaissance Stage" (PhD diss., Harvard University, 2016), ch. 2.

33. Samuel Harsnett, *A discouery of the fraudulent practises of Iohn Darrel* (London, 1599), image 3.

34. Stephen Greenblatt, "General Introduction," in *The Norton Shakespeare*, gen. ed. Stephen Greenblatt, 3rd ed. (New York: W. W. Norton, 2016), pp. 1–74 (at p. 32).

35. Robert Herrick, "Oberon's Chappell," in *The Complete Poetry of Robert Herrick*, ed. Tom Cain and Ruth Connolly, 2 vols. (Oxford: Oxford University Press, 2013), number 223, pp. 8689, ll. 12–18. Rimmon is a Syrian god.

36. Ben Jonson, *The Masque of Queens*, in *Ben Jonson: Selected Masques*, ed. Stephen Orgel (New Haven, CT: Yale University Press, 1970), p. 92.

37. John Milton, *A maske presented at Ludlow Castle, 1634*, in *John Milton, The Major Works*, ed. Stephen Orgel and Jonathan Goldberg (Oxford: Oxford University Press, 2003), pp. 44–71. Further references to this text will be from this edition, made by line number in the body of the text.

38. *English Professional Theatre, 1530–1660*, ed. Glynne Wickham, William Gladstone, Herbert Berry, and William Ingram (Cambridge, UK: Cambridge University Press, 2000), p. 132.

39. David Scott Kastan, "Performances and Playbooks: The Closing of the Theaters and the Politics of Drama," in *Reading, Society and Politics in Early Modern England,* ed. Kevin Sharpe and Steven N. Zwicker (Cambridge, UK: Cambridge University Press, 2003), pp. 167–184.

40. Kastan, "Performances and Playbooks," p. 169.

41. For Prynne and Puritanism, see the *ODNB.*

42. e.g. William Ames, *A fresh suit against human ceremonies in God's vvorship* (London, 1633), image 72; Henry Ainsworth, *Covnterpoyson considerations touching the poynts in difference between the godly ministers and people of the Church of England* (London, 1642; two editions; first pub. Amsterdam 1608), image 76; Anon, *A Confvtation of M. Lewes Hewes his dialogve* (London, 1641), image 21; Lancelot Andrews, *The morall law* (London, 1642), image 244.

43. *SR* 9 Geo. 2 c. 5.

44. John Milton, *Samson Agonistes,* in *John Milton, The Major Works,* ed. Stephen Orgel and Jonathan Goldberg (Oxford: Oxford University Press, 2003), ll. 1605–1610. Further reference will be made to this edition in the body of the text by line number. For Milton's "expulsion" of Shakespeare, see Nigel Smith, *Literature and Revolution in England, 1640–1660* (New Haven, CT: Yale University Press, 1994), p. 17.

45. For Milton's own identifications with Samson earlier in his career, see David Loewenstein, *Milton and the Drama of History: Historical Vision, Iconoclasm, and the Literary Imagination* (Cambridge, UK: Cambridge University Press, 1990), pp. 127–128. Loewenstein discusses the iconoclastic and anti-theatrical context of Samson's destruction (pp. 136–141). For a more sympathetic reading of Samson's violence, and a crisp survey of recent critical positions with regard to *Samson Agonistes,* see Susanne Woods, "Inviting Rival Hermeneutics: Milton's Language of Violence and the Invitation to Freedom," in *Milton's Rival Hermeneutics,* ed. Richard J. DuRocher and Margaret Olofson Thickstun (Pittsburgh, PA: Duquesne University Press, 2012), pp. 3–16.

15. Scripture

1. Alistair E. McGrath, *Christianity's Dangerous Idea: The Protestant Revolution—A History from the Sixteenth Century to the Twenty-First* (New York: Harper, 2007), p. 53.

2. McGrath, *Christianity's Dangerous Idea,* p. 53. See also David Daniell, *The Bible in English: Its History and Influence* (New Haven, CT: Yale University Press, 2003), pp. 126, 130.

3. See Sebastian Sobecki, *Unwritten Verities: The Making of England's Vernacular Legal Culture, 1463–1549* (Notre Dame, IN: University of Notre Dame Press, 2015).

4. For which see the brilliant and often theological essay by Milad Doueihi, *Pour un Humanisme Numerique* (Paris: Seuil, 2011).

5. Stephen Greenblatt, "The Word of God in an Age of Mechanical Reproduction," in *Renaissance Self-Fashioning: From More to Shakespeare* (Chicago, IL: University of Chicago Press, 1980), pp. 74–114. For the depth of reading culture in the English Reformation, see Alec Ryrie, *Being Protestant in Reformation England* (Oxford: Oxford University Press, 2013), ch. 11.

6. Diarmaid MacCulloch, *Reformation: Europe's House Divided* (London: Allen Lane, 2003), pp. 485–501.

7. See Alistair Fox, *Thomas More: History and Providence* (Oxford: Blackwell, 1982), pp. 71–74.

8. See Chapter 1.

9. C. Paul Christianson, "The Rise of London's Book Trade," in *The Book in Britain*, vol. 3: *1400–1557*, ed. Lotte Hellinga and J. B. Trapp (Cambridge, UK: Cambridge University Press, 2008), pp. 128–147. For early modern library formation, see Jennifer Summit, *Memory's Library: Medieval Books in Early Modern England* (Chicago, IL: University of Chicago, 2008).

10. See D. M. Loades, "The Theory and Practice of Censorship in Sixteenth-Century England," in his *Politics, Censorship, and the English Reformation* (London: Pinter, 1991), pp. 96–108, and Cyndia Susan Clegg, "Tudor Literary Censorship," in Oxford Handbooks Online, www.oxfordhandbooks.com/browse?to=ORR:AHU01560.

11. See David Daniell, *Bible in English*, p. 249, for dates of Biblical translations in other European states, most of which were produced in the late fifteenth century.

12. For late medieval literacy: M. T. Clanchy, *From Memory to Written Record: England 1066–1307*, 2nd ed. (Oxford: Oxford University Press, 1993). For later medieval writing and trust: Richard Firth Green, *A Crisis of Truth: Literature and Law in Ricardian England* (Philadelphia: University of Pennsylvania Press, 2002). For likely literacy rates of 10–15 percent of English people in the 1530s, see Ian Green, *Print and Protestantism in Early Modern England* (Oxford: Oxford University Press, 2000), p. 26. For early modern print practice and Protestantism: Green, *Print and Protestantism in Early Modern England*. For early modern history of the material book: *Book in Britain*, vol. 3: *1400–1557*, ed. Hellinga and Trapp.

13. Elizabeth L. Eisenstein, *The Printing Press as an Agent of Change: Communications and Cultural Transformation in Early-Modern Europe*, 2 vols. (Cambridge, UK: Cambridge University Press, 1979).

14. Richard Helgerson, *Forms of Nationhood: The Elizabethan Writing of England* (Chicago, IL: University of Chicago Press, 1992), and Cathy Shrank, *Writing the Nation in Reformation England, 1530–1580* (Oxford: Oxford University Press, 2004).

15. For the history of late antique and medieval Biblical scholarship, see Henri de Lubac, *Exégèse médiévale: les quatres sens de l'Écriture*, vols. 41, 42, and 59 of *Théologie*, 2 vols. in 4 (Paris: Aubier, 1959–1964), and Gilbert Dahan, *L'Exégése Chrétienne de la Bible en Occident Médiéval XII-XIV siècle* (Paris: Cerf, 1999).

16. See *JMEMS* 47 (2017), "English Bibles and Their Readers, 1400–1700," ed. Thomas Fulton, which leads the way.

17. See David Lawton, "Englishing the Bible," in *The Cambridge History of Medieval English Literature*, ed. David Wallace (Cambridge, UK: Cambridge University Press, 1999), pp. 454–482.

18. *The Holy Bible . . . made from the Vulgate by John Wycliffe and His Followers*, ed. Josiah Forshall and Frederic Madden, 4 vols. (Oxford: Oxford University Press, 1850). For a conspectus of scholarship on the Wycliffite Bible, see Anne Hudson, *The Premature Reformation: Wycliffite Texts and Lollard History* (Oxford: Clarendon Press, 1988), pp. 228–247. See also Lawton, "Englishing the Bible," and the important book by Mary Dove, *The First English Bible: The Text and Context of the Wycliffite Versions* (Cambridge, UK: Cambridge University Press, 2007).

19. See Introduction, n. 21

20. David Daniell, *William Tyndale, A Biography* (New Haven, CT: Yale University Press, 1994), and David Daniell, *Bible in English*, pp. 133–159. This book has descriptive chapters on each of the Bibles listed in the following discussion.

21. *The New Testament* (Cologne, 1525). For all the Bible translations between 1525 and 1611 surveyed here, see also Green, *Print and Protestantism in Early Modern England*, pp. 45–100. *EEBO* does not possess this facsimile. Neither does it possess the Worms facsimile.

22. E.g. *The New Testament* (Cologne, 1525), image 11.

23. *The Pentateuch* (Antwerp, 1530), also supplied with explicitly anti-papal marginalia (e.g. image 19).

24. *The prophete Ionas with an introduccion* (Antwerp, 1531).

25. *The new Testament as it was written* (Antwerp, 1534). This text is very sparely supplied with marginal comment, which is non-polemical.

26. *Biblia the Bible, that is, the holy Scripture of the Olde and New Testament* (?Cologne, 1535), a text without discursive annotation. See Daniell, *Bible in English*, pp. 173–189 (at p. 174).

27. *The Byble which is all the holy Scripture* (London, 1537); marginal annotation is very spare and non-polemical.

28. *The Byble in Englyshe that is to saye the content of all the holy scrypture, both of ye olde and newe testament* (London, 1539). The text has no discursive marginal annotation. For the official status and promotion of this translation, see *Concilia Magnae Britanniae et Hiberniae*, ed. David Wilkins (London: Bowyer, Richardson, Purser, 1737), 3:815.

29. *Concilia*, ed. Wilkins, 3:815.

30. See the plausible calculations of Daniell, *The Bible in English*, p. 135, n. 9. See also Green, *Print and Protestantism in Early Modern England*, pp. 50–52.

31. See Jean-François Gilmont, "Protestant Reformations and Reading," in *A History of Reading in the West*, ed. Guiglielmo Cavallo and Roger Chartier, trans. Lydia G. Cochrane (Cambridge, UK: Polity Press, 1999), pp. 213–237 (at p. 216).

32. Green, *Print and Protestantism in Early Modern England*, p. 50.

33. *The Holie Bible conteynyng the olde Testament and the newe* (London, 1568).

34. *The Nevve Testament of our Lord Iesus Christ* (Geneva, 1557), and *The Bible and Holy Scriptures conteyned in the Olde and Newe Testament* (Geneva, 1560). The citation is from Green, *Print and Protestantism in Early Modern England*, p. 73.

35. For overall format figures between 1530 and 1640, see Green, *Print and Protestantism in Early Modern England*, pp. 57 and 76. There is a sharp spike in quarto and octavo figures from 1610 to 1640.

36. Thus, for example, *The Bible and Holy Scriptures conteyned in the Olde and Newe Testament* (Geneva, 1560), Romans 9:15 at image 267. Many of the marginalia were not, however, polemically Calvinist: see Green, *Print and Protestantism in Early Modern England*, p. 75. For specific studies of the marginalia to the Geneva Bible, see George Moore, "'The Ornament of the Law': Vestments and the Translation of Judaism in the Geneva Bible," *Prose Studies: History, Theory, Criticism* 37 (2015), 161–180; and Thomas Fulton, "Toward a New Cultural History of the Geneva Bible," *JMEMS* 47 (2017), 487–516.

37. Thomas Fulton, "English Bibles and Their Readers," *JMEMS* 47 (2017), 415–435 (at p. 415).

38. *Nevv Testament of Iesus Christ, translated faithfully into English* (Rhemes, 1582); *The holie Bible faithfully translated into English, out of the authentical Latin* (Douai, 1609–1610).

39. *Nevv Testament of Iesus Christ, translated* (Reims, 1582), images 18, 19, 23 respectively.

40. *The Holie Bible conteynig the Old Testament, and the New* (London, 1611).

41. William Barlow, *The Summe and Substaunce of the Conference* (London 1604), image 28.

42. For Thomas More's very cautious promotion of vernacular scriptures, see his *A Dialogue Concerning Heresies*, in *CWSTM*, 6:331–344. For a conspectus of More's views on the appropriateness of a vernacular Bible, see Heinz Holeczek, *Humanistische Bibelphilologie als Reformproblem bei Erasmus von Rotterdam, Thomas More und William Tyndale* (Leiden: Brill, 1975), pp. 359–394.

43. For the Lollard version of sola-scriptura, see Anne Hudson, *The Premature Reformation: Wycliffite Texts and Lollard History* (Oxford: Clarendon Press, 1988), p. 389, for summary; and Kantik Ghosh, *The Wycliffite Heresy: Authority and the Interpretation of Texts* (Cambridge, UK: Cambridge University Press, 2002).

44. Cited in Luther's *Werke*, accessed at http://luther.chadwyck.com, *Schriften*, vol. 1, p. 236.

45. Martin Luther, *To the Christian Nobility of the German Nation*, in *Luther's Works*, 44, *The Christian in Society*, 1, ed. James Atkinson (Philadelphia, PA: Fortress Press, 1966), pp. 123–217 (at p. 133).

46. Luther, "Luther at the Diet of Worms, 1521," in *Luther's Works*, 32, *Career of the Reformer*, 2, ed. George W. Forell (Philadelphia, PA: Muhlenberg Press, 1958), pp. 101–132 (at p. 113). For the German insertion, see *Luther's Werke* (http://luther.chadwyck.com), 7:838a.

47. For further discussion, see James Simpson, *Burning to Read: English Fundamentalism and Its Reformation Opponents* (Cambridge, MA: The Belknap Press of Harvard University Press, 2007), ch. 4, and further references.

48. For a rich account of this fundamental issue, see George H. Tavard, *Holy Writ or Holy Church?* (London: Burns and Oates, 1959). For the issue in England, see Peter Marshall, "The Debate over 'Unwritten Verities' in Early Reformation England," in *Protestant History and Identity in Sixteenth-Century Europe*, ed. Bruce Gordon (Aldershot, Hampshire: St Andrews Studies in Reformation History, 1996), 1:60–77.

49. William Tyndale, *An Answer unto Sir Thomas Mores Dialogue*, ed. Anne M. O'Donnell and Jared Wicks (Washington, D.C.: The Catholic University of America Press, 2000), p. 23.

50. See Simpson, *Burning to Read*, ch. 5.

51. For More's forceful, witty, and legalistic defense of Church Councils, see More, *Confutation of Tyndale's Answer*, in *CWSTM*, 8, 3 Parts, 2:921–942.

52. Thomas Cranmer, *The Confutation of Unwritten Verities* (1556), in Thomas Cranmer, *Miscellaneous Writings and Letters of Thomas Cranmer*, ed. John E. Cox (Cambridge, UK: Cambridge University Press, 1846), pp. 7–19.

53. Luther, "Luther at the Diet of Worms, 1521," in *Luther's Works*, 32, *Career of the Reformer*, 2, ed. Forell, p. 111.

54. Luther, *On the Bondage of the Will*, in *Luther and Erasmus: Free Will and Salvation*, trans. E. Gordon Rupp, A. N. Marlow, Philip S. Watson, and B. Drewery (Philadelphia, PA: The Westminster Press, 1969), p. 129.

55. Martin Luther, *Against the Robbing and Murderous Hordes*, in *Luther's Works*, 46, *The Christian in Society*, 3, ed. Robert C. Schultz (Philadelphia, PA: Fortress Press, 1967), p. 49–55. Further citations of this text will be made by page number in the body of the text.

56. For Luther's rapid retreat from promotion of unmediated Bible reading, see Richard L. Gawthrop and Gerald Strauss, "Protestantism and Literacy in Early Modern Germany," *Past and Present* 104 (1984), 31–55. They argue that until 1525, Luther favored "everyman as his own Bible reader; thereafter he falls silent and effectively discouraged the unmediated encounter between sacred scripture and the untrained lay mind" (p. 34).

57. Cited in Brad M. Gregory, "Reforming the Reformation: God's Truth and the Exercise of Power," in *Reforming Reformation*, ed. Thomas F. Mayer and Ronald F. Thiemann (Farnham, Surrey: Ashgate, 2012), pp. 17–41 (at p. 24).

58. On the sacramental system, see Eamon Duffy, *The Stripping of the Altars: Traditional Religion in England, c. 1400–c. 1580* (New Haven, CT: Yale University Press, 1992), pp. 393–394 (for Purgatory); pp. 398 and 407 (for pilgrimage). For the effective abolition of the sacrament of penance, see the "Ten Articles" of 1536, in *Religion and Society in Early Modern England: A Sourcebook*, ed. David Cressy and Lori Anne Ferrell (London: Routledge, 1996), pp. 18–20; on iconic apparatus, see Margaret Aston, *England's Iconoclasts; Laws against Images* (Oxford:

Clarendon Press, 1988); on traditions of the saints, see Duffy, *Stripping of the Altars*, pp. 393, 443.

59. For theatrical perfomances, see Chapter 14 of the present book. For visionary writing, see James Simpson, "Visionary Writing in England, 1534–1550s," *The Cambridge Companion to Medieval Mysticism*, ed. Vincent Gillespie and Samuel Fanous (Cambridge, UK: Cambridge University Press, 2011), pp. 249–264.

60. Hooker, *Of the Laws of Ecclesiastical Polity*, in *The Folger Library Edition of the Works of Richard Hooker*, gen. ed. Speed Hill, 4.2.3.1, p. 280.

61. *The Book of Common Prayer: The Texts of 1549, 1559, and 1662*, ed. Brian Cummings (Oxford: Oxford University Press, 2011), p. 675.

62. Coverdale, *Biblia the Byble*, image 6.

63. *Goostly psalmes and spirituall songes drawen out of the holy Scripture* (London, 1535?), image 3. Coverdale is echoing Erasmus's *Paraclesis* here: see Erasmus, *Paraclesis*, in his *Novum Instrumentum* (Basel, 1516), facsimile edition, ed. Heinz Holeczek (Stuttgart: Fromann, 1986), aaa3v—aaa6v. The first English translation was first published in 1529: *An exhortation to the diligent studye of scripture, made by Erasmus Roterodamus* (Antwerp, 1529). See image 6 for Coverdale's source text.

64. Luther, *Assertio omnium articulorum per bullam Leonis X. novissimam damnatorum*, in *Luther's Werke* (http://luther.chadwyck.com), 7:94–151 (at p. 97). See also Walter Mostert, "Scriptura Sui Ipsius Interpres. Bemerkungen zum Verständnis der heligen Schrift durch Luther," *Luther-Jahrbuch* 46 (1979), 60–96, and, for Erasmus's perceptive critique of this Lutheran reading principle, C. Augustin, "Hyperaspistes I: la doctrine d'Érasme et de Luther sur la *claritas scripturae*," in *Colloquia Erasmiana Turonensia* (Paris : Vrin, 1972), 2:737–748.

65. See James Simpson, "Tyndale as Promoter of Figural Allegory and Figurative Language: *A Brief Declaration of the Sacraments*," *Archiv für das Studium der Neueren Sprachen und Literaturen* 245 (2008), 37–55.

66. Simpson, "Tyndale as Promoter of Figural Allegory."

67. More, *A Dialogue Concerning Heresies*, in *CWSTM* 6, 1:286–291 for "priest," "church," "charity," and "penance."

68. Thomas More, *The Confutation of Tyndale's Answer*, in *CWSTM* 8, 3 Parts, 1:164–173, for "congregation" versus "church." Tyndale had responded point by point to attacks of this kind made in the *Dialogue Concerning Heresies*: see William Tyndale, *An Answere unto Sir Thomas Mores Dialogue*, ed. Anne M. O'Donnell and Jared Wicks (Washington, D.C.: The Catholic University of America Press, 2000), pp. 13–23.

69. Tyndale, *Tyndale's New Testament*, ed. Daniell, p. 3.

70. Tyndale, *Tyndale's Old Testament*, ed. Daniell, p. 3.

71. John Foxe, *The Acts and Monuments Online*, 1570 edition, Book 8, p. 1271.

72. Tyndale, 'The Preface . . . that he made before . . . Genesis', in *Tyndale's Old Testament*, ed. David Daniell (New Haven, CT: Yale University Press, 1992), p. 8.

73. See Simpson, *Burning to Read*, ch. 3.

74. *SR*, 34 Henry 8 (1542), 3:894.

75. *SR*, 34 Henry 8 (1542), 3:894
76. *SR*, 34 Henry 8 (1542), 3:896.
77. *SR*, 34 Henry 8 (1542), 3:897, ch. 17.
78. Christopher St German, *An Answer to a Letter* (London, 1535). See John Guy, "Scripture as Authority: Problems of Interpretation in the 1530s," in Alistair Fox and John Guy, *Reassessing the Henrician Era: Humanism, Politics and Reform 1500–1550* (Oxford: Blackwell, 1986), pp. 199–220.
79. For Tyndale's understanding of "feeling faith," see Simpson, *Burning to Read*, ch. 4.
80. Tyndale, *Answer unto Sir Thomas More's Dialogue*, ed. O'Donnell, p. 47.
81. For especially clear statements by Luther to this effect, see Augustin, "*Hyperaspistes* I: la doctrine d'Érasme et de Luther sur la *claritas scripturae*," at pp. 74–42.
82. Tyndale, *Tyndale's New Testament*, ed. Daniell, p. 3. For a more virulent account of the plagues that will befall the non-elect who cannot read Scripture properly, see John Champneys, *The harvest is at hand, wherin the tares shall be bound, and cast into the fyre and brent* (London, 1548), image 14.

16. Private Scriptural Anguish

1. Katherine Little, *Confession and Resistance: Defining the Self in Late Medieval England* (Notre Dame, IN: University of Notre Dame Press), p. 90.
2. Christopher Marlowe, *Doctor Faustus*, in *The Norton Anthology of English Literature*, gen. ed. Stephen Greenblatt, 9th ed. (New York: W. W. Norton, 2012), 1023–1057 (this is the 1604 text), Scene 1.39.
3. Michel de Montaigne, *Les Essais de Michael de Montaigne*, ed. Pierre Villey, 2nd ed. (Paris: Presses Universitaires de France, 1978; first pub. 1924), Book 3.13, p. 1069. See Brian Cummings, *The Literary Culture of the Reformation: Grammar and Grace* (Oxford: Oxford University Press, 2002), p. 16.
4. Thus, for example, two best sellers: Calvin's *Institution of Christian Religion* (London, 1587) weighs in at 507 pages; or William Perkins's *A Golden Chaine* (London, 1592), at 334 pages.
5. For examples of all these aids, and more, see Ian Green, *Print and Protestantism in Early Modern England* (Oxford: Oxford University Press, 2000), pp. 113–151.
6. James Simpson, *Burning to Read: English Fundamentalism and Its Reformation Opponents* (Cambridge, MA: The Belknap Press of Harvard University Press, 2007), ch. 6.
7. Martin Luther, *Prefaces to the New Testament*, in *Luther's Works* 35, *Word and Sacrament* 1, ed. E. Theodore Bachmann (Philadelphia: Muhlenberg Press, 1960), p. 357
8. William Tyndale, *Tyndale's New Testament*, ed. David Daniell (New Haven, CT: Yale University Press, 1989), p. 207.
9. See Tyndale, *Tyndale's New Testament*, ed. Daniell, pp. 207–224, for the prologue; pp. 225–242, for the letter to the Romans.
10. Tyndale, *Tyndale's New Testament*, ed. Daniell, p. 207.

11. See James Simpson, *Reform and Cultural Revolution, 1350–1547* (Oxford: Oxford University Press, 2002), chs. 9 and 10 and further references.

12. John Bunyan, *The Pilgrim's Progress*, ed. David Hawkes (New York: Barnes and Noble, 2005), p. 21.

13. For Surrey's biography, see William A. Sessions, *Henry Howard, the Poet Earl of Surrey: A Life* (Oxford: Oxford University Press, 1999). For Surrey as the inventor of blank verse, see James Simpson, "The *Aeneid* Translations of Henry Howard, Earl of Surrey: The Exiled Reader's Presence," in *The Oxford History of Classical Reception in English Literature*, vol 1: *The Middle Ages*, ed. Rita Copeland (Oxford: Oxford University Press, 2016), pp. 601–623. For the precautionary nature of Surrey's execution: Peter R. Moore, "The Heraldic Charge against the Earl of Surrey, 1546–47," *English Historical Review* 116 (2001), 557–583 (at p. 581).

14. For Psalms 30 and 50: Henry Howard, Earl of Surrey, *Certayne chapters of the proverbs of Salomon drawen into metre by Thomas Sternholde* (London, 1549–1550). For a plausible argument that these are by Surrey, see C. A. Huttar, "Poems by Surrey and Others in a Printed Miscellany, c. 1550," *Miscellany* 16 (1965), 9–18 (at pp. 11–15). For the entire discussion of Surrey's psalm translations, see further James Simpson, "The Psalms and Threat in Sixteenth-Century English Court Culture," *Renaissance Studies* 29 (2015), 576–594. For Psalms 55, 73, and 88: *The Poems of Henry Howard Earl of Surrey*, ed. Frederick Morgan Padelford, rev. ed. (Seattle, WA: University of Washington Press, 1928). Citations from Surrey's Biblical translations are taken from this edition. Texts will be numbered in the body of the text, by Biblical locus (Masoretic numbering), and line number.

15. Matthew Parker, *The whole Psalter translated into English metre* (London, 1567), image 19.

16. I find the characteristic voice of the lonely and betrayed speaker in, for example, the following psalms: 2, 3, 5, 9b, 11, 16, 17, 30, 34, 35, 37, 43, 53, 54, 55, 58, 63, 68, 87, 108, 118, 139, 141.

17. By using the word "authors," I mean "authors." Of course the personae of these poems might be distinguishable from authors, but the condition in which these translations were produced was demonstrably one of extreme danger for their actual authors.

18. My discussion of Surrey in this essay replicates some of the material published in Simpson, *Burning to Read*, ch. 5.

19. For the same psalm translated, in equally vengeful spirit, by (?)John Dudley, Earl of Warwick, while in the Tower between 1553 and 1554, see *The Arundel Harington Manuscript of Tudor Poetry*, ed. Ruth Hughey, 2 vols. (Columbus, OH: Ohio State University Press, 1960), no. 289, and 2:433–435 for notes.

20. It is expressed as desirable, if not necessary: see Karl Gunther, *Reformation Unbound: Protestant Visions of Reform in England, 1525–1590* (Cambridge, UK: Cambridge University Press, 2014), pp. 68–76; and Simpson, *Burning to Read*, ch. 5. The quote is from Thomas Wyatt, "Stand Whoso List upon the Slipper Top," in *Sir Thomas Wyatt, The Complete Poems*, ed. Rebholz, p. 94 (ll. 1–2).

21. *The Boke of Psalmes* (Geneva, 1559), RSTC, 2384, image 2. This text of the Psalms was produced for the Geneva Bible of 1560.

22. *The Boke of Psalmes*, image 5.

23. This prologue is included in the Sternhold and Hopkins editions of 1562—*The whole booke of Psalmes collected into Englysh metre by T. Starnhold, I. Hopkins* (London, 1562)—and the majority of editions until 1577. I thank an anonymous reader for help on this point. See Hannibal Hamlin, *Psalm Culture and Early Modern English Literature* (Cambridge, UK: Cambridge University Press, 2004), pp. 29–30.

24. Thomas Sternhold, *Al such psalmes of Dauid as T. Sternehold didde in his life time draw into English metre* (London, ?1549), RSTC, 2420, image 10.

25. Sternhold, *Al such psalmes of Dauid*, images 10–11.

26. Respectively, *The Poems of Henry Howard Earl of Surrey*, ed. Padelford, Ps 88.22; Ps 38.7; Ps 38.7; Ps 88.21. That Surrey did adopt an evangelical spirituality has not by any means always been accepted. See H. A. Mason, *Humanism and Poetry in the Early Tudor Period* (London: Routledge and Kegan Paul, 1959), pp. 240–247, for the decisive step in favor of such a reading. For an argument suggesting that such accents could be politically strategic, see Elizabeth Heale, *Wyatt, Surrey, and Early Tudor Poetry* (Harlow, Essex: Longman, 1998), pp. 175–176. See also the finely nuanced account in Andrew Taylor, "Psalms and Early Tudor Humanism," Unpublished PhD Dissertation, University of Cambridge, 2002. Greg Walker, *Writing under Tyranny: English Literature and the Henrician Reformation* (Oxford: Oxford University Press, 2005), pp. 397–398, urges caution in assuming that "Surrey was necessarily consistently Lutheran in his beliefs."

27. See Paul Althaus, *The Theology of Martin Luther*, trans. Robert C. Schultz (Philadelphia, PA: Fortress Press, 1966; first pub. in German 1963), pp. 35–39.

28. Martin Luther, *The Freedom of a Christian*, in *Luther's Works*, 31, *Career of the Reformer*, 1, ed. Harold Grimm (Philadelphia, PA: Muhlenberg Press, 1957), pp. 327–377 (at pp. 346–347).

29. For the tradition of ethical exegesis from late Antiquity up to the pre-Reformation period, see Winthrop Wetherbee, "The Study of Classical Authors: From Late Antiquity to the Twelfth Century," and Vincent Gillespie, "The Study of Classical Authors: From the Twelfth Century to c. 1450," both in *The Cambridge History of Literary Criticism*, vol. 2: *The Middle Ages*, ed. Alastair Minnis and Ian Johnson (Cambridge, UK: Cambridge University Press, 2005), pp. 99–144 and 145–238.

30. Luther, *Freedom of a Christian*, ed. Grimm, p. 348. My emphasis.

31. John Bunyan, *Grace Abounding with Other Spiritual Autobiographies*, ed. John Stachniewski (Oxford: Oxford University Press, 1998), p. 38. All further citations are drawn from this edition and cited in the body of the text by page number.

32. Bunyan, *Grace Abounding*, ed. Stachniewski, pp. 97–122.

33. See Chapter 5 of the present book.

34. The fleeting quality of Bunyan's moments of joy resonates with the chapter on joy in Alec Ryrie, *Being Protestant in Reformation England* (Oxford: Oxford University Press, 2013), ch. 5. Ryrie divides his scant evidence of joy into "enduring joy" ("more aspired to than enjoyed," p. 80) and "fleeting joy." His discussion of the frequency of fleeting joy is vitiated by refusal to look at the syntax of emotion, or the way in which the logic of fleeting joy is intelligible only in the sequence of sustained, prolonged, chronic despair, something Ryrie wants to underplay (see Chapter 2).

35. The non-Biblical named figures are spiritual athletes: Mr Gifford (p. 34); Martin Luther (p. 38); Francis Spira (p. 45).

36. For the isolated autobiographical Calvinist subject, see the great book by John Stachniewski, *The Persecutory Imagination: English Puritanism and the Literature of Religious Despair* (Oxford: Clarendon Press, 1991), and the excellent essay by Katharine Hodgkin, "Autobiographical Writings," in *The Oxford Handbook of Early Modern English Literature and Religion*, ed. Andrew Hiscock and Helen Wilcox (Oxford: Oxford University Press, 2017), pp. 207–222.

37. Figures drawn from the machine readable text, supplied by *EEBO*, of John Bunyan, *Grace abounding to the chief of sinners* (London, 1666).

38. e.g. Mr Gifford's congregation in Bedford, from which Bunyan receives "more conviction," but which provoke "wicked thoughts and desires, which I did not regard before" (p. 24).

39. See Stachniewski, *Persecutory Imagination*, ch. 3.

40. Compare Bunyan's situation in *Pilgrim's Progress*, where, as Jason Crawford astutely points out, we hear no more of the book in Christian's hand once he has passed through the wicket gate; and why not?: "Christian ceases to carry the book because he has entered it." See Jason Crawford, *Allegory and Enchantment: An Early Modern Poetics* (Oxford: Oxford University Press, 2017), p. 190.

41. For an excellent account of Bunyan's reading practice, see Jennifer A. Herdt, *Putting on Virtue: The Legacy of the Splendid Vices* (Chicago, IL: University of Chicago Press, 2008), pp. 207–217.

42. Genesis 25:34, and, especially, Romans 9.13–14. For Bunyan's compulsive fear that he, too, has rejected his birthright, see Bunyan, *Grace Abounding with Other Spiritual Autobiographies*, ed. Stachniewski, pp. 41, 46, 50, 56, 59, 61, 64.

43. Herdt, *Putting on Virtue*, p. 217.

17. Escaping Literalism's Trap

1. Shakespeare's *King John* (1595–1596) decisively refuses to participate in the virulently anti-Catholic Protestant version of the reign of King John.

2. See Ian Green, *Print and Protestantism in Early Modern England* (Oxford: Oxford University Press, 2000), pp. 66–68.

3. For Tyndale's claim that the literal sense is the "root and ground of all," see *The Obedience of a Christian Man*, ed. David Daniell (London: Penguin, 2000), p. 156.

4. For Tyndale's frequent use of tropology and typology, despite his equally frequent dismissals of allegory, see James Simpson, *Burning to Read: English Fundamentalism and Its Reformation Opponents* (Cambridge, MA: The Belknap Press of Harvard University Press, 2007), ch. 6 and further references. The larger topic of Protestant allegorization is huge; for an exemplary example, see Barbara Kiefer Lewalski, *Protestant Poetics and the Seventeenth-Century Religious Lyric* (Princeton, NJ: Princeton University Press, 1979), pt. I.

5. For the basic lines of Reformation exegesis, see Green, *Print and Protestantism in Early Modern England*, pp. 104–109, and further references, including especially Jerry H. Bentley, *Humanists and Holy Writ: New Testament Scholarship in the Renaissance* (Princeton, NJ: Princeton University Press, 1983). For the essential point, that the hermeneutic issues were effectively claims to power, see Richard Duerden, "Equivalence or Power? Authority and Reformation Bible Translation," in *The Bible as Book: The Reformation,* ed. Orlaith O'Sullivan and Ellen Herron (London: The British Library, 2000), pp. 9–23.

6. "The Preface of Master William Tyndale that he made before the Five Books of Moses called Genesis," in William Tyndale, *Tyndale's Old Testament,* ed. David Daniell (New Haven, CT: Yale University Press, 1992), pp. 3–4.

7. Martin Luther, *Predigten, 1533–4,* in *Luther's Werke* (http://luther.chadwyck.com), 37:246; translation cited from Joseph Leo Koerner, *The Reformation of the Image* (Chicago, IL: University of Chicago Press), pp. 305–306.

8. *Obedience,* ed. Daniell, p. 161.

9. Cited from "A Fruitful Exhortation to the Reading and Knowledge of Holy Scripture," in *"Certain Sermons or Homilies" (1547) and "A Homily against Disobedience and Wilful Rebellion" (1570),* ed. Ronald B. Bond (Toronto: University of Toronto Press, 1987), pp. 61–67 (at p. 63).

10. *The Bible and Holy Scriptures conteyned in the Olde and Newe Testament* (Geneva, 1561), image 3.

11. Thomas Cartwright, *The second replie of Thomas Cartwright* (London, 1575), image 64. For discussion of Cartwright's call for the death sentence for idolatry see Margaret Aston, *England's Iconoclasts: Laws against Images* (Oxford: Clarendon Press, 1988), pp. 472–473.

12. Cartwright, *Second replie of Thomas Cartwright,* image 68.

13. Keith Thomas, "The Puritans and Adultery: The 1650 Act Reconsidered," in *Puritans and Revolutionaries: Essays in Seventeenth-Century History Presented to Christopher Hill,* ed. Keith Thomas and D. H. Pennington (Oxford: Clarendon Press, 1982), pp. 257–282. See also Chapter 8 of the present book. Cartwright, *Second replie of Thomas Cartwright,* image 74.

14. William Shakespeare, *Twelfth Night,* in *The Norton Shakespeare,* gen. ed. Stephen Greenblatt, 3rd ed. (New York: W. W. Norton, 2016), 3.1.10–12. *Twelfth Night* was written c. 1601. All further citations from Shakespeare's plays will be from this edition and made in the body of the text by act, scene, and line number.

15. For Luther's supercessionism, see Paul Althaus, *Die Theologie Martin Luthers* (Gütersloh: Gerd Mohn, 1962), pp. 86–87.

16. On Luther, see Heinrich Bornkamm, *Luther and the Old Testament*, trans. Eric W. and Ruth C. Gritsch (Philadelphia, PA: Fortress Press, 1969; originally pub. in German in 1948), pp. 1–21, esp.: "Luther detested the Jews and loved the Old Testament" (p. 1).

17. William Tyndale, *A briefe declaration of the sacraments* (London, ?1548), image 10. Further references to this text in this chapter will be made by image number in the body of the text.

18. George Moore, "'The Ornament of the Law': Vestments and the Translation of Judaism in the Geneva Bible," *Prose Studies: History, Theory, Criticism* 37 (2015), 161–180.

19. Francis Bacon, *New Atlantis*, in *Francis Bacon: The Major Works*, ed. Brian Vickers (Oxford: Oxford University Press, 1996), pp. 457–489 (at p. 465).

20. Bacon, *New Atlantis*, ed. Vickers, p. 465.

21. John Milton, *Of Reformation*, in CPWJM, 1:519–617 (at p. 524). All further references to this text will be made to this edition by page number in the body of the text.

22. John Milton, *Reason of Church Government*, in CPWJM, 1.750.

23. Milton, *Reason of Church Government*, in CPWJM, 1.750.

24. John Milton, *Paradise Lost*, in *John Milton: The Major Works*, ed. Stephen Orgel and Jonathan Goldberg (Oxford: Oxford University Press, 2003), 12.648–649. Further references to *Paradise Lost* will be to this edition, and cited by book and line number in the body of the text.

25. See Barbara K. Lewalski, *The Life of John Milton: A Critical Biography* (Oxford: Blackwell, 2000), pp. 154–185.

26. John Milton, *The Doctrine and Discipline of Divorce*, in CPWJM, 2.222–356. All further references to this text will be drawn from this edition, and made by page number in the body of the text.

27. Barbara K. Lewalski, "Interpreting God's Word—and Words—in *Paradise Lost*," in *Milton's Rival Hermeneutics*, ed. Richard J. DuRocher and Margaret Olofson Thickstun (Pittsburgh, PA: Duquesne University Press, 2012), pp. 77–99 (at pp. 80–85).

28. For the most lucid and powerful explication of which, see Erich Auerbach, "Figura," in *Scenes from the Drama of European Literature* (Minneapolis: University of Minnesota Press, 1984; first pub. 1959), pp. 11–26. For the flexibility with which different levels of Biblical interpretation in pre-modern practice, see Gilbert Dahan, *L'Exégèse Chrétienne de la Bible en Occident Médiéval XII-XIV siècle* (Paris: Cerf, 1999).

29. For Woodford see Kantik Ghosh, "Contingency and the Christian Faith: William Woodford's Anti-Wycliffite Hermeneutics," *Poetica* 49 (1998), 1–26. For Pecock see Kirsty Campbell, *The Call to Read: Reginald Pecock's Books and Textual*

Communities (Notre Dame, IN: University of Notre Dame Press, 2010). For More see Simpson, *Burning to Read*, chs. 3, 4, and 7 esp. For Whitgift see Patrick Collinson, *The Elizabethan Puritan Movement* (London: Methuen, 1967), pp. 131–145. For Hooker see Patrick Collinson, "Hooker and the Elizabethan Establishment," in *Richard Hooker and the Construction of Christian Community*, ed. Arthur Stephen McGrade (Tempe, AZ: Medieval & Renaissance Texts & Studies, 1997), pp. 149–181.

30. For an excellent discussion of the fascinating case of the Leveller William Walwyn, who ends up as a promoter of tolerance and a lover of Montaigne, see William Haller, *Liberty and Reformation in the Puritan Revolution* (New York: Columbia University Press, 1955), pp. 162–175. See also Rachel Foxley, "The Levellers," in *The Oxford Handbook of Literature and the English Revolution*, ed. Laura Lunger Knoppers (Oxford: Oxford University Press, 2012), pp. 272–286.

31. For Erasmus's defense of non-literalist, rhetorical understandings of Scripture, see Desiderius Erasmus, *De Libero Arbitrio (On the Freedom of the Will)*, in *Luther and Erasmus: Free Will and Salvation*, trans. E. Gordon Rupp, A. N. Marlow, Philip S. Watson, and B. Drewery (Philadelphia, PA: The Westminster Press, 1969), pp. 35–97.

32. For Augustine's brilliant injunction to read until one arrives at a charitable sense, see Augustine of Hippo, *Sancti Aurelii Augustini de doctrina christiana, libri IV*, Corpus Christianorum Series Latina 32 (Turnholt: Brepols, 1962), 3.15.23, p. 91.

33. For Langland, see James Simpson, "Desire and the Scriptural Text: Will as Reader in *Piers Plowman*," in *Criticism and Dissent in the Middle Ages*, ed. Rita Copeland (Cambridge, UK: Cambridge University Press, 1996), pp. 215–243. For Chaucer, see esp. the *Friar's Tale*; for Shakespeare, see the present chapter.

34. For Milton's non-exclusivist grounds of any claim to be illumined by the Holy Spirit, see Lewalski, "Interpreting God's Word," pp. 80–81.

35. Lewalski, "Interpreting God's Word," pp. 86–99.

36. Andrew Marvell, "On Mr Milton's *Paradise Lost*," in *The Poems of Andrew Marvell*, ed. Nigel Smith, rev. ed. (Harlow: Pearson Education, 2007), pp. 182–184, ll. 29–30. Further references will be made by line number in the body of the text.

37. For which see Gordon Teskey, *Delerious Milton: The Fate of the Poet in Modernity* (Cambridge, MA: Harvard University Press, 2006).

18. Liberty Taking Liberties

1. I gain the information about the Bolsheviks from Benjamin Nathan's review of Yuri Slezkine, *The House of Government: A Saga of the Russian Revolution* (Princeton, NJ: Princeton University Press, 2017), *New York Review of Books*, 23 November 2017. The full expression would be "Vsemirnaya revolyutsiya," for guidance with which I thank Vladimir Tarnopolski.

2. Lyndal Roper, *Martin Luther: Renegade and Prophet* (London: Vintage, 2016), p. 99.

3. See www.reformationsjubilaeum-bund.de, consulted 31 October 2017. Translation mine.

4. For a detailed account of the historiographical placing of religion in the English Revolution, and especially of Victorian Whig historiography, see Glenn Burgess, "Introduction: Religion and the Historiography of the English Civil War," in *England's Wars of Religion, Revisited*, ed. Charles W. A. Prior and Glenn Burgess (Farnham, Surrey: Ashgate, 2011), pp. 2–25.

5. Blair Worden, "Oliver Cromwell and the Cause of Civil and Religious Liberty," in *England's Wars of Religion, Revisited*, ed. Prior and Burgess, pp. 231–232.

6. See Peter Lake, "The Historiography of Puritanism," in *The Cambridge Companion to Puritanism*, ed. John Coffey and P. Lim (Cambridge, UK: Cambridge University Press, 2008), pp. 346–372.

7. Burgess, "Introduction: Religion and the Historiography of the English Civil War," in *England's Wars of Religion, Revisited*, ed. Prior and Burgess, p. 8.

8. For which, see esp. Greg Walker, *Writing under Tyranny: English Literature and the Henrician Reformation* (Oxford: Oxford University Press, 2005).

9. James Simpson, *Reform and Cultural Revolution, 1350–1547* (Oxford: Oxford University Press, 2002), p. 1.

10. Iconoclasm in both Reformation Europe and revolutionary France was always defended as a claim to freedom, since the idols enslaved the spirit. See James Simpson, *Under the Hammer: Iconoclasm in the Anglo-American Tradition* (Oxford: Oxford University Press, 2010), esp. ch. 3.

11. Emma Lazarus, "The New Colossus" (1883), cited from the plaque on the Statue of Liberty; Nathaniel Hawthorne, as reported in Nathaniel Hawthorne, *The Scarlet Letter*, ed. John Stephen Martin, 2nd ed. (Peterborough, Ont: Broadview, 2004), p. 310.

12. See Roy Walmsley, *World Prison Population List*, 11th ed. (London: Institute for Criminal Policy Research, 2015), available at www.prisonstudies.org/core-publications, consulted 8 December 2017.

13. Thus Thomas Hobbes, *Leviathan*, ed. Richard Tuck (Cambridge, UK: Cambridge University Press, 1991), ch. 14, p. 91: "By Liberty is understood . . . the absence of external impediments." That state produces war, and the state of war is (ch. 13) "solitary, nasty, brutish and short" (p. 89).

14. Cited from *OED*, sense I, 2.c.

15. John Milton, *A Ready and Easy Way to Establish a Free Commonwealth*, in *CPWJM*, 7:455.

16. Cf. also *OED*, senses II, 6(b) and (c).

17. See Alan Harding, "Political Liberty in the Middle Ages," *Speculum* 55 (1980), 423–443, and *Liberties and Identities in the Medieval British Isles*, ed. Michael Prestwich (Woodbridge: Boydell Press, 2008).

18. *OED*, sense P 2c: N. Ridley *Certein Conf. Ridley & Latimer* (1556).

19. For the crucial shifts in the concept of conscience from pre- to post-Reformation, see Paul Strohm, "Conscience," in *Cultural Reformations: Medieval*

and Renaissance in Literary History, ed. Brian Cummings and James Simpson (Oxford: Oxford University Press, 2010), pp. 206–226, and Brian Cummings, "The Conscience of Thomas More," in *Representing Religious Pluralization in Early Modern Europe,* ed. Andreas Höfele, Stephan Laqué, Enno Ruge, and Gabriela Schmidt (Berlin: LIT Verlag, 2007), pp. 1–14.

20. John Milton, *Second Defence of the English People* in Milton, *The Major Works,* ed. Stephen Orgel and Jonathan Goldberg (Oxford: Oxford University Press, 1991), pp. 308–330 (at p. 308).

21. See Milton, *The Major Works,* ed. Orgel and Goldberg, p. 842. For Milton as censor, see Barbara K. Lewalski, *The Life of John Milton: A Critical Biography* (Oxford: Blackwell, 2000), pp. 244–246 and 253.

22. Milton, *Second Defence of the English People,* in Milton, *The Major Works,* ed. Orgel and Goldberg, p. 310.

23. James Madison provides a crisp statement of the reverse case, in 1792: "In Europe, charters of liberty have been granted by power. America has set the example and France has followed it, of charters of power granted by liberty." Cited in Bernard Bailyn, *The Ideological Origins of the American Revolution* (Cambridge, MA: The Belknap Press, 1967), p. 55.

24. The authoritative work is J. G. A. Pocock, *The Ancient Constitution and the Feudal Law: A Study of English Historical Thought in the Seventeenth Century* (Cambridge, UK: Cambridge University Press, 1957). See also Corinne C. Weston, "England: Ancient Constitution and Common Law," in *The Cambridge History of Political Thought, 1450–1700,* ed. J. H Burns and Mark Goldie (Cambridge, UK: Cambridge University Press, 1991), pp. 374–411.

25. Cited in Pocock, *Ancient Constitution,* p. 41.

26. Pocock, *Ancient Constitution,* p. 32.

27. Pocock, *Ancient Constitution,* passim, and Weston, "England: Ancient Constitution and Common Law." See also Alan Cromartie, *The Constitutionalist Revolution: An Essay on the History of England, 1450–1642* (Cambridge, UK: Cambridge University Press, 2006), ch. 7.

28. For the larger history of the common law in England, see John H. Langbein, Renée Lettow Lerner, and Bruce P. Smith, *History of the Common Law: The Development of Anglo-American Legal Institutions* (Austin, TX: Wolters Kluwer, 2009), esp. chs. 1, 2, and 4.

29. M. J. Braddick, *God's Fury, England's Fire: A New History of the English Civil Wars* (London: Allen Lane, 2008), p. 258.

30. *CPWJM,* 7.337. For Milton's disillusionment with the Ancient Constitution, see Peter C. Herman, *Destabilizing Milton: Paradise Lost and the Poetics of Incertitude* (New York: Palgrave, 2005), pp. 78–79.

31. See the excellent essays by J. C. Davis, "Religion and the Struggle for Freedom in the English Revolution," *The Historical Journal* 35 (1992), 507–530, and Worden, "Oliver Cromwell and the Cause of Civil and Religious Liberty."

32. See Worden, "Oliver Cromwell and the Cause of Civil and Religious Liberty," for a neat encapsulation of its deeply paradoxical structure: "They [Puritans] exchange the 'yoke of bondage' for a glorious subjugation, the 'yoke' or 'absolute subjugation' of Christ's 'law of liberty'" (p. 235).
33. See Quentin Skinner, *Liberty before Liberalism* (Cambridge, UK: Cambridge University Press, 1998); for Hobbes's striking account of this theory as the product of humanist learning see *Leviathan*, ed. Tuck, pp. 149–150.
34. Skinner, *Liberty before Liberalism*, 36–57. For the Aristotelian influence on the theory, see also Jonathan Scott, *Commonwealth Principles: Republican Writing of the English Revolution* (Cambridge: Cambridge University Press, 2004), pp. 151–152.
35. Quentin Skinner, "Surveying the Foundations: A Retrospect and Reassessment," in *Rethinking the Foundations of Modern Political Thought*, ed. Annabel Brett and James Tully, with Holly Hamilton-Bleakley (Cambridge, UK: Cambridge University Press, 2006), pp. 236–261 (at p. 259).
36. Skinner, *Liberty before Liberalism*, p. 41.
37. Arthur Barker, *Milton and the Puritan Dilemma* (Toronto: University of Toronto Press, 1942), p. 141. Cited in Stephen M. Fallon, "Nascent Republican Theory in Milton's Regicide Prose," in *The Oxford Handbook of Literature and the English Revolution*, ed. Laura Lunger Knoppers (Oxford: Oxford University Press, 2012), pp. 310–324 (at p. 310).
38. For the address of Pauline Christianity to slaves, see e.g. Romans 6.16 (and passim), where the word "*doulos*" (Greek "slave") is translated in English Bibles as "servant." For the citizen-intellectuals, see Skinner, *Liberty before Liberalism*, pp. 43–44, for the importance of Tacitus and Livy especially.
39. See Chapter 1, n. 5 of the present book.
40. William Tyndale, *The Obedience of a Christian Man*, ed. David Daniell (London: Penguin, 2000), p. 51.
41. John Milton, *Of Reformation Touching Church-discipline in England* (London, 1641), *CPWJM*, 1.609.
42. See, e.g. John Milton, *Areopagitica* (1644), in *CPWJM*, 2.554: "Could we but forgo this Prelatical tradition of crowding free consciences and Christian liberties into canons and precepts of men"; and John Milton, *A soveraigne salve to cure the blind* (London, 1643), image 11.
43. Thomas Becon, *The flour of godly praiers* (London, 1550), image 11.
44. Milton, *Tenure of Kings and Magistrates* (1649), in Milton, *The Major Works*, ed. Orgel and Goldberg, pp. 273, 274–275.
45. Milton, *A Ready and Easy Way to Establish a Free Commonwealth*, in *CPWJM*, 7:455.
46. Anonymous, *Here begynneth the pystles and gospels, of euery Sonday, and holy daye in the yere* (London, 1538), image 183.
47. Quentin Skinner, *The Foundations of Modern Political Thought* (Cambridge, UK: Cambridge University Press, 1970), 2:15–19.

48. Tyndale, *Obedience of a Christian Man*, ed. Daniell, p. 39.
49. Tyndale, *Obedience of a Christian Man*, ed. Daniell, p. 57. See Richard Y. Duerden, "Justice and Justification: King and God in Tyndale's *The Obedience of a Christian Man*," in *William Tyndale and the Law*, ed. John A. R. Dick and Anne Richardson (Kirksville, MO: Sixteenth Century Journal Publishers, 1994), pp. 69–80: both the politics and the soteriology are motivated by a "sense of intolerable burdens and a longing for deliverance" (p. 73).
50. Skinner, *Foundations of Modern Political Thought*, 2:210–211.
51. See e.g. (perhaps surprisingly), William Prynne, *The divine right of kings asserted in general* (London, 1679).
52. Milton, *Tenure of Kings and Magistrates*, in Milton, *The Major Works*, ed. Orgel and Goldberg, p. 281. See also Fallon, "Nascent Republican Theory in Milton's Regicide Prose," in *The Oxford Handbook of Literature and the English Revolution*, ed. Knoppers, p. 313. These ideas are also expressed in the American Declaration of Independence of 1776: "But when a long train of abuses and usurpations, pursuing invariably the same Object evinces a design to reduce them under absolute Despotism, it is their right, it is their duty, to throw off such Government, and to provide new Guards for their future security," consulted at www.ushistory.org/declaration/document/index.htm, consulted 9 December 2017.
53. J. P. Sommerville, *Politics and Ideology in England, 1603–1640* (London: Longman, 1986), pp. 46–47, for decisive conclusions that absolutism was theorized in England as forcefully as it was in France, and that absolutism was, in England, primarily a Stewart, and therefore seventeenth-century phenomenon. See also J. P. Sommerville "Absolutism and Royalism," in *The Cambridge History of Political Thought*, ed. Burns and Goldie, pp. 347–373, and Ronald G. Asch, "Sacred Kingship in France and England in the Age of the Wars of Religion: From Disenchantment to Re-enchantment?," in *England's Wars of Religion, Revisited*, ed. Charles W. A. Prior and Glenn Burgess (Farnham, Surrey: Ashgate, 2011), pp. 27–47.
54. *The Political Works of James I*, ed. Charles Howard McIlwain (Cambridge, MA: Harvard University Press, 1918); *Patriarcha and Other Writings*, ed. Johann P. Sommerville (Cambridge, UK: Cambridge University Press, 1991); Hobbes, *Leviathan*, ed. Tuck.
55. Edmund Calamy, *Englands looking-glasse* (London, 1642), image 6; see also Chapter 2 of the present book.
56. Terry Eagleton, *The Ideology of the Aesthetic* (Oxford: Blackwell, 1990), p. 100.
57. Skinner, "Surveying the Foundations: A Retrospect and Reassessment," in *Rethinking the Foundations of Modern Political Thought*, ed. Brett and Tully, p. 256.
58. Michael Wilks, *The Problem of Sovereignty in the Later Middle Ages: The Papal Monarchy with Augustinus Triumphus and the Publicists* (Cambridge, UK: Cambridge University Press, 1963). Skinner, *Foundations of Modern Political Thought*, 1:49–68 and 2:113–173. For the constitutionalism of Sir John Fortescue, see James Simpson, "Pecock and Fortescue," in *A Companion to Middle English Prose*, ed.

A. S. G. Edwards (Woodbridge: Boydell and Brewer, 2004), pp. 271–288, and Cromartie, *Constitutionalist Revolution: An Essay on the History of England, 1450–1642*, pp. 4–32. Parliament in the reign of Henry IV (1399–1413) "enjoyed a greater influence over the business of central government than at any time before the seventeenth century." See John Gillingham, "Crisis or Continuity? The Structure of Royal Authority in England 1369–1422," in *Das Spätmittelalterliche Königtum in europäischen Vergleich*, ed. Reinhard Schneider (Sigmaringen: Thorbecke, 1987), pp. 59–80 (at p. 73).

59. See John Milton, "Of the New Forcers of Conscience under the Long Parliament," in *Milton, The Major Works*, ed. Orgel and Goldberg, l. 20, pp. 83–84.

60. For a recent and extensive example of which, see John Witte Jr, *The Reformation of Rights: Law, Religion and Human Rights in Early Modern Calvinism* (Cambridge, UK: Cambridge University Press, 2007), pp. 209–275.

61. See note 52 above.

62. For especially consistent special pleading in the face of republicans who act in less than republican manner, see David Norbrook, *Writing the English Republic: Poetry, Rhetoric, and Politics, 1627–1660* (Cambridge, UK: Cambridge University Press, 1999), pp. 18, 19, 20, 70, 113, 117, 131, 189, 201, 203, 246, 267, 270, 326, 335, 344, 367, 436, and 438 (for example). Norbrook's splendidly learned book must work very hard to avert its gaze from evangelical culture, and from military-backed republican despotism.

63. Lewalski, *Life of John Milton*, p. 224.

64. Milton, *Tenure of Kings and Magistrates*, in Milton, *The Major Works*, ed. Orgel and Goldberg, p. 273.

65. Milton, *Tenure of Kings and Magistrates*, in Milton, *The Major Works*, ed. Orgel and Goldberg, p. 274–275. For Milton's appeal to natural right over legal precedent for the act of regicide, see Elizabeth Sauer, "Milton's Defences and the Principle of *Sanior Pars*," in *The Oxford Handbook of Literature and the English Revolution*, ed. Knoppers, pp. 446–456: "In his tribute to the free nation, Milton registers the Puritan shift from legal precedent to the law of nature, and from historic to abstract rights" (p. 447).

66. Milton, *Tenure of Kings and Magistrates*, in Milton, *The Major Works*, ed. Orgel and Goldberg, p. 276.

67. Milton, *Tenure of Kings and Magistrates*, in Milton, *The Major Works*, ed. Orgel and Goldberg, p. 281.

68. Milton, *Tenure of Kings and Magistrates*, in Milton, *The Major Works*, ed. Orgel and Goldberg, p. 284.

69. Milton, *A Ready and Easy Way to Establish a Free Commonwealth*, in *CPWJM*, 7:455.

70. John Milton, *A Ready and Easy Way to Establish a Free Commonwealth*, in *CPWJM*, 7:433.

71. John Milton, *Eikonoklastes*, in *CPWJM*, 2:601.

72. Milton, *Second Defence of the English People* in Milton, *The Major Works*, ed. Orgel and Goldberg, pp. 308–309. For Milton's simultaneous appeal to and dismissal

of "the people" in his regicide prose, see Fallon, "Nascent Republican Theory in Milton's Regicide Prose," pp. 313–314.

73. John Milton, "The Verse," in John Milton, *Paradise Lost*, in *The Major Works*, ed. Orgel and Goldberg, p. 355.

74. Thus *Paradise Lost:* Mammon: 2.256; Gabriel: 4.958; Satan: 5.793; Abdiel: 5.823; Satan: 6.164; Satan: 6.420; Milton as narrator: 10.307; Sin: 10.368; Michael: 12.82, 83, 100, 526.

75. The formulation annually pronounced by the Harvard president to graduating law students.

Conclusion

1. Herbert Butterfield, *The Whig Interpretation of History* (London: Bell and Sons, 1931), p. 88.

Index

Absolutism, 85, 144, 149, 296, 319, 328, 329, 334, 335, 339, 342, 361n20, 430n53
Adams, Robert, 378n12
Adams, Thomas, 145–146
Admonition to the Parliament, 36, 37, 38
adultery, death sentence, 302
Aers, David, 358n8, 359n13, 366n20, 374n42, 378n12, 378n14
agency, 77, 78–80
Age of Literalism, 313
Aglionby, Edward, 129
Ahnert, Ruth, 382n4
Ainsworth, Henry, 42
allegory, typological, 300, 311–312
Althaus, Paul, 422n27, 425n15
Ames, William, 242
Ancient Constitution, 87, 327, 328, 428n30
Andrews, Lancelot, 414n42
Antinomianism, 99
Appleford, Amy, 403n23
Archibald, Elizabeth, 413n29
Arendt, Hannah, 388nn3–4
Arminianism, 96–97, 98, 99, 100, 102; in England, 99–100, 101
Armitage, David, 362n23
Arundel, Thomas, 164, 166, 266
Asch, Ronald G., 430n53

Askew, Anne, 27, 91, 214
Aston, Margaret, 360n17, 367n24, 371n14, 373n34, 375n55, 381n44, 396n7, 397n9, 397n12, 397n15, 397n18, 398n23, 398n26, 399nn33–35, 402n5, 402n10, 402nn14–15, 405n17, 411n8, 418n58, 424n11
atheist, as word, 40
Atwood, Margaret, 140
Auerbach, Erich, 425n28
Augustin, C., 419n64
Augustine of Hippo, 61, 62, 63, 313; *City of God*, 232, 233
Austin, J. L., 230
Auzépy, Marie-France, 396n1

Bacon, Francis, 307–308
Bailyn, Bernard, 428n23
Bale, John, 31, 33, 34, 51, 53, 128, 136, 142, 209, 214, 215, 224, 232, 408n1; *God's Promises*, 169–170, 209; *Image of Both Churches*, 31–32, 124–125; performativity in plays, 209–211, 212–213; *Three Laws*, 169, 209
Bancroft, Richard, 128
Barish, Jonas, 367n24, 392n32, 407n32, 407n34, 409n15, 411n51

433